THE HIGH COURT
OF CHIVALRY

Oxford University Press, Amen House, London E.C.4

GLASGOW NEW YORK TORONTO MELBOURNE WELLINGTON
BOMBAY CALCUTTA MADRAS KARACHI KUALA LUMPUR
CAPE TOWN IBADAN NAIROBI ACCRA

THE HIGH COURT
OF CHIVALRY

A Study of the Civil Law in England

BY

G. D. SQUIBB, Q.C.

WITH A FOREWORD BY
A. R. WAGNER

OXFORD
AT THE CLARENDON PRESS
1959

PRINTED IN GREAT BRITAIN

TO

THE MOST NOBLE

BERNARD MARMADUKE
DUKE OF NORFOLK

K.G., G.C.V.O.

Earl Marshal and Hereditary Marshal of England

THIS WORK IS

BY HIS GRACE'S PERMISSION

RESPECTFULLY DEDICATED

'This Court of honor is part of the
law of England': per Keeling C.J. in
R. v. *Parker* (1668), 2 Keb. 316.

FOREWORD

IN 1931, when I came into the College of Arms, the dust of the great controversy of twenty-five years earlier on the Right to Bear Arms had not yet quite settled. Of the chief participants A. C. Fox-Davies had indeed died three years earlier, but Oswald Barron was still living and I was later to know him well. A young and keen pursuivant was soon aware that though the fight had ended little had been settled and furthermore that, though the heralds had never been drawn in, the issue was of importance to them as affecting the credit of their estab lishment and practice.

I therefore soon found myself studying the whole subject with close attention and in time I came to two conclusions. The first was that the original controversy had been an *elephantocetomachia*, a fight between an elephant and a whale, incapable of decision because the adversaries lived in different elements and could not come to grips. Oswald Barron, a historian, was trying to settle a legal question by reciting history. Fox-Davies, a lawyer, hoped to settle history by quoting law. My second conclusion was that neither party had got to the bottom of his own case and that no decision could be looked for till much more was known both of the history and the law.

On the historical side I was able to make some headway, but on the legal side, though I noted much material relative to the Court of Chivalry, I soon realized that little progress was possible in its interpretation until a legal historian could be persuaded to study and analyse it. Two large boxfuls of seventeenth- and eighteenth-century documents of the Court kept in a strong room at the College of Arms and several manuscript volumes in the Record Room there called for examination with a knowledge of the forms and history not merely of law but of the Civil Law. Not only did I lack such knowledge myself, but for years I was unable to find anyone who both possessed it and was willing to undertake the labour of working through this material, which had lain undisturbed for two centuries.

In 1949 I myself wrote an article on the Court of Chivalry for *Chambers's Encyclopædia*, because I could find no one else to do it. Soon after this, however, I began to have hopes of Mr. Squibb. He examined my notes and in due course agreed to undertake a serious study of the subject if the Court Records in the College could be placed at his disposal. To this the College Chapter agreed and the present volume is the fruit of the work then begun.

It will not surprise those who have looked forward to its appearance to find that it sheds entirely new light on the Court's history. My own short article proves to need radical correction on several points and I confess this with the less shame since the same is true of all previous writers on the subject, including Sir William Holdsworth in his *History of English Law*, Horace Round in his paper on 'Peerage Cases in the Court of Chivalry', and L. W. Vernon Harcourt in *His Grace the Steward and the Trial of Peers*.

What is more surprising is to find so much new light thrown on social history by the Court's seventeenth-century records. The evidence of reputation and style of living brought forward to prove that litigants in Charles I's reign were or were not gentlemen is fascinating both in itself and in its wider implications. Mr. Squibb makes it clear that the Civil Law, as practised in the Court, though Roman in origin was distinctly English in its development. The social facts which shaped the Court's practice were still more distinctively national and their special character is reflected in it very clearly. For these reasons I believe that the value of this book will extend to all students of English social history and of the English seventeenth century.

ANTHONY R. WAGNER
Richmond Herald and
Joint Register of the Court of Chivalry

PREFACE

THIS book owes its being to the unrivalled knowledge
of the records and collections of the College of Arms
enjoyed by Dr. Anthony Wagner, for it was he who
told me of the existence of the records of the Court of
Chivalry and suggested to me that they were worthy of
study. So they have proved to be, whether considered
from the legal or from the heraldic point of view.

Unfortunately the surviving records of the Court cover
but a comparatively short part of the six centuries of its
erratic and eccentric existence. It has therefore been
necessary to set the material derived from the records in a
context derived from secondary sources. The manageable
bulk of the records (mostly contained in two large boxes
of files and loose documents and eight bound volumes)
has made it possible to read every document. A sabbatical
year would be required to enable the same to be said of
the secondary sources, and since sabbatical years are not for
the self-employed to wait for one would be to delay in-
definitely the publication of hitherto unexplored material
which throws new light on a much misunderstood subject.

I should like to record my gratitude to Dr. Wagner,
who not only aroused my interest in the records of the
Court, but has also guided me to valuable secondary
sources amongst the manuscripts in the College of Arms
and has in many other ways given me great help during
the progress of the work, and to the Chapter of the College
of Arms for generously giving me unrestricted access to
the records and to other relevant manuscripts in the
College. My thanks are also due to Sir Henry Dashwood,
lately Registrar of the Court of Arches, for permission to
make use of the Court of Chivalry records now amongst
those of the Court of Arches; to Mr. H. Stanford London, Norfolk Herald Extraordinary, and Mr. A. Colin
Cole, Portcullis Pursuivant, who amongst other kindnesses
have given me transcripts of manuscripts; to the late Sir

Geoffrey Ellis for advice on early peerage claims; to the owners and custodians of the various manuscripts cited; to others mentioned in the footnotes who have helped me in various ways; and to my colleagues on the Council of the Heraldry Society for allowing me to incorporate some material from my preliminary essay *The Law of Arms in England*. The last sentence must be one of thanks to the staff of the Clarendon Press for the care and skill with which they have guided me along the tiresome road between manuscript and publication.

G. D. S.

Temple
28 July 1958

CONTENTS

APPENDIXES

ABBREVIATIONS

A.C. (preceded by date)	Law Reports, Appeal Cases
A.P.C.	*Acts of the Privy Council*
A.P.C., Col.	*Acts of the Privy Council, Colonial Series*
Ant. Journ.	*Antiquaries Journal*
App. Cas.	Law Reports, Appeal Cases, 1875–90
Ashm.	Ashmolean
Atk.	Atkyns's Reports, 1736–54
B.	Baron of the Exchequer
B. & Ad.	Barnewall and Adolphus's Reports, 1830–4
B. & Ald.	Barnewall and Alderson's Reports, 1817–22
B.M.	British Museum
Bing (N C.)	Bingham's New Cases, 1834–40
Bodl.	Bodleian Library
C. & K.	Carrington and Kirwan's Reports, 1843–53
C.C.R.	*Calendar of Close Rolls*
C.J.	Chief Justice
C.J.	*House of Commons Journals*
C.P.	*Complete Peerage* (2nd ed., unless otherwise stated)
C.P.R.	*Calendar of Patent Rolls*
C.S.P.D.	*Calendar of State Papers, Domestic*
Ch. (preceded by date)	Law Reports, Chancery
Ch. D.	Law Reports, Chancery Division, 1875–90
Co. Inst.	Coke's Institutes
Co. Litt.	Coke upon Littleton (1 Inst.)
Co. Rep.	Coke's Reports, 1572–1616
Coll. Arm.[1]	College of Arms
Coll. Top. & Gen.	*Collectanea Topographica et Genealogica*
Cur. Mil.	Curia Militaris
D.N.B.	*Dictionary of National Biography*
Dow. & Ry. K.B.	Dowling and Ryland's King's Bench Reports, 1822–7
Dowl.	Dowling's Practice Reports, 1830–41
Dyer	Dyer's Reports, 1513–81
E.M.	Earl Marshal
East	East's Reports, 1800–12

[1] Used in references to manuscripts in the library of the College of Arms, but not in references to records of the Court of Chivalry, which, although housed in the College, are a separate archive group.

Foedera	T. Rymer and R. Sanderson, *Foedera*
Gent. Mag.	*Gentleman's Magazine*
H.E.L.	Sir William Holdsworth, *History of English Law*
Hag. Con.	Haggard's Consistorial Reports, 1789–1821
Harl. Soc.	Harleian Society
Her. Cas.	G. D. Squibb, *Heraldic Cases in the Court of Chivalry*
Her. & Gen.	*Herald and Genealogist*
Holt K.B.	Sir John Holt's Reports, King's Bench, 1688–1710
Hut.	Hutton's Reports, 1617–38
J.	Justice
K.B. (preceded by date)	Law Reports, King's Bench Division
Keb.	Keble's Reports, 1661–77
Keil.	Keilwey's Reports, 1327–1578
Knapp	Knapp's Privy Council Reports, 1829–36
L. & P. Hen. VIII	*Calendar of Letters and Papers Foreign and Domestic, Henry VIII*
L.J.	Lord Justice
L.J.	*House of Lords Journals*
L.J.C.P.	Law Journal Reports, Common Pleas
L.J.Ecc.	Law Journal Reports, Ecclesiastical
L.K.	Lord Keeper
L.Q.R.	*Law Quarterly Review*
Lev.	Levinz's Reports, 1660–96
M. & S.	Maule and Selwyn's Reports, 1813–17
M.R.	Master of the Rolls
Mag. Brit. Not.	J. Chamberlayne, *Magnae Britanniae Notitia*
Misc. Gen. et Her.	*Miscellanea Genealogica et Heraldica*
Mod.	Modern Reports, 1669–1755
Moo. P.C.	Moore's Privy Council Cases, 1836–63
O.E.D.	*Oxford English Dictionary*
P.	President of the Probate, Divorce and Admiralty Division
P. (preceded by date)	Law Reports, Probate, Divorce and Admiralty Division
P.C.C.	Prerogative Court of Canterbury
P.D.	Law Reports, Probate, Divorce and Admiralty Division, 1875–90
P.R.O.	Public Record Office
Proc. P.C.	Sir Harris Nicolas, *Proceedings and Ordinances of the Privy Council*

Q.B. (preceded by date) Law Reports, Queen's Bench Division
Q.B.D.   Law Reports, Queen's Bench Division, 1875–90
R.D.P.   *Report on the Dignity of a Peer*
Rawl.   Rawlinson
Rot. Parl.   *Rotuli Parliamentorum*
Salk.   Salkeld's Reports, 1689–1712
Show. K.B.   Shower's Reports, King's Bench, 1678–95
Show. P.C.   Shower's Cases in Parliament, 1694–9
Sid.   Siderfin's Reports, 1657–70
Sjt.   Serjeant-at-Law
St. Tr.   *State Trials*
Vent.   Ventris's Reports, 1668–91
W. Bl.   William Blackstone's Reports, 1746–79
W.N. (preceded by date) Law Reports, Weekly Notes
Y.B.   Year Book

TABLE OF STATUTES

TABLE OF CASES

WHERE a case is cited more than once from original documents there is a possibility of inconsistencies in the spelling of the names of the parties owing to the spelling in the document cited having been followed in each instance. The spelling of the first reference in the text is used in this table. All cases are cited in the form '*X* v. *Y*', irrespective of the courts in which they were heard. In the records of the civil law and ecclesiastical courts 'contra' is used instead of 'versus'. R. G. Marsden, *Select Pleas in the Court of Admiralty* (Selden Soc. VI, 1894), accordingly uses the form '*X* c. *Y*', but this was not the practice of the early admiralty and ecclesiastical reporters.

INTRODUCTION

THE High Court of Chivalry is unique in that it is the only surviving civil law court in England. It owed its escape from the Victorian law reformers to the fact that it had never sat since the early part of the eighteenth century and so attracted no attention in the nineteenth. Had it then been active there can be little doubt that its jurisdiction would have been transferred with the secular jurisdictions of all other courts in which the advocates in Doctors' Commons had formerly practised to the new High Court of Justice created by the Supreme Court of Judicature Act, 1873. If the framers of that Act had been entirely logical, we should now have a Probate, Divorce, Admiralty, and Chivalry Division of the High Court.

The long dormancy of the Court of Chivalry during the two centuries before its sleep was broken in 1954 by the Lord Mayor, Aldermen, and Citizens of the City of Manchester has not only secured its survival but has also caused its true nature to be largely forgotten. The vacuum has been filled by a variety of misconceptions, some of which will be dealt with hereafter. The only truth to survive in common currency is that it is a court for the settlement of disputes as to armorial bearings. That truth is rather like the visible fraction of an iceberg: it reveals less than it conceals. In its origin and in its hey-day the Court of Chivalry was much more than an heraldic tribunal. As a result of a series of vicissitudes which left it with a jurisdiction confined to heraldic matters the Court has primarily attracted the attention of those interested in the antiquities of heraldry, so that the emphasis in what has been written concerning it has been upon heraldry rather than upon the wider aspects of the place which the Court formerly held in the practice of the civil law. As will appear, to regard it as a court of heraldry is to misunderstand its true nature. The essential distinction between the Court of Chivalry and other courts is not that it has jurisdiction in heraldic disputes, but that it administers justice in relation to those military matters which are not governed by the common law. That these matters are now and have been for several centuries entirely heraldic is an accident of history.

That there should have been misapprehension as to the Court and its jurisdiction is not a matter for wonder, for there has been little reliable material for a study of the Court readily accessible. The fundamental material, the records of the Court, remained forgotten in the College of Arms until Dr. Anthony Wagner recognized their importance. Now it is possible to see the Court from the point of view of the civilians who practised in it during the seventeenth and eighteenth centuries and to form a detailed picture of their work. The perusal of the records leaves a feeling of regret that they cover but a fraction of the whole period of the Court's history, but, incomplete though they are, they shed a light which illuminates not only the period which they cover, but also the secondary sources which have to be relied upon for the remainder. Some of the chapters which follow are primarily derived from the records: the others could not have been written in their present form without the record evidence in the background.

I

THE ORIGIN AND MEDIEVAL
JURISDICTION OF THE COURT

ONE of the curiosities of English constitutional
history during the reigns of the Plantagenet
kings is the closeness of the association between
the Constable and the Marshal. Since they were the chief
military officers of the Crown, co-operation between them
might reasonably be expected, but instead of mere liaison
between commanders we find them acting jointly on
almost every occasion in such unison that it has been suggested that the Marshal was the recognized lieutenant of
the Constable.[1] The unison of the Constable and the
Marshal is nowhere more marked than in the Court over
which they jointly presided.

That the Constable and the Marshal had a joint court
and that it had jurisdiction over disputes relating to
armorial bearings seem to be the only facts upon which
all modern authors who have touched upon the subject
are agreed. Its origin, its nature, and the remainder of its
jurisdiction have all been the subject of misconceptions
of various kinds. The account of the Court of Chivalry
generally accepted today is that it had its origin either in
the reign of William the Conqueror or at least as early as
that of Edward I, and that it was originally concerned
with the enforcement of military discipline, and later
acquired jurisdiction over the trial of peers and claims to
peerages and baronetcies.

In order to test the accuracy of this generally accepted
account it is first of all necessary to have in mind that in
medieval England there were many constables and many
marshals. Some of them were great men and some of
them were men of but little importance. The greatest of

---

[1] Round, *The King's Serjeants*, p. 76.

B

them were the Constable of England and the Marshal of England, later known as the Lord High Constable and the Earl Marshal. It is with these two Great Officers of State alone that this work is concerned, and it is essential to avoid confusing them with other constables and other marshals, especially where a constable and a marshal are found mentioned together. The unison between the Constable and the Marshal mentioned above is paralleled by a similar unison between lesser constables and marshals, and when a constable and a marshal are found mentioned together it cannot be concluded that they are necessarily the two Great Officers of State bearing those titles.

This is the first possible cause of confusion in investigating the nature and origin of the Court of the Constable and the Marshal. The second is the nomenclature of the Court. During its long history it has been known by a variety of names—the Court of the Constable and the Marshal, the High Court of Chivalry, the Court Military, the Court of Honour, and, in its later days, the Earl Marshal's Court. For the purposes of the present work it will be called the Court of Chivalry, save in quotations. During the Middle Ages it was often referred to without a specific name—proceedings being described as being 'before the Constable and the Marshal'. In the few early formal documents of the Court of which copies are available it is styled in French 'Court de Chivalrie'[1] and in Latin 'Curia Militaris'.[2] This Latin name has been the cause of much confusion concerning the nature and identity of the Court. This confusion has arisen through 'Curia Militaris' being translated as 'Court Military' in the belief that *militaris* was connected with *miles* in its classical sense of 'soldier'. In English medieval Latin, however, *miles* did not mean 'soldier', but 'knight', and was the usual description of a knight until the expression *eques auratus* became fashionable in the sixteenth century. In an age when *miles* meant 'knight' the proper translation

---

[1] Young, *An Account of the Controversy between Reginald Lord Grey of Ruthyn and Sir Edward Hastings*, pp. 6 et seq.
[2] Ibid., pp. 32–33.

of 'Curia Militaris' would therefore not be 'Court Military', but 'Court of Knighthood', which corresponds exactly with the French 'Court de Chivalrie'. This is borne out by documents in English in the case of *Grey* v. *Hastings*, where the Court is referred to as 'this Court of Knighthode of Engeland'.[1]

Before proceeding to consider the effect upon the historiography of the Court of this mistranslation, it will be well to attempt to define this variously named Court. It is the Court held before the Constable and the Marshal or their lieutenants by virtue of their respective offices, from which there is an appeal to the Crown in Chancery. Its records can be readily identified, because it proceeded in accordance with the forms of the civil law, but references or apparent references to the Court in secondary sources require careful scrutiny before they can be accepted.

The Latin name of the Court—'Curia Militaris'—has led seekers after its origin to connect it with the disciplinary powers exercised by the Constable and the Marshal over the army. That the Constable and the Marshal had such disciplinary powers is not to be doubted. They derived them not from the common law but from Ordinances of War (sometimes termed 'Statutes and Ordinances'), which were promulgated by the King for the purposes of particular expeditions. These Ordinances prefaced detailed provision for the conduct of the soldier with a general rule as to obedience. Thus the first of the Ordinances made by Henry V in 1419 was

that alle maner of men of what soever nacion, estate, or condicion soever he be, be obeissaunt to our soverayn lorde the Kyng, and to his Constable and Mareshall, uppon peyn of asmoche as he may forfaite in body & in goodes.[2]

[1] Ibid., p. 18.

[2] Sir Travers Twiss (ed.), *The Black Book of the Admiralty*, i. 459. Cf. ibid., pp. 282, 453. Twiss suggests that this military matter was included in the *Black Book* because Thomas Howard, eighth Duke of Norfolk, filled the offices of Lord High Admiral and Earl Marshal at the same time (ibid., pp. xxxviii–xxxix). Norfolk, however, ceased to be Lord High Admiral in 1525 and was not created Earl Marshal until 1533, though he had held military commands whilst he was Lord High Admiral (*C.P.* ix. 615, 617).

It has been generally assumed that the Statutes and Ordinances of War were enforced by the Court of Chivalry.[1] This has led to the further assumption that the modern court martial was instituted on account of the inadequacy of the Court of Chivalry.[2]

There seems to be but little evidence of any judicial procedure for the enforcement of military discipline during the Middle Ages. Probably much of it was by the 'summary course' referred to in the commission of martial law issued by Charles I in 1625.[3] There is, however, an indication in Henry V's Ordinances of War that the more serious offences were the subject of judicial proceedings. Clause 30 commences—

Also, if any man be juged to the deth by the Kyng, Constable, Mareshall, or any other Juge Ordinarie, or any other officer lawefull . . . .[4]

We could wish for a precise description of the procedure which led to a man being 'juged to the deth', but clause 30 is not apt to describe the Court of Chivalry. That was a court held jointly by the Constable and the Marshal or their lieutenants, whilst clause 30 indicates that the Constable and the Marshal were only two of a number of officers who might act as judges and that the Constable and the Marshal could, like other officers, act severally. Furthermore, it cannot even be assumed that the Constable and the Marshal mentioned in the Ordinances of War were necessarily the Lord High Constable and the Earl Marshal. These Great Officers of State did not always take part in military expeditions. Although an army had to have its constable and its marshal, they could be military officers who were as distinct from the Great Officers of State as a modern field-marshal is from the Earl Marshal. As early as 1346 William Fraunk and Thomas de Haukeston were respectively appointed constable and marshal of the army then about to sail to

---

[1] Adye, *A Treatise on Courts Martial*, p. 11; Charge of Cockburn C.J. in *R. v. Nelson and Brand* (1867), Special Report (2nd ed.), p. 92; *H.E.L.* i. 573-8.
[2] *H.E.L.* i. 576.   [3] See p. 9 *post*.
[4] *Black Book of the Admiralty,* i. 468.

the King,[1] and in 1358 William de Brideport was secretary of the marshal of the army.[2]

The medieval Ordinances of War were the forerunners of the later Articles of War, which only differed from the Ordinances in that their provisions became progressively more detailed. Ultimately the Articles of War were given statutory force in 1689 by the first Mutiny Act, which was the forerunner of the Army Act, under which modern military courts martial are held. Although the court martial books amongst the records of the War Office only commence in 1684,[3] the Ordinances or Articles of War have expressly empowered the holding of courts martial for at least three centuries.[4] In the absence of positive evidence of a change in the procedure it seems more likely that discipline under the medieval Ordinances of War was enforced by military officers in substantially the same manner as it was enforced under the later Ordinances and Articles, which successively replaced them, and that clause 30 of Henry V's Ordinances refers to a court of the same nature as the modern court martial.

A proper understanding of the matter is not assisted by a passage in the *Black Book of the Admiralty* immediately preceding, though apparently unconnected with, a version of Henry V's Statutes and Ordinances of War. It is headed 'The Office of the Constable and Mareschalle', the words of the heading being part of the first sentence, and is for convenience set out below in two paragraphs, though it appears as one in the text.

The office of the Conestable and Mareschalle in the time of werre is to punysh all manner of men that breken the statutes and ordonnaunce by the kynge made to be keped in the oost [i.e. the army] in the said tyme, and to punysh the same accordyng to the peynes provided in the said statutes

---

[1] *Foedera*, v. 525.   [2] *Foedera* (Record Ed.), iii, pt. i. 401.
[3] Clode, *Military Forces of the Crown*, i. 475.
[4] e.g. 'Lawes and Ordinances of Warre', 1639, printed in Clode, op. cit., i. 438–9; 'Laws and Ordinances of Law [*sic*] Established for the Better Government of the Army', 1642, printed ibid. i. 444; 'Orders and Articles of Warr', 1666, printed ibid. i. 447.

The conestable and mareschall hath knowleche upon all maner crymes, contracts, pleets, querelle, trespas, injuries, and offenses don beyonde the see in tyme of werre between souldeour and souldeour, bytwene merchaunts, vytelers, leches, barbours, launders, corvesers, laborers, and artificers necessary to the oost, and yf any of the personnes be oone [i.e. our own subject] and the other person be a straunger, the conestable and mareschalle shall have knowleche in the said matere done in the werre beyonde the see, and of all maner dedes of armes here within the londe doone he [*sic*] hath cognoissaunce, and of the offenses doon beyonde the see he hath knowleche of here in the londe.[1]

At first sight this looks like a description of the Court of Chivalry and it is so treated by Holdsworth.[2] The second paragraph is (except for the inclusion of 'crymes')[3] a paraphrase of the jurisdiction of the Court as defined by the Statute 13 Ric. II, st. 1, c. 2, and the running together of the two paragraphs makes it appear that they both deal with the same subject-matter. The general subject-matter is not, however, the Court of the Constable and Marshal, but, as stated in the heading, the office of the Constable and Marshal, the word 'office' being used in the sense of 'function' or 'duty'.[4] If 'office' is understood in this sense, it becomes apparent that the two paragraphs relate to two different forms of jurisdiction, the first that exercised under the Statutes and Ordinances of War and the second that of the Court of Chivalry. The first jurisdiction was exercised in common with other officers, whilst the second was peculiar to the Lord High Constable and the Earl Marshal. To deduce from this account of the judicial functions of the Constable and the Marshal that the Court of Chivalry had jurisdiction over military discipline under the Statutes and Ordinances of War is as unjustifiable as it would be to deduce from an enumeration of the judicial functions of the present Recorder of London that indictable

---

[1] *Black Book of the Admiralty*, i. 281.
[2] *H.E.L.* i. 574, n. 1.
[3] For the criminal jurisdiction of the Court see pp. 22–26 *post*.
[4] Cf. Hall, *Chron. Hen. VII* (1548), p. 61, '... a king, whose office is to rule ...', cited *O.E.D.*, s.v. 'Office'.

offences are triable in the Mayor's and City of London Court.

The belief that military discipline was enforced in the Court of Chivalry seems to be no older than Sir Matthew Hale's *History of the Common Law*, which includes amongst the matters formerly determinable by the Court 'The Offences and Miscarriages of Soldiers contrary to the Laws and Rules of the Army' and proceeds to state

> For always preparatory to an actual War, the Kings of this Realm, by advice of the Constable, (and Marshal) were used to compose a Book of *Rules* and *Orders* for the due Order and Discipline of their Officers and Soldiers, together with certain Penalties on the Offenders; and this was called, *Martial Law*,[1]

The only writer before Hale who might be read as indicating some connexion between the enforcement of military discipline and the Court of Chivalry is Dr. (afterwards Sir) Thomas Ridley, who in his *View of the Civile and Ecclesiastical Law*, published in 1607, includes breaches of military discipline in his enumeration of matters determinable by the civil law.[2] Ridley's next category of such matters is the bearing of arms,[3] but he does not state that military offences and armorial disputes were dealt with in the same court, nor does he mention the Court of Chivalry anywhere in his work. Dr. Matthew Sutcliffe, on the other hand, in his *Practice, Proceedings, and Lawes of Armes*, published in 1593, treats of the

---

[1] 3rd ed, 1739, pp. 38–39. P. H. Winfield, *The Chief Sources of English Legal History* (Cambridge, Mass., 1925), p. 37, comments: 'Very little service was done either to Hale's reputation or to his wishes by this posthumous publication.' What Hale termed 'martial law' is more generally known as 'military law', the expression 'martial law' being used to denote 'that kind of military government of a country or district, by which the ordinary law is suspended, and the military authorities are empowered to arrest all suspected persons at their discretion, and to punish offenders without formal trial' (*O.E.D.*, s.v. 'Martial'). Martial law in this sense is, of course, unknown to the law of England (A. V. Dicey, *Introduction to the Study of the Law of the Constitution* (9th ed., London, 1948), p. 293). Hale regarded the two expressions as synonymous, for the sentence following the passage quoted in the text reads 'We have extant in the Black Book of the Admiralty and elsewhere several examples of such military laws.'

[2] pp. 87–89.

[3] Op. cit., p. 89.

enforcement of military discipline by courts martial, making no mention of the Court of Chivalry.[1]

Hale's elder contemporary, Sir Edward Coke, described the Court of Chivalry as 'the fountain of Marshal Law'.[2] It must have been directly or indirectly due to Hale that Coke has been misquoted as saying that the Court is 'the fountain of martial law in England'.[3]

Holdsworth's account of the Court of the Constable and the Marshal is based on the belief that it was originally the court which administered military law.[4] Having quoted Hale *in extenso*, he draws the conclusion: 'The maintenance, then, of the rules to be observed in the army was the main part of the jurisdiction of the court',[5] and proceeds on the basis that military law continued to be administered by this Court until the Civil War showed that the Court was quite useless to preserve discipline in a modern army, whereupon Parliament found it necessary to take further powers for the discipline of their troops.[6]

In fact the records of the Court of Chivalry do not include a single case relating to the 'offences and miscarriages of soldiers contrary to the laws and rules of the army'. There is nothing of desertion or mutiny or any other offence within the jurisdiction of the modern court martial. The belief that the Court of Chivalry administered martial law has led to the provisions of the Petition

[1] See p. 281, *post*.

[2] 4 Co. Inst. 123.

[3] Adye, *Treatise on Courts Martial*, p. 1. By the time that Adye wrote English orthography was sufficiently settled to justify the condemnation of this as a misquotation. Earlier phonetic spelling sometimes caused 'martial' to appear as 'marshal' and vice versa (e.g. 'Lord Martiall of England' in F. Moryson, *Itinerary* (London, 1617), ii. 27, and other citations in *O.E.D.*, s.v. 'Martial') and is a further possible cause of confusion in the interpretation of secondary sources. R. O'Sullivan, *Military Law and the Supremacy of the Civil Courts*, p. 6, also treats 'marshal law' as being synonymous with 'martial law' in the modern sense of military law.

[4] The point is made in a slightly different form in an opinion of Edward James and Fitzjames Stephen Q.CC., where modern military law is regarded as having superseded the 'law martial' exercised by the Constable and Marshal (W. Forsyth, *Cases and Opinions on Constitutional Law* (London, 1869), pp. 552–3).

[5] *H.E.L.* i. 573.

[6] Ibid., pp. 576–7. Holdsworth originally stated this view in 'Martial Law Historically Considered', *L.Q.R.* xviii (1902), 117–32.

of Right directed against martial law being read as limiting the powers of the Court.[1] This is a curious error, for the Petition makes no mention of the Court, but recites that

divers commissions under your Majesty's great seal have issued forth, by which certain persons have been assigned and appointed commissioners with power and authority to proceed within the land, according to the justice of martial law, against such soldiers or mariners, or other dissolute persons joining with them, as should commit any murder, robbery, felony, mutiny or other outrage or misdemeanour whatsoever, and by such summary course and order as is agreeable to martial law, and as is used in armies in time of war, to proceed to the trial and condemnation of such offenders, and them to cause to be executed and put to death according to the law martial [and prays that such commissions may be revoked and that] hereafter no commissions of like nature may issue forth to any person or persons whatsoever.[2]

At the time of the Petition of Right the Court of Chivalry had been but recently revived.[3] It was held by the Earl Marshal alone by virtue of his office without any special commission, and the commissions of martial law referred to in the Petition conferred a jurisdiction entirely different from that of the Court of Chivalry. The commissions referred to in the Petition of Right were directed to a number of persons and empowered the commissioners to proceed to trial and condemnation 'by summary course, as used in Armies in time of War'.[4] This was not the method of proceeding in the Court of Chivalry, and there was in truth no connexion between the Court and the commissions of martial law.

Holdsworth's theory that the Court administered martial law until the Great Rebellion showed that it was quite useless to preserve discipline cannot survive the fact

---

[1] *H.E.L.* i. 576; O'Sullivan, op. cit., p. 8.   [2] 3 Car. I, c. 1.
[3] See p. 48 *post.*
[4] e.g. Commission dated 28 December 1625, printed in *Foedera*, xviii. 254. This may have been thought to have had some connexion with the Court of Chivalry through a confusion between the first commissioner, Edward, Viscount Wimbledon, 'Lord Marshall of Our Army', and the Earl Marshal, but the Earl Marshal at that time was the Earl of Arundel.

that the Court was suppressed early in 1641,[1] for Charles I did not raise his standard at Nottingham until 22 August 1642.

The name 'Curia Militaris' has been the cause of misconception concerning the antiquity as well as the nature of the Court of Chivalry. It would be unnecessary even to mention the myth that the Court of Chivalry dates from the reign of William the Conqueror were it not that it received judicial authority in the charge of Cockburn C.J. to the grand jury in R. v. Nelson and Brand.[2] As will be seen below, the Conqueror had been dead for two and a half centuries before the Court of Chivalry appeared on the English scene. We owe the story of its Norman origin to an attempt by Edward IV to enlarge its jurisdiction. When Richard Woodville, Earl Rivers, was appointed Lord High Constable in 1467 the letters patent authorized him to exercise the powers there described as they had been exercised by his predecessors since the Conquest.[3] As Vernon Harcourt has pointed out, this was nothing less than fraudulent, the powers conferred upon Rivers not having even been conferred upon his immediate predecessor.[4]

Vernon Harcourt's theory of the origin of the Court requires more serious consideration. By the process of translating 'Curia Militaris' as 'military court' and then seeking for evidence of a court attached to an army[5] he formed the view that the Court of Chivalry was in existence at least as early as the reign of Edward I.[6]

The documents on which Vernon Harcourt based this

---

[1] See p. 66 post.

[2] (1867), Special Report (2nd ed.), p. 92.

[3] This patent is further considered at p. 26 post.

[4] His Grace the Steward, p. 392. The patents of Rivers and John Tiptoft, Earl of Worcester, his immediate predecessor, are printed ibid., pp. 407–11.

[5] The expression 'an army' is used advisedly, since it would be anachronistic to refer to 'the army' before a standing army was made lawful by the first Mutiny Act (1 Will. & Mar., c. 5).

[6] His Grace the Steward, p. 362. This assertion is made in respect of 'a military court . . . under the control of the Constable and Marshal of England', but on the following page this is treated as being identical with the Court of Chivalry. J. H. Round accepted Vernon Harcourt's view (The King's Serjeants, p. 77).

view are a roll of *Placita exercitus Regis* of 24 Edward I (1295–6)[1] and an entry on the *Coram Rege* Roll of Hilary term, 1325.[2] The first of these documents is a record of trials by jury and the second is a writ of *certiorari* in respect of the trial in 1322 of Roger Damory for treason before Fulk FitzWarin, a constable of the royal army, John de Weston, Marshal of the Royal Household, and Geoffrey le Scrope. These both relate to common-law proceedings, and whilst it is tempting to find in the appearance of a constable and a marshal amongst the judges of Roger Damory some similarity to the later Court of Chivalry, the temptation cannot survive the observation that neither of these officers was one of the Great Officers of State whose court was the Court of Chivalry. By 1322 the Constableship of England had become hereditary in the family of Bohun, whilst the Marshal of England at that time was Thomas of Brotherton, Earl of Norfolk,[3] and the proceedings against Roger Damory were not proceedings in their court, even if they had a court at so early a date.

Vernon Harcourt appears to have noticed that the early proceedings which he cited were governed by the common law, for he states that 'from and after (if not before) the reign of Richard the Second the proceedings seem to have been exclusively in accordance with the civil law'.[4] That a court should have changed from a common-law court to a civil-law court is highly improbable, and the difference in the law applicable seems rather to indicate a lack of identity between the early military tribunals and the Court of Chivalry.

One of the consequences of this identification has been that the nature of the undoubted jurisdiction of the Court of Chivalry over such matters as ransom and armorial bearings has been misunderstood. Holdsworth described them as being allied to the maintenance of the rules to be

---

[1] The first case on the roll is printed in Vernon Harcourt, op. cit., p. 363, n. 1.

[2] Printed ibid., p. 399. R. O'Sullivan, op. cit., p. 2, follows Vernon Harcourt in treating these documents as records of the Court of Chivalry.

[3] *C.P.* ii. 605, 611.

[4] Vernon Harcourt, op cit., pp. 365–6.

observed in the army.[1] The true reason why these matters fell within the jurisdiction of the Constable and the Marshal only becomes apparent when the nature and origin of the Court is considered.

Until the passing of the first Mutiny Act[2] legalized the maintenance of a standing army the legal basis of military discipline was of a purely temporary nature, resting upon whatever Ordinances or Articles of War happened for the time being to be in force. In times of peace when there were no Ordinances or Articles of War in force there was no military law. The Court of Chivalry, on the other hand, was a permanent institution. As Hale says in his unpublished treatise *De Praerogativa Regis*, although the Court of Chivalry is 'called *Curia Militaris* in respect of the subject matter, yet the jurisdiction is a formal settled jurisdiction, and may be exercised as well in time of peace as war'.[3]

This 'settled jurisdiction' did not depend upon transient Articles of War, but was derived from the Crown through a more enduring institution—the King's Council.

The Council dealt with cases which could not be tried by the common law because either the parties were aliens or the dispute arose outside the realm.[4] In the time of Edward III there arose a practice of delegating part of the Council's jurisdiction, which was the origin of the Court of Admiralty.[5]

One of the most striking features of the Court of Chivalry revealed by its records is its similarity in constitution and procedure to the Court of Admiralty. Not only was there this similarity between the two courts, but, as will appear below, their first recognizable appearances were almost contemporaneous. We might therefore fairly expect to find that their origins were similar.

There is no direct evidence that the Court of Chivalry originated in the same way as the Court of Admiralty.

---

[1] *H.E.L.* i. 573.   [2] 1 Will. & Mar., c. 5.

[3] B.M. MS. Hargrave 94, f. 186, cited in *Case of the Army of the Deccan* (1833), 2 Knapp 103, at p. 151.

[4] Baldwin, *The King's Council*, p. 272.   [5] Ibid., p. 273.

Both courts had, however, the same connexion with the Council in that some at least of the jurisdiction of each was originally exercised by the Council,[1] whilst an appeal to the Crown in Chancery lay from each court. Furthermore each court was governed by the civil law and neither court had any jurisdiction over matters which were triable at common law.

The reasons why this should be were similar in the case of each court. English seamen and their ships were continually in contact with those of other nations. That contact was often violent, resulting in disputes which set in motion the processes of law. Seaman could not be expected to submit themselves to the municipal laws of foreign countries; so there grew up a kind of legal *lingua franca*, a body of law acceptable to all sailors of all nations. This maritime law was compounded of a number of elements of diverse origins, such as the Laws of Oleron and the Laws of Wisby, but it contained a large measure of what had once been the law of the whole civilized world—the civil law of the *Corpus Juris Civilis*. In England the maritime law came to be administered by the Lord High Admiral.

The maritime contact with the men of other nations which brought the English Court of Admiralty into being had its counterpart in the military contact between Englishmen and their continental allies and enemies. Here also there was need for a body of law which was internationally acceptable, and here again those learned in the civil law satisfied the need. The military counterparts of the Lord High Admiral were the Lord High Constable and the Earl Marshal: the Court of Admiralty had its opposite number in the Court of Chivalry.

The Court of Admiralty came rather suddenly into existence in the middle of the fourteenth century, its origin being traced to the period between 1340 and 1357.[2] It seems possible to date the origin of the Court of

---

[1] Hale, *De Praerogativa Regis*, cc. 11, 12. See note 3, p. 12 *ante*.

[2] R. G. Marsden, *Select Pleas in the Court of Admiralty* (Selden Soc. vi, 1894), i, p. xiv; Senior, *Doctors' Commons and the Old Court of Admiralty*, p. 14.

Chivalry with rather more precision. The earliest recognizable reference to the Court appears to be the appointment by Edward III on 23 August 1348 of two of his serjeants-at-arms to arrest William le Counte, whom William de Wynchelez had taken prisoner of war in Normandy, and bring him before the King's Constable and Marshal to answer for his broken faith and other things to be put forward against him.[1] That the Court was probably not in existence much earlier than this is indicated by certain armorial proceedings tried during the siege of Calais between 1345 and 1348.

The first of these cases was a dispute between John de Warbeltone and Tibaud, son of Tibaud Russel alias Gorges, for the arms 'lozenge dor et daszeur'. It is known only from a single copy of an early eighteenth-century engraving of a document purporting to be the original letters patent (*lettres ouvertes*) containing the decision dated 19 July 1347.[2] This recites that Henry, Earl of Lancaster, Steward of England, William, Earl of Huntingdon, Reynold Cobham, Walter, Lord Manny, William Lovel, and Stephen de Cosington had been commissioned by the King 'oier trier et jugger toutes manieres de batz darmes et heaumes de dayntz son host en son siege devant Caloys' and goes on to state their decision and to authenticate it by the affixing of their seals. There is here no act of the Court of Chivalry. The personnel of the tribunal, the manner of their appointment, and the form of their decision are all entirely different. Since the Court of Chivalry had in later times exclusive jurisdiction in cases of this kind, the inference to be drawn from these proceedings is that there was no such Court in 1347. Otherwise there would have been no necessity for the granting of the commission to Lancaster and the others 'oier trier et jugger' such disputes.

The evidence afforded by the other case, which was a

---

[1] *C.P.R. 1348–50*, p. 174. Prynne, *Animadversions on the Fourth Institute*, p. 339, cites from the French Rolls a writ dated 10 Dec. 1347 to the Bailiffs and Jurats of Jersey to arrest William le Counte 'prout secundum jus armorum fuerit faciendum'.

[2] Bodl. MS. Ashm. 1137, f. 144; Wagner, *Heralds and Heraldry*, p. 23.

dispute between Nicholas, Lord Burnell, and Robert, Lord Morley, is somewhat equivocal. It cannot be more precisely dated than sometime during the siege of Calais. Furthermore, there is no contemporary record of the case, which is only known from reference to it by witnesses in *Lovel* v. *Morley* about forty years later.[1] All that we know of *Burnell* v. *Morley* is that it was tried before the Earl of Northumberland, Constable, and the Earl of Warwick, Marshal, sitting together 'tribunalement'. This is consistent with a sitting of the Court of Chivalry and were it a few years later there would be no difficulty about so identifying it. It is, however, equally consistent with Northumberland and Warwick having been included with Lancaster and the others in the commission under which *Warbeltone* v. *Gorges* was tried in 1347 and trying *Burnell* v. *Morley* under that commission, rather than by virtue of any jurisdiction vested in them as a Court of Chivalry. If *Burnell* v. *Morley* was earlier than *Warbeltone* v. *Gorges*, it was almost certainly tried under the commission: if later, it may have been one of the earliest cases in the Court of Chivalry. In either event the evidence seems to indicate that the origin of the Court is to be found between the decision in *Warbeltone* v. *Gorges* in 1347 and the appointment of the serjeant-at-arms to arrest William le Counte in 1348. This is also consistent with a commission issued on 28 November 1347 to John Bonde appointing him to arrest Robert Tillote and Thomas de Ramesdene, two prisoners of war who were alleged to have broken their parole, and to bring them before the Council to do what of right and according to the law of arms should be done in the premises.[2] Had there been a Court of Chivalry at this time, the case would have been an appropriate one to be dealt with in that Court.

There is little evidence of the existence of the Court during the next two decades. A petition to the Council in 1361 tells the tale of a parson, perhaps an army chaplain, who had his portmanteau stolen before Chartres and caused his servant to sue before the Constable and

---

[1] Wagner, op. cit., pp. 21–22.   [2] *C.P.R. 1345–8*, p. 468.

Marshal. When the parties were adjudged to combat the parson withdrew, being afraid of incurring irregularity by seeking a judgment of blood before a lay court. He then found himself the defendant in a suit for conspiracy before the Constable and Marshal, although they had no jurisdiction in such a matter, and he petitioned the Council on account of his opponent imprisoning him and making him agree under duress to pay 100 marks.[1]

From the 1370's onwards the business of the Court must have been substantial. Although there are no original records of the Court for the medieval period, the fact that an appeal lay to the King in Chancery caused many entries of commissions of appeal to be enrolled on the patent rolls. Behind the cases which are known from there having been an appeal there must lie many more in which there was no appeal and of which no record now remains.

The lack of original records of the Court is in some small measure remedied by the existence of transcripts of some or all of the documents in three cases in the reigns of Richard II and Henry IV—*Lovel* v. *Morley*,[2] *Scrope* v. *Grosvenor*,[3] and *Grey* v. *Hastings*.[4] It so happens that each of these cases concerns a dispute as to armorial bearings, but that does not mean that such cases formed the bulk of the Court's work. On the contrary, if the cases mentioned on the patent rolls are a fair sample of the whole, but a small portion of the business of the Court was concerned with heraldic matters.[5] Whilst in each of the three cases

[1] *Parson of Langar* v. *Conynsby*, J. S. Leadam and J. F. Baldwin, *Select Cases before the King's Council* (Selden Soc. xxxv, 1918), p. 47.

[2] P.R.O., C. 47/6/1; P.R.O. 30/26; Coll. Arm. MS. Processus in Curia Marescalli, ii, pt. 2.

[3] P.R.O., C. 47/6/2–3; printed by Sir Harris Nicolas as *The Scrope and Grosvenor Controversy*.

[4] Coll. Arm. MS. Processus in Curia Marescalli, i and ii, pt. 1. Some of the documents in this case were privately printed by C. G. Young, York Herald, in *An Account of the Controversy between Reginald Lord Grey of Ruthyn and Sir Edward Hastings* (1841). For a transcript of the evidence of one of the witnesses, see A. R. Wagner, 'A Fifteenth-Century Description of the Brass of Sir Hugh Hastings at Elsing, Norfolk', in *Antiquaries Journal*, xix (1939), 421.

[5] In addition to the three cases mentioned in the text there was protracted litigation between Thomas Baude and Nicholas de Syngleton concerning the

the transcripts include depositions which contain material of the greatest value to the heraldic historian, the value of the transcripts for the present purpose lies in the formal documents which disclose the manner of proceedings in the Court, showing that it closely followed the forms used in the Court of Admiralty and that the officers and legal practitioners of the Court were civilians.

Many of the matters which came before the Court at this period are what one would expect to find before a tribunal concerned with matters of war. There were proceedings in respect of the unjust detention of prisoners from their captors,[1] the exchange of prisoners,[2] and the payment of ransom.[3] Litigation concerning the division of the ransom of the Count of Denia, a nobleman of Aragon, who was captured at the battle of Najara in 1367 by three English esquires, dragged on for nearly half a century.[4]

By the last quarter of the fourteenth century the Court was dealing with litigation which had no apparent connexion with war. Whilst an allegation of broken faith could be used, as in Wynchelez's case,[5] to found proceedings relating to a prisoner of war, it could also be used for the purposes of a complaint of the non-payment of a debt or some other matter determinable by the common law. Although it is not possible to cite instances from so early a period, it is apparent that it had become a common practice before 1384, by which time the encroachment on

arms *Gules, 3 chevrons argent* (*C.P.R. 1391–6*, pp. 332, 576; *1396–9*, p. 89), and *Wyght* v. *Tannere* (1394), *C.P.R. 1391–6*, p. 380, seems to be a unique case of a female plaintiff complaining of the usurpation of her arms. In 1378 an armorial dispute in the Court between two members of the Cheshire family of Massey was referred to the arbitration of four knights and an esquire (*The Ancestor*, ix (1904), 217).

[1] e.g. *More* v. *Basset* (1374), *C.P.R. 1374–7*, p. 54.

[2] e.g. *Waldeshef* v. *Wawe* (1383), *C.P.R. 1381–5*, p. 354.

[3] e.g. *Hoo* v. *Bretvill* (1385), ibid., p. 596.

[4] It was still under appeal in 1412 (*C.P.R. 1408–13*, p. 391). By this time the captors were dead and the litigation was proceeding between an assignee of the heiress of one and the executor of another. There are many references to this case in the patent rolls. The date of the Count's capture is given in *C.P.R. 1399–1401*, p. 524. His son was being held as a hostage as late as 1380 (*Foedera*, vii. 275).

[5] See p. 14 *ante*.

C

the common-law courts had become so serious that it had to be arrested by Parliament. The first statutory attempt to curb the Constable and the Marshal made no attempt to define their jurisdiction, but simply provided that they should confine themselves to what belonged to their Court and not hold pleas touching the common law.[1]

This enactment had no sanction and was quite ineffective. Shortly after it was passed we find a cause of alleged prevarication, forgery or breach of pact,[2] and in 1386 debt appears as a cause of action.[3] In 1389 the Court rejected an exception declinatory against the jurisdiction in a cause concerning the non-payment of an annuity based upon breach of faith (causa fidei lesione pretense).[4]

It is small wonder that this extension of the jurisdiction of the Court in the face of the statutory prohibition of 1384 caused the Commons to complain in 1389 that the Court of the Constable and the Marshal was encroaching contracts, covenants, trespasses, debts, detinues, and other actions pleadable at common law to the great prejudice of the King and his courts and the great grievance of the people.[5] On this occasion Parliament positively stated the limits of the jurisdiction of the Constable and the Marshal and provided a remedy if those limits were overstepped. The jurisdiction was defined as

cognisance of contracts touching deeds of arms and of war out of the realm, and also of things that touch [arms or] war within the realm, which cannot be determined nor discussed by the common

---

[1] 8 Ric. II, c. 5. The statute concludes with a declaration that the common law should be executed and used as was customary in the times of the King's progenitors, which indicates that the cause for complaint had arisen since the death of Edward III. For the petition which led to this statute see *Rot. Parl.* iii. 202.

[2] *Etton* v. *Merton* (1385), *C.C.R. 1385–9*, p. 103.

[3] *Tottenas* v. *Mareschal*, *C.P.R. 1385–9*, p. 85. At first sight *Salisbury (Earl)* v. *Montague*, a cause *de fide lesa* concerning the detention of an indenture and a statute merchant, appears to be a contravention of the statute, but it had been commenced in 1383, when the defendant had submitted to the jurisdiction of the Court of Chivalry (*C.P.R. 1385–9*, p. 67).

[4] *Asthorpe* v. *Dynham*, *C.P.R. 1388–92*, p. 130.

[5] *Rot. Parl.* iii. 265.

law, with other usages and customs to the same matters pertaining, which other constables heretofore have duly and reasonably used in their time.[1]

The statute went on to provide that one who complained that a plea commenced before the Constable and Marshal might be tried by the common law could have a writ under the privy seal directed to the Constable and the Marshal ordering them not to proceed with the case until the King's Council had discussed whether it ought to pertain to the Court of the Constable and Marshal or should be tried by the common law. A defendant applying for a writ under the privy seal had to enter into a recognizance before the Chancellor to appear before the Constable and the Marshal should the Council determine that it was triable in their Court.[2] The Council authorized the continuance of the proceedings by a writ called a *procedendo*. It appears that in determining whether to issue a *procedendo* the Council had to be assisted by at least one of the common-law judges, for in *Pounteney* v. *Borney*[3] a second writ under the privy seal ordering the Constable and the Marshal not to proceed was obtained on the ground that although the *procedendo* mentioned all the names of the bishops and knights who were of the Council, it made no mention of any judge being present when it was granted. When the question of jurisdiction came before the Council a second time, they referred it to the judges, who heard it in the Exchequer Chamber. When the case was argued before the judges Sir William Fulthorpe, the Constable's lieutenant, appeared in court and unsuccessfully argued that the case could not be determinable by the common law because a *procedendo* had already been issued.

The inclusion in the jurisdiction defined by the statute of 1389 of 'contracts touching deeds of arms and of war

---

[1] 13 Ric. II, st. 1, c. 2. The words in brackets are in the French text, but are omitted from the common English translations.

[2] *Gournay* v. *Trote* (1393), *C.C.R. 1392–6*, p. 153, where the recognizance was for £500, which was the amount claimed by the plaintiff.

[3] (1411), Y.B. 13 Hen. IV, Mich., pl. 10.

out of the realm' is of interest because it may indicate
the reason of the original necessity for the Court. The
commonest 'contracts touching deeds of arms and of war'
must have been the indentures of war, by means of which
armies were raised in the later Middle Ages. By such
indentures commanders contracted with the Crown to
provide specified numbers of troops and in turn sub-
contracted their obligations to smaller men.[1] By the
beginning of the Hundred Years War indentured troops
had practically replaced the old feudal force based upon
tenure by knight service,[2] so that disputes arising out of
indentures of war must have started to engage the attention of lawyers by the time when the Court of Chivalry
first appears. By 1374 the jurisdiction of the Court of
Chivalry over such disputes had become so well established that Belknap C.J. held that the Court of Common
Pleas had no cognizance of an action of debt upon a
retainer in London to serve in the war in France.[3]

So far as can be judged from the matters which went
to appeal, the statute of 1389 seems to have been more
effective than its predecessor of 1384, as might be expected from the fact that it was provided with a sanction.
There is, moreover, direct evidence that care was taken to
keep the Court within bounds. There were references to
the Council under the statute of 1389 to determine
whether the Court had jurisdiction in particular cases,[4]
and in 1393 the Court itself decided that it had no jurisdiction to try a claim on a charter-party for the carriage
of wine from Bordeaux to England, notwithstanding that
the plaintiff had already sued unsuccessfully at common
law and in the Admiralty Court of the North.[5]

Even so, encroachments on the jurisdiction of the

---

[1] For examples of such indentures see Nicolas, *History of the Battle of Agin-court*, App. pp. 8 (king and subject), 10 (subject and subject).

[2] J. W. Fortescue, *A History of the British Army*, i (London, 1910), 21–22.

[3] A. Fitzherbert, *La Graunde Abridgement* (London, 1577), Dett. 1.

[4] e.g. *Gournay* v. *Trote* (1393), *C.C.R. 1392–6*, p. 153; *Pounteney* v. *Borney* (1411), Y.B. 13 Hen. IV, Mich., pl. 10.

[5] *Copyn* v. *Snoke* (1393), *Select Pleas of the Admiralty* (Selden Soc., ix, 1897), ii, lix; *C.P.R. 1391–6*, p. 340. An appeal against this decision was still pending in 1397 (*C.P.R. 1396–9*, p. 103).

common-law courts were not entirely prevented. In the second year of Henry IV's reign (1400–1) the Commons complained that the officers of the Court of Chivalry had arrested and imprisoned the King's subjects and compelled them to answer concerning matters done within the realm which ought to be determined in the common-law courts, whereupon the King ordered that the laws and statutes should be obeyed.[1]

In spite of this the encroachments seem to have continued. Thus in 1403 there was an appeal by an unsuccessful plaintiff in a case concerning certain pieces of money to the value of 15,000 doubles of gold of Spanish coinage and jewels to the value of £100.[2] On the face of it this was a common-law matter, though it may be that the cause of action arose outside England in some military context.[3] Nevertheless, some regard was had to the limits of the Court's jurisdiction in debt. In a cause in 1469 the defendant questioned the jurisdiction of the Court on the ground that the pretended contract was made in England and not beyond the seas.[4]

In addition to the power of determining the limits of the jurisdiction of the Court of Chivalry conferred on the Council by the statute of 1389, the exercise of the Court's jurisdiction was controlled by means of the appellate jurisdiction of the King in Chancery. This appellate jurisdiction was exercised by commissioners, who often included one or more civilians, appointed by letters patent for the purposes of each case,[5] though the King could take the case back into his own hands and decide it, as was done in *Scrope* v. *Grosvenor* on account of 'les grandes delayes et frivoles' in the proceedings before the Commissioners.[6]

[1] *Rot. Parl.* iii. 475.

[2] *Blethlowe* v. *Dowesto, C.P.R. 1401–5,* p. 211.

[3] A late example of a non-military cause was *Zeboll* v. *Wattys* (1472), *C.P.R. 1467–77,* p. 307, which was concerned with a contract made by Spanish merchants in Flanders for the sale of white soap.

[4] *Curteys* v. *Spicer, C.P.R. 1467–77,* p. 169.

[5] The commission in *Scrope* v. *Grosvenor* is printed in *The Scrope and Grosvenor Controversy,* i. 2.

[6] Ibid. i. 350. See further as to appeals pp. 221–4 *post.*

All the cases to which reference has been made were causes of instance, i.e. *inter partes*. No example of a medieval cause of office in the Court of Chivalry has so far been found. Indeed, the requirement in the statute of 1389 that every plaintiff should declare plainly his matter in his petition seems to show that the draftsman considered the cause of instance to be the normal form of proceeding in the Court. Yet there must have been some causes of office, for on 8 October 1471 Thomas Appleton was appointed by letters patent to be 'clerk of the King's Constableship of England and promoter of business concerning the King's Majesty'. Moreover, this was not an innovation, for Appleton's appointment was stated to be in succession to Thomas Brouns.[1]

The principal criminal jurisdiction of the Court at this period was of an entirely different character, being an appeal—a formal accusation, which the accuser (appellant) offered to support in single combat, and which, in default of evidence, could result in a trial by battle. This form of trial was not peculiar to the Court of Chivalry. It was also used in certain archaic proceedings in the common-law courts, where it remained a legal possibility until it was abolished by Act of Parliament in 1819.[2] It had, however, become practically obsolete in the common-law courts long before the Court of Chivalry came into existence. In the Court of Chivalry it was primarily used for the trial of treasons and homicides committed abroad, for which there was no remedy at common law, though it could also be used for a 'deed or action of arms'.[3]

The proceedings were commenced by a petition to the King in Council, to which was annexed a schedule of the articles of complaint.[4] The matter was then referred to the Court of Chivalry, where the parties joined battle and the Court assigned a day for the combat.[5] If, however, the

[1] *C.P.R. 1467–77*, p. 110.
[2] 59 Geo. III, c. 46. See p. 120 *post*.
[3] *Black Book of the Admiralty*, i. 325; W. Dugdale, *Origines Juridiciales* (3rd ed., London, 1680), p. 85.
[4] *Talbot (Lord)* v. *Ormond (Earl)* (1423), *Rot. Parl.* iv. 198.
[5] *Lyalton* v. *Norres* (1453), *Proc. P.C.* vi. 129, 137.

appellant was in a position to prove his case by evidence, he could do so instead of proceeding to battle.[1]

The manner in which a trial by battle was conducted in the Court of Chivalry was the subject of many detailed rules, which it would be tedious to set out at length.[2] The form of the lists, the weapons of the combatants, and the functions of the various officers of the Court were all precisely defined and the whole procedure was highly formalized.[3] The King paid for the preparation of the field of battle and also provided the parties with weapons and the services of armourers and others.[4] The manner of trial was the same, whatever the nature of the accusation, but the result of defeat varied with the crime. If the appeal was one of treason, the vanquished party, whether he was the appellant or the defendant, was disarmed in the lists and drawn behind a horse in the charge of the Marshal to the place of execution, where he was beheaded or hanged. In the case of any other crime the indignity of being drawn behind a horse was spared, and if the appeal related only to a 'deed or action of arms', the only penalty was being disarmed and put out of the lists.[5] The same result followed a confession of the charge.[6]

---

[1] *Hereford (Duke)* v. *Norfolk (Duke)* (1398), *Rot. Parl.* iii. 383. It is not certain that this was actually a proceeding in the Court of Chivalry, for Norfolk was the Earl Marshal at the time, but it was ordered that the process should take the course of the 'law of chivalry'.

[2] There are several versions of these rules, the most authoritative being 'The Ordenaunce and Fourme of Fightyng within Listes', addressed to Richard II by his uncle, Thomas of Woodstock, Duke of Gloucester and Lord High Constable, printed in French and English versions in *Black Book of the Admiralty*, i. 300–29. See also Dugdale, op. cit., pp. 76–86, and Viscount Dillon, 'A MS. Collection of Ordinances of Chivalry of the Fifteenth Century', *Archaeologia*, lvii (1900), 61–66. For an account of a combat fought according to these rules see Neilson, *Trial by Combat*, pp. 171–6. The procedure at tournaments was very similar to this judicial combat: see 'Tournament between Lord Scales and the Bastard of Burgundy', *Excerpta Historica* (London, 1831), pp. 171–212. This no doubt explains the erroneous belief referred to on p. 282 *post* that this tournament took place in the Court of Chivalry. As to the distinction between tournaments and judicial combats see Dillon, op. cit., p. 38.

[3] In a case in 1453 both the appellant and the defendant refer to 'the custume in the seid courte of old tyme used' (*Proc. P.C.* vi. 132, 137).

[4] Ibid. vi. 55, 130, 133, 135. In 1446 Henry VI paid for lessons in fighting for two appellants (ibid. vi. 59).

[5] *Black Book of the Admiralty*, i. 325; 4 Co. Inst. 124.

[6] *Aleyn's Case* (1398), *C.P.R. 1396–9*, p. 433.

The battle did not always take place, for the King could by a writ under the Privy Seal directed to the Constable and the Marshal stop the proceedings and order them to be deleted from the records of the Court.[1] In the famous dispute between the Dukes of Hereford and Norfolk in 1398 the King not only forbade the battle, but also banished the parties.[2]

Although most of the appeals in the Court of Chivalry concerned treason,[3] the Court also entertained charges of attempted murder,[4] whilst one of the articles of complaint against Richard II after his deposition was that he caused appeals to be brought in the Court of Chivalry against persons alleged to have spoken words which might tend to the abuse, scandal, or disparagement of the King.[5] An appeal of a less common type was *Annesley* v. *Catreton*,[6] in which the defendant was accused of treacherously surrendering to the French for money a castle in Normandy of which he was the keeper and in which the appellant's wife had a one-third share. It was even claimed that there could be a combat on a debt because the defendant had been guilty of a breach of faith in denying it.[7]

The common-law courts recognized this jurisdiction of the Court of Chivalry, so that to kill a man in judicial combat was justifiable homicide.[8]

Apart from the risk that the party killed might not be the defendant, but the appellant, an appeal was a some-

---

[1] *Talbot (Lord)* v. *Ormond (Earl)* (1423), *Rot. Parl.* iv. 199; cf. *Proc. P.C.* vi. 57.

[2] *Rot. Parl.* iii. 383. As to this case see note 1, p. 23 *ante*.

[3] e.g. *Aleyn's Case, supra*; *Kighlee* v. *Scrope* (1400), *C.P.R. 1399–1401*, p. 401; *Barnolby's Case* (1407), *C.C.R., 1405–9*, p. 300; *Bradley's Case* (temp. Ric. II), *C.C.R. 1405–9*, p. 416; *Belsham* v. *Wolf* (1438), *C.P.R. 1436–41*, p. 265; *Davy* v. *Catour* (1446), *Proc. P.C.* vi. 55; *Kilmain (Prior)* v. *Ormond (Earl)* (1446), ibid. vi. 59; *Lyalton* v. *Norres* (1453), ibid. vi. 129.

[4] *Scrope* v. *Kighlee* (1400), *C.P.R. 1399–1401*, p. 401.

[5] *Rot. Parl.* iii. 420b.

[6] (1380), *C.P.R. 1377–81*, p. 485. For an account of the battle in this case, see Neilson, op. cit., pp. 171–6.

[7] Per Fulthorpe, Lieutenant of the Constable *arguendo* in *Pounteney* v. *Borney* (1411), Y.B. 13 Hen. IV, Mich., pl. 10. No actual case of battle for debt has been found, but in 1415 the plaintiff offered himself in combat on a claim for damages for breach of a contract for service in war in Guienne (B.M. MS. Add. 9021, f. 196).

[8] *Paston* v. *Ledham* (1495), Y.B. 37 Hen. VI, Pasch., pl. 8, per Nedham J.

what unsatisfactory proceeding because the Court of Chivalry could only levy execution on the body and goods of a convicted person and could not distrain upon his lands and tenements.[1] In consequence the Court was powerless against an alleged traitor if he could not be brought before it in person. Thus the proceedings commenced against Henry Percy, Earl of Northumberland, and Thomas, Lord Bardolf, for treason in 1406 were ineffective, Northumberland and Bardolf being later condemned in Parliament in their absence to suffer death and the forfeiture of their lands and chattels.[2]

The attempt of the Court of Chivalry to encroach on the civil jurisdiction of the common-law courts was paralleled by an attempt to obtain jurisdiction over appeals of treason and homicide committed within the realm. This led to a petition by the Commons in 1379. At that time the Constableship was vacant, the last Constable, Humphrey de Bohun, Earl of Hereford, having died in 1373, leaving two infant daughters as his coheirs, and the Lords made this an excuse for not dealing with the matter,[3] although Thomas of Woodstock, who had married the elder daughter, had been appointed Constable in 1376 for so long as the King had the wardship of the Bohun lands.[4] Twenty years were to pass before the Court's jurisdiction over appeals was limited by statute.

Meanwhile there was another innovation with respect to appeals of treason. In 1388 it was the turn of the Court of Chivalry to have its jurisdiction encroached upon. Instead of proceeding in the Court of Chivalry, the Lords Appellant brought their appeals in Parliament. Either on account of this precedent or for some other reason, in 1397 the Constable and the Marshal were unwilling to proceed in appeals and were ordered to do so by a warrant under the privy seal.[5] In order to prevent this precedent being followed in the future, the first Parliament of Henry IV enacted that thenceforth no appeals should be pursued in Parliament and that all appeals to be made of

---

[1] *Rot. Parl.* iii. 473.   [2] Ibid. iii. 604–7.   [3] Ibid. iii. 65.
[4] *C.P.R. 1374–7*, p. 279.   [5] *Proc. P.C.* i. 65.

things done out of the realm should be tried and determined before the Constable and Marshal of England.[1]

Whilst this Act preserved the jurisdiction of the Court of Chivalry over crimes committed abroad, it also met the petition of 1379 by providing that all appeals to be made of things done within the realm should be tried and determined by 'the good laws of the realm', i.e. the common law, and so prohibited the Court of Chivalry from dealing any more with appeals of treason committed at home, such as that of the Duke of Hereford against the Duke of Norfolk in 1398. Nevertheless, in spite of the statutory prohibition, it seems that such appeals continued to be brought in the Court, for in 1429 the Commons petitioned against breaches of the statute.[2]

This criminal jurisdiction of the Court of Chivalry must be distinguished from another form of criminal jurisdiction in treason exercised by the Constable with or without the Marshal during the latter half of the fifteenth century. This latter jurisdiction was conferred first on Richard Woodville, Earl Rivers, when he was appointed Lord High Constable in 1467. As Vernon Harcourt has demonstrated,[3] the recital in Rivers's patent that the power to try cases of treason 'summarie et de plano sine strepitu et figura judicii sola facti veritate inspecta' had been conferred upon his immediate predecessor, John Tiptoft, Earl of Worcester, is a fabrication.[4] Nevertheless, it seems likely that Tiptoft was the originator of this summary method of trial. This was probably the reason for the contemporary complaint that a few days after his appointment in February 1462, 'the butcher of England', as Tiptoft came to be called on account of his cruelty in

---

[1] 1 Hen. IV, c. 14; S. B. Chrimes, 'Richard II's Questions to the Judges', *L.Q.R.* lxxii (1956), 390. For the petition which led to the statute see *Rot. Parl.* iii. 442. This statute was interpreted as making it essential for there to be a Lord High Constable before an appeal could be brought in the Court of Chivalry. It was for this reason that the Earl of Lindsey was twice appointed Lord High Constable during the reign of Charles I: see pp. 52, 53 *post.*

[2] *Rot. Parl.* iv. 349.

[3] *Op. cit.,* p. 392.

[4] R. J. Mitchell, *John Tiptoft* (London, 1938), p. 65, accepts this recital at its face value.

doing justice,[1] condemned the Earl of Oxford and his eldest son and Sir Thomas Todenham 'by lawe padowe'.[2] This reference to Tiptoft's studies at the University of Padua cannot relate to the application of the civil law in the Court of Chivalry, for that had been well established for many years and was recognized as lawful by the common-law courts,[3] and so cannot have been the cause of any grievance. The manner in which Oxford and others were tried must have been an innovation, the origin of which was attributed, possibly wrongly, to the Constable's studies abroad.[4]

In the absence of the formal records it is difficult to distinguish these trials 'by lawe padowe' from appeals of treason in the accounts of contemporary chroniclers, but it seems likely that they became the customary method of disposing of political opponents in the last four decades of the fifteenth century. Although at first it was the Constable alone who presided over trials of this kind, they were later also conducted before the Marshal as well as the Constable,[5] and by 1497 it was possible to describe proceedings against traitors 'sine strepitu et figura judicii sola rei veritate inspecta' (the exact words used in Rivers's patent of 1467) as being 'secundum leges et consuetudines coram constabulario et marescallo hactenus usitatas'.[6] In so far as such proceedings had any legal

---

[1] B.M. MS. Cotton Vitellius A. 16, f. 130, cited in Vernon Harcourt, op. cit., p. 394, n. 2.

[2] J. Warkworth, *A Chronicle of the . . . Reign of King Edward the Fourth* (Camden Soc., 1839), p. 5. Warkworth later records with satisfaction that Tiptoft himself 'was juged be suche lawe as he dyde to other menne' before the son and heir of the Earl of Oxford (ibid., p. 13).

[3] See p. 165 *post.*

[4] Possibly Tiptoft was proceeding by analogy with the summary causes 'absque strepitu judicii et de simplici et plano' in the ecclesiastical courts: see Conset, *Practice of the Ecclesiastical Courts*, p. 23.

[5] The trial of the Duke of Somerset and others before the Constable and the Marshal in 1471 after the battle of Tewkesbury appears to have been of a summary nature. Waurin's statement that the Constable and the Marshal 'estorient commis leurs juges de par le roy' seems to indicate that they were not dealing with appeals of treason under their inherent jurisdiction (J. de Waurin, *Recueil des Croniques*, v (Rolls Series 39), 672).

[6] Letters patent appointing commissioners for the trial of James, Lord Audeley, after the Cornish rising, printed in Vernon Harcourt, op. cit., pp. 414–15.

validity at all, they derived it by direct grant from the Crown, and they cannot properly be classified as proceedings of the Court of Chivalry, although the combination of the Constable and the Marshal has sometimes led to them being so described.[1] There is no evidence that the officers of the Court of Chivalry were in any way concerned in them and, as will appear in the next chapter, such trials continued to be held at a time when the ordinary business of the Court was temporarily at a standstill.

[1] Vernon Harcourt, op. cit., pp. 394, 397; *H.E.L.* i. 575.

II

THE CIVILIANS ECLIPSED
1485–1622

THE year 1485 is traditionally regarded as a resting-place for the general historian. In the annals of the Court of Chivalry it seems to have a special significance. The union of the houses of Lancaster and York put an end to war within the realm and so to the possibility of litigation concerning it. Another branch of the jurisdiction of the Court defined by the statute of 1389—contracts touching deeds of arms and of war out of the realm—was rendered obsolete by the replacement of indentured troops by the national militia as the principal military force of England.[1] Appeals of treason had been replaced in fact, though not in law, by the summary jurisdiction mentioned in the previous chapter, so that the Court was left with nothing but the 'other usages and customs to the same matters [i.e. arms and war] pertaining' under the statute of 1389[2] and appeals of crimes, other than treasons, arising outside the realm under the statute of 1399.[3] This must have been insubstantial fare for the civilians, so that it is not surprising that no contemporary references to the Court during the reign of Henry VII have been found. Holdsworth cites the trial of Perkin Warbeck in 1500 as a Court of Chivalry case.[4] In fact the Constable and the Marshal were authorized to try Warbeck according to martial law by a special commission under the Great Seal.[5]

Not only has no reference to the Court of Chivalry at this period been found, but there is a clear indication that in 1496 the Court was inactive. There was then a dispute

---

[1] See Fortescue, *History of the British Army*, i. 109–10.
[2] See p. 19 *ante*. [3] See p. 25 *ante*. [4] *H.E.L.* i. 574.
[5] *Calvin's Case* (1607), 7 Co. Rep. 1, at f. 6b, citing an extract from a book of Hobart A.-G. temp. Hen. VII in a book of Griffith A.-G.

between two Lancashire knights, Sir Thomas Ashton and Sir Piers Legh, concerning the bearing of the arms *Argent, a mullet of five points sable.* This dispute was decided in favour of Ashton by the Lord High Constable, the Earl of Derby, sitting in the King's Chamber at Westminster. So far this is consistent with the Constable sitting alone in the Court of Chivalry, but the significant fact is that Derby ordered that his decision, which took the form of a 'bill endented', should be registered in the books of Garter and Norroy Kings of Arms.[1] This would have been quite inappropriate had the Court of Chivalry been properly constituted with a Register keeping its records. The only tenuous link between these proceedings and the Court of Chivalry is that amongst those present before the Earl of Derby was a doctor of civil law.

If the Court of Chivalry was not active in 1496, it seems a fair inference in the absence of direct evidence to relate its inactivity back to the events of 1485. This interpretation of the very scanty and mostly negative evidence antedates by thirty-six years the break in the continuity of the Court's work, which had been generally attributed to the fact that after Edward, Duke of Buckingham, was executed on Tower Hill on 17 May 1521 the office of Lord High Constable was left vacant, save on a few special occasions, mostly coronations. As will appear later, this vacancy in the office of Constable was many years afterwards made the basis of an argument that the Court of Chivalry could not be properly constituted without a Constable, so that Buckingham's execution has been given a significance which was almost certainly not apparent at the time. For all practical purposes the office of Constable had been vacant since the death of the Earl of Derby in 1504. Buckingham had been appointed for the coronation of Henry VIII in 1509, but his claim to the office as of right was rejected in 1514.[2] In all probability the vacancy in the Constableship had no immediate

---

[1] *Visitation of Lancashire, 1533* (Chetham Soc. cx, 1882), p. 161.
[2] *Duke of Buckingham's Case* (1514), 3 Dyer 285b.

effect upon the Court, which remained as dormant afterwards as it had been for many years previously.

Scanty though the evidence for the years before 1521 may be, the position is not much more satisfactory with regard to the years which immediately followed. For the next half-century we have to rely on hearsay evidence of uncertain weight contained in a manuscript entitled 'An Abstract of such causes as have received a judicial hearing in the Earle Marshalls Court before the Erles Marshalls of England or the Lords Commiss^rs for that Office since the death of Edward Stafford Duke of Buckingham the last Constable of England'.[1] The reference to the Lords Commissioners shows that the 'Abstract' was not compiled before 1590, when the office of Earl Marshal was first put into commission. Indeed, it is likely that it must be dated after the power of the Earl Marshal to sit alone had been questioned in 1613, its object being to prove that he had done so since the death of the Duke of Buckingham.[2]

If the 'Abstract' is to be believed, Thomas, Duke of Norfolk, who was Earl Marshal at the time of the execution of the Duke of Buckingham, exercised the jurisdiction of the Court alone after Buckingham's death. Before he died in 1524 Norfolk had heard several controversies between Garter King of Arms and the two provincial kings concerning their rights at the funerals of the nobility, which Garter claimed under an order in the Black Book of the Order of the Garter and the provincial kings by virtue of letters patent under the Great Seal. These controversies were continued in the time of the next Earl Marshal, Charles, Duke of Suffolk. There is cited a replication of Garter dated 22 Henry VIII (1530–1) asking that the Earl Marshal would be pleased to hear and determine the cause and that he would compel Clarenceux to bring in his rejoinder within six months.

---

[1] Coll. Arm. MS. R. 19, ff. 179 et seq. Where no other reference is given this chapter is based on this 'Abstract'.

[2] Most of the cases in the 'Abstract' were cited by counsel in argument before the Privy Council on 11 July 1622 (see p. 130 *post*), so it may have been prepared for that occasion.

This litigation was protracted over the five succeeding Earl Marshalships, and did not receive a final judgment and determination until 1563.

The 'Abstract' does not refer to any cases other than this lengthy dispute until 1 February 1567, when a question concerning the arms of Heneage of Heinton, co. Lincoln, which it was alleged he had no right to bear, received a full hearing and final determination before the Earl Marshal, who heard the matter fully debated and argued amongst all the kings of arms and heralds.[1] Shortly afterwards there was a dispute between Fitz-william of Sprotborough, co. York, and one Gascoigne concerning arms and pedigree. This was referred by the Earl Marshal to the Earl of Leicester and Sir William Cecil, Secretary of State, to hear and determine by a commission dated 16 May 1567, after which the Earl Marshal gave judgment.

A controversy of a somewhat different kind was that between the Dean and Chapter of Westminster and the officers of arms concerning the right to a hearse set up 'in Westminster', presumably in the Abbey. This was referred by the Earl Marshal to the Marquess of Winchester for examination. The Marquess certified his findings to the Earl Marshal on 24 February 1569 and the latter then gave a final judgment.

In 1582 there was another armorial case. This was a dispute between two Cheshire gentlemen, Thomas Legh and Richard Legh, both of High Legh, which was heard and determined by George, Earl of Shrewsbury E.M. at Chapel-en-le-Frith, co. Derby, in July of that year in the presence of sundry knights, esquires, and gentlemen of the 'blood, surname and alliance' of the parties. Here again the procedure differed from that of the Court of Chivalry, for instead of pronouncing a definitive sentence, the Earl Marshal more than two years later (4 December 1584) embodied his decision in a warrant declaring the right to bear the disputed arms to belong to the plaintiff and requiring Norroy King of Arms and Somerset Herald,

---

[1] Her. Cas. 3.

his marshal, to enter and record the decision in the books and registers of their office, thereby indicating that there were then no court books in which such decisions were recorded.[1]

During the Earl Marshalship of Robert, Earl of Essex (1597–1601), one Dakins, 'a forger of armes & pedegrees', was apprehended by virtue of a warrant from the Earl Marshal, and being found guilty was committed to prison and 'received such further punishmt as the said Erle Marshall thought fitting for such an offence'.

The Commissioners who executed the office of Earl Marshal during most of the reign of James I exercised judicial or quasi-judicial functions on a number of occasions. There were several disputes between peers for precedence.[2] There were also disputes for precedence between the serjeants-at-law and the knights bachelor;[3] the knighted aldermen of London and other knights bachelor;[4] the elder sons of barons and the knights of the Privy Council in Ireland; burgesses and aldermen of boroughs; ex-mayors of Reading;[5] the younger children of peers;[6] and Sir James Stanley and Sir Richard Wilbraham.

On 29 March 1609 the Commissioners at a 'Marshal's Court' at Whitehall decided that Sir Thomas Smith, late Ambassador to the Emperor of Russia, was entitled to

---

[1] G. Ormerod, *History of Cheshire* (2nd ed. London, 1882), i. 457; Coll. Arm. MS. Heralds IX, p. 444; Bodl. MS. Ashm. 857, p. 199.

[2] Lord Abergavenny and Lord Spencer (20 May 1604); the Lord of Kerry and Lord Slane (Irish); and Viscount Gormanston and Viscount Roche (Irish).

[3] Having failed to obtain satisfaction from the Earl Marshal's Court, the serjeants petitioned the King (*C.S.P.D. 1611–1618*, p. 82).

[4] Ibid., p. 166.

[5] Coll. Arm. MS. R. 19, f. 138. Roger Knight claimed precedence over Christopher Turnor as having been mayor first, whilst Turnor claimed precedence as being the elder burgess. It was held on 24 April 1619 that by the usage and custom of all other cities and corporate towns if a junior burgess or alderman be elected mayor before his senior, he afterwards holds his place, although the senior be afterwards made mayor. The Commissioners had previously given a contrary decision 'by unfair contrivance of parties interested', which they reversed after referring the matter to the judges of assize (*C.S.P.D. 1619–1623*, p. 17). In the following year the Mayor of Oxford certified that the contrary rule applied in that city (ibid., p. 123).

[6] *C.S.P.D. 1611–1618*, p. 157.

precedence over certain knights bachelor of the City of London who had been knighted before him because he had the honour to stand covered in the presence of a king. This decision was stated to be 'according to the grounds of Honour, as well as the Presidents of former tymes' and to be given by virtue of the power and authority under their commission to decide doubts and questions of this nature.[1]

There were armorial cases—a petition by Viscount Montagu against Sir Edward Montague concerning the arms of Montagu and Monthermer; a question between Sir Richard Blunt and Sir Francis More, serjeant-at-law, concerning the arms of More of Burcester;[2] and one Wolmer was punished for assuming a coat of arms. In 1605 Sir Richard Musgrave received a royal pardon after having been condemned by the Commissioners for engraving seals and using the arms of Edward the Confessor, of Richard, Earl of Cambridge, and of Scotland quartered with his own without difference.[3] The Commissioners also determined a dispute between Thomas Knight, Chester Herald, and William Penson who pretended to the same office.

Upon a complaint by the kings of arms and heralds that achievements of arms falsely and erroneously quartered had been set up without their knowledge or consent over the grave of one Aske in the church of St. Clement Danes, the Commissioners by warrant dated 3 January 1606 directed the rector and churchwardens to suffer the heralds to take down the achievements which had been set up contrary to 'the Lawe, and Custome of the Lawe of Armes'.[4]

---

[1] Bodl. MS. Ashm. 862, p. 67.

[2] Coll. Arm. MS. R. 19, f. 137. More was held to have no right to the arms of More of Burcester and not to be in any way allied to that family, but upon further inquiry it was certified by the officers of arms that he was a gentleman of blood and coat armour, lineally descended from the family of More of Burghfield. co. Berks., who bore *Arg., a moor-cock ppr.* This case is wrongly dated 1637 in Grazebrook, *The Earl Marshal's Court*, p. 15, through a misreading of Dallaway, *Inquiries into the Origin . . . of Heraldry*, p. 297. The true date was 1618 (Her. Cas. 3).   [3] Coll. Arm. MS. R. 19, f. 99.

[4] Coll. Arm. MS. Heralds IX, p. 377.

Those who refused to appear at visitations were summoned before the Commissioners to show cause for their contempt, the summons being issued by the herald making the visitation.[1]

The rights of the heralds to serve at funerals were the subject of proceedings against the sons of Sir Richard Conquest, a Bedfordshire knight. They were charged with combining with Ralph Treswell, a painter, and others not to have any of the officers of arms at Sir Richard's funeral, whereby the officers of arms were defrauded of their fees. The Commissioners ordered £10 to be paid to the Office of Arms for the officer whose turn it was to serve at the funeral and 40s. for the fee of Clarenceux King of Arms, with York Herald's charges in riding into the country to bring the defendants before the Commissioners, whilst Treswell was committed by warrant to the Marshalsea.[2]

The funeral of a Devonshire knight, Sir George Smith, at Exeter in 1619 was the scene of even greater irregularity. Not only did Thomas Wastcote provide more hatchments than befitted the dignity of a knight, setting up a standing hearse of velvet in the church, but one Hart, a painter, 'most presumptuously invested himselfe in the Kings Coat of Armes takeing upon him to discharge the office of an Herald', a proceeding which the Commissioners stigmatized as a 'foule offence'.[3]

[1] Summons dated 22 Aug. 1615 issued by Richard St. George, Norroy King of Arms, to those who refused to appear at the visitation of co. Durham (ibid., p. 323) and a similar summons relating to Northumberland (Coll. Arm. MS. Heralds IV, p. 261). Cf. citation of — Spurstow to appear before the Earl Marshal to answer for his contempt in having refused to appear at the visitation of Cheshire in 1580 that he might be punished according to the law and custom of arms (Bodl. MS. Ashm. 840, f. 451), and warrant by Rouge Croix Pursuivant as marshal for Clarenceux King of Arms to one who refused to appear at a visitation in 1591 to appear before the Earl Marshal (B.M. MS. Add. 6297, f. 4).

[2] Bodl. MSS. Ashm. 836, f. 607; 857, pp. 410–11; Coll. Arm. MS. I. 25, p. 42.

[3] Bodl. MS. Ashm. 857, pp. 412–13. At 'a Marshal's Court' held at Worcester House on 15 Nov. 1619 Sir Nicholas Smith, the son and heir of the deceased, and Wastcote were discharged upon making submission in writing acknowledging their error and craving pardon and upon paying the fees of the pursuivants for fetching them up to London. Hart could not be brought up at that time by reason of an accident to one of his legs, and he was ordered to be brought up later

One of these 'funeral' cases is of interest because the defendant was William Le Neve of Aslacton, co. Norfolk. Le Neve, then a young man of about eighteen,[1] was accused on 16 May 1618 of giving instructions for the making of certain escutcheons used at the funeral of Robert Wolme of Flixton, co. Suffolk. It could not, however, be proved that he had done this or anything else prejudicial to the Office of Arms, 'but only for his private pleasure had taken pains in the study of armory'. The Commissioners for executing the office of Earl Marshal were 'no ways displeased therewith, but rather encouraged him therein, accompting it a study best deservinge a gentlemans practise: Provided it be donne lawfully, and not to the detriment of the Officers of Armes'.[2] Six years later, in 1624, Le Neve received further encouragement by being appointed Mowbray Herald Extraordinary, becoming York Herald in the following year, and in 1635 he was finally promoted to be Clarenceux King of Arms.

Sometimes it was the heralds who were in the position of defendants. The commission for executing the office of Earl Marshal issued in 1592 authorized the Commissioners to call before them all officers of arms and to cause 'due inquisition' to be made of arms by them given to any person 'without good warraunt by the Lawe of Armes'.[3] In the exercise of this authority the Commissioners dealt with a complaint presented by Henry, Earl of Kent, in 1597 alleging that William Dethick, Garter King of Arms, had made and published a false pedigree showing one George Rotheram to be lineally heir general to Edmund, Earl of Kent, and depicted a shield of the arms of the Earl quartered without any difference with Rotheram.[4] The Commissioners adjudged the arms of the

to receive such 'condigne punishmt as to their Lop⁵ should bee thought fitt'. What the punishment was does not appear. Perhaps he was committed to the Marshalsea, like Treswell (see p. 45 post) and Robert Kniby, another painter, who was so committed by the Earl Marshal on 21 Sept. 1624 for painting arms without the allowance of the officers of arms (Bodl. MSS. Ashm. 832, p. 627; 857, p. 116).

[1] D.N.B., sub. nom.   [2] Coll. Arm. MS. I. 25, f. 43v.
[3] B.M. MS. Add. 6297, f. 1; Grazebrook, The Earl Marshal's Court, p. 52.
[4] Collins, Proceedings ... on Claims ... concerning Baronies, p. 144.

Earl to be unlawfully borne by Rotheram and also determined the part of the pedigree by which Rotheram was
made to be the Earl's cousin and heir general to be unlawful.[1]

Dethick appeared again at a 'Court Marshal' on
26 January 1604, when the Commissioners declared the
King's pleasure that 'upon some approved misdemeanours'
committed in the execution of his office of Garter, he
should be put from it and that William Segar should be
Garter in his place.[2]

Whilst not nearly so common as they were afterwards
to become,[3] complaints regarding insulting acts and words
were not unknown during this period. *Felton* v *Withepole*[4]
in 1598 may not have been determined in the Court of
Chivalry, but not long afterwards we find James I trying
to eliminate duelling by making the Court the forum for
such matters. He issued proclamations against duels on
15 October 1613 and 4 February 1614, pointing out that
the 'Courts of Honour' offered satisfaction for breaches
of honour.[5]

James's efforts met with some success, though what
proportion of disputes of this kind found their way to the
Court is not capable of estimation from the few records
surviving. The disputes were frequent. On 3 January
1610 the Commissioners said 'Wee see daily the daungerous eventes of theire sodaine quarrells'.[6] They were
calling upon Laurance Warton of Hatfield in Holderness
and Christopher Constable to answer for abuse offered to
Sir William Eure in an 'honourable assembly' in Lincoln-
shire by Warton, who sent Eure a challenge by Constable.[7] When Thomas Gates, a member of Gray's Inn,

---

[1] Ibid., p. 147. The Star Chamber had declined jurisdiction as to the arms in
earlier proceedings against Dethick in which Clarenceux King of Arms and York
Herald were co-plaintiffs with the Earl of Kent (J. Hawarde, *Les Reports del
cases in camera stellata* (London, 1894), p. 66).

[2] Coll. Arm. MS. I. 25, p. 12.

[3] See pp. 57–60 *post*.   [4] See p. 39 *post*.

[5] B.M. MS. Add. 6297, f. 284; R. R. Steele, *Bibliography of Royal Proclamations*,
i, nos. 1134, 1142.

[6] Coll. Arm. MS. R. 19, f. 123.

[7] Ibid. The Commissioners asked the Lord President of the North to take bond

complained to the Commissioners of having received 'most disgracefull and disparagable Tearmes from one Sr Baptist Hickes knight' he stated that he was doing so in obedience to the King's 'edicte'.[1] In January 1618 John Smyth of Nibley, the author of *Lives of the Berkeleys*, complained of slanderous words spoken of him by Giles Addis of Frampton, co. Gloucester, 'a fellowe of meane quallitie', which tended not only to provoke him to break the peace, but also (which was probably much more important in his eyes) to disgrace him in his employment under 'a great and honorable person in this Kingdome', namely the Earl of Berkeley.[2] Addis was attached by Lancaster Herald[3] and brought before the Commissioners for executing the office of Earl Marshal, by whom he was committed to the Marshalsea until he gave security to the King's use to make satisfaction to Smyth by asking forgiveness and acknowledging under his hand that the words which he had spoken were scandalous and unjust. This he had to do in the office of the Court of Wards and in the court leet of the hundred of Berkeley, being the two places where he had 'in a boasting manner' called Smyth 'Knave, Villaine & Beggar'.[4]

As indicated at the beginning of the chapter, there does not seem to be any legal continuity between the hearing of the cases referred to in the 'Abstract' and the medieval Court of Chivalry. The 'Abstract' cites as authority 'the several bills, answers, replications, rejoinders and articles' in the controversies between the kings of arms, whilst Gascoigne is said to have commenced his proceedings against Fitzwilliam by exhibiting 'a formal bill' to the Earl Marshal. Documents described in this manner seem to indicate a procedure similar to that of the Court of

---

of the defendants for their appearance before the Commissioners on the ground that their condition and estate were such as would not well bear the charge of a pursuivant to be sent from London to summon them. Perhaps the acknowledgement before the Commissioners by James Maxwell on 1 June 1612 that he had done Hatton Hawley gent., very great wrong without any cause was another case of this nature (ibid., f. 97).

[1] Bodl. MS. Tanner 236, f. 33b.   [2] Coll. Arm. MS. I. 25, f. 42v.
[3] Coll. Arm. MS. R. 19, f. 103.   [4] Coll. Arm. MS. I. 25, f. 43.

Chancery or the Court of Requests rather than the civil-law procedure of the Court of Chivalry in causes of instance. Indeed, it may be that the successive Earl Marshals in dealing with the disputes amongst the kings of arms between 1521 and 1563 were not even purporting to exercise the old jurisdiction of the Court of Chivalry, but were merely exercising in a formal quasi-judicial manner their domestic jurisdiction over the College of Arms and the heralds. However, whether the jurisdiction was actually exercised at the time or not, contemporary opinion did not consider that the vacancy in the office of Lord High Constable prevented the Earl Marshal from having a court. In an undated petition addressed to the Duke of Suffolk, who was Earl Marshal from 1524 to 1533, the officers of arms prayed (*inter alia*) that they should not be 'arrested, troubled, vexed or sued for actions, demands of debt or trespasses in any Court but only in the Lord Marshall's Court'.[1] Later in the century references to the Earl Marshal's Court are frequent. Thus in 1597 Garter Dethick in a letter to Lord Keeper Pickering wrote of a complaint made against him to the 'Court of Earl Marshal'.[2]

It is not safe to assume that whenever we find the Earl Marshal acting in a judicial capacity he was holding a Court of Chivalry properly so called. In the first place it was not uncommon for disputes to be settled by uncon-ventional tribunals composed partly of the judges of a court and partly of other persons. Thus a decree made in 1562 by the Lord Treasurer and other persons has been held not to be a decree of the Court of Exchequer.[3] Therefore the association of other persons with the Earl Marshal may indicate that he was not sitting in a Court of Chivalry. An example of such an association is to be found in the case of *Felton* v. *Withepole* in 1598, in which the defendant had offered disgrace by the bastinado to the

---

[1] Bodl. MS. Ashm. 857, p. 515.

[2] Noble, *History of the College of Arms*, App., p. xv. On 30 Dec. 1601 the Com-missioners held a 'Marshal's Court' at Whitehall (B.M. MS. Add. 6297, f. 244). For later instances see pp. 33, 35, 37 *ante*.

[3] *Rogers* v. *Wood* (1831), 2 B. & Ad. 245.

plaintiff. Here the Earl of Essex E.M. called to his assistance Thomas, Lord Howard de Walden, John, Lord Lumley, Thomas, Lord Darcy of Chiche, Sir William Knollys, Comptroller of the Queen's Household, Sir Walter Raleigh, Captain of the Queen's Guard, Sir Robert Sidney, Lord Governor of Flushing, and Sir Edward Dyer, Chancellor of the Order of the Garter.[1] While the rank of some of these 'assistants' probably indicates that the Earl Marshal was not sitting in a Court of Chivalry on this occasion, the fact that the Earl Marshal was sometimes accompanied on the bench by one or more noblemen at undoubted sittings of the Court[2] makes it difficult to identify apparent sittings of the Court with complete certainty.

Conversely the Earl Marshal sitting alone did not necessarily constitute a Court of Chivalry, for he had a jurisdiction *virtute officii* which was distinct from that of the Court of Chivalry. This is expressly stated in a letter of 28 September 1584 from the Earl of Shrewsbury E.M. to the Lord Mayor of London. The Earl Marshal complained that Windsor Herald had been arrested and imprisoned in the City of London, although this had been forbidden by letters from the Privy Council to the Lord Mayor and his brethren in June 1566, and went on to state that if any had cause to sue or implead any of the officers of arms and should bring his suit 'either before me as Erle Marshall of England or in the Courte of my said Office and authoritie' they would find 'such uprightness of Justice with expidicion as the equitie of their cause will beare and shall in reasonne seem meete'.[3]

The lack of records properly so called and the paucity of secondary evidence for this period makes it difficult to determine in which capacity the Earl Marshal was acting in any particular case. This is hardly surprising, for despite the distinction drawn by the Earl of Shrews-

[1] Bodl. MS. Ashm. 856, pp. 105–6; Dallway, *Inquiries into . . . Heraldry*, p. 295. The precedence of the parties was also in dispute (B.M. MS. Cott. Faustina, C. viii, f. 21, quoted in Grazebrook, op. cit., pp. 46–48).

[2] See pp. 48, 88, 103 *post*.

[3] Bodl. MS. Ashm. 857, pp. 274–5.

bury E.M. in the letter quoted above, there seems to have been some contemporary confusion between the two jurisdictions. This is shown in the record of the proceedings in 1609 for settling a dispute between the Lord Mayor of York and the Earl of Sheffield, Lord Lieutenant of the County and the City of York, concerning the bearing of the city's sword in the Lord Lieutenant's presence. These proceedings were very similar to a peerage case in that they were begun by a petition to the Crown. This petition, like a peerage claim, was referred to the Commissioners for executing the office of Earl Marshal, but it is noteworthy that the Commissioners were described in the reference as 'Commissioners for Causes determinable by the Earl Marshal's Court'.[1] The Commissioners heard the allegations of the parties in the Council Chamber at Whitehall and considered the wording of a charter granted to the Corporation by Richard II and the letters patent of lieutenancy. Feeling unable to determine the matter without certain legal questions arising upon the wording of these documents being resolved, the Commissioners stayed the proceedings and directed letters to Coke C.J.C.P. and Tanfield C.B. asking for their opinion.[2] The two judges advised 'That the Mayor of York ought not to deliver up the Sword of Justice which he holdeth by Charter, nor to abase and bear down the same (especially in Time of Peace) in the presence of the Lord Sheffield, his Majesty's Lieutenant there'.

This opinion was considered by the Commissioners, who finding no reason to differ from it reported it to the King. The King's reply was characteristic. He said that 'for his own Part he had been of the same Mind ever since his first Reading of the Petition, though it pleased him for his own better Satisfaction, to require the Judgment of the Lords Commissioners for the Office of Earl Marshal, which do commonly examine Matters of this Nature with great Judgment and Equity; wherefore

---

[1] For the mistaken belief that peerage claims were decided in the Court of Chivalry at this period see pp. 153–60 *post*.
[2] Coll. Arm. MS. R. 19, f. 89.

finding now that upon further consideration, the Laws of Honour do so fitly suit and concur with the Laws of the Land, and the Judges of the Court of Chivalry in their Opinion with the Judges of the Point in Law, his Majesty doth likewise declare himself to agree resolutely with both their Opinions'.

Not only did the King refer to the Commissioners as 'the Judges of the Court of Chivalry', but when the Commissioners made their order in accordance with these unanimous opinions they did not direct it to be entered in the books of the College of Arms as was done by the Earl of Shrewsbury E.M. in *Legh* v. *Legh*,[1] but it was enrolled by John Guillim, then Portsmouth Pursuivant Extraordinary, who described himself as 'Registrum Officii Curie Mariscal'.[2]

Despite the description of the Commissioners as Commissioners for Causes determinable by the Earl Marshal's Court and 'Judges of the Court of Chivalry' and the common use of the expression 'Earl Marshal's Court',[3] the proceedings before the Commissioners were as far removed from the sphere of the civilians' practice as those in the courts of common law or equity. Proceedings were initiated by documents described as 'bills'[4] or 'complaints',[5] and the later steps bore no resemblance either in name or in form to the civil-law procedure of the medieval Court of Chivalry. Furthermore, the parties were represented by common lawyers.[6]

Later in the reign of James I the jurisdiction of the Commissioners fell to be considered in the Court of Chancery. William Penson, who claimed the office of Chester Herald, brought suits against Garter and Norroy Kings of Arms and against Chester Herald for official fees. In June 1612 Lord Ellesmere L.C. dismissed both suits with costs on the ground that the nature of the suits

---

[1] See p. 32 *ante*.
[2] *The History and Antiquities of the City of York* (York, 1785), ii. 7–11.
[3] See p. 39 *ante*.
[4] See p. 38 *ante*.
[5] e.g. *Kent (Earl)* v. *Rotheram and Dethick* (1597), Collins, 141, at p. 144.
[6] B.M. Add. MS. 9021, f. 58. See p. 133 *post*.

was not fit for the Court of Chancery, leaving Penson to attend the Commissioners.[1]

A few months afterwards Ralph Brooke, York Herald, preferred a similar bill in Chancery against Henry St. George, Bluemantle Pursuivant, in respect of fees due to the heralds collected by St. George. The defendant pleaded to the jurisdiction, alleging that because the parties were officers of arms the Court of Chancery could not hold plea between them. On 3 March 1613 the Lord Chancellor made an order that the plaintiff should show cause why his bill should not be dismissed and the cause referred to the Commissioners for the office of Earl Marshal.[2]

On 28 April 1613 counsel for the plaintiff moved before Phelips M.R. to retain the plea in court. He argued that there was no such court as the Earl Marshal's Court, but only the Court of the Constable and Marshal, which could only be held at such time as there was a Constable or Commissioners for executing his office, whereupon it was ordered that the dismission should be stayed. After the entry of this order the defendant, through his father, Richard St. George, Norroy King of Arms, reported it to the Earls of Northampton and Suffolk, the principal Commissioners for executing the office of Earl Marshal, and caused them to complain to the Lord Chancellor. As a result counsel for the defendant was appointed to move to reverse the order on the last day of Easter term (17 May) before the Lord Chancellor and the Master of the Rolls.[3]

When the motion was heard the Lord Chancellor treated counsel for the plaintiff with scorn and taxed him with denying the King's power to give authority to the Commissioners to keep a court. Counsel replied that a court could be held under a commission of constableship

[1] Coll. Arm. MS. R. 19. f. 179, where Penson is styled Lancaster Herald, though he did not obtain that office until the following year. Further particulars of his Chancery suit against Garter and Norroy are in Bodl. MS. Ashm. 857, pp. 135–6.
[2] *Liber Famelicus of Sir James Whitelocke* (Camden Soc., lxx, 1858), p. 34.
[3] Ibid., pp. 34–35.

as well as of marshalship[1] and therefore only the validity of the commission as granted and not the King's power of granting it was in question.[2] After dinner the next day the Lord Chancellor, with the Lord Privy Seal and the Lord Chamberlain, took the Master of the Rolls' order of 28 April to the King at Whitehall,[3] whereupon the plaintiff's counsel was summoned to the Council Chamber that afternoon and committed by warrant to the Fleet Prison.[4] There he remained until 13 June, when he was discharged on making a humble acknowledgement of his offence in writing. This concluded with a sentence out of Tacitus ('Tibi summum rerum imperium Dii dederunt, nobis obedientiae gloria relicta est') of which the King took 'special notice and good liking'.[5] On 4 November the Lord Chancellor dismissed the cause and referred it to the Commissioners as being a matter most proper to be heard in their Court.[6]

Counsel might make his submission, but he could not unsay what he had said, and his argument that the Earl Marshal had no jurisdiction in the absence of a Constable was adopted by other counsel from time to time during the next hundred years.[7]

Brooke was less submissive than his counsel and would have none of the Earl Marshal's Court. He refused to prosecute his suit there. On 9 October 1621 he filed a second bill in Chancery against his brother heralds for fees of office, declaring that there was no Earl Marshal's Court and that he would overthrow the Earl Marshal's office and authority.[8] Brooke also commenced several

---

[1] Half a century later such a joint commission was drafted, though it never passed the Great Seal, see p. 78 *post*.

[2] *Liber Famelicus*, p. 36.   [3] Ibid., p. 37.

[4] Ibid., p. 38. The Earls of Northampton and Suffolk were amongst the signatories of the warrant (ibid., p. 40).

[5] Ibid., pp. 39–40.

[6] Coll. Arm. MS. R. 19, f. 179. In an entry in the Register of the Privy Council made in 1622 it is stated that the suit was dismissed on 28 Apr. 1613 (*A.P.C. 1621–1623*, p. 365), but this was the date on which the dismission was stayed: see p. 43 *ante*.

[7] The last case in which this point was taken seems to have been *Lowther* v. *Murgatroyd* in 1716: see p. 105 *post*.

[8] *C.S.P.D. 1619–1623*, p. 321; *A.P.C. 1621–1623*, p. 365.

suits in the Court of Common Pleas for fees of office.[1] Somewhat inconsistently, he also joined with Robert Treswell, Somerset Herald, in complaining to the Commissioners of the alleged misdeeds of their fellow-members of the College of Arms,[2] but when they failed to get redress they appealed to other courts and put in pleas derogatory to the Earl Marshal's Court.[3]

These further aspersions on the Earl Marshal's Court were reported to the King by Thomas, Earl of Arundel, who had been appointed Earl Marshal for life on 29 August 1621. The King took the view that his own honour was engaged to defend the power and reputation of the Court, 'which is of so high a nature, so auncient, so imediatelie derived from us, who are the fowntaine of all honor', and referred the complaint to the Privy Council on 8 December 1621 with instructions that if the two heralds could not clear themselves, they were to be punished in such a way as to deter others from similar evil ways.[4] The Privy Council commanded Brooke and Treswell to appear before them, and on 14 December they issued a warrant to the keeper of the Marshalsea to receive the two heralds into his custody, and to keep them prisoners until further order.[5] Treswell was released on 3 January 1622,[6] but Brooke remained in prison for many months more. On 7 December 1622 a petition from him was exhibited to the Council, but since he obstinately persisted in his former offence, it was ordered that he should remain a prisoner until he submitted.[7] It was not until 25 March 1623 that he brought himself to acknowledge his error and to submit his cause for fees to be heard and decided by the 'Court Marshall', whereupon he was ordered to be set at liberty.[8]

Meanwhile on 25 June 1622 the King, as 'the supreame and proper Judge and limitter both of Judges and the Jurisdiction of the Courts', enlarged the scope of the

---

[1] *A.P.C. 1621–1623*, p. 267.   [2] *C.S.P.D. 1619–1623*, p. 110.
[3] Bodl. MS. Ashm. 857, p. 242; *A.P.C. 1621–1623*, p. 99.
[4] Ibid.   [5] Ibid., pp. 99, 100.
[6] Ibid., p. 111.   [7] Ibid., pp. 364–5.
[8] Ibid., p. 450.

Privy Council's inquiry by desiring them, as his representatives, to consider whether the Earl Marshal was a judge with the Constable in the 'Court Marshal', and consequently a judge during a vacancy in the Constableship, or whether he was only the minister of the Constable to see his judgments executed.[1] Three days later the Council ordered that Brooke's suits in the Court of Common Pleas concerning heralds' fees should be referred entirely to the jurisdiction of the Earl Marshal's Court.[2]

It did not take the Privy Council long to remove the King's doubts. In July they reported that they were clearly of opinion that the Earl Marshal was always a joint judge with the Constable, and that in the vacancy of the office of Constable he had full and absolute power to judge of all causes belonging to the jurisdiction and cognizance of the Court of the Constable and Marshal.[3] On 1 August 1622 letters patent were issued to the Earl Marshal authorizing and commanding him to proceed 'judicially and definitively' in all causes within the jurisdiction of the Court of the Constable and Marshal. The letters patent not only clarified the Earl Marshal's position. They opened the way to a new era in the history of the Court of Chivalry by requiring the Earl Marshal to endeavour to 'restore and settle' the procedure of the Court with the assistance of ancient records and precedents.[4]

Thus were the civilians restored.

[1] Bodl. MS. Ashm. 857, pp. 242–3.
[2] *C.S.P.D. 1619–1623*, p. 413; *A.P.C. 1621–1623*, p. 268.
[3] *A.P.C. 1621–1623*, pp. 365–6. See also p. 130 *post*.
[4] See Appendix III, p. 239 *post*. Apparently the Earl Marshal had but few ancient precedents on which to rely: see Appendix I, p. 225 *post*.

III

THE CIVILIANS RESTORED

1622–40

DESPITE the confident tone of the letters patent of 1 August 1622, there seems to have been some thought of making assurance doubly sure by conferring upon the Earl Marshal the powers of the Lord High Constable. This appears to be the proper interpretation of an order of 16 April 1623 to the Auditor of the Exchequer and others to deliver to the Earl Marshal the staff of the Constable of England and certain ancient seals of a former Constable, Humphrey de Bohun, Earl of Hereford and Essex.[1] If there was such a proposal, it was soon abandoned, for in the following June John Chamberlain told Sir Dudley Carleton, the Ambassador in Holland, that the office of Lord High Constable was to be revived and conferred on the Duke of Buckingham.[2] Whilst this project may have been seriously considered, the office of Lord High Constable was not revived at this time, and the Earl Marshal was left to proceed alone in accordance with his letters patent.

It was easier for the King to order the Earl Marshal to 'restore and settle' the procedure of the Court of Chivalry than it was for the Earl Marshal to obey. The procedure in heraldic litigation had been of a makeshift character for more than a century, whilst the old records of the Court had almost wholly disappeared.[3] Considerable research must have been necessary before the old machinery could be put into working order. One of the Earl Marshal's difficulties was that it was uncertain what fees were due

---

[1] *C.S.P.D.1619–1623*, p. 559. The possibility of the granting of a 'commission of the office of constable and marshal' seems to have been under consideration some years earlier (*Anon.* (1618), Hut. 3).

[2] Ibid., p. 608.

[3] See Appendix I, p. 225 *post*.

to the various officials of the Court. In order to put an end to this uncertainty the King issued a warrant to Sir Thomas Coventry, the Attorney-General, to draw a bill to be signed by the King authorizing the Earl Marshal to settle such court fees as he might think fit, and to increase or diminish them from time to time, provided that he had regard to the fees warranted by the precedents and records of the Court or to the usual fees of other courts whether common law, civil law, equity, or ecclesiastical.[1] The Earl Marshal accordingly drew up a list of fees which was approved by Royal Warrant.[2]

Having settled the fees, the Earl Marshal was able to appoint a Register, a Cryer, and an Usher, and all was made ready for the first sitting of the reconstituted Court on 24 November 1623. In addition to the officers appointed by the Earl Marshal, the King appointed Dr. Arthur Duck, one of the foremost civilians of the time, to be King's Advocate in the Court.

The venue was in the Palace of Westminster in the Painted Chamber, so called on account of its fine thirteenth-century wall-paintings, which survived until 1834, when they perished in the fire which destroyed the Houses of Parliament.[3] A bench three feet higher than the ordinary benches was set up under the Royal Arms 'newly depicted very fair'. There was a table twelve feet square covered with green cotton and surrounded by benches stuffed with wool or flocks, also covered with green cotton.[4]

The Earl Marshal took his seat immediately under the Royal Arms with the Earl of Dorset on his right and his uncle, Lord William Howard, on his left and a number of other peers on either side. At the Earl Marshal's feet sat the Register, with Garter King of Arms on his right and

[1] B.M. MS. Add. 6297, pp. 368–9; Queen's Coll., Oxf. MS. CXXII, f. 38b.
[2] Folger Shakespeare Library MS. 393.4. I am indebted to Professor P. H. Hardacre of Vanderbilt University, Nashville, Tennessee, for drawing my attention to this warrant. The list of fees is set out in Appendix XXVI, p. 271 post.
[3] T. Borenius and A. W. Tristram, English Medieval Painting (Florence, 1927), p. 14.
[4] The account of this sitting is based on B.M. MS. Add. 6297, pp. 387–93.

Norroy on his left. The Earl Marshal's Gentleman Usher sat on Garter's right, and the Earl Marshal's Secretary on Norroy's left. On the other side of the table, opposite the Earl Marshal, was Dr. Duck, flanked by Sir Thomas Trevor, Solicitor-General to the Prince of Wales, and a Mr. Hackwell, who had been counsel to the late Queen Consort. The Usher was on the right-hand side at the lower end of the Court, and the Cryer was on the left next to the door. The Heralds were on the right of the Court with the Pursuivants on the left, and some 'gentlemen of quality' were placed within the Court by the Earl Marshal's command.

It is interesting to compare this arrangement of the court-room with Segar's account of the arrangement when the Court sat at the Earl Marshal's residence. In the great hall at Arundel House there was

a large Table or Stage four square, built with Rails thereabout, and Benches therein, and an half Pace raised above the same; there the Earl sitteth in the midst thereof, being accompanied on either Side with divers Noblemen, and sometimes Judges.[1]

Clearly the present interior of the hall of the College of Arms, which was fitted up in the reign of Queen Anne, was based upon well-established precedents.

Returning to the events of 24 November 1623, the proceedings opened with three cries being made and silence commanded. Then, after the patents appointing the Earl Marshal and authorizing him to keep a Court by himself without a Constable had been read, the Earl Marshal made a 'good pithy speech'. He declared his intention to revive that which had 'lain long in the dust', and that he had made all the searches that he possibly could into the precedents of ancient times to the end that he might not encroach upon other courts as he hoped that other courts would not encroach upon his.

After his speech was finished, the Register ordered the Cryer to call for the Earl Marshal's Messenger to return

---

[1] 'The Earl Marshal his Office both in Peace and War' (Bodl. MS. Ashm. 856, p. 431), printed in J. Guillim, A Display of Heraldry (6th ed., London, 1724), App., p. 40.

his mandate. The Messenger returned a mandate on parchment under the Earl Marshal's seal for summoning Sir Thomas Harris, baronet. The Register read the mandate and caused the Cryer to call for Harris, who appeared in person.

Harris, a Master in Chancery, had been created a baronet in December 1622 on the recommendation of Christopher Villiers, brother of the Duke of Buckingham, and shortly afterwards created Earl of Anglesey.[1] In order to show that he was qualified to be a baronet, Harris produced a certificate signed by Garter, Norroy, Richmond, Chester, and Bluemantle purporting to show that his father and paternal grandfather had been armigerous.[2] This certificate was called into question by Simon Leeke, one of Harris's neighbours in Shropshire, who, having been employed for a fee by Harris's son to act as agent in obtaining the patent, now alleged that Harris was not qualified to be a baronet.

Harris took exception to the plaintiff's libel on the ground that it was scandalous, but without success.[3] The libel was written on parchment with a spacious margin in which were depicted the supposed arms of Harris and another escutcheon showing those arms quartered with other arms. When Harris was called upon for his answer it was not ready and the Earl Marshal gave him further time until 1 December.

The only other cause to come before the Court on 24 November was the one in which Ralph Brooke, York Herald, claimed from Sir Richard St. George, Norroy King of Arms, and Henry St. George, Richmond Herald, certain fees of office which he alleged had been collected by them and should have been distributed amongst the other heralds and which had led to Brooke's fifteen months in the Marshalsea. Brooke's counsel put in exceptions to the defendants' answer, and the defendants

---

[1] *C.S.P.D. 1623–1625*, p. 506.

[2] *Leeke* v. *Harris* (1623), Her. Cas. 1.

[3] The document is termed a 'bill' in the account of the proceedings in B.M. MS. Add. 6297, p. 392, but if the King's command to 'restore and settle' the procedure of the Court had been obeyed, the plaintiff's pleading was a libel.

were given until 1 December to amend or maintain their answer.

It does not appear what happened in *Brooke* v. *St. George*, but *Leeke* v. *Harris* came before the Court again on no fewer than twenty-three occasions during the following twelve months.[1] In the course of this protracted litigation certain pleas and exhibits of the defendant were disallowed, whereupon he exhibited a petition to Lord Keeper Williams for a commission of appeal. The Lord Keeper referred the consideration of the petition to the Attorney-General and the Solicitor-General, who after making a long search of the records and precedents in the Tower certified that the appeal was just and lawful. Whilst this petition was pending Leeke exhibited a counter-petition to the Lord Keeper. Meeting with no success with his counter-petition, Leeke went back to the Court of Chivalry and procured a sentence against Harris by default. Harris then petitioned the King for his appeal to proceed[2] and on 1 June 1625 letters patent were issued appointing delegates to hear the appeal.[3] There seems to be no record of the result of the appeal extant. The baronetcy continued in the Harris family until it became extinct in 1685, but nothing can be deduced from that, for it is doubtful whether Harris could have been deprived of his baronetcy. Although the King ordered the Earl Marshal to proceed judicially to 'actuall degradation' in such a case,[4] Coke took the view that the Court could not question a patent under the Great Seal, the proper procedure being by way of *quo warranto* or *scire facias*.[5]

Evidence as to the other business before the Court of Chivalry at this period is very scanty, but its powers were invoked to deal with certain recalcitrant painter-stainers. The painting of arms without their licence had long been

---

[1] Her. Cas. 5.

[2] P.R.O., S.P. Dom. James I, vol. clxxxv, no. 92, printed in F. W. Pixley, *A History of the Baronetage* (London, 1900), p. 138.

[3] *Foedera*, xviii. 241; Her. Cas. 5.

[4] P.R.O., S.P. Dom. James I, vol. cliii, no. 54, printed in Pixley, op. cit., p. 136.

[5] *C.J.* i. 692. Cf. *C.S.P.D. 1623–1625*, p. 401.

a sore point with the officers of arms. In 1620 and 1621 agreements were entered into with the Painter-Stainers' Company governing the manner in which arms painting for funerals was to be carried out.[1] Notwithstanding these agreements some painters and other tradesmen continued to paint and marshal arms without the allowance of the heralds, and on 19 September 1624 James I ordered the Earl Marshal to cause such delinquents to appear before him and to be punished by imprisonment or otherwise 'that by their examples others may be fore warned & dishartened from attempting the like in tyme to come'.[2] The Earl Marshal responded by committing Robert Kniby, a painter, to the Marshalsea two days later.[3]

The next landmark in the history of the Court was the case of *Rea* v. *Ramsey* in 1631.[4] Donald, Lord Rea accused a Scots courtier, Donald Ramsey, of high treason alleged to have been committed on board ship near Elsinore in Sweden. Since Rea was the only witness, it would not have been possible to obtain a conviction at common law, where at least two witnesses were essential,[5] so Rea proceeded by way of appeal in the Court of Chivalry. Such an appeal was not within the jurisdiction of the Earl Marshal alone, so in order to enable the matter to proceed Robert, Earl of Lindsey, was appointed Lord High Constable on 24 November 1631.[6]

On 28 November 1631 the new Lord High Constable, together with the Earl Marshal, the Earls of Pembroke, Dorset, Carlisle, Mulgrave, and Morton, Viscounts Wimbledon, Wentworth, and Falkland, and Sir Henry Vane, sat in the Painted Chamber at Westminster. Rea

---

[1] W. A. D. Englefield, *History of the Painter-Stainers' Company* (London, 1950), p. 92.

[2] Bodl. MS. Ashm. 857, pp. 111, 112, 353.

[3] Bodl. MSS. Ashm. 832, p. 627; 857, p. 116.

[4] 3 St. Tr. 483.   [5] 3 Co. Inst. 26.

[6] Coll. Arm. MS. R. 19, f. 238v. William Noy in a letter to an unnamed correspondent dated 6 Aug. 1631 expressed the view that a combat would be 'altogether unlawfull'. He also took the view that to appoint a Constable for this purpose 'in this time wherein men are ready to dispute of all things' would cause 'talke that the Marshall hath no Connsuans in any cause without the Constable' (ibid., f. 32). Noy became Attorney-General on 27 Oct. 1631.

and Ramsey having been ushered in by heralds, the proceedings were opened with a speech by the Earl Marshal.
Dr. Duck, the King's Advocate, then made a speech
concerning the antiquity, jurisdiction, and necessity of
the Court of Chivalry, especially in cases of treason.[1] The
case then proceeded in accordance with the civil law until
the Lord High Constable and the Earl Marshal adjudged
a duel between the parties.[2] The duel was appointed to
take place on 12 April 1632 in Tothill Fields in Westminster in the presence of the King, each combatant to be
armed with a spear, a long sword, a short sword, and a
dagger, each of them with a point. Meanwhile Lord Rea
was forbidden to go westward beyond Charing Cross,
and Ramsey to go eastward of Whitehall without special
licence of the Court, or some just and reasonable cause.[3]
On 10 April the day of combat was prorogued to 17 May
at the King's pleasure. In the event the combat never took
place, for the King came to the conclusion that Ramsey,
though not blameless, was not guilty of treason and decided that he and Rea should not fight. On 12 May the
Court reassembled and the Lord High Constable declared
that whilst they had not found Ramsey guilty of treason,
he had seditiously committed many contempts against
the King. The Court then decreed that both Rea and
Ramsey should be committed to the Tower of London
until they gave sufficient caution by sureties to be approved by the King that neither would attempt anything
against the other. The parties were then arrested and
delivered by the serjeants-at-arms to Sir William Balfour,
Lieutenant of the Tower.[4] The proceedings closed by
Sir Richard St. George, Clarenceux King of Arms, bringing a letter from the King revoking the letters patent for
the trial of the cause.[5]

On 11 February 1634 the Earl of Lindsey was again
appointed Lord High Constable by letters patent authorizing him to hear and determine with the Earl Marshal

---

[1] 3 St. Tr., at pp. 486, 498.   [2] For the procedure see pp. 219–20 *post*.
[3] 3 St. Tr., at p. 510.
[4] Balfour's warrant is in Cur. Mil. Boxes 7/3.   [5] 3 St. Tr., at p. 514.

all murders and homicides committed by any of the King's subjects outside England, Scotland, and Ireland.[1] This appointment was rendered necessary by an appeal of murder brought against William Holmes, late purser of the good ship *Thomas* of the port of London by Katherine Hocker alias Wise, who alleged that he had killed her former husband, William Wise, cooper of the *Thomas*, in a duel in Newfoundland. The jurisdiction of the Court was founded upon evidence that Wise received the fatal wound on land 'about a flight's shot[2] from any flowing of the sea'.[3] The object of this evidence was to show that the crime was not committed within the jurisdiction of the Court of Admiralty, but its form is somewhat curious. At first sight it would seem to indicate that the Admiralty jurisdiction extended inland for the distance of a shot's flight, but this was not the case in England, where it ended at high-water mark,[4] and there is no reason to believe that any different rule applied in the colonies. It would appear that the reference to a shot's flight was nothing more than a picturesque way of saying that the crime was committed well away from tidal waters, which fell within the jurisdiction of the Court of Admiralty. It is possible that the original intention may have been to take proceedings in that Court, for the earliest surviving documents are some depositions sworn on 10 October 1632 before Sir Henry Marten, Judge of the High Court of Admiralty,[5] but this evidence is equivocal, since Marten was also surrogate in the Court of Chivalry.

Mrs. Hocker entered into a bond with two sureties for the prosecution of the appeal on 25 January 1634.[6] On 29 January a warrant was issued for the arrest of the defendant and on the following day he was committed to the custody of the keeper of the Poultry Compter.[7] There

---

[1] Cur. Mil. Boxes 7/114*i*.
[2] Presumably 'a shot's flight' was intended.
[3] Cur. Mil. Boxes 8/17.   [4] *Constable's Case* (1601), 5 Co. Rep. 107.
[5] Cur. Mil. Boxes 8/17. Amongst the deponents was the defendant himself, whose explanation was that after receiving ten wounds in a duel with Wise he fell down and as he held up his sword Wise fell upon it and soon afterwards died.
[6] Ibid. 7/114*a*.   [7] Ibid. 7/114*b, c.*

he remained until 25 February, when he was transferred to the custody of Sir Edmund Verney, the Knight Marshal of the Royal Household, in readiness for the sitting of the Court the next day.[1]

On 26 February the Lord High Constable and the Earl Marshal took their seats in the Court of Requests in the Palace of Westminster, where they were accompanied by Henry, Earl of Manchester, Keeper of the Privy Seal, Francis, Earl of Bedford, Edward, Earl of Dorset, Henry, Lord Matravers, and Sir Henry Marten. The proceedings began with the usual reading of the letters patent, after which the bill was read and witnesses sworn in order that they could be examined before Sir Henry Marten in Doctors' Commons.[2] The next sitting was on 1 March, when the depositions were read by the Register and confirmed by the witnesses. The defendant then gave in his defence, which was read by the Register. The defence pleaded provocation and self-defence, it being alleged that Wise was a ringleader in a mutiny in which the defendant was loyal to the captain and master of the ship.[3] On 5 March the depositions of the defendant's witnesses were read and acknowledged by the deponents, and a further witness for the defence was examined in open court.[4] At a further sitting on 14 April Dr. Eden, the defendant's advocate, argued unsuccessfully that Mrs. Hocker had lost her right by marrying again.[5]

It was not until 26 April that the definitive sentence was pronounced. On this occasion the Constable and Marshal sat in the Painted Chamber and were accompanied by the Earls of Manchester, Huntingdon, and Essex, Garter King of Arms also being present.[6] The defendant's pleas were not accepted. The sentence was that he should be taken to the Marshalsea prison and thence to the 'accustomed place of execution' and there hanged by a noose fixed around his neck until he was dead.[7]

The sentenced man petitioned the King, stating that

---

[1] Ibid. 7/114f, g.   [2] Ibid. 7/114i; 8/21.   [3] Ibid. 7/114j; 8/20.
[4] Ibid. 7/114k.   [5] Ibid. 7/9.   [6] Ibid. 7/114m.
[7] Ibid. 7/114n.

he was provoked into fighting and that there had been no proceedings for homicide in the Court Military for many years, upon which a royal pardon was granted on condition that he gave good and sufficient security for his good behaviour according to the form of the statute.[1] On 30 June the Earl Marshal issued his warrant to the Marshal of the Marshalsea to set Holmes at liberty.[2] So ended the last capital cause in the Court of Chivalry. The subsequent records are concerned with matters of a very different character.

Apart from the numerous documents relating to *Rea* v. *Ramsey*, the records of the Court do not begin until 1633.[3] It is not clear whether this date is of any significance in the history of the Court or whether the absence of earlier records is accidental, but from then on to 1640 the records survive in considerable numbers.[4] Though obviously incomplete, the records for this period are much more copious than those for the whole of the rest of the history of the Court. From them it is apparent that it was a period of great activity. Since each cause had to come before the Court at each session, even though it might only be in order to be adjourned to the next session, it is possible to ascertain from the Act Books how many cases there were pending at a time. The series of Act Books is nothing like complete, but there are records of fifty-five sessions between 9 June 1634 and the last session on 4 December 1640. On the first of these days there were nineteen causes and on the other forty-one.[5] During the intervening six and a half years the numbers fluctuated quite considerably, but were frequently over sixty and on 20 October 1638 they reached eighty-one.[6] The total number of causes commenced during this period of which

---

[1] Cur. Mil. Boxes 7/1140.

[2] Ibid. 9/4/53. In August 1634 Holmes petitioned for a pursership in the Navy (*C.S.P.D. 1634–1635*, p. 436).

[3] The earliest document is a defence dated 12 Nov. 1633 (Cur. Mil. Boxes 7/1/1).

[4] It may be a coincidence, but the earliest record of a cause in which damages had been given for scandalous words which could be produced to the House of Commons Committee in 1640 was dated 1633 (see p. 66 *post*).

[5] Cur. Mil. Boxes 8/24; 1/11*l.*

[6] Ibid. 1/7*a.*

records survive is 606, many only represented by a single document, others by documents at every stage from petition to sentence.

In addition to the sessions in court, there were interlocutory proceedings in chambers. Unlike the sessions in court, which were frequently presided over by the Earl Marshal or by Lord Matravers as his lieutenant, the work in chambers was always done by the Earl Marshal's professional surrogate, Sir Henry Marten LL.D., sometimes at his chambers in Doctors' Commons, sometimes at Arundel House, and sometimes at his house in Aldersgate Street.[1]

Of this substantial volume of litigation comparatively little was concerned with heraldic disputes. If it can be assumed that the surviving documents represent a fair sample of the work of the Court during this period, it is apparent that the bulk of the causes related to duelling. Sometimes the cause of action was a challenge to a duel,[2] but far more often it arose out of 'scandalous words provocative of a duel'. Causes of this nature seem to have been comparatively rare in earlier times[3] and the royal proclamations against duelling in 1614[4] do not seem to have resulted in much litigation. Despite the smug allegation in the petition in *Malett* v. *Stokes*[5] that the plaintiff 'in obedience to his Mats declaracons & comaunds doth forbeare to take revenge . . . by way of single Combatt', the sudden increase in numbers was really due to the advice given to the Earl Marshal by Sir Henry Marten and other civilians that the Court had power to award damages for scandalous words—advice which in the end brought about the temporary downfall of the Court.[6]

The subject-matter of such causes is usually exceedingly dull, the 'scandalous words' consisting of various combinations of defamatory nouns, such as 'rascal', 'rogue', 'liar', and 'villain', coupled with adjectives of

---

[1] Ibid. 1/6b.
[2] e.g. *Bowne* v. *Throgmorton* (1634), Cur. Mil. Boxes 9/4/65.
[3] For an example, see *Eure* v. *Warton*, p. 37 *ante*.
[4] See p. 37 *ante*.   [5] (1639), Cur. Mil. Boxes 6/118.
[6] *Life of Edward Earl of Clarendon*, i. 64, and see p. 63 *post*.

mere vulgar abuse, such as 'base', 'vile', and 'stinking'. Richard Beare was quite refreshingly original when he called William Southcott of Bovey Tracey, co. Devon, 'the squirt of a Kite and the spawne of a Crablouse'.[1] Occasionally a party is found using a word now obsolete. Thus John Wheeler, a Fleet Street apothecary, was provoked by being described by his lodger, Sampson Sheffield, a Gentleman Pensioner to the King, as 'one that liveth by the turdes of gentlemen', not to a duel, but to retort that Sheffield was a 'bafler'.[2] Sometimes attention is arrested by the unusual form of the invective, such as Henry Vincent's statement that Francis Brabant of the Inner Temple had betrayed his master, Sir Richard Greenvill, and was 'an Iscariot',[3] whilst William Haskett said of William Fillioll of Knightstreet, co. Dorset, amongst other things, that he fed on 'sheepes henges or gathers'.[4] A half-forgotten trade is recalled by the defendant in *Ivat* v. *Harding*, who had disparaged the plaintiff by saying that his brother was but a 'crowde string maker'.[5] Sometimes it was not only words but actions which were alleged to be provocative of a duel, as in *Leonard* v. *Engham*,[6] where the defendant was not content with calling the plaintiff, a doctor of medicine, 'a base stinkinge and a pispott doctor', but also struck him with a cane. In *Mackworth* v. *Owen*[7] one of the defendants endeavoured to hire some shoemakers in their shops in Shrewsbury to ring and beat with hammers when the plaintiff, Humphrey Mackworth, gentleman, being newly married, brought his wife (being the Baron of Kinderton's sister) and passed through the street towards his house, 'which kind of ringing and beating with hammers is not used, but by way of disgrace, scorn and obloquy when notorious and common offenders

---

[1] *Southcott* v. *Beare* (1637), Cur. Mil. Boxes 12/1*l*.
[2] *Wheeler* v. *Sheffield* (1640), Cur. Mil. 1631–42, 39–40, 175–7. 'Baffler'=a juggler, trickster; a trifler (*O.E.D.*, s.v.).
[3] *Brabant* v. *Vincent* (1637), Acta Cur. Mil. (5), 45.
[4] *Fillioll* v. *Haskett* (1638), Cur. Mil. i. 267. 'Henge'=the 'pluck' (heart, liver, &c.) of an animal (*O.E.D.*, s.v.). 'Gather' has the same meaning (ibid).
[5] (1637), Cur. Mil. II. 64. 'Crowd'=a fiddle (*O.E.D.*, s.v.).
[6] (1640), Cur. Mil. II. 46.   [7] (1639), Cur. Mil. Boxes 2/97.

or most infamous persons pass by and so commonly known and observed in that place'.

The circumstances which gave rise to *Southcote* v. *Crossen*[1] and the words complained of are sufficiently out of the ordinary to be worth citing at length. Sir Popham Southcote, knight, held a patent for making and ordering the making of soap in the county of Devon and the city and county of Exeter and other western counties. Thomas Crossen, a merchant, being Mayor of Exeter in 1638, Southcote asked for his assistance because some of the inhabitants of Exeter resisted an attempt to seize for non-payment of duty some soap made by one John Glide.[2] The Mayor was not co-operative. According to Southcote, he:

asked mee . . . whether I had no more manners than to require the Kings Lieftenant & challenged mee for wearing my hatt before him, hee being . . . at all tyms and in any place as good a man as I, said that a veryer scum of base Rascalls than those that followed mee were not to bee found againe, they were worse than the tin bailiffs, he made comparisons wth mee, vilifying the dignity of knighthood, most rudely squirting pughing and saying it was a greate peece of matter to bee a knight now, sayd that hee w[as able] to take up two such as I was one on the one shoulder and a nother on the other shoulder, and throwe them both, That hee the sayd Thomas was able to buy mee out of all I had, [with a]ll my Clowts: badd mee goe and swagger in my Country thatch ale-howses, and threatned to send mee to Goale [*sic*] and during the tyme of such his reproachful speeches he walked up and [dow]n chafing, and stamping, and expressing lookes and gestures full of scorne contempt and indignation.

The Mayor admitted that he refused to assist South-cote, but denied speaking in derogation of his knighthood, and in the end obtained a definitive sentence in his favour.[3] The records are not complete enough to show whether Southcote fared any better in a cause in which he alleged that William Morrell, a fuller of Exeter, had

[1] (1639), Acta Cur. Mil. (4), 12.
[2] The citizens of Exeter were puritans and the soap monopolists were regarded as 'popish' (C. Hill, *Economic Problems of the Church* (Oxford, 1956), pp. 5, 9).
[3] Cur. Mil. Boxes 15/4*b*, 18/1*s*.

said that if he had not been a 'base beggerly knight' he
would not have taken the business concerning the soap-
makers,[1] or in that which he brought against John
Spiller, a soap-maker, for scandalous words spoken at
Curland, co. Somerset, when Southcote was there about
the execution of his letters patent.[2]

The main interest of this type of case lies in the inci-
dental information to be found in the pleadings and the
evidence. Such information is to be found in all records
of litigation and the records of the Court of Chivalry are
by no means peculiar in this respect. There is, however,
one feature of cases of 'scandalous words' which makes
them of special value to the biographer and the genealo-
gist. The Court of Chivalry was only concerned with
wrongs done to gentlemen. That the plaintiff was a
gentleman and descended from gentlemen was a common form matter of inducement in every libel alleging
'scandalous words'. Frequently this was pleaded in very
general terms, such as that 'the plaintiff is a gentleman of
very ancient descent and family in the county of Devon'.[3]
Occasionally matters supporting this averment were
alleged in the libel itself, as in *Somerset* v. *Perkins*,[4] where
the plaintiff alleged that he was of the family of the Earls
of Worcester. More frequently it is in the depositions that
particulars of the plaintiff's pedigree appear. Sometimes
it only amounts to a vague statement that the plaintiff
and his father have always lived in the manner of gentlemen and been reputed to be such in the county in which
they lived. Often the evidence is more detailed and sometimes the witnesses take the pedigree back for many
generations.[5] In *Mascall* v. *Sole*[6] the defendant was
alleged to have coupled with the words spoken of the
plaintiff the statement that the plaintiff's wife was no

---

[1] *Southcote* v. *Morrell* (1639), Cur. Mil. II. 184–8.

[2] *Southcote* v. *Spiller* (1639), Cur. Mil. Boxes 6/54.

[3] *Coppleston* v. *Bayly* (1640), Cur. Mil. Boxes 2/12.

[4] (1634), Acta Cur. Mil. (5), 18.

[5] e.g. *Stepney* v. *Williams* (1638), Her. Cas. 119, where both parties called such evidence.

[6] (1637), Acta Cur. Mil. (4), 32.

gentlewoman, although she was the daughter of an esquire.

There is a glimpse of early colonial history to be obtained from *Hawley* v. *Futter*[1] and *Futter* v. *Hawley*.[2] Henry Hawley, Captain-General and Governor of the Island of Barbados under the Earl of Carlisle, took proceedings against James Futter for saying that he was a base, cheating knave and had none to wait on him but a hangman. It would seem that even if the hangman was not the whole of the Governor's entourage, he was a prominent member of it, for in cross-proceedings brought by Futter on the ground that the addition of 'gentleman' to his name was not inserted in Hawley's libel, Hawley stated that had he not thought that Futter was distracted, he would have hanged him for saying that the island did not belong to the King of England nor to the Earl of Carlisle, but to the King of Spain, and that Hawley and others lived there but as rebels, and that if the Spaniards should come, he would revolt and submit to them.

Whilst armorial causes were in the minority, there were enough of them to form a well-defined branch of the Court's business. Heraldic questions arose in two ways. Sometimes a plaintiff alleged that the defendant was pirating his arms, and proceeded by libel in the usual way.[3] The other type of heraldic case was criminal in form, the office of the judge being promoted by the person, usually the King's Advocate or one of the kings of arms, alleging that the defendant was bearing arms to which he was not entitled. During the period under review we have the records of but few causes of this type. Such a case was *Duck* v. *Woodall*.[4] There the defendant sought to justify his use of the arms in question by producing a certificate purporting to bear the signature of Robert Cooke, Clarenceux King of Arms from 1567 to 1592. This was countered by the evidence of William Sedgwick, who deposed that whilst he was servant to

---

[1] (1638), Cur. Mil. Boxes 20/3f.   [2] (1638), Cur. Mil. Boxes 13/2r.
[3] *Perrot* v. *Perrocke alias Perrot* (1639), Her. Cas. 44.
[4] (1640), Her. Cas. 40.

Henry Lillie, Rouge Dragon Pursuivant, he was instructed by his master to erase the arms from a painting signed by Cooke and to substitute the arms used by the defendant.[1]

The large number of cases in the 1630's shows that the Court was popular amongst plaintiffs, but towards the end of that decade defendants began to take an unfavourable view of it. In 1639 Humphrey Abdy of All Saints, Lombard Street, mercer, was alleged to have said that it was a 'base Court'.[2] John Mundy of St. Columb the Lower, co. Cornwall, spoke 'verry unbeseeminge words concerninge the Court Militarie'.[3] John Waters of Bensington, co. Oxford, when told to remember the Court of Honour, replied that 'he cared not a turd for the Lord Marshal of England nor his Court'.[4] Robert Googe of Bigglesworth, co. Bedford, was slightly more polite when he said that the Court of Honour was 'a fool's Court'.[5] When the mandatory of the Court went to arrest Richard Rogers of Allingomery, co. Hereford, for contempt, he was told that it was a trick to get money, that all the 'fetches and ways' of the Court were but to get money out of men, and that Rogers hoped shortly to see the Court put down.[6]

Rogers did not have to wait long to see his hopes fulfilled, for the Court attracted the unfavourable notice of an ambitious barrister of the Middle Temple, Edward Hyde, whose green bag was later to be exchanged for a Lord Chancellor's purse.[7] Hyde first entered Parliament

---

[1] Sedgwick is described in his deposition as household servant to Sir Christopher Hatton of Kirby, co. Northampton, knight. He was employed to paint some of the 'Hatton-Dugdale' series of facsimilies of rolls of arms, deeds, and church monuments: see *Sir Christopher Hatton's Book of Seals* (Oxford, 1950), p. xxiv, and A. R. Wagner, *A Catalogue of English Mediaeval Rolls of Arms* (Harl. Soc. c, 1950), p. xxii. Lillie by his will dated 24 July 1638 (P.C.C. 106 Lee) left 'To my servant William Sedgewicke my second Book of ordinarys'. (I am indebted to Mr. H. Stanford London, Norfolk Herald Extraordinary, for this reference).

[2] *Draper* v. *Abdy* (1639), Cur. Mil. Boxes 2/60.

[3] *Cosowarth* v. *Mundy* (1639), Cur. Mil. Boxes 2/95.

[4] *Machen* v. *Waters* (1640), Cur. Mil. Boxes 11/24.

[5] *Poultney* v. *Googe* (1640), Cur. Mil. Boxes 5/172.

[6] *Office of the Judge* v. *Rogers* (1640), Cur. Mil. Boxes 11/10.

[7] The Duke of Gloucester said that Hyde's daughter, the Duchess of York,

as one of the members for Wootton Basset in his native Wiltshire in the Short Parliament of 1640. This gave him an opportunity of ventilating a long-standing resentment against the Court of Chivalry, due, it is said, to a near relation having been disclaimed at a visitation in 1623.[1] Parliament met on 13 April and Hyde soon found an opportunity to make his maiden speech. On the 17th petitions from Middlesex, Northamptonshire, and Sussex complaining of various grievances were delivered to the House of Commons by their respective members. On the 18th there were two more petitions from Essex and Hertfordshire.[2] There followed a debate, in which John Pym, one of the members for Poole, spoke for two hours on a large number of 'grievances'.[3] Hyde's turn to speak came the next day. He told the House that Pym had omitted one grievance, more heavy (as he thought) than many of the others. This was the Earl Marshal's Court, which he described as 'a court newly erected, without colour or shadow of law, which took upon it to fine and imprison the King's subjects, and to give great damages for matters which the law gave no damages for'.[4] He said that he was not ignorant that it was anciently a court in time of war, but he hoped that as the youngest man there could remember the beginning of the manner in which it was then used and of the greatness into which it was swollen, so the oldest might see the end of it.[5]

Hyde went on to tell the story of a citizen who, being rudely treated for more than his fare came to, by a waterman, who, pressing him, still shewed his crest, or badge upon his

<hr />

smelt of her father's green bag (*D.N.B.* x. 369). For barristers' green bags see *L.Q.R.* (1955), lxxi. 487.

[1] Dallaway, *Inquiries into . . . . the Science of Heraldry*, pp. 293–4. Probably the 'near relation' was Hyde's uncle, Robert Hyde of Hatch, co. Wilts. Robert Hyde was not in fact disclaimed, but having complained about being ordered as a justice of the peace to assist the heralds who visited Wiltshire in 1623, he had the tables turned on him by being summoned to appear before the Earl Marshal to answer for his unjust complaint (Coll. Arm. MS. Heralds II, p. 866; *C.J.* i. 692–3).

[2] *Parliamentary History of England* (London, 1751), viii. 420.

[3] Ibid., pp. 425–34.   [4] *Life of Edward Earl of Clarendon*, i. 60.

[5] Coll. Arm. MS. Heralds II, p. 871.

coat, the citizen bade him be gone *with his goose*; whereas it was in truth, a swan, the crest of an earl, whose servant the waterman was: whereupon the citizen was called into the Marshal's Court, and, after a long and chargeable attendance, was, *for the opprobrious dishonouring the earl's crest, by calling the swan a goose*, fined and imprisoned, till he had paid considerable damages to the lord, or at least to the waterman; which really undid the citizen.[1]

The story of the citizen and the goose was followed by one of a gentleman who, being dunned by his tailor, called him a base fellow, which provoked the tailor into saying that he was as good a man as his customer, for which words the tailor was condemned by the Marshal's Court to release his demands in lieu of damages.[2]

Hyde concluded his diatribe with an attack on the heralds, who, he said, 'were as grievous to the gentry, as the Court was to the people', especially on account of the fees which they took for the funerals of the nobility and gentry,[3] and moved that the commission, under pretence of which the heralds demanded their fees, might be sent for.[4] All this was 'very acceptable to the House', and Hyde smugly closed his account of it by observing that 'this being the first part he had acted upon that stage, brought him much applause; and he was ever afterwards heard with great benignity'.[5]

Support for Hyde came on 30 April, when Michael Wharton, one of the members for Beverley, reported to the House a cause in the Court of Chivalry which Ralph Pudsey of Stapleton, co. York, had instituted against him

---

[1] *Life*, i. 61. This is clearly a reference to *Dover (Earl)* v. *Fox* (1638), Cur. Mil. Boxes 11/32/3, but the interrogatories show that the plaintiff's complaint was not merely that his swan had been called a goose, but that the defendant said to the waterman, 'Thou fellowe with the goose on thy sleeve, whose fooles coate doest thou weare ?', and when the waterman replied that his master the Earl of Dover gave him the coat, the defendant said that it was a fool's coat and a knave's coat. The defence (Cur. Mil. Boxes 10/12/11) puts the matter in a still more different light from Hyde's speech, but no record of the sentence survives.

[2] This cause has not been identified in the records of the Court with certainty, but it may be *Gardiner* v. *Gilbert*, Cur. Mil. Boxes 2/74, 75, in which the Town Clerk of New Sarum sued a tailor of that city in respect of scandalous words in January 1640. Being a recent Wiltshire case, it would probably have been known to Hyde.

[3] *Life*, i. 61.   [4] *C.J.* ii. 6.   [5] *Life*, i. 62.

for scandalous words.[1] It was thereupon ordered that the proceedings should be stayed during the privilege of that Parliament; that John Rainshaw, who had served Wharton with a warrant to attend the commission for the examination of the plaintiff's witnesses, should be sent for; and that the contempt should be referred to the Committee for Privileges for examination.[2] Wharton did not inform the House that there was also a cause pending in the Court of Chivalry which he had instituted against Pudsey.[3] The privilege of that Parliament did not last long. Parliament was dissolved on 8 May and Pudsey was free to continue his proceedings against Wharton. This he did, but with what result the records do not disclose.[4]

The dissolution of Parliament also temporarily removed Hyde's more general threat to the Court. Litigation continued on the same scale as before.[5] It was not long, however, before Hyde was able to return to the attack. On 3 November 1640 a new Parliament assembled with Hyde as one of the members for Saltash. Within a few days Hyde renewed the motion against the Court of Chivalry which he had made in the last Parliament. He described the proceedings in the Court since the dissolution of Parliament, and said that more damages had been given there for 'contumelious and reproachful words', of which the law took no notice, in two days, than had been given by all the juries in all the Courts in Westminster Hall in the whole term and the days for trial after it was ended.[6] On 23 November Hyde and thirty-two other members, including John Selden, one of the members for Oxford University, were appointed a committee

to receive all Petitions that are or shall be delivered concerning the

---

[1] *Pudsey* v. *Wharton*, Cur. Mil. Boxes 5/105.   [2] *C.J.* ii. 16.

[3] *Wharton* v. *Pudsey*, Acta Cur. Mil. (5), 115–17. On 15 June 1640 Wharton obtained a definitive sentence for damages and costs against Pudsey (Cur. Mil. Boxes 17/6a).

[4] Pudsey's witnesses were examined on 22 July 1640 (Cur. Mil. II. 99–106).

[5] Records of eight sittings between May and October 1640 survive. There were forty-nine cases pending at the first session in Michaelmas term (Cur. Mil. Boxes 1/11h) and forty-one at the last session (ibid. 1/11l).

[6] *Life*, i. 64. The judges were authorized by the statute 18 Eliz. I, c. 12 to sit for four days after the end of term.

High Constable and Earl-Marshal's Court; and to inquire after the Fees of the High Constable and Earl-Marshal's Court, and the Herald's Fees; and to consider of the Proceedings and Power of the High Constable and Earl-Marshal's Court; and to report the state of the whole Matter to the House.[1]

The committee, of which Hyde was chairman, was ordered to meet in the Star Chamber on 25 November.[2] At that meeting they ordered the commission and other instruments by which the heralds claimed fees on the death of persons of 'several degrees' to be brought before them in Middle Temple Hall on the 27th, the notice of the order to the officers of arms being signed by Hyde.[3] The committee found that the first precedent in the records of the Court for the giving of damages for words went back no farther than 1633, on which Hyde stigmatized it as 'that upstart court', entirely leaving out of account the centuries of jurisdiction in heraldic and other military matters.[4]

These proceedings must have alarmed the officers of the Court of Chivalry, but the sittings of the Court were continued until the last session of Michaelmas term on 4 December.[5] On 8 December the House of Commons ordered that the committee, then adjourned *sine die*, should meet the following day and that all the lawyers in the House should be added to it.[6] Since there were seventy-five barristers in the House at the time,[7] the enlarged committee must have been somewhat unwieldy. However, Hyde managed the matter to his satisfaction, for on 19 February 1641 he had what must have been the congenial task of reporting the result of the committee's deliberations to the House. Upon this report the House resolved that the Court had no jurisdiction to hold plea of words; that the Earl Marshal could hold no Court without the Constable; and that the Court was a grievance. The House then ordered that it be referred to the committee

---

[1] *C.J.* ii. 34.
[2] *Life*, i. 64; *C.J.* ii. 34.
[3] Dallaway, op. cit., p. 294 n.
[4] *Life*, i. 64.
[5] Cur. Mil. Boxes 1/11*l.*
[6] *C.J.* ii. 47.
[7] D. Brunton and D. H. Pennington, *Members of the Long Parliament* (London, 1954), p. 5.

to consider who had been guilty of the grievance which the House had voted the Court to be; to consider the nature of the crime of which those who had laid this grievance upon the subject had been guilty; and to consider of some fit way for reparation to be made to the parties aggrieved. The committee were also instructed to prepare and draw up a charge, to be transmitted to the Lords, against those who had usurped this jurisdiction.[1]

It does not appear that the committee proceeded any farther in the matter. The resolution of the House was sufficient to put a stop to the work of the Court. Three causes—all of 'scandalous words'—had been instituted on 1 December 1640, but they were never heard.[2]

The latest surviving document of this period is a bond dated 27 January 1641.[3]

The Commons had one last kick at the Court on 1 December 1641, when one of the items in the 'Remonstrance of the State of the Kingdom' presented to Charles I at Hampton Court was the assertion that 'The pretended Court of the Earl Marshal was arbitrary, and illegal, in its being and proceedings'.[4]

After that there is silence. Hyde did not have to concern himself about the Court of Chivalry any more. He had been dead for nearly thirteen years before the Court next sat.

---

[1] *C.J.* ii. 89. There are further details concerning the proceedings of the committee in *The Journal of Sir Simonds D'Ewes* (ed. W. Notestein) (New Haven, 1923), *passim.*

[2] Cur. Mil. Boxes 5/179, 180, 183. A few days earlier Dr. Charles Tooker, one of the advocates in Doctors' Commons, had instituted a cause against Humphrey Terricke, the Register of the Court, but there is nothing to show its nature (ibid. 168).

[3] Ibid. Boxes 5/187.

[4] *Parliamentary History of England,* x. 69.

IV

THE PARLIAMENTARY HERALDIC TRIBUNAL
1645–60

U NPOPULAR though the Court of Chivalry had become before it was denounced in Parliament in 1640, the cessation of its sitting proved to be a not unmixed blessing. The use of armorial bearings was not confined to Cavaliers. The Parliamentarians numbered many armigerous men in their ranks and the prospect of heraldic chaos can have held no attraction for them.[1] The state of affairs which followed the suspension of the Court of Chivalry is described in the preamble to the 'Ordinance to prevent abuses in Heraldry' of 19 March 1646 as follows:

Whereas divers Persons have assumed to themselves the Use and Bearing of the Arms of several of the Nobility and Gentry of this Kingdom, whereby many Errors are crept in, and divers Abuses committed, since the sitting of this Parliament [i.e. 3 November 1640], which may produce great Inconveniences and Debate hereafter, if seasonable Remedy be not provided.

It was accordingly ordained that Algernon, Earl of Northumberland, together with forty-four peers and members of the House of Commons, should have power

to settle and regulate the Office and Officers of Arms, and all abuses therein or otherwise committed; and to hear and determine all Manner of Offences and Abuses since the beginning of this Parliament committed, or that shall be committed, in or by the bearing, assuming, giving, granting, or allowing, of any Coat or Scutcheon of Arms, or of any Crest thereto belonging; and in those Particulars only to supply the Offices of the Constable and Marshal of England,

---

[1] There is much Commonwealth heraldry in J. Prestwich, *Prestwich's Respublica* (London, 1787), *passim*.

in such sort and Manner as to the Office of Constable and Marshal of England doth belong, or of Right have heretofore belonged.

The quorum was to be five, including at least one peer and two members of the House of Commons.[1]

The Commissioners soon got to work.[2] Ten of them (the Earl of Warwick, Lord North, Lord Roberts, Sir William Lewis, Sir Simonds d'Ewes, Sir John Curzon, Sir Philip Stapleton, Bulstrode Whitelocke, Denis Bond, and Edward Bysshe) assembled for their first sitting on 14 April 1646 in the house of Sir Abraham Williams, knight, situate by the Palace of Westminster. The proceedings were similar *mutatis mutandis* to those at the opening of the Court of Chivalry in 1622. The Ordinance was recited and the Commissioners accepted the burden of executing it. They then appointed a notary public, John Watson, to be their Register. Next Dr. John Exton was admitted 'Advocate of the Court or Promoter of Causes', and a Sub-Marshal or Serjeant-Marshal and a Messenger were appointed.[3]

The next sitting was held on 21 April, when four proctors were appointed,[4] but there was no judicial business at this time, the Commissioners devoting themselves to 'settling and regulating' the College of Arms in accordance with the Ordinance, which they interpreted as authorizing them to appoint officers of arms. Amongst the officers appointed by the Commissioners were one of their own number, Edward Bysshe, who became Garter, and Arthur Squibb, who became Clarenceux, the father-in-law of another Commissioner, John Glynne.[5]

On 13 August the Commissioners prepared for litigation by ordering a seal of the Court to be made.[6] The seal

---

[1] C. H. Firth and R. S. Rait, *Acts and Ordinances of the Interregnum*, i. 838–9.

[2] No record of their proceedings seems to have been preserved, save in a copy of their Act Book in the College of Arms made by Stephen Martin Leake, Garter 1754–73 (Coll. Arm. MS. SML 3, ff. 185–201), and some notes in Bodl. MS. Ashmole 857.

[3] Coll. Arm. MS. SML 3, ff. 185–7.   [4] Ibid., f. 188.

[5] Ibid., ff. 189, 190. Bysshe went through the form of getting a petition on his behalf presented to his fellow Commissioners (Coll. Arm. MS. Heralds IX, p. 361).   [6] Coll. Arm. MS. SML 3, f. 189.

was ready by 3 September, when the Commissioners approved it and authorized the Register to seal citations with it in cases in which libels and complaints were signed by advocates and left with him. The first libel on which process was ordered was exhibited by Edmund Langley, but the nature of his complaint does not appear.[1]

On 13 October the Commissioners appointed John Watson, the Register, to act as Bluemantle Pursuivant at the funeral of the Earl of Essex, and on 22 December appointed him Bluemantle for life.[2]

No further step seems to have been taken in Langley's cause and there was no more judicial business until 30 March 1648, when Sir Ralph Ashton, baronet, and Ralph Ashton, esquire, exhibited a complaint against one William Ashton of St. Martin-in-the-Fields, co. Middlesex, in a cause relating to the unlawful use and usurpation of arms at the funeral of Sir William Ashton.[3]

Hitherto the Commissioners themselves sat on each occasion, but on 28 April 1648 they appointed Dr. Exton, the Advocate of the Court, to be their Lieutenant in all causes or complaints instituted before them, with power to pronounce a definitive sentence. Dr. Walter Walker was appointed Advocate of the Court in place of Exton.[4]

Dr. Exton did not take his seat in Court until the following 5 October, when the Ordinance and his deputation were read. To the pending cause of *Ashton* v. *Ashton* there were added two causes promoted by Arthur Squibb, Clarenceux, against Walter St. John, esquire, and John Gomershall, the painter who made the escutcheons for the funeral of Sir William Ashton.[5] Later in the same month Edward Bysshe, Garter, promoted a cause on behalf of Sir John Strangways, knight, against Richard Cuthberd, and two other causes against Abraham Stanion of St. Catherine Creechurch and Thomas Bludworth.[6] In November Squibb promoted a cause against

---

[1] Coll. Arm. MS. SML 3, f. 191.
[2] Ibid., ff. 192, 193.
[3] Ibid., ff. 194, 199.
[4] Ibid., f. 195.
[5] Ibid., ff. 195, 196, 199.
[6] Ibid., ff. 197, 198.

Anthony Maria Smith, so bringing the number of pending causes up to seven. With the exception of *Ashton* v. *Ashton* there is no information in the Act Book as to the subject-matter of these causes, but it is known from other sources that the cause against St. John concerned the undue pomp with which he as executor solemnized the funeral of Sir John St. John at Battersea.[1] Anthony Maria Smith was a prominent herald-painter, and the proceedings against him probably related to the funeral of John Chamberlain, the Sheriff of Oxfordshire, who died during his shrievalty in November 1648, his funeral being ordered by a Mr. Smith, a herald-painter, 'instead of Clariencieux King of Arms, whose office he thus boldly usurped, as well as at other times'.[2]

A sitting was held in a chamber in the Court of Wards and Liveries on 6 November at which Edward Norgate, Windsor Herald, appeared personally and exhibited a supplicatory libel. This was read by the Register, and the Commissioners ordered Norgate to be restored to the profits and emoluments of the office of Windsor Herald.[3]

On 30 November 1648 the Court was adjourned until the following 17 January with five causes still pending, sentence having been given in *Squibb* v. *St. John*, and *Squibb* v. *Gomershall* having apparently been discontinued. Whether the Court was held on 17 January is open to doubt, since on that day some of the Commissioners were engaged in preparing for the King's trial, which began on the 20th. There is no record of any subsequent proceedings in the pending causes, but the Commissioners were still acting judicially later in the year. Winifred, Viscountess Brouncker, died on 30 July 1649. Her husband had been raised to the peerage on 12 September 1645 and died later in the same year. In the eyes of the Parliamentarians she was not a peeress at all, for the Commissioners had been ordered by Parliament to cancel and deface all patents conferring honours

---

[1] H. S. London and G. D. Squibb, 'A Dorset King of Arms', in *Proc. Dorset N.H. & Arch. Soc.* lxviii (1947), 58, and the authorities there cited.

[2] *C.S.P.D. 1648*, p. 336.   [3] Coll. Arm. MS. SML 3, f. 199.

after 4 January 1641.[1] Her son and heir was charged by the officers of arms as 'Sir William Brouncker' with having ordered an achievement with a viscountess's coronet over two coats impaled to be fixed on his mother's house in Westminster, where it was exposed to view for 'divers months'.[2] The result of the cause does not appear, though presumably the defendant's answer that he believed his father to have been a viscount of Ireland was of little avail, having regard to the cancellation of the patent.

No later causes before the Commissioners have been found, but the commission seems to have remained in being until the Restoration, when the Ordinance of 1646, in common with all the other legislation passed without the Royal Assent after 1640, ceased to have effect.[3]

[1] *C.P.* ii. 299, note (a).

[2] *Officers of Arms* v. *Brouncker*, Bodl. MS. Ashm. 836, p. 637.

[3] The proceedings of the Commissioners were not included in the Act for the confirmation of judicial proceedings since 1 May 1642 (12 Car. II, c. 12).

V

RESTORATION HERALDIC LITIGATION
1660–87

AT the Restoration there was not only no Lord High
Constable, but no Earl Marshal. Thomas, Earl of
Arundel and Surrey, who had been appointed Earl
Marshal for life in 1621, had died at Padua in 1646. His
son Henry, who succeeded him as Earl of Arundel, is
said to have been created Earl Marshal for life in reversion
on 1 July 1640,[1] but he died in 1652 and the office remained vacant.

James, Earl of Suffolk, was appointed Earl Marshal
for the Coronation in April 1661, after which the office
again became vacant and remained so until 26 May 1662,
when Thomas, Earl of Southampton, Lord Treasurer, and
a number of other peers were appointed Commissioners
for executing the office of Earl Marshal.[2]

The appointments of any surviving officers of the Court
of Chivalry expired upon the death of the Earl of Arundel
and Surrey,[3] and there is no evidence that the Commissioners appointed fresh officers. Nevertheless, the
Commissioners exercised judicial powers in relation to

---

[1] Petition by Henry, Lord Howard of Castle Rising (Coll. Arm. MS. R. 19,
f. 218, cited in *C.P.* ix. 627, note (e)); Plott, 'A Defence of the Jurisdiction of the
Earl Marshal's Court', in *Curious Discourses*, ii. 268.

[2] It is stated in the report of *Parker's Case* (1668), 1 Lev. 230, that the Earl
Marshal at that time was a lunatic. Thomas, Duke of Norfolk, the grandson and
heir of the last Earl Marshal, was *non compos mentis*. The office of Earl Marshal
had, however, been granted to his grandfather (and possibly also to his father)
for life, so that he was not Earl Marshal by descent, but his insanity was no
doubt the reason why Commissioners were appointed. He was still alive when his
brother was created hereditary Earl Marshal in 1672.

[3] This appears from the fact that the officers were reappointed when there was
a change in the office of Earl Marshal, e.g. Sir Richard Raines was reappointed
Surrogate in 1701 after the appointment of the Earl of Carlisle D.E.M., and
Dr. Isham was reappointed in 1733 on the succession of Edward, Duke of
Norfolk.

heraldic matters in a number of cases. An early example of such a case was *Dugdale* v. *Meinill and Nower*. Here William Dugdale, Norroy King of Arms, complained to the Commissioners that William Meinill with the help of Francis Nower, a painter-stainer in London, had made 'irregular and unjustifiable' arms, and had on 27 October 1666 marshalled 'a great and solemn funeral' at Bradley, co. Derby, for Francis Meinill, an alderman of London. Dugdale prayed for letters directed to the justices of the peace and other royal officers in Derbyshire 'exciting' them to give him assistance in pulling down and defacing the escutcheons and achievements and that the Commissioners would send for Meinill and Nower to answer their misdemeanours. A warrant signed by the Duke of Albemarle, the Marquess of Dorchester, and the Earls of Manchester and Carlisle was issued on 6 November 1666. It may be that this was the first case after the Restoration, for the petition prays that the Commissioners will exercise their powers 'as your Lo^{pps} predecessors have heretofore done in the like cases'.[1]

The heralds continued to have trouble with the painters as they had done before the Civil War. In January 1668 the Commissioners on a complaint by Sir Edward Walker, Garter, committed to the Marshalsea until further order one Parker, a member of the Painter-Stainers' Company, for painting escutcheons, trophies, and other ensigns for the funeral of Lord Gerard and ordering and marshalling it without licence of the Commissioners, 'Judges of the Court of Honour'.[2]

Parker was brought before the Court of King's Bench by a writ of *habeas corpus* on 27 January. The Court expressed the view that being but a painter-stainer he could not paint any coat of arms to be used at funerals or other solemnities without the direction of a king of arms— Garter in the case of a nobleman and in the case of gentry Clarenceux if south of the Trent and Norroy if beyond.

---

[1] Bodl. MS. Ash. 857, pp. 417–18, printed in J. Guillim, *A Display of Heraldry* (6th ed., London, 1724), App., p. 53.

[2] *Parker's Case* (1668), 1 Lev. 230; *sub nom. R.* v. *Parker*, 1 Sid. 352.

The Court would have Parker submit, 'and if it were only a mistake, it would make an end of all'. The defendant, however, said that he was an arms-painter and not bound to take licence from the Commissioners, so the matter was adjourned.[1] Parker was brought before the Court again on 31 January, when the matter was argued by counsel, but although all the judges were of the opinion that he had been rightly committed, he refused to acknowledge his fault and was refused his discharge.[2] Ultimately, seeing the opinion of the Court against him, he submitted to Garter; compounded with him for the misfeasance; and was brought up again and discharged.[3]

Later in the year 1668 it was the heralds whose conduct gave rise to a complaint before the Commissioners. William Waller, son and heir of Sir William Waller, knight, who died 19 September 1668,[4] presented a petition to the Commissioners. In this he alleged that his father was a colonel of horse beyond the seas. Being minded to make a public funeral for his father, the petitioner caused certain 'achievements' to be made and informed Sir Edward Bysshe, Clarenceux King of Arms. Bysshe took exception to five pennons[5] as being more than the proper number, and refused to be present to marshal the funeral. Thereupon the petitioner caused all the achievements to be carried before the corpse and afterwards caused them to be hung up in the New Chapel in Tothill Fields, Westminster. Shortly afterwards three officers of arms upon pretence of an order from the Commissioners 'rudely, disgracefully and dishonorably' pulled down all the achievements, and not only defaced them, but carried them away.

The officers of arms gave in an answer pleading:

1. That the petitioner ought to prove his father to have

---

[1] *R. v. Parker* (1668), 2 Keb. 310.

[2] 2 Keb. 316.

[3] 1 Lev. 230. There is a detailed account of this case in Coll. Arm. MS. R. 28 (not foliated).

[4] Sir W. Musgrave, *Obituary* (Harl. Soc. xlix, 1901), vi. 190.

[5] Pennon—a long narrow flag or streamer, triangular and pointed, or swallow-tailed (*O.E.D.*, s.v.).

been a colonel beyond the seas, otherwise no guidon[1] ought to have been carried at the funeral.

2. That the achievements ought not to have been prepared without the licence of Clarenceux.

3. That Clarenceux refused to marshal the funeral because the petitioner required more pennons to be used than belonged to the degree of a knight.

4. That the arms and crest depicted in the achievements were erroneous.

5. That no coat of arms, helm, crest, &c., ought to be carried at a funeral, otherwise than by an officer of arms.

6. That the taking down of the achievements was done by lawful authority in the day-time, and not 'rudely, disgracefully and dishonorably'.

The Commissioners after hearing counsel found that the taking down of the achievements was by virtue of a visitation commission granted to Sir Edward Bysshe by letters patent; that the number of pennons carried at the funeral were more than were due and belonging to the degree of a knight 'by any lawful practise or Constitution'; that some of the achievements were not truly painted; that the marshalling of the funeral belonged to Sir Edward Bysshe by virtue of his office; and that the carrying of the coat of arms, helm, crest, sword, and target belonged to the officers of arms and to no other person 'according unto ancient presidents and constant practice'.

It was accordingly ordered that the three supernumerary pennons taken down by the officers of arms should not be hung up again, yet 'in regard of the former meritt & service performed by the said Sir William Waller in asserting the quarrell of his Maties Aunt the Queen of Bohemia in the German Warr; And that in the year 1659, he was ready to have actively engaged in Armes in order to his Maties restitution', and since they believed that the petitioner had been misguided by arms-

[1] Guidon—a flag or pennant, broad at the end next the staff and forked or pointed at the other (*O.E.D.*, s.v.).

painters, the Commissioners ordered him to address himself to Clarenceux and the other officers of arms concerned so that the errors in the painting of several of the achievements might be reformed. When that had been done, the officers of arms were to cause the guidon, standard, two pennons only, the coat of arms, helm, crest, sword, target, gauntlet, and spurs to be again hung up in the chapel, the petitioner paying the officers of arms their 'due and accustomed fees'.[1]

On 5 November the painters, Wright, Gale, and Williams, who had irregularly painted the achievements for the funeral without Sir Edward Bysshe's allowance, were called before the Commissioners, told of their irregularities and invasion of the rights of the officers of arms, and ordered to ask the officers of arms' pardon, which they did, whereupon they were further told by the Commissioners that if they offended thereafter they would be 'severely proceeded against'.[2]

This did not end the matter for the petitioner. The crest carried at his father's funeral was a walnut tree on which hung an escutcheon of the arms of Charles, Duke of Orleans, taken prisoner at Agincourt by Richard Waller. The Commissioners referred the bearing of this crest to the King. On 13 November, upon the rising of the King from Council at Whitehall, two of the Commissioners, the Duke of Albemarle and the Earl of Carlisle, asked the King to declare his pleasure touching the crest. The King declared that for the time being the crest was to be hung up with the other achievements of Sir William Waller according to the Commissioners' order, but that within a year his son should make further and other proof than what he had already produced of his right to bear and use the crest. If he failed, he was not to use it for the future, but to have 'some such Marke or part of the Duke of Orleance his Armes assigned him as may preserve the memory & merit of his Ancestor'.[3]

---

[1] Misc. Cur. Mil. 179–81.   [2] Ibid. 171.
[3] Ibid. 175. See Sir H. Nicolas, *History of the Battle of Agincourt*, p. 168. The family of Waller now bear a single fleur-de-lis on the escutcheon, but they

At the time when Sir William Waller's 'achievements' were taken down, the officers of arms also caused four pennons formerly set up for his wife to be taken down, on the ground they were unduly set up and more than were due to the degree of a knight's wife. However, 'at the desire of some persons of Honour & quality', the Commissioners on 15 December 1668 authorized the officers of arms to cause two of the pennons of the arms of Lady Waller and her two husbands to be hung up again in the chapel.[1]

In another case in November 1668 the officers of arms, instead of taking down supernumary pennons by virtue of the visitation commission, complained to the Commissioners first. They alleged that whilst only two pennons were carried at the funeral of Sir Robert Page, knight, which was directed and marshalled by the officers of arms, two more pennons were set up in the New Chapel at Westminster 'contrary to the established rules'. The Commissioners thereupon ordered that Clarenceux or his deputy should take down the two supernumerary pennons, and that 'all justices of the peace, constables, church-wardens, and other officers civil and military' should assist in the execution of the order.[2]

In July 1669 there was a suggestion that the Court of Chivalry should be used for trying certain officers and soldiers for offences committed in the attempt to regain the island of St. Christopher from the French *secundum legem armorum* and the civil law,[3] but there seems to be no evidence that any such trials ever took place.

At about this time it was proposed to put the office of Lord High Constable into commission and to give the Commissioners together with the Commissioners for executing the office of Earl Marshal power to hear and determine all questions, differences, and complaints concerning arms, titles, and registration of the descents of

were credited with the crest embodying the shield of the Duke of Orleans in successive editions of Burke's *Peerage* down to 1902. The present form of the crest, however, appears in the 1880 edition of Foster's *Peerage*.

[1] Misc. Cur. Mil. 183.   [2] Bodl. MS. Ashm. 836, p. 629.
[3] *A.P.C., Col.* i. 527.

the nobility and gentry 'in as full and ample manner and form to all intents and purposes as any Constable and Earl Marshal of England or either of them have or hath done or might, could or ought to have done by virtue of their several offices'.[1]

Nothing seems to have come of this project, and matters went on as before until the office of Earl Marshal was taken out of commission on 19 October 1672. Henry, Lord Howard of Castle Rising, was created Earl of Norwich and hereditary Earl Marshal by letters patent which recited the letters patent of 1 August 1622, whereby the power of the Earl Marshal to proceed judicially without a Constable was declared.[2]

After the passing of the Test Act in March 1673 the new Earl Marshal was disabled from executing his office, but under the Act he was empowered to appoint a deputy or deputies approved by the King under the privy signet.[3] Accordingly in the following June the Earl Marshal obtained the King's approval to the appointment of the Marquesses of Worcester and Dorchester and the Earls of Bedford, Suffolk, Peterborough, Carlisle, and Ailesbury to be his deputies.[4]

Like the Commissioners, the Deputy Earl Marshals continued to deal with matters falling within the jurisdiction of the Court of Chivalry. Their powers for so doing were reinforced by a royal declaration dated 16 June 1673 and confirmed by Order in Council on 22 January 1674 that

it appertains to the office of Earl Marshal to order, judge and determine all matters touching arms, ensigns of nobility, honour and chivalry according to the law of arms and to make and prescribe rules, ordinances and decrees for the due regulation and settlement

---

[1] Draft letters patent (Coll. Arm. MS. Heralds IX, pp. 412–15). The draft may be dated between 6 July 1668, when the Duke of Buckingham became Master of the Horse, and 5 May 1671, when the Earl of Manchester died. The two sets of Commissioners were to appoint a register and such other officers and ministers as might be necessary.

[2] See p. 46 ante. The relevant portion of the 1672 patent is printed in 'X', The Right to Bear Arms, pp. 68–86.

[3] 25 Car. II, c. 2, s. 11(6).   [4] C.S.P.D. 1673, p. 414.

thereof, to revive and put in execution the laws and ordinances heretofore made by any Constable or former Earl Marshal touching the same.[1]

One case of this period is of some interest in that the defendant was Daniel Wycherley of Clive, co. Salop, the father of William Wycherley, the dramatist. Daniel Wycherley had had his pedigree and arms registered and allowed by William Dugdale, Norroy King of Arms, at the visitation of Shropshire in 1663. Notwithstanding this, in July 1675, when the son was at the height of his fame, a petition was exhibited to the Earl of Suffolk against the father by Sir Vincent Corbet, baronet, Sir Richard Corbet, baronet, and seven other persons representing the gentry of Shropshire, alleging that they were aggrieved by the pretences to gentry made by Daniel Wycherley; that they could not discover that his father, grandfather, or great-grandfather had or used any arms, or other addition than that of 'yeoman'; and that nevertheless he assumed arms and boasted himself to be a gentleman of blood and antiquity equal to the best of the petitioners. They prayed that his arms and pedigree might be inspected, examined, and proceeded upon, so that they might receive judgment and determination; and that his pedigree might be expunged and that he might be prohibited from bearing arms in future.[2]

On 27 September the Earl of Suffolk D.E.M. ordered the kings of arms and heralds to report on the petition. This they had not done by 4 November, when the Earl issued a further order.[3]

A start was then made, and on 13 November the defendant appeared before Richmond, Chester, Somerset, and Windsor Heralds and produced various documents in support of his case.[4] The kings of arms and heralds found themselves unable to agree on the matter. After more delay and yet another order from the Earl of Suffolk, Richmond, Chester, York, and Lancaster Heralds pro-

---

[1] Coll. Arm. MS. I. 26, ff. 55, 57.
[2] Coll. Arm. MS. Heralds IX, p. 230.
[3] Ibid., p. 234.   [4] Ibid., p. 1.

duced a report in favour of the petitioners on 8 May 1676:[1] two days later Garter and Clarenceux Kings of Arms and Somerset Herald reported in favour of the defendant.[2] Faced with these conflicting reports, the Earl of Peterborough referred the latter to Richmond, Chester, York, and Lancaster for their consideration on 22 May, and at the same time William Dugdale, Norroy King of Arms, was required to explain in writing the circumstances in which the pedigree and arms of the defendant came to be entered in the visitation of Shropshire.[3]

Norroy produced his explanation on 27 May. This throws some light on the standard of proof required at visitations. In 1662 Dugdale had been deputed by Sir Edward Bysshe, then Clarenceux, to visit Shropshire, that county being in the southern province. Daniel Wycherley was summoned to appear at the 'Raven' in Shrewsbury for the registration of his descent and arms. He there produced a draft of the pedigree of Wycherley of Cleve, 'pieced or knit' to four descents of Wycherley of Wycherley, together with the arms, and asked for them to be registered. Dugdale was not satisfied of Wycherley's right to the arms, so ('as former Kings of Armes had done in like cases') he registered the arms with the pedigree and gave Wycherley respite for the proof until he came to London. Later Wycherley saw Dugdale at the College of Arms and there 'affirmed confidently' that his family had anciently borne the arms in question, and that they were entered with his pedigree in a book of arms and pedigrees of Shropshire gentry collected by 'Mr. John Langley of that county, then lately deceased'. Dugdale regarded Langley as 'not only a person of good knowledge in Antiquitie, Armes and Genealogies, but of great Integrity'.[4] Nevertheless, he would not allow the arms until he had the approval of Clarenceux, so Wycherley attended on Clarenceux and Sir Thomas St. George,

---

[1] Ibid., pp. 143–62.   [2] Ibid., pp. 167–70.
[3] Ibid., pp. 232–3.
[4] Langley was of Brosely, co. Salop, and one of Dugdale's correspondents (W. Hamper, *Life . . . . of Sir William Dugdale* (London, 1827), p. 278).

Somerset Herald, and repeated the affirmation which he had made to Dugdale. Clarenceux and Somerset stated that in their opinion this was sufficient proof for the allowance and registration of the pedigree and arms, which were accordingly allowed and registered by Dugdale.[1]

On 14 June Richmond, Chester, York, and Lancaster produced their certificate, which contained severe reflections upon the report of Garter, Clarenceux, and Somerset.[2] This certificate in its turn was referred back to Garter, Clarenceux, and Somerset for their comments by the Earl of Peterborough on the defendant's petition on 15 November.[3] Finally, on 23 December 1676 they submitted a further certificate answering the four heralds point by point at great length and stating that in their opinion the defendant was justified in bearing 'the three spread eagles'.[4]

The Deputy Earl Marshals appear to have been still unsatisfied, for the day for determination was postponed until 23 February 1677, and thence to 5 April, to 7 June, and to 2 August. On 2 August the defendant requested that the matter should not then proceed to determination and delivered a paper of allegations, which he prayed might be admitted.[5] The defendant relied on a number of deeds amongst his muniments of title, the earliest being one dated 10 Henry IV, by which Richard Young granted to Roger, son of Richard de Wycherley, the elder lands in Clive and Sonsawe, which had descended to the defendant. He also pleaded that arms had been allowed to him and his pedigree entered at the visitation of Shropshire in 1663.[6] To this the petitioners prepared an 'answer',[7] and a 'further supplemental answer',[8] but since the paper of allegations was not admitted, the

---

[1] Coll. Arm. MS. Heralds IX, pp. 175–6. Dugdale had produced a similiar report on 13 Nov. 1675 (ibid., pp. 235–6).

[2] Ibid., pp. 113–38.   [3] Ibid., p. 252.

[4] Ibid., pp. 33–59, 79–109. The arms were *Per pale arg. and sa., 3 eagles displayed counterchanged* (ibid., p. 249).

[5] Ibid., p. 253.   [6] Ibid., pp. 73–77.

[7] Ibid., pp. 63–66.   [8] Ibid., pp. 67–68.

answers were not delivered.[1] The determination was further postponed from time to time, the last date fixed being 10 January 1678, when the matter was respited.[2]

On the death of the Earl Marshal on 13 January 1684 the appointments of the Deputy Earl Marshals determined and his son, also named Henry, succeeded to the office by virtue of the letters patent of 1672. The new Earl Marshal, having conformed to the Church of England, was able to execute his office in person. One of the first matters he had to deal with was a complaint made on 28 February 1684 by the Earl of Huntingdon that William Hastings of Hinton, co. Northampton, had contrary to the law of arms given for his coat *Argent, a maunch sable*, the paternal arms of the Earl's family. By way of answer the defendant produced an escutcheon on vellum, showing the arms with the addition of a *trefoil gules*, said to have been entered at the visitation of Bedfordshire in 1669 and signed 'Ed. Bish Clarencieux', but could not give any 'reasonable proof or account' of any relationship to the Earl's family. A search of the records of the College of Arms revealed that in the 1669 visitation of Bedfordshire there was a descent entered for the defendant, but it was dated 1674 and there were no arms entered with it, nor did it indicate any relationship to the Earl's family. The Earl Marshal held that the escutcheon signed by Sir Edward Bysshe was no sufficient authority for the defendant to bear the arms there shown and ordered him to give an undertaking to the Earl of Huntingdon not to continue to use the arms and to deliver the escutcheon to an officer of arms to be defaced. It was further ordered that any seals, paintings, carvings, engravings, or monuments with the arms upon them should also be defaced and broken.[3]

Although the Court of Chivalry was not formally reconstituted, the Commissioners, the Deputy Earl Mar-

---

[1] Ibid., p. 253.   [2] Ibid.

[3] Misc. Cur. Mil. 227. Cf. the opinion expressed by Bysshe's colleagues about some other visitations made by him that they were 'so erroneous and defective' that they were 'not only useless but scandalous' (A. R. Wagner, *Records and Collections of the College of Arms* (London, 1952), p. 74).

shals, and the Earl Marshal purported to be acting according to the law of arms,[1] and proceeded with some formality in dealing with the complaints which were brought before them. There were written pleadings by petition and answer,[2] and counsel were heard.[3] Nevertheless, the procedure was not that of the civil law, though there is an echo of the civil-law procedure in the petitioner's allegation in *Corbet* v. *Wycherley* that the object of the defendant's answer was 'to obstruct and delay the diffinitive sentence of the Deputy Earl Marshal and not upon any real hopes of gaining any other advantage thereby'.[4] In fact definitive sentences do not seem to have been pronounced at this period, any action upon a petition being by way of order or warrant. The manner of recording the proceedings was quite different from that of the old Court of Chivalry. Instead of acts being entered in an act book, minutes were drawn up in a form similar to those of meetings of the Privy Council.[5] There being no act book, when a permanent record of an order was required to be kept, the Registrar of the College of Arms was instructed to enter the order on record in the College.[6]

There was no machinery for enforcing the orders so made, though a warrant issued by the Earl Marshal or those executing his office might possibly have afforded a defence to a common-law action in respect of an act done in its execution.

[1] 'Forasmuch as the ordering Judgeing and determining all Matters touching Armes and Ensignes of Nobility &c (amongst other authorities) are vested in the Earle Marshall according to the Law of Arms. . . :' Order dated 4 Dec. 1684 in *Huntingdon (Earl)* v. *Hastings,* Misc. Cur. Mil. 227. Cf. the royal declaration quoted on p. 79 *ante.*

[2] In *Corbet* v. *Wycherley* the petitioners prepared a reply to the defendant's answer (Coll. Arm. MS. Heralds IX, p. 63).

[3] e.g. *re Waller* (1668), Misc. Cur. Mil. 179.

[4] Coll. Arm. MS. Heralds IX, p. 63.

[5] e.g.
> 'At the Court at Whitehall
> 'the 5th of November 1668
> 'Present
> 'Duke of Albemarle   Marquess of Dorchester
> 'Earle of Carlisle'

(Misc. Cur. Mil. 171).

[6] e.g. *Huntingdon (Earl)* v. *Hastings* (1684), Misc. Cur. Mil. 228.

The exact nature of the proceedings during this period seems not to have been entirely clear at the time. In 1666 Dugdale invited the Commissioners to exercise their powers 'as your Lo^pps predecessors have heretofore done in the like cases'.[1] If by that he meant 'by holding the Court of Chivalry' his invitation was not accepted. Two years later in *R. v. Parker*,[2] counsel for the defendant argued that it was an ancient Court, in which the Earl Marshal alone without the Constable could not commit. The contrary argument that the Court could be held before the Constable and the Marshal, or either of them, was upon the same footing. Keeling C.J. also spoke of 'the Court of honor', but it is submitted that Windham J. drew the correct distinction when he said:

This is not done by the Court of Chivalry, who may hold pleas of debt on contract in another kingdom; but the Earl Marshal is by himself a conservator of the peace in the laws of arms, as an officer, like the Chamberlain, Treasurer, &c. and upon any abuse or invasion, or contempt to the heralds, he may reform it by imprisonment.[3]

The exercise of these powers was not confined to cases in which complaints were made by the officers of arms or aggrieved parties. Sometimes action was taken on personal knowledge. Thus on 7 November 1683, Dame Sarah How, widow of Sir Richard How, knight, sometime one of the Sheriffs of the City of London, obtained leave from the Earl of Ailesbury D.E.M. to continue a hatchment set up after the death of her husband, alleging that she could make sufficient proof of the coat (*Or, a fess engrailed between three wolves' heads erased sable*) shown on it. No proof having been made by 19 June 1684, the new Earl Marshal issued an order to Clarenceux to cause the hatchment to be pulled down and defaced and to endeavour to find the name of the painter responsible for it.[4]

---

[1] See p. 74 *ante*.   [2] (1668), 2 Keb. 316.
[3] 2 Keb., at p. 317.
[4] Coll. Arm. MS. Heralds IX, p. 378. A similar order was made on 29 Jan. 1684/5 after John Head had failed to prove the arms of his father-in-law, John Dawes, painted on a hatchment set up after his wife's death (ibid., p. 375).

Despite these strong measures the son and daughter of the deceased Sheriff did not take out a grant of arms until 1691.[1]

The Commissioners, the Deputy Earl Marshals, and later the Earl Marshal himself continued to act as 'conservators of the peace in the laws of arms' for nearly twenty years after *R.* v. *Parker*, but in the end the unsatisfactory nature of their proceedings led to the recognition of the necessity for the reconstitution of the Court of Chivalry in its ancient form.

---

[1] *Grantees of Arms* (Harl. Soc. lxvi, 1915), p. 130. The petition and certificate of fitness are in Coll. Arm. MS. Heralds IX, pp. 379–80.

VI

THE CIVILIANS RESTORED AGAIN
1687–1731

AFTER a lapse of forty-seven years the Court of Chivalry was revived in 1687. The necessity for this step was due to the fact that the quasi-judicial proceedings which had been conducted by the Earl Marshal and those executing his office since the Restoration lacked any effective sanction. It may be that the immediate occasion for taking action was the unsatisfied complaint of Lord Leigh of Stoneleigh that Edward Lye, late Secondary to the Sheriffs of London, and John Lye of Enfield, co. Stafford, had not only assumed his name by changing Lye into Leigh, but had also assumed a coat of arms and crest very near to those of Lord Leigh's family. On 28 February 1685 the Earl Marshal ordered the Lyes to appear before him to answer the complaint and either justify their right for so doing within the ensuing month or abide such further order as he should think fit to make 'according to the Law of Arms'.[1] This clearly had no effect, for *Leigh* v. *Lye*[2] and *Leigh* v. *Lye* (*No. 2*)[3] were amongst the first causes in the revived Court of Chivalry.

On 13 August 1687 letters patent were issued to Henry, Duke of Norfolk, Earl Marshal, by virtue of a writ under the privy seal.[4] This patent, after reciting that the Court had been disused ever since the 'horrid Rebellion ... by reason whereof very many abuses not determinable in any other Court hath been unreformed and gon unpunished', ordered the Earl Marshal to hold a Court of Chivalry from time to time 'as judicially and definitively as any Constable or Marshall of this Our Realm either

---

[1] Misc. Cur. Mil. 231.　　　　　　　　[2] (1687), Her. Cas. 52.
[3] (1687), Her. Cas. 53.
[4] Printed in Appendix IV, p. 240 *post*, from a copy in the College of Arms.

joyntly or severally heretofore have or hath done' and to 'endeavour to restore and settle the Honorable Proceedings of that Court with the Rights thereunto belonging'.

The Earl Marshal's first step in obedience to the royal command was to appoint as Register of the Court Dr. Robert Plot, the Secretary of the Royal Society, of which the Earl Marshal was also a fellow.[1] The King appointed Dr. William Oldys, one of the advocates of the Court of Arches, to be 'Advocate General in the Court Military'. After these appointments had been made citations were issued on 3 October 1687 against two painter-stainers, Henry Howell and Richard Wallis.[2]

The first sitting of the reconstituted Court was held in the Painted Chamber on 5 October. The Earl Marshal, attended by the officers of arms,[3] was accompanied on the bench by the Earls of Bath, Craven, and Dunbarton, Lord Thomas Howard the Earl Marshal's brother, and Robert, Lord Hunsdon.[4] After proclamation for silence had been made three times by the Cryer, Dr. Plot read the letters patent of 19 October 1672, by which the Howard family was restored to the hereditary office of Earl Marshal, and the recent letters patent commanding the holding of the Court. Next the Earl Marshal took the oath faithfully to administer justice in the Court so far as in him lay. Then Dr. Oldys presented to the Earl Marshal the commission by which he had been appointed Advocate General in the Court, and the Earl Marshal took the commission and ordered that it should be publicly read. Dr. Plot exhibited the commission under the Earl Marshal's hand and seal by which he was appointed Register and took the oath to execute his office faithfully. The preliminaries concluded with the appearance of four notaries public, proctors in the Court of Arches,[5] who

---

[1] Noble, *History of the College of Arms*, p. 327, wrongly dates Plot's appointment as 'Registrar of the Court of Honor' as 1695.

[2] Cur. Mil. Boxes X/23/1, 2.

[3] Luttrell, *Brief Historical Relation of State Affairs*, i. 415.

[4] The following account of the proceedings is based upon the Act Book.

[5] Samuel Francklin, Everard Exton, Francis Nixon, and Robert Chapman. Francklin was the Procurator-General (E. Chamberlayne, *Angliae Notitia* (1684), pt. ii, p. 291 (misprinted 281)).

petitioned to be admitted proctors of the Court of Chivalry and took the oath faithfully to execute the office of proctor.

The substantive business began when Dr. Oldys exhibited the petitions of Lord Leigh of Stoneleigh against Edward Lye and John Lye and prayed for them to be cited to appear at the next sitting to reply to the complaint, which was decreed by the Earl Marshal.

There then appeared a link with the past in the person of Ralph Suckly, another proctor of the Court of Arches, who alleged that he had practised in the Court Military in the time of Thomas Earl of Arundel and petitioned to be admitted a proctor of the Court, whereupon he was admitted and sworn in.[1]

The proceedings concluded with the appearance of John Currey, the Mandatory or Marshal of the Court, who exhibited two original mandates, with certificates upon oath of their execution endorsed, against the two painter-stainers, Howell and Wallis. Sir Henry St. George, Clarenceux King of Arms, the promoter of the office of the judge against Howell and Wallis, petitioned for them to be declared in contempt and to be attached. The Earl Marshal pronounced them to be in contempt, but ordered that the attachments should not issue under seal before the next sitting on 8 October. On 8 October both Howell and Wallis appeared, so that it became unnecessary to seal the attachments.[2]

The Court settled down to work at the second sitting, when the Earl Marshal was accompanied on the bench by Sir Richard Raines LL.D., the Judge of the Court of Admiralty and Master of the Prerogative Court of Canterbury, who was described as 'Lieutenant', although he was not formally appointed until a month later.

---

[1] Suckly does not seem to have been engaged as a proctor in any of the subsequent litigation in the Court, but perhaps the Earl Marshal and the Register drew upon his recollections of nearly half a century before in order to obey the precept in the letters patent 'to restore and settle the Honourable Proceedings of that Court with the Rights thereunto belonging'.

[2] For the further proceedings in these causes see *St. George* v. *Howell* (*No.* 2) (1687), Her. Cas. 51, and *St. George* v. *Wallis* (1687), Her. Cas. 49. See also p. 92 *post.*

There were further sittings on 21 October and 9 November, at the latter of which Sir Thomas Exton LL.D., Official Principal of the Court of Arches, and Sir Richard Raines were appointed surrogates of the Earl Marshal during his pleasure.

On 21 October the King's Advocate commenced the first purely armorial proceedings in the revived Court against a Cornish knight, Sir James Tyllie, who had received the accolade on the previous 14 January and was celebrating his new rank by displaying arms to which he had no right, which bogus arms he supported with a pair of angels.[1]

The sitting on 9 November was marked by the appearance in person of a celebrated and pertinacious litigant, James Percy, the Dublin trunk-maker and claimant of the earldom of Northumberland, who presented a petition against Charles, Duke of Somerset, and his wife Elizabeth, daughter and heiress of the last Earl of Northumberland, and George FitzRoy, who had been created Duke of Northumberland by his father, Charles II, on the ground that they had impugned his right to the earldom. The hearing was fixed for 24 November, but did not take place because Percy was arrested in his lodgings that morning at the instance of the Duke of Somerset. The Duke might have saved himself the expense of the arrest, for when the cause finally came on for hearing on 19 January 1688 a copy of an order of dismissal by the House of Lords between Percy and Elizabeth, Countess Dowager of Northumberland, in 1673 was read and the cause was dismissed with costs, but with power reserved to admit Percy's petition as to his genealogy and 'to notice and determine concerning it according to law'.

On 15 November the Court sat in the hall of the College of Arms, which was thenceforward the usual place of sitting, though there were occasional sittings in the Painted Chamber and in the hall of Doctors' Commons and on at least two occasions (16 March 1688 and 17 April 1692)

[1] See *Oldys* v. *Tyllie* (1687), Her. Cas. 59, and *Le Neve's Pedigrees of the Knights* (Harl. Soc. viii, 1873), p. 409.

at the Earl Marshal's house in Spring Garden. Inter-locutory work was done in the chambers in Doctors' Commons of one of the surrogates.

The Court sat frequently, though at irregular intervals, until 18 November 1690, when it was adjourned until 3 December. There is no record in the Act Book of a sitting on 3 December and the next recorded sitting was not until 1 September 1691. The reason for this hiatus is not apparent, but it is not due to the loss of records, for there is clearly nothing missing from the Act Book between 18 November 1690 and 1 September 1691. Then came several more months of considerable activity until 29 April 1692, when the Court was adjourned until 9 May. There was no sitting on 9 May and the sittings were not resumed until 5 September 1693. Regular sittings then followed until 15 March 1695, after which there is another unexplained and much longer interval until 29 June 1699. Thereafter the sittings continued without further abnormal interruptions until the last entry in the Act Book on 27 March 1702.[1] In this last period of two and three-quarter years there were fifty-four sittings in Court and thirty-nine in chambers.

The work which came before the Court during the period covered by this chapter was of a more varied nature than was usual during the period ending with the Civil War. A determined attempt was made by means of causes of office promoted by the King's Advocate to put a stop to the unlawful assumption of arms.[2] Such cases usually arose out of the display of arms at funerals and on hatchments, though other forms of public display, e.g. on a coach and on a silver collar worn about a foot-man's neck, also gave rise to proceedings.[3] Sometimes the complaint related to the surname as well as the arms.[4]

---

[1] Notes of eleven cases dealt with on 15 Sept. 1699 are contained in the Diary of Peter Le Neve, Norroy (*Gent. Mag.* xviii, N.S. (1842), 266), but the information there given is no substantial addition to the record in the Act Book.

[2] For examples of such causes see *Oldys* v. *Mowbery* (1688), Her. Cas. 61; *Oldys* v. *Booth* (1693), Her. Cas. 79; and *Oldys* v. *Fowle* (1694), Her. Cas. 87.

[3] See *Oldys* v. *Feilding* (1702), Her. Cas. 102.

[4] e.g. *Oldys* v. *Mowbery* (1688), Her. Cas. 61.

The net was thrown quite widely and caught all kinds of heraldic offences, such as publishing 'the genealogy or succession of the Kings of England' without licence or lawful authority;[1] using a coat of arms in an advertisement for the sale of 'Issue Plaisters';[2] and failing to register arms with Clarenceux King of Arms when required to do so.[3]

Proceedings were not only taken against those who used false arms, but also against those who assisted them by painting the arms. At the first sitting of the revived Court Sir Henry St. George, Clarenceux King of Arms, promoted a cause of office against Richard Wallis, who 'kept a shopp adjoining or neare to St. Bartholomew's Church against the North doore of the Royall Exchange London', where he 'set forth signes and tokens of Armes, Escutcheons and Banners as is usually done by persons called Armes Painters within the City of London',[4] and who had painted false arms for a funeral. On the same occasion a similar cause was promoted against another arms-painter, Henry Howell of Russell Street near Covent Garden, for painting false arms on trumpet banners for the High Sheriff of Derbyshire and on funeral escutcheons. Wallis was fined £20 and Howell 10 marks.[5] If Richard Penson, porter to the Company of Herald Painters, was right when he gave evidence that

. . . it is usuall for Armes painters to paint Escutcheons for funeralls for any person who shall employ them, and that they do the same upon such persons producing an old Escutcheon or Coat of Armes engraven on a seal for their direction, but not without consulting the Heraulds office whether the said Armes belong to the deceased partyes,[6]

the activities of painters like Wallis and Howell must

[1] *Oldys* v. *Croome* (1687), Cur. Mil. Boxes X/23/27.

[2] *Oldys* v. *Burrard* (1700), Her. Cas. 95.

[3] *St. George* v. *Brerewood; St. George* v. *Bowater and Abney*, Act Book, 10 Mar. 1687/8.

[4] Deposition of John Barrobie in *St. George* v. *Wallis*, Deposition Book, 12 Nov. 1687.

[5] Act Book, 28 Jan. 1688.

[6] *Oldys* v. *Domville* (1691), Deposition Book, 14 Oct.

have resulted in considerable losses of fees to the College of Arms.

Another form of heraldic impropriety which gave rise to a number of cases in the Court was the marshalling of funerals and the letting of velvet palls without a licence from the appropriate provincial king of arms. 'Marshalling' was described by Richard Penson in the following terms:

That he calls marshalling a funerall, placing of People according to their qualities, receiving them out of a house and putting them into Coaches, ordering Mourners to ride before the hearse, ordering the hearse and Coaches to halt then to move again, and riding before this train in the order they were put, and then when they come to the Church putting the corners of the Pall into the hands of the Holders, placing the persons attending the funerall in the order they are to go, and giving orders for their moving. And this, Sr Henry St. George told the Respondent, was or is marshalling.[1]

The kings of arms claimed not only the 'cognizance, correction and disposing of arms and ensigns', but also the 'ordering, directing and marshalling of funeral pomps'.[2] About 1685 they started granting licences to shopkeepers who furnished funerals with coffins, shrouds, and other necessaries to have 'the representacons of what they sell, and of a herse and funerall painted on the outside of their Balconyes Penthouses or Shops'.[3] Some of the heralds also granted 'deputations' to paint escutcheons and to let out palls for funerals.[4]

The marshalling or ordering of funerals by persons

---

[1] Answer to interrogatory in *Oldys* v. *Domville*, Deposition Book, 14 Oct. 1691.

[2] Deposition of John Giles, clerk to Sir Henry St. George, Clarenceux, in *Oldys* v. *Morris* (1692), Deposition Book, 9 Apr. 'Funeral pomp' was 'a more solemn Ceremonious and orderly procession than usual in common Burials' (Deposition of Robert Dale, late clerk to Sir Henry St. George, Clarenceux, Deposition Book, 14 Apr.).

[3] *Oldys* v. *Domville* (1691), Deposition Book, 21 Oct. Such persons are described as 'undertakers' in a deposition in *Oldys* v. *Russell* (1692), Deposition Book, 16 Apr., six years earlier than the first citation of the word in this sense in *O.E.D.*

[4] Such 'deputations' were granted to one Starr of Bristol about 1676 and to one Paine of Reading about 1688 (*Oldys* v. *Domville* (1691), Deposition Book, 21 Oct.).

who were not so licensed was regarded by the kings of arms as a particularly heinous offence, since it tended to the use of false arms and to prevent the heralds earning their fees for attending the funerals of 'persons of coat armour and worship'.[1]

Sir Henry St. George, Clarenceux, felt so strongly about this that he was not above sending out his clerk and the porter of the College of Arms to funerals to collect the necessary evidence.[2]

It was cases of this type which first brought the Court of Chivalry into conflict with the common-law courts. The leading case is a cause of office promoted against Charles Domville of St. Peter Cornhill, cheesemonger. In August 1691 Domville undertook the funeral of a Mrs. Barkstead, a daughter-in-law of John Barkstead, the regicide. He not only furnished the funeral with shroud, coffin, mourning cloaks, and 'other necessaries', and hired the hearse, coaches, and horses, but also provided painted escutcheons of arms to be affixed to the hearse and mourners in mourning cloaks to ride before it; he received the people attending the funeral and put them into coaches; he rode in front of the funeral procession from Chelsea to the upper end of the Haymarket and through the City of London into Essex, where the body was to be buried; and he provided a velvet pall to be laid upon the coffin in the house before it was put into the hearse. All this was done without the licence of Clarenceux King of Arms and was observed by Richard Penson, the porter of the Company of Herald Painters, who attended the funeral, being paid for his attendance and loss of time by Clarenceux and some of the Company of Herald Painters.[3] The herald painters, one of whom was

[1] *Cheshire and Lancashire Funeral Certificates* (Lancashire and Cheshire Record Soc. vi, 1882), p. vi. At the beginning of the seventeenth century these fees ranged from 20s. for a knight to 3s. 4d. for a citizen buried with the arms of his company (ibid., p. vii).

[2] See *Oldys* v. *Morris* (1692), Her. Cas. 75. On another occasion the porter and an arms-painter went to observe a funeral and were greeted by the undertaker with the words: 'Well! How do you like it? Is it not very fine? We want nothing but two of your Officers of Arms here' (*Oldys* v. *Russell* (1692), Misc. Cur. Mil. 272).   [3] Deposition Book, 14 Oct. 1691.

Richard Wallis, their Treasurer, who had been in trouble
for painting false arms four years before,[1] were responsible
for the bringing and prosecution of the suit. Apparently
Domville expected trouble, for when Penson asked the
postilion of the hearse for one of the escutcheons and
promised him something for it, he was told that Domville
had taken away all the escutcheons, telling the postilion
and the horseman that he would not pay them unless they
delivered the escutcheons to him. Presumably Domville
knew that it was a common practice in 'funeral' cases to
annex one of the escutcheons to the articles.[2]

Domville was also accused of marshalling the funerals
of Elizabeth, daughter of Michael Godfrey of Woodford,
co. Essex, in August 1691 and Sir William Sprignol in
September 1691. A witness, who was sent to Sprignol's
house at Highgate by Richard Wallis to collect evidence
against Domville, gave the following account of what he
saw there:

a piece of Black Base hanging over the dore of the said house with
three paper Escutcheons thereon bearing the Armes of the said
Sr Wm Sprignol and a roome or parlor in the said house hung round
with black base and Escutcheons and the roome wherein the Corps
of the said Sr Wm Sprignol lay covered with black base on the
Cieling and floor and the sides hung round with the same and
Escutcheons upon it and silver sconces with lights, and in the
middle of the Roome the Corps lay covered with a black velvet pall
and Escutcheons upon it and four men standing by the same with
their Hats on, as Mutes, and stands with Candlesticks and Candles
standing by the said Corps.[3]

---

[1] See p. 92 *ante*.

[2] Several of these escutcheons, painted on buckram or some similar cloth,
survive amongst the records of the Court, e.g. *St. George* v. *Wallis* (1687), Cur.
Mil. Boxes X/13; *Oldys* v. *Wyseman* (1691), Cur. Mil. Boxes X/14.

[3] Deposition Book, 21 Oct. 1691. Cf. the description of the lying in state of
Lady Herne at Brewers' Hall: 'The Room in the said Hall where the Corps lay
was hung from the bottom to the Top with Black, and the cieling covered with
Black, the Corps covered with a Pall of Velvet with white sarcent about it, upon
the Pall were ten or twelve silk Scocheons pinned, and at the head of the said Roome
was a Majestie or an Atchievement in form of a Majestie and about Twenty
Scucheons Silk or Buckrom hung about the Roome, and upon stands on each
side the Corps were about Thirty Candles that seemed to be wax besides those
that were up in Sconces about the Roome to the number of about 50, and this

The charges against Domville may be summarized as follows: (1) he painted and caused to be painted arms and escutcheons, and caused them to be fixed to hearses; (2) he provided and lent velvet palls for funerals; (3) he marshalled funerals; and (4) he had publicly hanging out at his balcony paintings of escutcheons, coaches, hearses, and funeral processions to entice people to come to his shop—all without any licence from Clarenceux.[1]

As soon as the evidence was completed Domville commenced an action in the Court of Exchequer for a prohibition against Dr. Oldys, the King's Advocate, who had promoted the office against him, on the ground that this was an illegal prosecution contrary to c. 29 of Magna Carta.[2] To this Oldys pleaded (1) that the suit complained of concerned arms, escutcheons, and funerals, which lay within the exclusive jurisdiction of the Court of Chivalry; (2) that if Domville wished to complain of the plea begun in the Court of Chivalry, his proper remedy was that given by the statute,[3] namely to obtain a privy seal to supersede the plea until it had been decided by the King in Council whether it belonged to that Court or to the common law; and (3) that prohibition did not lie to the Court of Chivalry.

After issue joined Domville's action was adjourned from the Court of Exchequer into the Exchequer Chamber *propter difficultatem.* By the advice of the judges in the Exchequer Chamber the Court gave judgment for the plaintiff, which was affirmed by the Chancellor and Treasurer of the Exchequer.[4]

The prohibition was granted on 11 November 1691. On 4 December the Earl Marshal presented a petition to the House of Lords praying that the prohibition might

was within a Raile covered with Black, and there was a step or two up to the Corps' (*Oldys* v. *Morris* (1692), Deposition Book, 11 Apr.).

[1] *Oldis* v. *Donmille* (1696), Show. P.C. 58 (House of Lords); *sub. nom.* *Oldys* v. *Domville*, Her. Cas. 72 (Ct. of Chivalry).

[2] 'Nullus liber homo capiatur vel imprisonetur aut dissesiatur de libero tenemento suo vel libertatibus vel liberis consuetudinibus suis aut utlagetur aut aliquo modo destruatur nec super eum mittemus nisi per legale judicium parium suorum vel per legem terre.'

[3] 13 Ric. II, st. 1, c. 2.   [4] Show. P.C., at p. 59.

be declared null and void on the ground that Domville's proper remedy was to obtain a privy seal.[1] The petition was referred to the Committee for Privileges, before whom it was argued on 11 December by counsel for the Earl Marshal and two of the judges of the Court of Exchequer, but no decision was given.[2] Oldys then brought the matter before the House of Lords in its judicial capacity in the usual manner by a writ of error to reverse the judgment of the Court of Exchequer.[3]

Meanwhile similar proceedings in the Court of Chivalry had been commenced against other undertakers. Two of them, Thomas Powell and William Lamb, obtained prohibitions in the Court of Exchequer at the same time as Domville.[4] Another, William Russell of St. Bride's, Fleet Street, joiner, also had recourse to the common law, but in a different manner from the others, for he went to the Court of King's Bench for a writ of prohibition.[5]

The arguments put forward in the King's Bench were similar to those in the Exchequer.[6] A prohibition was granted on the ground that if the matter complained of in the Court of Chivalry were true, there was a wrong done to the kings of arms, in respect of which they might maintain an action on the case.[7]

When *Oldys* v. *Domville* reached the House of Lords there was, in addition to the points which were argued below, considerable argument whether the Earl Marshal had any power to hold a Court of Chivalry without a Constable— a point which was not raised in *Russel's Case*.[8] Before the

---

[1] Hist. MSS. Comm., *House of Lords MSS., 1690–1691*, pp. 347–9.

[2] Ibid., p. 348; *L.J.* xiv. 672, 684.   [3] Show. P.C. 58.

[4] *House of Lords MSS., 1690–1691*, p. 349; *Oldys* v. *Powell* (1691), Her. Cas. 74. Lamb was accused of having marshalled the funerals of the daughter of — Denn of Bread Street, London, and of — Cann, widow, of Brentwood, co. Essex, in March and July 1691.

[5] *Russel's Case* (1692), 4 Mod. 128; *sub nom. Russel* v. *Oldish*, 1 Show. K.B. 353; *sub nom. Oldys* v. *Russell*, Her. Cas. 76 (Ct. of Chivalry).

[6] Cf. 4 Mod., at p. 128, and Show. P.C., at pp. 58, 59.

[7] The Court of King's Bench referred to 'the matter set forth in the libel' (4 Mod., at p. 129), but the proceedings in the Court of Chivalry were a cause of office, in which articles took the place of a libel.

[8] (1692), 4 Mod. 128. It was admitted in argument (at p. 129) 'that the Court of Honour has jurisdiction to marshal arms'.

appeal was determined, the following questions were referred to the judges for their opinion:

1. 'whether the Earl Marshal's Court is now the same as it was when there was a Constable and Earl Marshal joined';
2. whether prohibition lay to the Court; and
3. whether the power to direct a privy seal under the statute 13 Ric. II, st. 1, c. 2, had been taken away by the statute 16 Car. I, c. 10.

The reply of Holt C.J., given on 10 March 1696 after six of the judges had met, was that the power to direct a privy seal had been repealed, so that if prohibition was not allowed, the subject would have no remedy. No specific answer was given to the first question, but in the reply reference is made to 'the Court of the Earl Marshal' and no doubt is cast upon its legality.[1] After receiving the opinion of the judges the House of Lords affirmed the judgment of the Court of Exchequer.[2]

The report of *Oldis* v. *Donmille*[3] contains a valuable collection of references bearing upon the power of the Earl Marshal to hold a Court of Chivalry during a vacancy in the office of Lord High Constable, but the case decided no more than (1) that Domville's offence, if any, was not a breach of the rules of honour and did not relate to arms, but was an encroachment upon the office of Clarenceux King of Arms, which was an injury at common law, for which an action would lie; (2) that prohibition lay to the Court of Chivalry; and (3) that a privy seal under the statute 13 Ric. II, st. 1, c. 2 could no longer be granted.

Whilst it was fortunate for the officers of the Court of Chivalry and the practitioners there that the decisions in *Oldis* v. *Donmille* and *Russel's Case* were of so limited a

---

[1] Hist. MSS. Comm., *House of Lords MSS.*, *1695–1697*, p. 155. The taking away of the privy seal is there attributed to 'the Act of 16 Car. II, that takes away the Star Chamber', but 'II' is an error for 'I' and the reference intended is to 16 Car. I, c. 10, s. 5. The reference to the judges is not mentioned in the report in Show. P.C.

[2] The order of the House of Lords is printed in *L.J.* xv. 701.

[3] Show. P.C. 58.

character, they nevertheless had the result of depriving the Court of a good deal of business. Indeed, the causes of office were thenceforward limited to cases of a purely armorial nature. In order to reduce the risk of further successful applications for writs of prohibition the Earl Marshal ordered the revival of the earlier practice whereby a cause of instance could only be begun by petition subscribed by the King's Advocate that the cause was cognizable in the Court of Chivalry.[1]

Funerals still continued to be the subject of litigation in the Court, but only when it was alleged that arms were displayed which did not belong to the deceased by the laws of arms.[2] This was frequently coupled with an allegation that the offending arms had been displayed on a hatchment outside the house of the deceased.[3]

Although the bulk of the litigation consisted of causes of office promoted by either the King's Advocate or one of the kings of arms, there were some causes of instance where the complainant was a private person.

The most persistent private litigant was Percy the trunk-maker. Having failed in his cause against the Duke and Duchess of Somerset and the Duke of Northumberland referred to above, he went on to promote a cause against all persons denying or impugning his right to bear the arms and insignia of the family of Henry, fifth Earl of Northumberland. These proceedings were started by affixing the monition on the columns of the Royal Exchange on 1 February 1688 between the hours of 11 a.m. and 2 p.m. 'during the time of the concourse of merchants'.[4] At the next sitting of the Court proclamation

---

[1] Note on table of fees (Northamptonshire Record Office MS. I. C. 3311). I am indebted to Miss Shelagh M. Lewis, Assistant Archivist at Lamport Hall, for drawing my attention to this and other documents, among the Isham Muniments at Lamport Hall, whither they presumably found their way amongst the papers of Sir Edmund Isham, Earl Marshal's Assessor and Surrogate from 1732 until his death in 1772.

[2] e.g. *Oldys* v. *Hide* (1699), Her. Cas. 94.

[3] e.g. *Oldys* v. *Sweetapple* (1699), Her. Cas. 91.

[4] Act Book, 28 Jan. 1687/8. Endorsement of citation (Cur. Mil. Boxes X/23/12). Notice of later steps in the cause was given in the same manner (ibid. X/23/16).

was made for those summoned, and since none of them appeared, the Surrogate pronounced them contumacious and admitted the libel and exhibits.[1] Between the following 10 May and 12 July Percy produced twenty-five witnesses in an endeavour to show that he was descended from one of the four children of Sir Ingleram Percy who were sent from the north in hampers to the house of their maternal kinswoman, Lady Vaux, 'in the time of the Percy's troubles in Queene Elizabeth's time'.[2] Any doubt of the descent from the ancient Percys, who used a crescent for a badge, was sought to be dispelled by the evidence of the seventy-six-year-old parish clerk of Irthlingborough, co. Northampton, who deposed that 'the said James hath a marke or mole on or neare his belly like a halfemoone which this deponent hath seene'.[3] Neither this evidence nor the documents which he exhibited in support of his case had the convincing effect which Percy hoped for, and the cause was adjourned from court day to court day all through the rest of 1688 and the whole of 1689. Meanwhile on 11 June 1689 the House of Lords had adjudged that the pretensions of Percy to the earldom of Northumberland were 'groundless, false and scandalous', and had ordered that he should be brought before the four Courts in Westminster Hall, wearing upon his breast a paper, on which was to be written 'THE FALSE AND IMPUDENT PRETENDER TO THE EARLDOM OF NORTHUMBERLAND'.[4] The order of the House of Lords was exhibited in the Court of Chivalry on the following 17 December, and the cause was finally dismissed on 13 January 1690. On 24 November 1690 Percy presented a petition to the House of Commons praying that the Earl Marshal might be ordered to re-hear his claim in the Court of Chivalry.[5]

[1] Act Book, 11 Feb. 1687/8.

[2] Deposition of Mary Inglesby, 14 May 1688.

[3] Deposition of John Pyburne, 10 May 1688. For the Percy crescent, see A. G. Dickens, 'The Tudor-Percy Emblem in Royal MS. 18 D ii', in *Archaeological Journal*, cxii (1955), 97, and the authorities there cited.

[4] C. G. Y[oung], 'Claim of James Percy, the Trunk–maker, to the Earldom of Northumberland', in *Coll. Top. & Gen.* vi (1840), 271.

[5] *C.S.P.D. 1690–1691*, p. 169.

That petition met with no better success than Percy's previous attempts to prosecute his claim, which had begun twenty years before with his assumption of the title shortly after the death of the last Earl, and which had involved him in five actions in the common-law courts in addition to the proceedings in the House of Lords and the Court of Chivalry.[1]

Whilst they no longer formed the bulk of the work of the Court as they did in the days before the Civil War, causes of 'scandalous words provocative of a duel' were again promoted. The first cause of this kind during this period was commenced in November 1687.[2] This was followed in 1688 by ten more causes of the same nature,[3] and there were others later.

It was not until 1700 that a defendant questioned the legality of proceedings for 'scandalous words'. Cuthbert Chambers, an apothecary of Ripon, against whom Sir Jonathan Jennings[4] instituted proceedings for saying 'You a knight! You are a pitiful fellow, and an inconsiderable fellow', applied to the Court of King's Bench for a prohibition to stay the suit. Two questions were raised on the pleadings:

First, whether there is such a Court of Honour in England, as gives remedy for words not actionable at law, tending to the dishonour of knighthood, or of anybody bearing arms?

Secondly, if the Court of Honour have such a jurisdiction, whether it ought not, in such case to be held before the constable and the marshal and not before the marshal alone?[5]

---

[1] For accounts of Percy's litigation see his own *The Case of James Percy, Claymant to the Earldom of Northumberland* (1685) and *Coll. Top. & Gen.* vi. 266–83.

[2] *Wilcocks* v. *Hall*, Citation 24 Nov. 1687 (Cur. Mil. Boxes X/23/8).

[3] *Fowler* v. *Clinch*, Act Book, 19 Jan. et seq.; *Master* v. *Ford*, Cur. Mil. Boxes X/23/17 (plaintiff an advocate in Doctors' Commons); *Wase* v. *Newman*, Act Book, 23 Feb. et seq.; *Spyller* v. *Manning*, Act Book, 10 Mar. et seq.; *Hamilton* v. *Spernick*, Act Book, 15 Mar. et seq.; *Tichborne* v. *Allden*, Act Book, 3 May; *Selwin* v. *Blythwood*, Cur. Mil. Boxes X/23/22; *Fane* v. *Barethorpe*, Deposition Book, 10 Oct.; *Wyke* v. *Ems*, Cur. Mil. Boxes X/23/24; *Hicks* v. *Ward*, Cur. Mil. Boxes X/23/25.

[4] In 1699 Jennings had prosecuted one who took his coat of arms (Luttrell, *Brief Historical Relation of State Affairs*, iv. 560).

[5] *Chambers* v. *Jennings* (1703), 7 Mod. 125; Holt K.B. 597. In the Court of

As in the 'funeral' litigation a few years earlier,[1] it became unnecessary to decide the second question, because both judges were of opinion that the answer to the first question was in the negative. On this question Powell J. said:

> If they have jurisdiction of words concerning coats of arms, that is not this case: but here you say the words tend to breach of the peace, and are provoking to fight a duel, and if so they are indictable

When the case came on in the paper no one appeared for the defendant, and the Court said 'that whatever colour there might be to hold plea of some things before the marshal alone, there was no pretence to hold plea of words'.[2]

Chambers v. *Jennings* decided no more than that the Court of Chivalry could not entertain an action for words.[3] Both Anson and Holdsworth, however, cite it as authority for the proposition that the Court of Chivalry is not properly constituted in the absence of a Constable.[4] This view, which is inconsistent with the fact, mentioned by both writers, that the Court continued to function for many years after the decision in *Chambers* v. *Jennings*, is based on the judgment of Holt C.J., of which there are three conflicting reports.[5] In one of them Holt is reported as having gone so far as to describe the Court as 'a pretended Court', but neither of the other two reports contains these words. As was pointed out by Lord Sumner in *Clifford and O'Sullivan*,[6] if ever uttered at all, these words were unnecessary to the decision and have never been followed. Furthermore, it is to be observed that Holt had not given

Chivalry, *sub nom. Jennings* v. *Chambers*, the surviving documents are the libel (Cur. Mil. Boxes X/17a) and commission to take a bond with proceedings on the commission (ibid. 21/17, 18). The libel was admitted in the Court of Chivalry on 25 Oct. 1700, but the prohibition was not granted until Hilary term, 1703.   [1] See p. 98 *ante*.

[2] 7 Mod., at p. 128.

[3] *Manchester Corporation* v. *Manchester Palace of Varieties Ltd.*, [1955] P. 133, per Lord Goddard, Surrogate, at p. 149.

[4] Anson, *Law and Custom of the Constitution* (4th ed., Oxford, 1935), ii, pt ii, p. 214; *H.E.L.* i. 579.

[5] 7 Mod. 125; 2 Salk. 553; Holt K.B. 597.

[6] [1921] 2 A.C. 570, at p. 590; cf. per Lord Cave at p. 583.

this advice to the House of Lords in *Oldys* v. *Domville* in 1696, although the question had been specifically put to him and his brother judges,[1] nor did he act upon it subsequently.[2]

The last entry in the Act Book which was started on 5 October 1687 is dated 27 March 1702. From that date onwards reliance has to be placed upon isolated documents. The next surviving documents relate to proceedings in 1707. Whilst it is possible that there were cases during the intervening years, the proceedings on 26 April 1707 were so elaborate as to have the appearance of being another revival of the Court. The possibility of a revival is increased by the fact that a new Deputy Earl Marshal, the Earl of Bindon, had been appointed the previous August. In any case no sitting could have taken place between 24 August 1706 and 26 April 1707, since Bindon was not sworn in until the latter date.[3]

The venue was the Painted Chamber. The Deputy Earl Marshal was accompanied on the bench by the Dukes of Somerset and Beaufort, the Earls of Berkshire and Carlisle, and Lord Fitzwalter. With them was Sir John Cooke LL.D., Dean of the Arches, who had that day been appointed to be the Earl Marshal's Surrogate.[4] The proceedings were opened by the reading of the Duke of Norfolk's letters patent, the Deputy Earl Marshal's deputation and the Queen's approbation, and the swearing-in of the Deputy Earl Marshal. Next Dr. Nathaniel Lloyd's warrant of appointment as Queen's Advocate in the Court was read. The establishment of the Court was completed by the swearing-in of Godfrey Lee as Earl Marshal's Proctor and Henry Farrant as Register.

During the next few months about thirty causes of the

---

[1] See p. 98 *ante*.   [2] See p. 104 *post*.

[3] Luttrell, *Brief Historical Relation of State Affairs*, vi. 156, states that Bindon 'open'd his commission in the painted chamber, and adjourned to the Heralds Office' on 5 Apr. 1707, but this cannot have been a judicial proceeding. The inclusion of Bindon's arms amongst the heraldic carvings above the bench in the hall of the College of Arms seems to indicate that the revival in 1707 was the occasion for fitting up the hall as a court-room in its present form.

[4] Coll. Arm. MS. R.R.G. LXIV A, f. 5. Cooke had previously been appointed Surrogate by the Earl of Carlisle D.E.M. in 1701.

limited class left within its jurisdiction after the decisions in *Oldis* v. *Donmille*[1] and *Chambers* v. *Jennings*[2] came before the Court. In July 1707 there were five causes pending, all of them heraldic causes of office.[3]

There was a recurrence of the doubt whether the Earl Marshal could act judicially during a vacancy in the office of Lord High Constable. In Trinity term 1707 the defendant in *Lloyd* v. *Collet*[4] applied to the Court of Queen's Bench for a writ of prohibition on this, together with another ground. The application was unsuccessful, for in Easter term 1708 a writ of consultation was granted, whereby the cause was returned to the Court of Chivalry.[5]

During Queen Anne's reign there was a proposal that the Earl Marshal's powers should be declared by statute. A bill was prepared for this purpose, providing that the Earl Marshal should have power to proceed judicially and definitively in all cases within the cognizance and jurisdiction of the Court of Chivalry as fully as if there were a Constable in being, with the exception of appeals made of things done out of the realm which were to be tried and determined according to the statute 1 Hen. IV, c. 14, but it never reached the statute book.[6] The bill is not dated, but since it refers to 'that part of Great Britain called England', it must have been drafted after the Union with Scotland, which took effect on 1 May 1707.[7] Perhaps it was prepared after the application for a writ of prohibition in *Lloyd* v. *Collet* and was thought to be no longer necessary after the Earl Marshal's jurisdiction had been upheld by the granting of the writ of consultation in that case.

---

[1] (1696), Show. P.C. 58.   [2] (1703), 7 Mod. 125.

[3] Bodl. MS. Rawl. B. 378, f. 211.

[4] (1707), Her. Cas. 107.

[5] Coll. Arm. MS. J.P. 199. This manuscript consists of an examination of *Chambers* v. *Jennings*, which, it is there suggested, was not properly reported in 7 Mod. 125. The anonymous author points out that Holt C.J. presided in both cases and that if his *obiter dictum* in *Chambers* v. *Jennings* concerning the power of the Earl Marshal to sit alone in the Court of Chivalry is correctly reported, he acted inconsistently in granting a writ of consultation in *Lloyd* v. *Collet*.

[6] Coll. Arm. MS. R. 19, f. 233, printed in Appendix V, p. 241 *post*. For the statute 1 Hen. IV, c. 14, see p. 26 *ante*.

[7] Union with Scotland Act, 1706, art. I.

Despite the affirmation of the Earl Marshal's jurisdiction in *Lloyd* v. *Collet,* there are no records of any causes in the immediately succeeding years, with one exception in 1710.[1] Whilst there may have been losses, the total lack of documents may be due to the work of the Court having fallen off, for when Sir John Cooke, the Earl Marshal's Surrogate, died in 1710 no successor seems to have been appointed.[2]

The next surviving record is that of a remarkable case in 1716. Notwithstanding the decision in *Chambers* v. *Jennings,*[3] Sir William Lowther, a Yorkshire baronet, commenced a cause of 'scandalous words provocative of a duel' against one John Murgatroyd. This cause came before the Court on three occasions in April and May 1716. It is not surprising that Murgatroyd applied to the Court of King's Bench for a writ of prohibition, but what is surprising is that he did not make his application on the ground that such a case was outside the jurisdiction of the Court of Chivalry, but on the ground that causes within the jurisdiction of the Court ought to be heard and determined before the Constable and Marshal of England jointly and not before one of them.[4] What became of Murgatroyd's application does not appear, nor is there any record of any further proceedings in the Court during the remainder of the reign of George I.

Despite the lack of work, the Court was regarded as being still in being. Lists of the officers and proctors continued to appear in the successive editions of *Magnae Britanniae Notitia,* but these lists also show that the Court had become moribund. No new proctors were appointed after 1708, and as the posts of Earl Marshal's Proctor, Secretary and Seal Keeper, and Marshal fell

---

[1] *Re Wither,* Her. Cas. 113. It is possible that this is not a Court of Chivalry case. The only extant document is an affidavit, which is not intituled in any court and could be a 'stray'.

[2] *The Laws of Honour* (London, 1714), App., p. 52, contains a list of the officers of the Court, but no mention is made of a surrogate.

[3] (1703), 7 Mod. 125.

[4] *Lowther* v. *Murgatroyd* (1716), Coll. Arm. MS. R.R.G. LXIV A, ff. 54–55. There was another cause of office against one Church relating to a shield of arms, but no particulars of this are given.

vacant they were left unfilled. The lists also show that there must have been some intention of putting new life into the old Court at the beginning of the reign of George II. In 1727 Dr. Humphrey Henchman appears as King's Advocate,[1] and in the following year there is evidence of a crop of new appointments. Dr. Edmund Isham, the Admiralty Advocate, was Surrogate, Mark Holman, Register, William Jones, Earl Marshal's Proctor, and Grey Longueville, Secretary and Seal Keeper.[2] Whatever may have been the reason for these appointments, the Court did not sit at this time, but continued to be dormant for some years longer.

[1] *Magnae Britanniae Notitia* (1727 ed.), p. 215.
[2] Op. cit. (1728 ed.), p. 218. This edition also contains a list of sixteen proctors of this Court, but it seems to be a misplaced list of the proctors of the Court of Admiralty. It does not contain any of the three names in the list in the 1727 edition.

VII

THE CIVILIANS' LAST CASES
1732–7

ON 24 September 1729 Peter Le Neve, Norroy King of Arms, died. That night Stephen Martin Leake, who had been Lancaster Herald since 1727, wrote to the Earl Marshal and to the Deputy Earl Marshal soliciting the vacant office.[1] He received favourable answers from both, but the nomination was delayed until the Earl Marshal, who was then at Worksop, returned to London, and it was not until 6 December that Leake had the opportunity of waiting upon the Earl Marshal at Norfolk House.[2] This interview contained a surprise for Leake, for although he was kindly received, he was told that the Earl Marshal intended to hold a Court of Honour, 'which would be a benefit to the Office and not any to him', and that with the concurrence of Garter it had been decided that whoever came into the College of Arms should pay a sum towards the expenses of holding the Court, that for a king of arms being a hundred guineas and that for a herald being fifty guineas. Leake could only comply, and paid his money to the Earl Marshal's bankers that afternoon. Leake took it hardly that after purchasing the place of Lancaster he should have to pay for the exchange, and thought that he was being ill-requited by Garter, to whom he considered that he had made himself useful in the past.[3]

Leake's patent for the office of Norroy passed the Great Seal on 17 December 1729, but nothing was done

---

[1] Where no other authority is cited this chapter is based on Martin Leake's 'Heraldic Annals of my own Time' (Coll. Arm. MS. SML 65). Leake seems to have compiled his 'Annals' some time after the events which he recorded, and his recollection must be accepted with reserve: see p. 116 *post*. No records of the Court of Chivalry appear to have survived from this period.

[2] Coll. Arm. MS. SML 65, p. 20.　　　　　　　　[3] Ibid., p. 21.

about the Court of Chivalry. Having paid his money, Leake was anxious that the Court should be set in motion, but nearly two years went by before he was able to get anything done. On 27 October 1731 the Deputy Earl Marshal died and on the following 9 December Francis, Earl of Effingham, was appointed in his place.[1] One of the first acts of the new Deputy Earl Marshal, apparently on the instigation of Martin Leake, was to reappoint Dr. Isham to be his Assessor and Surrogate in the Court Military.[2]

The first sitting of the reconstituted Court was held on 3 March 1732. At noon the officers of the Court met in the room over Waghorn's coffee-house adjoining the House of Lords, and walked in procession from the north end of the Court of Requests to the court at the upper end of the Painted Chamber in the following order:

Cryer & Messenger (one) Usher & Marshal (one)
Proctors in their gowns
two and two according to seniority in the Court of Arches
Doctors of Civil Law in their black gowns
two and two according to seniority
Earl Marshal's Proctor (Mr. Sandford Nevile)
Register of the Court (Mr. Mark Holman)
King's Advocate (Dr. Henchman)
Pursuivants
two and two in their tabards
Heralds
two and two in their tabards and collars of SS.
Norroy   Garter
Earl Marshal's Secretary (Mr. Huchenson)
Deputy Earl Marshal with his staff of office
Peers
two and two according to degrees without order
Gentry
Dr. Isham in his scarlet doctor's robes[3]

[1] Coll. Arm. MS. SML 3, f. 212.
[2] Ibid., f. 220. The commission was dated 3 Dec. 1731 and sealed 10 Feb. 1731/2 (Coll. Arm. MS. SML 65, p. 45).
[3] London Gazette, No. 7073, as corrected in manuscript by Martin Leake (Coll. Arm. MS. SML 3, f. 224). According to Leake, the account of the proceedings in the Gazette was compiled by the Earl Marshal's secretary (Francis

The Deputy Earl Marshal was accompanied by the Lord President of the Council (the Earl of Wilmington) and the Lord Great Chamberlain (the Duke of Ancaster), together with the Duke of Manchester, the Marquess of Lothian, and four other earls and nine barons.

'The Manner of Sitting and Opening of the Court of Honour' is given in the *London Gazette* as follows:

Dr. Isham   Peers   Earl Marshal [sic]   *Peers*

These sat on the highest Seat

Another Seat where some Peers sat which the uppermost could not Contain

These on the lower Seat at the Table under the Earl Marshal [sic]

Garter   Register   Norroy   Lord Marshal's Secretary

| *Heralds in the Marshal's place* | TABLE | *Pursuivants in the Messenger & Usher's Place* |

Doctors   King's   Doctors   L.M.
Advocate   Proctor

U		C
s	*Proctors to be admitted & Drs more than could*	r
h	*sitt standing behind*	y
e	*Bar*	e
r.		r.

After the proclamation, the letters patent of Charles II constituting the Duke of Norfolk Earl Marshal and Hereditary Marshal of England were presented to the Deputy Earl Marshal by Dr. Henchman and read by the Register, followed by the Earl Marshal's nomination of

Huchenson, nephew to the Earl of Effingham) and the Registrar of the College of Arms (Charles Whinyates, Richmond Herald) and was 'so Erroneous that shewed they neither knew how it was or how it ought to have been, and Convinced everybody that Anstis had no hand in it' (Coll. Arm. MS. SML 64, f. 49).

the Deputy Earl Marshal and the King's approbation of it. Then the Deputy Earl Marshal took the oaths of allegiance and supremacy, with the oath of office, tendered to him by the King's Advocate, Garter holding the book. Next were read the appointment of Dr. Henchman as King's Advocate and the commissions of the Register and the Earl Marshal's Proctor and they took the oaths of allegiance and supremacy, with the oath of office. The constitution of the Court was completed by swearing-in six proctors of the Court of Arches to be proctors of the Court of Chivalry. Then the King's Advocate addressed the Deputy Earl Marshal on the inconvenience which had happened by the bearing of false arms and the discontinuance of the Court.

The only business on this occasion was the exhibition by the King's Advocate of a complaint against Sarah Radburne, the widow of John Radburne, a merchant of Mark Lane, London, for using ensigns of honour not belonging to his condition at his funeral; and also certain arms both at the funeral and since upon her coach, not being entitled thereto in her own or her husband's right. On this the Deputy Earl Marshal granted a process and adjourned the Court to the Hall of the College of Arms on 30 March.[1]

According to Martin Leake, there was a great deal of confusion previous to the opening of the Court. Anstis was greatly disgusted and did not come to London until the morning the Court was opened. Indeed, no one believed that the Court would be held until they saw it, and then said it was a trick of Anstis's and would not continue. Perhaps not knowing that Mrs. Radburne was being supported by the undertakers, the newspapers commented unfavourably on making a beginning with a widow. The lawyers said that it was no Court without a Constable and that a prohibition would soon put an end to it. This made many uncertain what to do and dis-

---

[1] *London Gazette*, No. 7073; R. Seymour, *Survey of the Cities of London and Westminster* (London, 1734), i. 153–4, reprinted in Noble, *History of the College of Arms*, p. 373; Coll. Arm. MS. SML 3, f. 324; *Gent. Mag.* ii (1732), 673.

couraged business. Martin Leake was disappointed by the King's Advocate's opening speech, which he thought very short and insufficiently considered. Leake felt that an opportunity had been missed of making a 'florid speech', setting forth the antiquity and dignity of the Court and showing the use and estimation of arms as distinctions of families and marks of nobility. There was a rumour of an agreement between Anstis and the undertakers, who displayed no uneasiness over the prosecution.

There was also a cause of office promoted about this time by the officers of arms against William Shiers, a member of the Painter-Stainers' Company, who pretended to keep an office of arms in Dean's Court near Doctors' Commons, but no records of this cause have survived.[1]

The sitting on 30 March was held in the Hall of the College of Arms. Dr. Isham sat alone. He was attended by the three kings of arms and several other officers of arms, but without their tabards, which they only wore when the Earl Marshal or his Deputy was present. Several more proctors and also the court keeper were sworn. The cause against Mrs. Radburne had to be adjourned because her proctor had not been legally appointed. Then the Court admitted articles exhibited against one Charles Baynton, the executor of Richard Ladbrooke, for using arms and other distinctions of honour not belonging to the testator's family, and against Sir John Blunt, baronet, who had been the chief projector of the South Sea Scheme, for assuming and usurping the arms of the Blounts of Sodington to which he was not entitled.[2]

The next sitting was held on 25 April 1732. Dr. Andrews, counsel for Mrs. Radburne, argued that she

[1] Noble, op. cit., p. 409; Coll. Arm. MS. Heralds V, p. 41. It appears that Shiers claimed the following rights under the Painter-Stainers' Charter of 9 July 1581: (1) painting arms, &c.; (2) painting pedigrees and consequently drawing and attesting them; (3) undertaking funerals; (4) making searches for coats of arms, for which he took a fee of half-a-crown, the fee due to the heralds on such occasions; (5) giving out arms in uncoloured tricks and sketches; and (6) performing 'all things correctly which relate to heraldry'.

[2] Gent. Mag. ii (1732), 677.

was not liable to a prosecution until she had neglected or refused to prove her right to the arms at a visitation, which she was ready to do. He said that until a visitation was held it was a grievance to the subject to put upon him proof of his arms, which had been rendered impracticable by the neglect of the kings of arms, and which was more difficult and expensive than to obtain a new grant, which seemed to be the object of the prosecution. The King's Advocate concluded his reply by stating that the Earl Marshal had asserted the authority of his office to settle matters of honour and arms with the King's consent and at his command. Dr. Andrews then desired to retract what he had said, but was not allowed to do so, that being contrary to the practice of the Court.[1] The process against Sir John Blunt was returned and the certificate continued to the next court day, and the process against Baynton was also returned.[2]

On 8 May the Deputy Earl Marshal sat with Dr. Isham on his right, and the officers of arms attended in their tabards. Two witnesses for the prosecution were sworn and examined in Mrs. Radburne's cause. Dr. Andrews also appeared as counsel in the other two causes. In Sir John Blunt's cause he denied the jurisdiction of the Court, but the argument was overruled and an attachment was ordered against Blunt for not appearing. Dr. Andrews also argued the Ladbrooke cause, which is noteworthy in that in order to prove the arms borne by the testator, his son obtained leave from the rector of Solihull, co. Warwick, to take the brass plate showing the arms from the gravestone of the testator's father, a former rector, who had died in 1655.[3]

On this occasion[4] Anstis had suggested to the Earl Marshal that no arms should ever be granted to persons

---

[1] Martin Leake states that Dr. Andrews was afterwards known as the 'Scurrilous Doctor' on account of his conduct in this case (Coll. Arm. MS. SML 65, p. 51).

[2] Gent. Mag. ii (1732), 721.

[3] Noble, op. cit., p. 375; Mill Stephenson, List of Momumental Brasses (London, 1926), p. 524.

[4] Gent. Mag. ii (1732), 772; Coll. Arm. MS. SML 64, f. 51.

who had stood in contempt of Court, which led Dr.
Andrews to observe that it was done in order to frighten
people into grants and thereby to advantage the kings
of arms.[1]

Anstis took the view that the Court could not be supported without visitations, and sought to obtain a joint
commission with Clarenceux. Norroy again tried to
persuade the Earl Marshal that a commission ought to be
granted for his province alone, using the argument that
without visitations the Court would be thought oppressive and illegal. The only result of these manœuvres was
to intensify the ill feeling between Garter and Norroy.

Further sittings of the Court were held on 23 May and
3 and 8 June. On 26 June Dr. Henchman declared that
he would not proceed any further against Sir John Blunt
on account of a mistake in the citation. The cause was
accordingly dismissed, but a new process was decreed
against the defendant.[2] Little further progress was made
with the pending causes, and soon afterwards counsel for
Mrs. Radburne and Boynton moved for writs of prohibition in the Court of King's Bench on the ground that
the Constable and the Marshal had no jurisdiction in
matters relating to coats of arms.[3] This put a stop to the
proceedings for the time being. The matter was further
complicated by the death of the Earl Marshal on the
following 23 December.

The new Earl Marshal reappointed the Earl of
Effingham as Deputy Earl Marshal on 28 December,
and this received the King's approval on 22 January 1733.
When the officers of arms attended the Earl Marshal to
pay their compliments, he declared his resolution to go on
with the Court of Chivalry. The first step was to present
to the King a memorial relating to the motions for writs

---

[1] There was some truth in what Dr. Andrews said, for after this sitting it was
agreed by the officers of arms in chapter that a process should be moved against
Dr. Barrowby, who had declared that he would try the jurisdiction of the Court.
Afterwards Rouge Croix (Pomfret), with Garter's consent, told Dr. Barrowby
of what was intended and persuaded him to have a grant of arms (Coll. Arm.
MS. SML 65, pp. 51, 52).

[2] *Gent. Mag.* ii (1732), 825.   [3] Coll. Arm. MS. SML 3, f. 240.

of prohibition on the ground that they concerned the royal prerogative. This was presented to the King by the Earl of Effingham. The King said that he would consider it and directed the Duke of Newcastle to remind him of it. The Duke, however, was heard to say that he should take care to forget it.[1]

On 7 March 1733 the Court sat in Doctors' Commons, when the new Deputy Earl Marshal took the oaths. Several persons were called upon to answer to their pretensions of arms and ordered to attend the Court on the following 19 May.[2]

Meanwhile the trial of the prohibitions was delayed for several reasons. Anstis had undertaken to prepare the brief for counsel, but had not done so. Then the Earl Marshal lost his two leading counsel by promotion, the Attorney-General (Sir Philip Yorke) becoming Lord Chief Justice of the King's Bench on 31 October 1733 and the Solicitor-General (Charles Talbot) becoming Lord Chancellor on 29 November. Next Anstis made the preparations for the wedding of the Princess Royal an excuse for further delay, and it was not until the Christmas holidays that he could be persuaded to discuss the draft brief with the solicitor. After the close of the pleadings the applicants for the prohibitions put themselves upon a trial by a jury within the City of London,[3] and it was proposed that the trial should take place at Guildhall during the following term. This led to further difficulty with Anstis, for those concerned to uphold the Court of Chivalry wished to have a special jury, whilst Anstis was of the contrary opinion. Rightly or wrongly Martin Leake thought that Anstis's object was to wreck the Court, for the ignorance and prejudice of a City jury would lead them to bring in either a verdict directly against it or a special verdict, which would have been almost the same, because in that case there could never be any determination without the consent of the Ministry, who were

[1] Coll. Arm. MS. SML 3, f. 240.
[2] *Gent. Mag.* iii (1733), 154. What took place on 19 May does not appear.
[3] Coll. Arm. MS. SML 3, f. 240.

known to be set against it. What Martin Leake wanted was for things to be so managed that there could ultimately be an appeal to the House of Lords.

In the end the trial never took place. The plaintiff Baynton decided to settle the matter and pay the costs. On 25 April 1734 it was agreed that the notice of trial should be countermanded and that a writ of consultation should be awarded.[1] It was also agreed that all further proceedings both in the King's Bench and in the Court of Chivalry should cease upon the following terms: (1) that Baynton might have recourse to the books in the College of Arms, paying the usual fee, in order to make out the right of Richard Ladbrooke to the coat of arms used at his funeral; (2) that if it should be made appear to the satisfaction of Dr. Isham that Ladbrooke was entitled to such arms, then the cousin and devisee of Ladbrooke might apply by petition to the proper officer for a confirmation of the arms, paying the usual fee; (3) that if Dr. Isham should not be satisfied of Ladbrooke's right to the arms, the cousin and devisee should apply by petition for a grant of arms and have a grant, paying the usual fee.[2] No confirmation or grant was ever made.

Of the other two causes which had been commenced in 1732, that against Sir John Blunt lapsed on the death of the defendant on 24 January 1733.[3] It does not clearly appear what happened to the cause of *Henchman* v. *Radburne*, in which there had been a motion for a prohibition. Since Mrs. Radburne was represented by the same counsel as Baynton,[4] the proceedings in the King's Bench were presumably discontinued in both cases at the same time, but if nothing more were agreed, that would leave *Henchman* v. *Radburne* pending in the Court of Chivalry.

---

[1] A writ of consultation was issued for the return of proceedings to an inferior court when no prohibition was granted (G. Jacob, *A New Law-Dictionary* (10th ed., London, 1782), s.v. 'Consultation').

[2] Coll. Arm. MS. SML 3, f. 232.

[3] The statement in G.E.C., *Complete Baronetage* (Exeter, 1906), v. 49, that Blunt was fined by the Court of Chivalry and that it was an appeal which was pending at the time of his death is not supported by any citation of authority.

[4] Strange and Kettleby (Coll. Arm. MS. SML 65, p. 54).

There certainly was one cause pending at this time and this seems to have been *Henchman* v. *Radburne*, for after the lapse of nearly another year it was decided in April 1735 to drop it, 'unless they should proceed and begin anew in Middlesex, in Order to have a Middlesex Jury',[1] a proviso which could only apply to a cause in which there had been some similar proceedings.

Instead of proceeding with the pending cause, it was decided to make a fresh start against six persons nominated by the officers of arms. Apparently the memory of Dr. Andrews's diatribes in the earlier causes had not faded, for on this occasion he was retained by the promoters for the sake of peace.[2]

One of the defendants was Sir Henry Blunt, the son of Sir John Blunt who had been unsuccessfully prosecuted in 1732. Sir Henry was alleged to have assumed and usurped arms which neither he nor any of his family ought to bear. During the progress of the cause an allegation was exhibited by the defendant, setting forth that all pedigrees must be signed by the proper hands of the parties requesting such entries to be made in the books belonging to the College of Arms, and then objecting to the validity of some of the entries in the books as not being signed and therefore not worthy of credit. This allegation was rejected, whereupon the defendant petitioned the Court of Chancery for a commission of Delegates to determine his appeal. Against this there was a cross-petition on the ground that an appeal only lay from a definitive sentence or a final interlocutory decree having the force of a definitive sentence. The matter came before Lord Hardwicke L.C. on 9 June 1737, when the petition was dismissed on the ground that the interlocutory sentence appealed from was not *gravamen irreparabile*.[3]

---

[1] Coll. Arm. MS. SML 65, p. 62.

[2] Ibid.

[3] *Blount's Case* (1737), 1 Atk. 295. For sentences *gravamen irreparabile*, see p. 223 *post*. Martin Leake's account of this case does not tally with the report. He states that on 13 Dec. 1735 sentence was passed against Blunt, requiring him to disclaim within thirty-five days and to deface the arms wherever painted or engraven, paying £100 costs. According to Leake it was *after* this that Blunt

It does not appear that the proceedings against Sir Henry Blunt were ever brought to a conclusion. According to Martin Leake a commission of Delegates was appointed, composed of the 'principal persons in the Ministry' and the Judges, but they could never agree upon a meeting, which put a stop to all further proceedings.[1] The arms were still said to be 'in suspense' in 1741,[2] and Blunt's descendants continued to use the disputed coat (*Barry nebuly of six, or and sable*) until a new coat (*Per pale or and sable, barry nebuly of six counterchanged*) was granted to the eighth baronet in 1910.[3]

According to Martin Leake, the last sitting of the Court was held on 4 March 1737, but it was a purely formal matter and nothing was done. It was an inglorious end. Contemporary opinion was that the 'whole business was imprudently begun, and unskilfully conducted'.[4]

appealed on a point concerning the validity of unsigned pedigrees (Coll. Arm. MS. SML 65, pp. 62–63). In any event, Leake's date must be wrong, for on 19 Mar. 1735/6 the cause was adjourned, the charge not having been proved (*Gent. Mag.* vi (1736), 165). The cause is wrongly assigned to the year 1720 in Dallaway, op. cit., p. 294.

[1] The Delegates must have been appointed after a definitive sentence had been given, since Lord Hardwicke L.C. refused to grant a commission of Delegates on the appeal against the interlocutory sentence.

[2] *English Baronetage* (London, 1741), v. 193.

[3] A. C. Fox-Davies, *Armorial Families* (7th ed., London, 1929), *sub nom.*

[4] Noble, op. cit., p. 375. 'The lawyers who were consulted laughed at it' (ibid.).

VIII

THE DORMANT YEARS
1737–1954

THE rising of the Court on 4 March 1737 was not regarded at the time as the end of an era. The list of the officers and proctors of the Court appeared as usual in the next edition of *Magnae Britanniae Notitia* and continued to appear in successive editions until it ceased publication in 1756, though with an ever-increasing number of gaps as the officers died and their places remained unfilled. In 1737 there were fourteen proctors: by 1756 they had been reduced by death to four.

Although the Court was never to sit again during the lifetime of any of those who knew it in 1737, there arose in 1740 what appeared to Martin Leake to be a good opportunity to revive it. An Italian merchant, John Baptista Meyer, had been using what he called his arms on his tillets[1] in order to distinguish them from the tillets of other merchants. Claude Passevant and Company of Exeter painted the same arms on their tillets, in order to pass off their goods as Meyer's. Upon this Meyer applied to Garter Anstis the elder to know what relief he could obtain. Anstis told him that he did not appear to have any right to the arms in question, but that if he had a right, he might have his remedy. This persuaded Meyer to take out a grant of the arms,[2] and when Passevant continued to paint his tillets as before, Meyer wished to prosecute him in the Court of Chivalry. Anstis was now for acting cautiously and suggested taking the opinion of Dr. Strahan. The opinion was disappointing. Strahan advised that if Passevant had used the arms on seals, plate, his coach or the like, the matter might be properly cognizable

---

[1] Cloths used for wrapping goods (*O.E.D.*, s.v.).
[2] Dated 29 Oct. 1740 (*Grantees of Arms* (Harl. Soc. lxviii, 1917), ii. 248).

in the Court of Chivalry, but being used for mercantile purposes it was not so much to be considered a coat of arms as a mark for the better vending of his merchandise, and that a more effectual remedy might be had in the common-law or equity courts. The tillets, which before they were applied to the merchandise were a complete achievement of the arms of Meyer, ceased to be arms when they were so applied.[1]

Anstis was then asked to advise in the light of Dr. Strahan's opinion.[2] He was doubtful whether an action would lie at common law, but thought that as a fraud was intended, a bill might be brought in the Court of Chancery to inhibit the use of the tillets and for costs, which was as much as could be expected in the Court of Chivalry. Anstis, however, thought that the latter Court had jurisdiction in the matter by virtue of the grant of arms. Upon this difference of opinion the matter rested.

Martin Leake thought that Anstis was very ill advised not to give any encouragement to proceed, for had he done so, Meyer would have been at any expense to prosecute his right. In Leake's view

the fairest opportunity to revive the Court of Chivalry was lost; for this being a matter of Right and Property, a Sentence thereon would have been an Act of Justice, not obtainable in any other Court.[3]

More than two centuries were to pass before there was another opportunity to obtain such an 'Act of Justice'. During that time the Court of Chivalry was not left untouched by the legislature, though probably few, if any, of the legislators realized it, for by the 1760's Blackstone could write that the Court had fallen into contempt and

---

[1] This opinion seems to have been at variance with that given by Dr. Oldys in *Oldys* v. *Burrard* (1700), Her. Cas. 95, where the defendant had used a coat of arms in an advertisement for 'issue plaisters'. Cf. *Manchester Corporation* v. *Manchester Palace of Varieties Ltd.*, [1955] P. 133, where it was not suggested that arms ceased to be arms by being displayed for commercial purposes in a theatre.

[2] Anstis was a common lawyer, having been called to the Bar by the Middle Temple in 1699. He also took an interest in the law of Doctors' Commons, for he was one of the subscribers to Oughton's *Ordo Judiciorum*, published in 1728.

[3] Coll. Arm. MS. SML 65, p. 111.

disuse,[1] whilst in 1828 it was declared by the editor of the second edition of Blackstone's *Reports* to be 'now obsolete'.[2]

In 1819 the criminal jurisdiction of the Court in appeals of treason and homicide was abolished by the Act 59 Geo. III, c. 46, which was passed in consequence of the revival of trial by battle in *Ashford* v. *Thornton*.[3]

The next change in the general law which affected the Court of Chivalry was the abolition of the High Court of Delegates in 1832 and the substitution of the Judicial Committee of the Privy Council as the tribunal of appeal from the Court.[4]

Of all the legislative changes of the nineteenth century which affected the Court of Chivalry the most important were those concerning the ecclesiastical courts and the Court of Admiralty, which involved the end of the civilians as a separate profession.[5] Although the Court of Chivalry had not sat for over a century, there were still in the latter half of the nineteenth century practitioners to whom its procedure would have seemed perfectly familiar. Parliament left the Court of Chivalry to be the last civil-law court, but deprived it of its civilians.

So far from appreciating that their activities were affecting the jurisdiction and procedure of the Court, the legislators apparently took the view that it was obsolete, for by section 3 of the Statute Law Revision and Civil Procedure Act, 1881, they repealed the medieval statutes[6] which defined its jurisdiction. This repeal has not, however, had any practical effect upon the Court. Neither of the repealed statutes conferred any jurisdiction on the Court: the purpose of each of them was to curb the Court's encroachments on the jurisdictions of other courts and to

---

[1] *Commentaries*, iii. 105.
[2] 1 W. Bl., at p. 614 n.   [3] (1818), 1 B. & Ald. 405.
[4] See p. 223 *post*.   [5] See p. 134 *post*.
[6] 8 Ric. II, c. 5; 13 Ric. II, st. 1, c. 2. 1 Hen. IV, c. 14, which safeguarded the jurisdiction of the Constable and Marshal with respect to appeals of treason and felony (see p. 26 *ante*), had become obsolete on the abolition of such appeals by the statute 59 Geo. III, c. 46, and had been repealed by the Statute Law Revision Act, 1863.

confine it to its original jurisdiction, which did not depend upon statutory authority.

The official view that the Court of Chivalry was obsolete persisted into the present century. In 1907 Sir Alfred Scott-Gatty, Garter King of Arms, suggested to the Departmental Committee on the Baronetage that the Court should be resuscitated as the tribunal for determining claims to baronetcies. This proposal was elaborated by W. A. Lindsay K.C., Windsor Herald, in his evidence, but the Committee reported

we regret that we cannot advise the revival of this obsolete Court. Apart from the fact that its procedure is not in accordance with modern practice, its anomalous position with regard to the Superior Courts of Justice in this country would, we think, give rise to all kinds of difficulties.[1]

The belief that the Court of Chivalry was obsolete received further statutory recognition in the Trade Marks Act, 1905. Section 68 of that Act provided for the restraint by injunction of the use of the Royal Arms (or arms so closely resembling them as to be calculated to deceive) in connexion with any trade, business, calling, or profession in such a manner as to lead to the belief that such use was duly authorized.[2]

This provision was re-enacted in section 61 of the Trade Marks Act, 1938, and is the obvious inspiration for a section in a local Act which the Kingston-upon-Hull Corporation sought and obtained in 1952, conferring a similar power (*mutatis mutandis*) with respect to the 'armorial ensigns of the City'.[3]

This initiated a new parliamentary fashion. In the following session the Huddersfield Corporation obtained

[1] *Report of the Departmental Committee . . . to inquire into certain matters connected with the Baronetage* [Cmd. 3445] (1907), p. 3. Claims to baronetcies are now determined by the Privy Council by virtue of a Royal Warrant dated 10 Mar. 1922.

[2] This was also made a criminal offence, punishable by a fine not exceeding £20 by the Patents Act, 1949, s. 92 (2).

[3] Kingston-upon-Hull Corporation Act, 1952, s. 99. As in the Trade Marks Act, 1938, s. 61, there is a proviso preserving the right (if any) of the proprietor of a registered trade mark.

a similar section in their local Act.¹ 1954 saw still more encroachments on the jurisdiction of the Court of Chivalry. Birkenhead obtained a section similar to those in force in Kingston-upon-Hull and Huddersfield,² whilst Birmingham and Coventry went a step farther by obtaining powers which were not limited, as in the earlier Acts, to the use of their arms in connexion with a trade, business, calling, or profession.³

The Coventry Act received the Royal Assent on 30 July 1954. The Manchester Corporation Act, 1954, received the Royal Assent on the same day, but contained no provision relating to the Corporation's arms, for on 5 May in that year the Corporation had presented to the Earl Marshal the petition which led to the first appearance of the Court of Chivalry in the *Law Reports*.⁴

A court of law does not cease to exist by falling into disuse.⁵

¹ Huddersfield Corporation Act, 1953, s. 57.

² Birkenhead Corporation Act, 1954, s. 173.

³ Birmingham Corporation Act, 1954, s. 60; Coventry Corporation Act, 1954, s. 47.

⁴ *Manchester Corporation* v. *Manchester Palace of Varieties Ltd.*, [1955] P. 133, 136.

⁵ *R.* v. *Mayor and Jurats of Hastings* (1882), Dow. & Ry. K.B. 148 (lapse of 52 years); *R.* v. *Wells Corporation* (1836), 4 Dowl. 562 (lapse of 200 years).

IX

THE COMMON LAWYERS' FIRST CASE
1954

THE presentation of the petition of the Manchester Corporation to the Earl Marshal on 5 May 1954 set the long-silent machinery of the Court in motion.[1] The petition complained of two matters—that Manchester Palace of Varieties Ltd. had displayed publicly on a pelmet above the main curtain in the auditorium of the Palace Theatre in Whitworth Street, Manchester, the arms, crest, and supporters which had been granted to the Manchester Corporation in 1842, and that the company had displayed the arms, crest, and supporters on their common seal. The Earl Marshal had first to satisfy himself that these were matters within the jurisdiction of the Court. This he signified by subscribing the petition 'Let Process issue as is desired'.

The next step was for the Earl Marshal to issue a citation under seal dated 20 October requiring the defendants to enter an appearance in the registry of the Court at the College of Arms and to appear on the next court day to answer the complaint. This was served on the defendants on 25 October.

The Earl Marshal then proceeded to appoint officers of the Court. By a warrant dated 24 October the Lord Chief Justice of England, Lord Goddard, was appointed Lieutenant, Assessor, and Surrogate. This warrant was, *mutatis mutandis*, in the same form as that used for the appointment of Sir Edmund Isham in 1731. Three days later Mr. A. R. Wagner, Richmond Herald, and

---

[1] Copies of the petition and other documents cited in this chapter are printed in *The Full Report of the Case of the Mayor . . . of Manchester versus the Manchester Palace of Varieties Limited*, pp. 63–82. Copies of the petition and the citation are also printed in *Manchester Corporation* v. *Manchester Palace of Varieties Ltd.*, [1955] P. 133, 135–7.

Mr. W. M. Phillips, a notary public, were appointed joint Registers of the Court. This was the first occasion on which joint Registers had been appointed in the Court of Chivalry, though it was not without precedents in the ecclesiastical courts.[1]

The defendants entered an appearance on 8 November and executed a bond for £100, conditioned for their due appearance in court. Next came the plaintiffs' libel, which set out their complaint in more detail than the petition. The pleadings were closed by the defendants lodging an answer in which they admitted the display of the arms complained of, but denied that it was unlawful.

Since all the allegations of fact in the libel were admitted in the answer, it was not necessary to make any arrangements for the taking of evidence.[2] There being no other interlocutory proceedings, the hearing of the cause was appointed for 21 December. Although the hall of the College of Arms has remained fitted up as a courtroom since the last sitting of the Court, the venue was changed to the Lord Chief Justice's Court in the Royal Courts of Justice in order to provide more room for members of the public.

As has been usual when the sittings of the Court have been resumed after long intervals, the Earl Marshal presided in person. The Earl Marshal, in levée dress, was accompanied on the bench by the Surrogate, wearing his Oxford D.C.L. robe with a short bench wig and a doctor's round velvet bonnet. On either side of the bench were Chester, York, Somerset, and Lancaster Heralds and Bluemantle and Rouge Dragon Pursuivants in levée dress.

After the Lord Chief Justice's clerk, who acted as Cryer, had proclaimed the opening of the sitting, the Earl Marshal's style was rehearsed by Mr. Wagner in his Oxford M.A. gown and hood. Mr. Wagner then read

[1] During the first half of the nineteenth century there were at one time two joint registrars and three joint deputy registrars of the Prerogative Court of Canterbury.

[2] At the hearing the defendants produced an affidavit to which the plaintiffs did not object, but this was an irregularity.

extracts from an English translation of the letters patent of 19 October 1672, by virtue of which the Earl Marshal holds his office.[1] Mr. Phillips, wearing the livery gown of the Scriveners' Company, followed by reading the Earl Marshal's warrant appointing the Surrogate. The formalities concluded with the Earl Marshal, the Surrogate, and the joint Registers making the declarations required by s. 12 (4) of the Promissory Oaths Act, 1868.

Both parties had of necessity to be represented by barristers. Counsel for the plaintiffs formally exhibited their grants of arms and supporters, opened his case, and porrected the definitive sentence sought by the plaintiffs. Three principal points were taken in the argument for the defendants. (1) Upon a proper interpretation of the statute 13 Ric. II, st. 1, c. 2, the case was excluded from the jurisdiction of the Court. The expression 'deeds of arms' in the statute was a translation of 'faits darmes', which had nothing to do with armorial bearings, but only with deeds of arms performed at jousts or tournaments. The 'things that touch arms or war within the realm' referred to in the statute should be construed in the same manner. The medieval armorial causes in the Court all arose out of the use of arms on military expeditions. The jurisdiction of the Court in relation to armorial bearings only concerned disputes arising on military expeditions either outside or within the realm, or at tournaments within the realm. In the post-medieval causes relating to arms the Court had exceeded its jurisdiction; (2) in any event the Court only had jurisdiction over disputes between natural persons, there being no record of any proceedings in the Court in which the arms of a body corporate had been in dispute; (3) wrongful 'bearing or using' of arms was a term of art which meant more than mere display. A display of the arms of another for ornamental purposes did not affect the right of the armiger because it was not necessarily an assertion of right to the

[1] In *Manchester Corporation* v. *Manchester Palace of Varieties Ltd.*, [1955] P. 133, 134 n. it is stated that the patent of 1 Aug. 1622 (see p. 46 *ante*) was read. This was not read, though it was recited in the patent of 1672, which was read.

arms. The defendants were not using the plaintiffs' arms as their own. Their name was on their seal as required by s. 108 (1) (*b*) of the Companies Act, 1948, and the representation on it of the plaintiffs' arms was mere decoration.

At the conclusion of the argument for the defendants the Surrogate stated that he proposed to hold that the Court had jurisdiction to deal with the case. Counsel for the plaintiffs then replied on the other two points and informed the Court that it had been agreed that the party to be condemned in costs should be condemned in the sum of £300. It only remained for counsel for the defendants to porrect the definitive sentence which they sought. The Court retired for a short time and on returning the Surrogate gave judgment for the plaintiffs, stating that the reasons would be put into writing and delivered later. The Cryer then proclaimed the adjournment of the Court.

The reasoned judgment was delivered on 21 January 1955 by the Surrogate sitting alone. He rejected the argument that the legislation of Richard II relied on by the defendants limited the power of the Court in relation to armorial bearings to those carried in war or displayed at a tournament: the object of that legislation was to prevent the Court from entertaining matters cognizable by the ordinary courts. The jurisdiction of the Court of Chivalry in matters relating to armorial bearings had been recognized by such high authorities as Coke, Comyns, Blackstone, and Hawkins. Hawkins's opinion was of particular value, since he had been in practice as a serjeant-at-law when the Court had last sat in 1737. The Surrogate then dealt with the two matters of complaint. He held that the use of the plaintiffs' arms on the defendants' common seal was a legitimate subject of complaint. If the only complaint had been of the display of the arms in the auditorium, he would have felt that it raised a matter of some difficulty. He was by no means satisfied that it would be right for the Court to be put into motion merely because arms had been displayed by way of decoration or embellishment. In view, however, of the use by the defendants of the arms of the city on their common seal, and the contentions which they had set up in the case, he thought that the Court might properly inhibit and enjoin them from any display of the plaintiffs' arms.

The substantive part of the definitive sentence, which in accordance with the practice of the civil law courts was in writing, was as follows:

We the said Bernard Marmaduke Duke of Norfolk with the counsel of those skilled in the law whom We have consulted in this behalf pronounce decree and declare that the Plaintiffs lawfully bear the arms crest motto and supporters in this cause libellate and that the defendants have displayed representations of the said arms crest motto and supporters in the manner in this cause libellate and contrary to the will of the Plaintiffs and the laws and usages of arms and We inhibit and strictly enjoin the Defendants that they do not presume to display the said arms crest motto and supporters or any of them.

X

THE PERSONNEL OF THE COURT

The Constable and the Marshal

BOTH the Lord High Constable and the Earl Marshal have from time to time acted in person as judges of the Court of Chivalry. The sentence in *Scrope* v. *Grosvenor* was pronounced on 12 May 1389 by Thomas, Duke of Gloucester, the Constable.[1] There is not sufficient evidence to make it possible to deduce whether this was usual at this period, but we may guess that it was exceptional. Many of the proceedings in that case were heard by lieutenants, and in *Grey* v. *Hastings* in 1409 the sentence was pronounced by the Constable's lieutenant.[2] In the seventeenth century Robert, Earl of Lindsey, sat in person with the Earl Marshal in *Rea* v. *Ramsey*[3] and in *Wise* v. *Holmes*.[4] Although Lindsey was appointed Lord High Constable for the purposes of these two cases because it was thought that the statute 1 Hen. IV, c. 14, made it necessary to have a Constable as well as a Marshal for the trial of appeals of treason and murder,[5] he also sat with the Earl Marshal on 30 June 1634 to deal with ten other causes, all of which appear to have been ordinary causes of instance or of office.[6]

The office of Earl Marshal has suffered a number of vicissitudes. Since 1672 it has been hereditary in the family of the present Duke of Norfolk, but in earlier times it was often vacant and was executed by Commissioners appointed under the Great Seal. During the seventeenth and eighteenth centuries the fact that the Earl Marshal was a Roman Catholic made it necessary to appoint a

---

[1] Nicolas, *Scrope and Grosvenor Controversy*, i. 330.
[2] Young, *Controversy between . . . Grey . . . and . . . Hastings*, p. 31.
[3] (1631), 3 St. Tr. 483.   [4] (1633), Cur. Mil. Boxes 8/20, 22.
[5] See p. 52 *ante*.
[6] Agenda Paper, Cur. Mil. Boxes 8/23.

Deputy Earl Marshal from time to time.[1] A Deputy Earl Marshal must be distinguished from an Earl Marshal's lieutenant. The latter is appointed by the Earl Marshal for the sole purpose of acting for him in the Court of Chivalry, but a Deputy Earl Marshal was appointed with the approval of the Crown to exercise all the functions of the Earl Marshal and could himself appoint a lieutenant to act in the Court of Chivalry.

The occasions on which the Earl Marshal has sat in person in the Court of Chivalry have been comparatively infrequent, but he (or the Deputy Earl Marshal) has presided when the sittings of the Court have been resumed after long intervals in 1622, 1687, 1707, 1732, and again in 1954.[2]

When the Lord High Constable and the Earl Marshal have sat in person they have often been accompanied on the bench by a number of other noblemen, who appear to have taken no active part in the proceedings.[3] On three occasions in 1689, once in 1690, and twice in 1694 a Baron of the Exchequer (Turton, B.) sat with the Earl Marshal,[4] presumably because a common-law question was raised in one of the causes.

Before acting, any judge or other officer of the Court must make a declaration under the Promissory Oaths Act, 1868, s. 12 (4).[5]

From time to time between 1613 and 1716 litigants raised the point that the Earl Marshal was not entitled to sit in the Court of Chivalry without a Constable.[6] The arguments for and against the point are set out at length

[1] See p. 79 *ante*.

[2] See pp. 48, 88, 103, 108, 124 *ante*, and *Manchester Corporation* v. *Manchester Palace of Varieties Ltd.*, [1955] P. 133.

[3] Thus on 28 Nov. 1631 the Earls of Pembroke, Dorset, Carlisle, Mulgrave, and Morton and Viscounts Wimbledon, Wentworth, and Falkland sat with the Lord High Constable and the Earl Marshal (3 St. Tr. 486), and on 5 Oct. 1687 the Earls of Bath, Craven, and Dunbarton and Lord Thomas Howard sat with the Earl Marshal (Act Book).

[4] Act Book, 7, 17, and 20 Dec. 1689, 13 Jan. 1689/90, 14 and 31 Jan. 1693/4.

[5] For the declarations made in 1954 see *The Full Report of the Case of the Mayor Aldermen and Citizens of the City of Manchester versus The Manchester Palace of Varieties Limited*, p. 5.

[6] See pp. 43, 97, 105 *ante*.

and the authorities cited in the report of *Oldis* v. *Don-mille*[1] in the House of Lords, though the case was decided on another point.[2] The Earl Marshal's capacity to sit alone may be taken to have been established as long ago as 11 July 1622. It was then argued at length before the Privy Council in the Inner Star Chamber on behalf of the Earl Marshal, who was represented by Sir Thomas Coventry, then Attorney-General, and two other counsel. After hearing the argument, Williams L.K. said that he was of opinion that the Earl Marshal was a judge and had power of judicature in the vacancy of a Constable as well as with the Constable, adding that 'there hath been as much said to prove the authority of that Court as can be said for any Court in Westminster Hall'.[3] On the following 1 August letters patent were issued in accordance with that opinion, and the Earl Marshal has since continued to sit alone without any successful challenge, his right to do so having been again recognized and confirmed by letters patent in 1672 and 1687.[4]

Lieutenants, Assessors, and Surrogates

The usual practice has been for the judicial functions of the Lord High Constable and the Earl Marshal to be performed by persons appointed by them for the purpose. These persons have usually been styled lieutenants, but they have sometimes also been styled assessors or surrogates. Thus Sir John Cooke, Dean of the Arches, was appointed Surrogate in the Court Military in 1707[5] and Dr. Edmund Isham was appointed Assessor and Surrogate in 1731,[6] whilst in 1954 Lord Goddard was appointed Lieutenant, Assessor, and Surrogate.[7] Strictly speaking an assessor is but an assistant, whilst a lieutenant

---

[1] (1692), Show. P.C. 58, at pp. 59–61, 65–66.

[2] See p. 98 *ante*.   [3] Coll. Arm. MS. R. 28 (unfoliated).

[4] See pp. 79, 87 *ante*. The position in France was similar. After the supression of the dignity of Constable of France in 1607 the jurisdiction of the Tribunal of the Constable and the Marshals was exercised by the Marshals alone (R. Mathieu, *Le Système héraldique français* (Paris, 1946), pp. 59–60).

[5] Coll. Arm. MS. R.R.G. LXIV A, f. 5.

[6] Coll. Arm. MS. SML 3, f. 220.   [7] *Full Report*, p. 66.

or surrogate acts as a substitute, but the distinction in terminology has not been observed very precisely. Thus on 8 October 1687 Sir Richard Raines sat with the Earl Marshal, but is described in the Act Book as 'Lieutenant in the Court Military'.

During the early days of the Court the lieutenants were usually military men appointed for a particular cause or even for some step in a cause. Thus in *Scrope* v. *Grosvenor* Lord Fitzwalter acted as the Constable's lieutenant on 17 August 1385, but on 7 May 1386 the Constable's lieutenant was Sir Hugh de Calverley.[1] A lieutenant did not hold anything in the nature of an office. On 11 October 1388 the Constable appointed Sir John Lakyngheth merely to hold a court in his place on 15 October and to adjourn it until 10 November.[2] A succession of temporary lay judges cannot have been wholly satisfactory and a change for the better in both respects was made when Thomas Kent LL.D. was appointed Vice-Constable for life with a fee of 100 marks a year on 7 January 1445.[3]

When the formal sittings of the Court were resumed in the seventeenth and eighteenth centuries the lieutenants were almost always civilians in Doctors' Commons, though Henry, Lord Matravers, who was not a lawyer of any kind, acted as his father's lieutenant on numerous occasions in the 1630's.

It is possible for there to be more than one lieutenant at a time. This was not unusual at the end of the seventeenth century. On 21 February 1700 no fewer than four, Dr. George Oxendon, Sir Charles Hedges, Sir Richard Raines, and Sir Thomas Pinfold, were appointed simultaneously.[4] The appointments were during the Earl Marshal's pleasure and terminated on his death.[5]

---

[1] Nicolas, *Scrope and Grosvenor Controversy*, i. 35, 39.
[2] Ibid., i. 329.
[3] *C.P.R. 1441–6*, p. 348. Kent's will was proved in 1468 (P.C.C. 26 Godyn).
[4] Act Book.
[5] Henry, Duke of Norfolk E.M., died on 2 Apr. 1701, and on the following 4 June Oxendon and Raines were reappointed. Hedges and Pinfold were not reappointed, being replaced by Sir John Cooke and Dr. George Bramston (Act Book).

A lieutenant can himself appoint an assessor. The evidence for this is an indenture dated 20 February 1392 made between John, Lord Cobham, and John Barnet witnessing the payment of £10 to Barnet on behalf of himself, William Cawode, and William Sondeye to act as assessors in the cause of arms then pending between Lord Lovel and Lord Morley, the parties each having contributed £5 towards the £10.[1]

The King's Advocate

The most important of the officers of the Court in the seventeenth and eighteenth centuries was the King's Advocate. His position was similar to that of the King's Advocate in the Court of Admiralty. The office existed as early as the fifteenth century, the earliest known holder of it being Thomas Brouns, who was succeeded by Thomas Appleton in 1468.[2] Appleton was not styled 'King's Advocate', but 'promoter of business concerning the King'. This, however, is an apt description of the officer who was later known as the King's Advocate. In addition to promoting the office of the judge in causes of office, the King's Advocate also decided whether any cause of action was disclosed by the petition in a cause of instance in much the same manner as the Attorney-General grants his *fiat* in a modern relator action in the High Court.

The office of King's Advocate was not inconsistent with private practice. Dr. Duck, who was King's Advocate from 1623 until 1640, appeared as counsel in many causes, despite the possibility of conflict between his public duty and his duty to his client. Thus in *Bingham* v. *Joyce*[3] he subscribed the petition in the following terms:

Mr. Dethick, divers of the words here expressed ar fitt for action in my L. Marshalls Court. Others are fitt to bee omitted wch I will make choyce of [when] they come to me to drawe their Libell.

---

[1] Kent County Record Office MS. U 601 O 3. Cobham acted as the Constable's lieutenant at this time (*C.P.R. 1391–6*, pp. 17, 41). Barnet and Cawode were doctors of laws (ibid.) and Sondeye was probably another.

[2] *C.P.R. 1467–77*, p. 110.

[3] (1637), Cur. Mil. Boxes 3/107.

The Register

The functions of the Register are to register the formal acts of the Court, to authenticate copies of those acts, and to preserve the records of the Court. It was the usual custom of the courts in which the civilians practised that the register should be a notary public, since a record made by a notary is evidence in every court according to the civil and canon law,[1] though a person who is not a notary is legally eligible for appointment.[2] In accordance with this custom the office of the Register of the Court of Chivalry has always been held by a notary public.[3]

Advocates

Doctors of civil law were not *ipso facto* entitled to practise as advocates, but they were eligible to be admitted as advocates of the Court of Arches by rescript of the Archbishop of Canterbury. The method of obtaining admission is described in detail in *R. v. Archbishop of Canterbury*.[4] After having been admitted as an advocate in the Court of Arches, an advocate was qualified to practise in the other ecclesiastical courts and the civil-law courts.[5]

When the sittings of the Court of Chivalry were resumed in 1623 the common lawyers sought to obtain audience there. Their argument 'That the Professors of the Common Lawes of England ought not to be excluded from practizeing in Cases of honor' survives in a number of copies.[6] It was stated that they had been admitted to practise in such cases within living memory without denial, a fact which tends to emphasize the nondescript

---

[1] J. T. Law, *Forms of Ecclesiastical Law* (London, 1831), p. 21.

[2] *Norwich Notaries, Eaton v. Watson*, [1904] W.N. 24.

[3] One of the two joint Registers appointed in 1954 was a notary public.

[4] (1807), 8 East 213.

[5] It is stated in *R. v. Archbishop of Canterbury, supra*, at p. 214 that a candidate was introduced into the Court of Admiralty by two advocates and admitted by the Judge. There may have been a similar ceremony in the Court of Chivalry, but there is no record of it.

[6] e.g. B.M. MS. Add. 9021, f. 58; Cambridge University Library MSS. Dd. iii. 64, f. 21, and Mm. vi. 69, f. 3.

character of the heraldic litigation in the sixteenth century rather than to support the common lawyers' claim to audience in the Court of Chivalry.[1] The civil law rule 'in honoribus decernendis inspicienda est consuetudo regionis'[2] was construed as a rejection of jurisdiction, it being argued that 'consuetudo regionis' in England was the common law.[3] This argument was so far successful that at the sitting of the Court on 24 November 1623 an 'utter Barrester of the Temple' was heard as counsel for Ralph Brooke, York Herald,[4] but that seems to have been the only occasion on which a barrister had audience before a properly constituted Court of Chivalry whilst the civilians practised in Doctors' Commons.[5]

For the civilians the beginning of the end came on 25 August 1857 with the passing of the Court of Probate Act, 1857. This abolished the testamentary jurisdiction of ecclesiastical and other courts, and set up the Court of Probate. The Act contained consequential provisions giving rights of audience in the new Court to the advocates of the ecclesiastical courts and to serjeants and barristers.[6] Conversely the advocates were given the right to practise in any court of law or equity in England as if they had been called to the bar on the days on which they had been admitted as advocates.[7] 'The College of Doctors of Law exercent in the Ecclesiastical and Admiralty Courts' were authorized to sell their real and personal estate.[8] The College were also authorized to surrender the charter granted to them by George III in 1768 and were to be dissolved upon such surrender.[9] Three days later

---

[1] See p. 39 *ante*.   [2] See p. 164 *post*.

[3] For a curious argument that the 'the Marshall lawe' must be either common law or ecclesiastical law because England is governed only by these laws and that therefore the 'Courte Marshall', having no dependence on either of these laws, 'cannot be but superflouse & unnecessary', see P.R.O., S.P. Dom. James I, vol. cxxiv, 38, quoted in P. H. Hardacre, 'The Earl Marshal, the Heralds, and the House of Commons. 1604–1641' in *International Review of Social History*, ii (1957), 113.

[4] B.M. MS. Add. 6297, f. 197.

[5] In *Rea* v. *Ramsay* (1631), 3 St. Tr. 483, 502, Selden and Littleton, both of the Inner Temple, are named amongst the appellants' counsel, but they had two civilians with them and do not seem to have addressed the Court.

[6] S. 40.   [7] S. 41.   [8] S. 116.   [9] S. 117.

the Matrimonial Causes Act, 1857 received the Royal Assent. This set up the Court of Divorce and Matrimonial Causes and provided that all persons admitted to practise as advocates in any ecclesiastical court and all barristers should be entitled to practise in the new Court.[1]

The real end of the advocates came on 8 August 1859 with the passing of 'An Act to enable Serjeants, Barristers-at-Law, Attorneys, and Solicitors to practise in the High Court of Admiralty'.[2]

Having been successively deprived of their monopolies of probate, matrimonial, and admiralty work, the advocates ceased to obtain further recruits, but the statutes which effected these changes made no provision for representation in the ecclesiastical courts and in the Court of Chivalry after the death of the last of the advocates then practising. However, the possibility of a similar position with regard to the Court of Common Pleas had been considered as long ago as 1462, when Littleton J. said: 'If all the serjeants were dead, we could hear the apprentices to plead here by necessity, and in ease of the people',[3] and Tindal C.J. agreed in *In the Matter of the Serjeants at Law*[4] that this might be requisite in order to prevent a failure in the administration of justice. The ecclesiastical courts accepted this principle by admitting barristers to practise in them *ex necessitate rei*[5] and this precedent has been followed by the Court of Chivalry.[6]

Proctors

The proctors who practised in the Court of Chivalry seem always to have been first admitted as proctors of the

---

[1] S. 15.   [2] 22 & 23 Vict., c. 6.

[3] *Parton* v. *Genny*, Y.B. 2 Edw. IV, Trin., f. 2, pl. 4. The serjeants had an exclusive right of audience in the Common Pleas until 1846, when it was opened to barristers by the statute 9 & 10 Vict., c. 54.

[4] (1840), 6 Bing. (N.C.) 235, at p. 239.

[5] Sir R. Phillimore, *Ecclesiastical Law* (2nd ed., London, 1895), ii. 936. In *Mouncey* v. *Robinson* (1867), 37 L.J. Ecc. 8, it was held that a barrister is competent to sign articles which are required by the Church Discipline Act, 1840, s. 7, to be signed by an advocate practising in Doctors' Commons. Cf. *Marson* v. *Unmack*, [1923] P. 163, 165.

[6] *Manchester Corporation* v. *Manchester Palace of Varieties Ltd.*, [1955] P. 133.

Court of Arches. However, not all the proctors of the Arches Court practised in the Court of Chivalry. In 1707 there were twenty-four proctors of the Arches Court, of whom only seven practised in the Court of Chivalry.[1] Unlike those of the advocates, the admissions of the proctors in the Court of Chivalry are formally recorded in the Act Book. It seems that the proctors did not have the same exclusive rights in the Court of Chivalry as the advocates, for in *Hungerford* v. *Broad*[2] one Nicholas Webbe of Burford, co. Oxford, a 'student of the Common lawes', deposes that 'hee doth sollicite this Cause in the Court of Honor' on behalf of the defendant. In *Somersett* v. *Good*[3] the plaintiff's solicitor was said to be an attorney who had been put out of the roll by some of the judges at Westminster.

One of the proctors was appointed to be the Earl Marshal's Proctor or Procurator-General.

In addition to being formally admitted, a proctor had to exhibit a written proxy in respect of each client for whom he acted.[4]

The nineteenth-century legislation which brought about the end of the advocates had a similar effect on the proctors. The Court of Probate Act, 1857 took away the proctors' monopoly of probate work and gave them in return the right to be admitted as solicitors.[5] The Matrimonial Causes Act, 1857 allowed all attorneys and solicitors entitled to practise in the superior courts at Westminster to practise in the new Court of Divorce and Matrimonial Causes,[6] and in 1859 the Act 22 & 23 Vict., c. 6 enabled attorneys and solicitors to practise in the High Court of Admiralty. The Solicitors Act, 1877[7] provided that solicitors should be eligible to practise in ecclesiastical courts, but nothing was done to provide

---

[1] *Present State of Great Britain*, pp. 168, 183.

[2] (1639), Acta Cur. Mil. (5), 151–2.

[3] (1637), Cur. Mil. I. 232.

[4] A party could appoint two proctors by one proxy (*Coventry (Earl)* v. *King* (1702), Cur. Mil. Boxes 21/19).

[5] Ss. 42, 43.   [6] S. 15.

[7] S. 17, now replaced by the Solicitors Act, 1957, s. 2 (1) (d).

substitutes for the proctors in the Court of Chivalry.[1] The result has been that solicitors, like barristers, have been admitted to practise in the Court of Chivalry *ex necessitate rei*.[2]

Inferior Officers

There have been various inferior officers of the Court, but it is not certain that there has always been a complete establishment of them. At various times we find a Secretary and Seal Keeper, a Messenger, a Sub-Marshal or Serjeant-Marshal, a Cryer, an Usher, and a Court Keeper.

The Messenger (sometimes styled Marshal or Mandatory) was employed to serve citations, to arrest contumacious litigants, and generally to execute the process of the Court.

The Cryer proclaimed the opening and the closing of the Court.[3] In addition to these ceremonial functions, he had to call an absent defendant three times before a warrant could be issued for his arrest.

Edmund Thorold, the Usher in 1640, was also Marshal of the Court of Exchequer. His social standing was such that he entered his pedigree and arms at the Visitation of London in 1634[4] and was the plaintiff in a cause of scandalous words.[5]

In 1732 the offices of Cryer and Usher were combined.

---

[1] The Solicitors Act, 1957, s. 88 (3), provides that references in any enactment to proctors are to be construed as references to solicitors, but the proctors did not enjoy their right to practise in the Court of Chivalry by statute.

[2] *Manchester Corporation* v. *Manchester Palace of Varieties Ltd.*, [1955] P. 133.

[3] The forms of proclamation are set out in Cur. Mil. Boxes 8/20.

[4] *Visitation of London . . . 1633, 1634 and 1635* (Harl. Soc. xvii), ii. 286.

[5] *Thorold* v. *Trumboll* (1640), Cur. Mil. Boxes 5/72.

XI

THE POST-MEDIEVAL JURISDICTION
OF THE COURT

As has already appeared,[1] the end of the Wars of the Roses left the Court of Chivalry with but two small remnants of its former jurisdiction: (a) the ill-defined 'other usages and customs to the same matters [i.e. arms and war] pertaining' referred to in the statute of 1389,[2] and (b) appeals of crimes arising outside the realm referred to in the statute of 1399.[3] This chapter will demonstrate from the records of the Court how the seventeenth-century civilians developed these remnants into the basis of a substantial body of litigation.[4]

The residuary matters mentioned in the statute of 1389 were, and still are, the basis of the Court's jurisdiction in causes relating to the bearing of coat armour.[5]

The armorial causes were of two kinds—those in which the defendant was alleged to have taken the arms of another person,[6] and those in which he was alleged to have used arms wrongfully without infringing another's rights.[7] Sometimes the alleged offence consisted of the fabrication of coats of arms[8] and sometimes it consisted of the use of armorial insignia, such as supporters, to which

---

[1] See p. 29 *ante*.   [2] 13 Ric. II, st. 1, c. 2. See p. 19 *ante*.
[3] 1 Hen. IV, c. 14. See p. 26 *ante*.

[4] In using the records for this purpose there has to be applied *mutatis mutandis* the principle laid down by Lord Esher M.R. in *The Gas Float Whitton No. 2*, [1896] P. 42, at p. 48: 'If you find that the Court of Admiralty has affirmatively stated that it has jurisdiction in certain cases, you cannot affirm that it has jurisdiction in other cases merely on the ground that the Court of Admiralty has not expressly excluded them by negative words.'

[5] Blackstone, *Commentaries*, iii. 103–4.

[6] e.g. *Office of the Judge* v. *Hurt* (1634), Her. Cas. 5 (cause of office); *Pauncefote* v. *Pauncefote* (1638), Her. Cas. 33 (cause of instance).

[7] e.g. *St. George* v. *Tuckfield* (1637), Her. Cas. 24. The defendant was fined £100, which was later mitigated to £5.

[8] e.g. *Prust* v. *Saltren* (1637), Her. Cas. 25.

the defendant was not entitled.[1] There was at least one case in which proceedings were taken for unlawfully using an escutcheon of pretence.[2] It was not only an offence to use false arms, but also to paint them for a customer.[3]

The jurisdiction over arms was extended to surnames. Sometimes, in addition to alleging that his arms had been wrongfully assumed, a plaintiff would allege that his name had been taken and that the defendant had falsely pretended to be of the same family.[4] Similar allegations with respect to surnames were made in causes of office.[5]

Akin to the causes for the wrongful assumption of arms were those in which the alleged offence was the wrongful assumption of the style of 'esquire' or 'gentleman'. Sometimes these causes were promoted by the King's Advocate,[6] or by one or more of the officers of arms,[7] and sometimes they were promoted by private persons who wished to put their neighbours in their places.[8] In *Constable* v. *Constable*[9] a defendant whose gentility was unchallenged was alleged by one of his kinsmen to have arrogated and assumed the title of 'esquire' without any right or just claim to it.[10] In *Leeke* v. *Harris*[11] the object of the proceedings was not simply to prove that the defendant was no gentleman, but also to show that he was thereby disqualified for being created a baronet. In *Longvyll* v. *Hawthorne*[12] the defendant was not proceeded against directly for having falsely assumed the style of gentleman, but for having said that the plaintiff was no better gentleman than himself. This put the

---

[1] *Oldys* v. *Tyllie* (1687), Her. Cas. 59.
[2] *Oldys* v. *Feilding* (1702), Her. Cas. 102.
[3] *Office of the Judge* v. *Winchell* (1634), Her. Cas. 6.
[4] *Perrot* v. *Perrocke alias Perrot* (1639), Her. Cas. 44.
[5] e.g. *Oldys* v. *Mowbery* (1687), Her. Cas. 61.
[6] e.g. *Duck* v. *Hanslopp* (1637), Her. Cas. 27.
[7] e.g. *Chitting* v. *Willymott* (1635), Her. Cas. 20.
[8] e.g. *Stepkin* v. *Dobbins* (1638), Her. Cas. 30.
[9] (1639), Her. Cas. 35.
[10] It was alleged that the defendant had no right or just claim to the title of esquire and was not descended of any knight of his family.
[11] (1623), Her. Cas. 1. See also p. 50 *ante*.
[12] (1634), Her. Cas. 9.

defendant's gentility in issue, for such words could only be provocative of a duel if the defendant was not a gentleman, and accordingly the defendant was not only fined and ordered to pay costs, but was also kept in custody until he had made a public confession that he had wrongfully assumed and used the title of gentleman.

Conversely the Court had cognizance of cases in which a gentleman alleged that he had been denied his proper title.[1] In *Constable* v. *Carlyle*[2] the defendant admitted that the plaintiff was a gentleman, but said that he was 'but of the second or third head or two or three descents at the most'.

The issue of gentility arose in another form in *Duck* v. *St. George*,[3] which was a cause of office promoted against Norroy King of Arms and Somerset Herald for granting arms without the Earl Marshal's warrant to one who was not a gentleman, contrary to the decrees and statutes of Thomas, Duke of Norfolk E.M.

It is, however, as plaintiffs rather than as defendants that the officers of arms normally appear in the records of the Court. The direction of the funerals of the nobility and gentry and the supervision of the painting of the arms used at such funerals was a lucrative part of their work, but it was rendered less lucrative than it might have been because frugally minded heirs and executors dispensed with elaborate funerals and the attendance of officers of arms. In order to counteract such parsimony the Commissioners for executing the office of Earl Marshal made an order dated 10 November 1618 that after the funeral of an archbishop, peer, peeress, bishop, baronet, knight, esquire, or gentleman buried without the ancient ceremonial rites attended by the officers of arms a certificate of the death, place of burial, marriage, issue and arms should be returned to the College of Arms and certain fees paid. For the better execution of this order the kings

---

[1] *Hudleston* v. *Pattison* (c. 1638), Her. Cas. 5. The plaintiff, the grandson of one knight and the brother of another, complained that one of the coroners for Cambridgeshire had described him as 'yeoman' in an inquisition. Cf. *Keresforth* v. *Scamadine* (1640), Her. Cas. 48.

[2] (1640), Her. Cas. 48.   [3] (1638), Her. Cas. 33.

of arms and heralds appointed deputies in various parts of the country.[1] At first these fees, if unpaid, were recovered by judgments and decrees of the Court of Chancery and the Court of Wards and Liveries.[2] About 1632 a new practice of recovering such fees in a cause of office in the Court of Chivalry was devised.[3] This was an unwarrantable extension of the jurisdiction of the Court over matters cognizable at common law, but it seems to have gone unchallenged for many years. Such proceedings were later covered by the decision in *Russel's Case*,[4] by which time funeral certificates were falling into desuetude.

Even worse than not paying the fees for dispensing with funeral pomp was the performance of funeral pomp without the attendance of officers of arms. In such a case both the executor and the tradesman who carried out the work were liable to be sentenced in a cause of office to pay a fine to the King, as well as the officers of arms' fees and the King's Advocate's costs.[5] If it was feared that a funeral was about to be conducted in this unlawful manner, the officers of arms could petition the Earl Marshal for a notice to be served on the executors warning them that, if they proceeded, they would be called upon to account for it.[6]

The right to direct and order all funerals other than those of peers and knights of the Garter belonged to the provincial kings of arms in their respective provinces.[7]

---

[1] Bond dated 5 May 1635 for the performance of their duties by Dominick Fisher of Taunton Magdalen, co. Somerset, and Joseph Thatcher of Exeter, co. Devon, painter-stainers, who had been appointed deputies for Somerset and Dorset on 18 Jan. 1633/4 (Cur. Mil. Boxes 11/1).

[2] *Kings of Arms and Heralds* v. *Twysden* (1637), Her. Cas. 27, 28, where it is somewhat surprisingly stated that such fees had also been recovered in the Prerogative Court of Canterbury.

[3] Ibid. An early example of such a cause is *Officers of Arms* v. *Yelverton* (*c.* 1630), Her. Cas. 5.

[4] (1692), 4 Mod. 128, 129. See p. 97 *ante*.

[5] e.g. *Duck* v. *Mosely* (1638), Her. Cas. 33 (£200 fine, 200 marks damages, and £5 costs); *Duck* v. *Myles* (1639), Her. Cas. 41 (100 marks fine and 100 marks fees and costs).

[6] Warning to executors of Sir Edward Mosely (Coll. Arm. MS. I. 25, f. 74). The warning was unheeded: see *Duck* v. *Mosely, supra*.

[7] *Le Neve* v. *Wiseman* (1635), Her. Cas. 20, 21. Although the right is there

After the revival of the Court in 1687 cases of alleged infringement of the rights of the kings of arms formed a large proportion of the business until the decision of the House of Lords in *Oldis* v. *Donmille*[1] put an end to them.

The painting of false arms brought many craftsmen before the Court, as in *St. George* v. *Howell*,[2] where the defendant was fined twenty marks for painting false arms on trumpet banners for the High Sheriff of Derbyshire. In order to sustain such proceedings the most trifling divergence from the correct blazon would be seized upon. In *St. George* v. *Howell* (*No. 2*)[3] the same defendant was fined ten marks for having painted a cross fleuretty instead of a cross flory.

Not only were proceedings taken against painters for painting false arms, but the kings of arms also sought to prevent the painting of arms without their licence.[4] This was the subject of a protracted quarrel between the Painter-Stainers' Company and the kings of arms which dragged on from 1578 until 1738, though it ceased to concern the Court of Chivalry after the decision in *Russel's Case*[5] that even if the claim of the kings of arms was well founded their proper remedy lay in an action on the case at common law.[6]

In *Duck* v. *Woodall*[7] the defendant was alleged to have exhibited a forged certificate of arms in proceedings in the Court. The placing of false inscriptions on coffin-plates and monuments by an officer of arms also fell within the jurisdiction of the Court.[8]

The Court enforced the control of the publishing of

---

pleaded as having existed from time immemorial, it was in fact derived from an order of Thomas, Duke of Norfolk E.M., made in 1568 (*Lancashire Funeral Certificates* (Chetham Soc. lxxv, 1869), p. 2).

[1] (1692), Show. P.C. 58. See p. 98 *ante*.
[2] (1687), Her. Cas. 51.   [3] Ibid.
[4] e.g. *Oldys* v. *Wyseman* (1691), Her. Cas. 74.
[5] (1692), 4 Mod. 128.
[6] For the dispute with the Painter-Stainers' Company, see W. A. D. Englefield, *History of the Painter-Stainers' Company* (London, 1950), pp. 69–71, 91–93, 104–6, 111–13, 116–17, 126–30, 150–1, 160–5, 169, 173.
[7] (1639), Her. Cas. 40.
[8] *Coventry* (*Earl*) v. *King* (1701), *Her. & Gen.* vii. 101.

books and prints relating to matters of heraldic interest. In March 1620 the Commissioners for executing the office of Earl Marshal considered that the proposed publication by one Grafton, a 'solicitor of causes in the law', of the arms of all the gentlemen of the Inns of Court and of Chancery would not only be a 'great wrong and preiudice' to the nobility and gentry, but also a 'scandall and impeachment' of the officers of arms. The Commissioners accordingly issued an order forbidding the Master and Wardens of the Stationers' Company to print or suffer to be printed any book, pamphlet, or other paper containing pedigrees, descents, arms, or matters of heraldry not first seen and allowed by the Commissioners.[1] This was reinforced on 11 July 1637 by a decree of the Court of Star Chamber, which provided that all books concerning heraldry, titles of honour and arms or otherwise concerning the office of Earl Marshal should be licensed by the Earl Marshal or by his authority, and that the licence should be printed at the beginning of each book.[2] Accordingly we find John Amery, a bookseller in Fleet Street, submitting in 1690 to a charge of printing and publishing a catalogue of the peers of England without licence or lawful authority.[3] There were at least three similar causes of office in respect of the publication of representations of the funeral pomp of Queen Mary II.[4]

It has been held by the Court of King's Bench that the Court of Chivalry has jurisdiction over disputes as to precedence,[5] but no trace of the exercise of such a jurisdiction has been found amongst the records of the Court, although there were instances of such disputes being determined by the Commissioners for executing the office of Earl Marshal before the revival of the Court in 1622.[6]

[1] Coll. Arm. MS. Heralds III, p. 1140.
[2] Coll. Arm. MS. SML 3, f. 173. The latter part of this decree seems to have been generally disregarded.
[3] *St. George* v. *Amery* (1690), Her. Cas. 71.
[4] *Oldys* v. *Overton* (1695), Her. Cas. 88; *Oldys* v. *Onley*, ibid.; *Oldys* v. *Smith* (1695), Her. Cas. 89.
[5] *Ashton* v. *Jennings* (1675), 2 Lev. 133.   [6] See p. 33 *ante*.

The great innovation of the early part of the seventeenth century was the devising of the cause of 'scandalous words provocative of a duel',[1] which was available whether the words were spoken at home or abroad.[2] Although it was ultimately decided that the Court of Chivalry had no jurisdiction in such proceedings,[3] they met a need which the common law was unable to satisfy, for the speaking of words of mere abuse, such as 'villain' or 'rogue', or even to say of a man that he was forsworn was not actionable.[4]

Once the Court had embarked on the hearing of causes of 'scandalous words' it was not long before the ingenuity of the civilians found ways of extending this jurisdiction. Although a woman could not be plaintiff in a cause of 'scandalous words', because women could not be provoked into duelling, a husband could sue in respect of words spoken of himself and his wife.[5] Proceedings could also be taken when the scandalous words were spoken of the plaintiff's wife alone.[6] Similarly a man could sue in respect of words spoken of his mother,[7] his daughter,[8] or his deceased father and grandfather.[9]

Although it might be thought that the clergy were as much debarred from duelling by their cloth as women by their sex, there were clerical defendants. There was even a cause of scandalous words against a clergyman for words

[1] See p. 57 *ante.*
[2] *Manwaring* v. *Johnson* (1639), Cur. Mil. Boxes 14/3*aa* (words spoken in Venice).
[3] See p. 102 *ante.*
[4] *Stanhope* v. *Blith* (1585), 4 Co. Rep. 15*a.*
[5] *Constable* v. *Carlisle* (1637), Cur. Mil. Boxes 3/61.
[6] *Madox* v. *Crome* (1639), Cur. Mil. Boxes 2/121; *Farnefold* v. *Bonnyman* (1637), Cur. Mil. Boxes 3/95. The plaintiff's wife was less directly responsible for *Heber* v. *Michell* (1640), Cur. Mil. Boxes 5/130, where the plaintiff, who had been scandalized by his tenants, stated that his wife was 'a gentlewoman descended of so noble a family as ye Cliffords Earles of Cumberland whose mind agreeth wth her birth so y^t y^{or} pet^r dares neuer looke her nor her freinds in ye face, vntill he hath gayned so much yor lop^s fauour, as to heare it publiquely in ye Court Military'.
[7] *Poyntz* v. *Cox* (1639), Cur. Mil. Boxes 11/37*b.*
[8] *Powis* (*Lord*) v. *Vaughan* (1638), Coll. Arm. MS. R. 19, f. 5; *C.S.P.D. 1639–1640,* p. 261.
[9] *Coryton* v. *Peryman* (1638), Cur. Mil. Boxes 13/2*t, u.*

concerning the plaintiff's wife spoken before the congregation in church.[1]

A cause of scandalous words came to an end on the death of the plaintiff, when the defendant could petition for his bond to be delivered up to him.[2]

The 'scandalous words' complained of were not always mere vulgar abuse. Sometimes heraldic issues came to trial under the guise of a complaint of scandalous words. The defendant might have said that the plaintiff was using arms to which he was not entitled,[3] or called in question the plaintiff's pedigree[4] or name.[5] A variant of this type of case was *Pember* v. *Phillippes*,[6] where one of the defendants said that the plaintiff's coat of arms 'came down by the last carrier'.[7] There was presumably an innuendo to the same effect in *Cooper* v. *Billop*,[8] where the defendant said that he was a better gentleman than the plaintiff and that he also could buy a coat of arms for 40s. or five marks.

A cause for 'scandalous words' could be used for purposes other than the solace of wounded pride. When William Mansergh, the Under-Sheriff of Westmorland,

---

[1] *Farnefold* v. *Bonnyman* (1637), Cur. Mil. Boxes 3/95. Presumably the plaintiff and his wife were not present, for quarrelling, chiding, or brawling in a church was an offence punishable by the ordinary under the Brawling Act, 1551, and one who had been presented to his ordinary under that Act could not be proceeded against in the Court of Chivalry in respect of scandalous words spoken in the quarrel (*Little* v. *Palmer* (1638), Cur. Mil. Boxes 15/29 (quarrel concerning overseers' accounts)).

[2] *Boswell* v. *Savage* (1638), Cur. Mil. Boxes 13/2a.

[3] *Weaver* v. *Pye* (1693), Her. Cas. 43. The defendant said that he would bring the plaintiff's ring on which his arms were engraved under the heralds' hammer.

[4] *Constable* v. *Constable* (1640), Her. Cas. 35. The depositions in this case contain an exceptionally large amount of information concerning the pedigrees and arms of the parties. *Kirton* v. *Davies* (1640), Cur. Mil. 1631–42, 137–8, seems to be a case of this type, but only a deposition survives.

[5] *Keresforth* v. *Scamadine* (1640), Her. Cas. 48, where the defendant said that the plaintiff's name was Kesforth and not Keresforth, and that the arms 'the milrines quartered with the three butterflies' did not belong to the plaintiff, but to the family of Keresforth.

[6] (1639), Her. Cas. 43.

[7] Since there seems to be no printed record of such a grant, it may be worth recording that the grantee was Thomas Pember of Leonhalls, co. Hereford.

[8] (1639), Her. Cas. 42. In *Baker* v. *Spenser* (1638), Her. Cas. 28, the defendant was alleged to have said, 'Aske Baker when you see him what his armes or gentery cost him'.

was trying to apprehend Roger Moore by virtue of a warrant from the Secretary of State, he called upon James Moore of Midleton for his assistance, and the words spoken by James Moore when he refused were the subject of a cause instituted by the Under-Sheriff.[1] *Pointz* v. *Coxe*[2] was an abuse of the process of the Court, for when it was referred to a knight and three esquires for hearing, examination, and ending (if it might be), the referees certified that the suit had been brought to hinder the defendant in a suit which he had instituted against the plaintiff's mother in another court. *Richardson* v. *Hardwicke*[3] seems to have been an attempt to bring a case of ancient light before the Court, for the 'scandalous words' alleged were: 'Thou art a base stinckinge knaue, thou hast damned upp my lights and by God's wounds I wilbe reuenged of thee.' Somewhat nearer to the usual proceedings in the Court was *Carnabie* v. *Johnson*,[4] where one of the defendants was a kinsman of the plaintiff, and on being asked to give his arms with due distinction, not only refused to do so, but boasted himself to come of a branch of the family superior to the plaintiff.

Somewhat similar to, but much rarer than, causes for scandalous words, were causes for derogating the rank and dignity of a nobleman. These were causes of office. Such a cause was *Duck* v. *Pinchbeck*,[5] where the King's Advocate promoted the office of the Judge against John Pinchbeck for writing an allegedly opprobrious letter to Philip, Earl of Pembroke and Montgomery, the Chamberlain of the King's Household, complaining of his treatment with respect to a post under Prince Henry's tutor— a grievance then more than twenty years old.

Even more serious than provoking another to a duel by speaking scandalous words was the arranging of a duel. In May 1638 Thomas Doubleday and Robert Walsh, both of the City of London, came to blows at a horse-race in Hyde Park and arranged to fight a duel in an open

---

[1] *Mansergh* v. *Moore* (1639), Cur. Mil. Boxes 6/122.
[2] (1639), Cur. Mil. Boxes 16/1n.   [3] (1640), Cur. Mil. Boxes 18/4a.
[4] (1640), Her. Cas. 47.   [5] (1635), Cur. Mil. Boxes 10/10/6.

field in Westminster, called 'Calliesands'. In order to prevent the duel the Earl Marshal issued warrants for their arrest. Doubleday was arrested and taken into the custody of John Coxe, the Messenger of the Court of Chivalry, but by Coxe's negligence in leaving his prisoner in charge of his deputy, Doubleday escaped. He was recaptured within two hours, but in that time he and Walsh had attempted to fight. The result was the promotion by the King's Advocate of a cause of office against Doubleday, together with Coxe and one Cassia Borrough, who acted as second.[1] The fines were extremely heavy. Doubleday had to pay £1,000, Walsh and Borrough 1,000 marks each, and Coxe £300, in addition to which Doubleday and Walsh each had to pay £12 costs. Doubleday, Walsh, and Burrough were also sentenced not to wear any weapon during the Earl Marshal's pleasure and not to come within five miles of the cities of London and Westminster, whilst Coxe was suspended from his duties for a year, saving to the Earl Marshal or his lieutenant power to absolve him from the suspension. All the defendants were to remain in custody until they produced sureties approved by the Court for the performance of their sentences.[2]

The other branch of the Court's jurisdiction—that over appeals of treasons and murders committed outside the realm—was less profitable to the later civilians, although it produced the Court's one case in the *State Trials*—*Rea* v. *Ramsey*.[3] The general rule of the common law is that offences committed by British subjects out of England are not punishable by the criminal law of this country.[4] Accordingly in its early days the Court of Chivalry had exclusive cognizance over crimes committed beyond the sea.[5] This monopoly was broken by the Treason

---

[1] *Duck* v. *Doubleday* (1638), Cur. Mil. Boxes 13/2*p*, *q*, *w*, *x*. A second cause was promoted against one William Browne for failing to arrest Walsh (*Duck* v. *Browne*, Cur. Mil. Boxes 12/2*e*).

[2] *Duck* v. *Doubleday*, (1638), Cur. Mil. Boxes 10/12/4.

[3] (1631), 3 St. Tr. 483.

[4] *R.* v. *Page*, [1954] 1 Q.B. 170, per Lord Goddard C.J. at p. 175.

[5] *Rea* v. *Ramsay* (1631), 3 St. Tr. 483, per the Earl of Arundel E.M. at p. 506, as to treason.

Act, 1543, section 1, which provided that treason committed out of the realm could be tried by jury before the judges of the Court of King's Bench in any county or before commissioners.[1] Section 7 of the Treason Act, 1554, provided that all trials for treason should be 'had and used only according to the due order and course of the common laws of the realm', but it was held in 1631 by Lord Coventry L.K. and all the judges of the Court of King's Bench (Hyde C.J. *dissentiente*) that neither this Act nor the Act of 1543 took away the jurisdiction of the Court of Chivalry in respect of treasons committed out of the realm.[2]

A conviction in an appeal of treason in the Court of Chivalry did not cause corruption of blood or forfeiture at the common law.[3] Nevertheless, such proceedings had the advantage that one witness was sufficient, whereas two were required at common law.[4] *Rea* v. *Ramsey*[5] was the last case of this kind.

Although after the passing of the Treason Act, 1543, the common-law courts had a concurrent jurisdiction in cases of treason committed abroad, the position with regard to murders is not so clear. It was not until the passing of the Act 9 Geo. IV, c. 31, s. 7, that express powers similar to those of the Act of 1543 were given with respect to murder. Meanwhile no suggestion that the jurisdiction of the Court of Chivalry over murders committed abroad was not exclusive seems to have been made before 1709. It was then argued successfully in *R.* v. *Chambers*[6] that the Act 33 Hen. VIII, c. 23, authorized the trial by jury in any county of an indictment for murder committed abroad, and this has been followed

---

[1] This is one of the few enactments by virtue of which a bill of indictment may still be preferred before a grand jury (Administration of Justice (Miscellaneous Provisions) Act, 1933, Sch. I). S. 2 of the Act of 1543 saved the right of peers to trial by their peers. Privilege of peerage in relation to criminal proceedings was abolished by the Criminal Justice Act, 1948, s. 30 (1).

[2] *Rea* v. *Ramsey* (1631), 3 St. Tr. 483, 495. The Treason Act, 1554 (1 & 2 Ph. & M., c. 10) is there incorrectly cited as 1 Mar., c. 10.

[3] *Rea* v. *Ramsey, supra,* at p. 495.

[4] 3 Co. Inst. 26.   [5] *Supra.*

[6] (1709), Unrep., cited in *R.* v. *Sawyer* (1815), 2 C. & K. 101.

recently in *R.* v. *Page*.[1] The Act 33 Hen. VIII, c. 23, provided that commissioners of oyer and terminer should have power to hear and determine treasons, misprisions of treasons, and murders in any shire or place 'in whatsoever other shire or place within the King's dominions, *or without*, such offences . . . were done or committed'. Despite the words 'or without', contemporary opinion seems not to have regarded the extra-territorial operation of this Act as clear, for the preamble to the Treason Act, 1543, recites that 'some doubts and questions have been moved' whether by the common law treasons committed abroad could be tried in England. If 33 Hen. VIII, c. 23 had then been construed in the way in which it was later, the Act of 1543 would not have been necessary, for whatever may have been the extra-territorial operation of 33 Hen. VIII, c. 23, it specifically referred to treason as well as to murder. When the trial of Lord Rea was under consideration in 1631 the judges were of opinion that the Act of 1543 'devised a way how to try these foreign Treasons in England'[2] and made no mention of 33 Hen. VIII, c. 23. Furthermore, when the trial of offences committed in Newfoundland was under consideration by the Privy Council in January 1634, the Attorney-General, William Noy, advised that murder and theft committed in that country 'cannot be here impeached'.[3] By 'impeached' Noy must have meant tried by jury, for there was no doubt at that time that such a murder could be tried in the Court of Chivalry, the case of *Wise* v. *Holmes* being then pending.[4] If the Act 33 Hen. VIII, c. 23, had then been considered to bear the construction which it has borne since *R.* v. *Chambers*, Noy would not have given this advice. It is of some interest to notice that Noy's suggestion was that the King should exercise his prerogative of legislating for newly acquired dominions by issuing letters patent making murder or theft com-

---

[1] [1954] 1 Q.B. 170.   [2] 3 St. Tr. 495.
[3] *A.P.C. Col.* i. 193. I am indebted to Dr. A. R. Wagner, Richmond Herald, for this reference.
[4] See p. 54 *ante*.

mitted in Newfoundland triable by the Earl Marshal.[1]
It is, however, apparent that such a trial was not intended
to be a proceeding in the Court of Chivalry, for it was
provided that the evidence of two or more witnesses should
be required. Furthermore, the letters patent were to give
the Earl Marshal sole jurisdiction, whereas under the
Act 1 Hen. IV, c. 14, the Court of Chivalry had no power
to try an appeal of murder without a Constable. It would
appear that since Noy did not look with favour upon a
Court of Chivalry composed of a Constable and a Marshal,[2]
he wished the Earl Marshal to have an independent jurisdiction over murders committed in Newfoundland and that
there should be a similar jurisdiction over larcenies committed there.

During the period under consideration there were very
few cases of murder tried in the Court of Chivalry. The
jurisdiction was a very limited one, extending only to
cases in which one of the King's subjects was killed by
another of his subjects in a foreign country. Then the
widow or heir of the deceased could have an appeal.[3] The
Court had no jurisdiction over aliens.[4]

The Court had no jurisdiction in an appeal of murder
unless it was held before a Constable as well as the Earl
Marshal.[5] This was the reason for the failure of the attempt
made to bring Sir Francis Drake to trial in this Court in
1583 on an appeal of murder brought by John Doughty
in respect of the execution of the latter's brother after
a purported court martial during the voyage round the
world: the Queen was unwilling to appoint a Constable
and so 'the appeal slept'.[6] It appears that proceedings of

---

[1] *A.P.C. Col.* i. 194.   [2] See p. 52 *ante*.
[3] Co. Litt. 74. Cf. *Pounteney* v. *Borney* (1411), Y.B. 13 Hen. IV, Mich., pl. 10,
per Ireby J.
[4] Admission of defendant in *Wise* v. *Holmes* (1634), Cur. Mil. Boxes 8/21
that he and the party slain were the King's subjects.
[5] 1 Hen. IV, c. 14; *Parker's Case* (1668), 1 Lev. 230; *Cabala*, pt. i, 201.
[6] Co. Litt. 74*a* (Coke was counsel for Doughty (*Cabala*, loc. cit.); Inner
Temple MS. Petyt 538, f. 7; Duck, *De Usu et Authoritate Iuris Civilis*, p. 389.
The conflicting explanations of the abandonment of the proceedings given in
J. S. Corbett, *Drake and the Tudor Navy* (2nd ed., London, 1899), i. 320, and
E. F. Benson, *Sir Francis Drake* (London, 1927), p. 181, are both incorrect.

this kind were contemplated in 1618, for in Trinity term in that year the judges assembled in Serjeants' Inn to consider whether if a 'commission of the office of constable and marshal were granted by the King, the King might have any remedy before them by indictment, or information by the Attorney-General'.[1] In 1634 William Holmes was less fortunate than Drake, for the Earl of Lindsey was appointed Lord High Constable for the purpose of his trial for a murder committed in Newfoundland.[2]

Henry VIII's view that the Constableship was 'very [sic] hault et daungerous, et auxy verye [sic] chargeable al Roy in fees'[3] was apparently also held by Charles I, for the Earl of Lindsey was only appointed Lord High Constable for the specific purpose of trying particular appeals.[4] To appoint a Lord High Constable for the purposes of each particular trial was a cumbersome procedure. In the autumn of 1640 an ingenious attempt was made to obviate the necessity for it. During a quarrel at Bantam in the East Indies Thomas Godfrey, a mariner of Ratcliffe, co. Middlesex, beat another Ratcliffe mariner, William Hunter, with such severity that he afterwards died. Instead of instituting an appeal of murder, Hunter's widow commenced an ordinary cause of instance. Her libel, signed by Dr. Thomas Rives, alleged that by reason of Godfrey's acts she had lost the maintenance of herself and her family out of Hunter's wages of 40s. a month and further alleged loss of *consortium* ('et ulterius viri solatio carni et in presenti careo et in futurum durante vita caritura sum').[5] Unfortunately before it could be decided whether this libel disclosed any cause of action within the jurisdiction of the Court, the Court had been voted by the House of Commons to be a grievance and its sittings suspended.[6]

---

[1] *Anon.* (1618), Hut. 3.   [2] See p. 53 *ante*.

[3] *Duke of Buckingham's Case* (1514), Dyer 285b.

[4] His patent of appointment for *Rea* v. *Ramsey* is set out in 3 St. Tr. 496.

[5] *Hunter* v. *Godfrey* (1640), Acta Cur. Mil. (4), 11 (libel); Cur. Mil. Boxes 5/147, 176 (defendant's bonds).

[6] See p. 66 *ante*.

The Court had full power to deal with contempt of itself. In the case of parties obedience to interlocutory orders was obtained by means of commital for contempt.[1] Contempt by one who was not a party to a cause could be the subject of separate proceedings. Thus at the execution of the commission for the examination of the defendant's witnesses in *Owen* v. *Lloyd*[2] one of the commissioners, 'appearing as a party rather than an indifferent commissioner', interrupted the witnesses, not suffering them to depose anything but what he instructed them, and refused to sign any deposition in which anything was proved for the defendant. Upon the reading in open court of a certificate from the other commissioners, the Earl Marshal declared it fit that he should be examined upon interrogatories 'touching his carriage and abuse', and ordered process of monition against him to answer articles in a cause of contempt. Persons who were not litigants could also be proceeded against by means of a cause of office promoted by a litigant. Thus Thomas Bowen of the Middle Temple, who was plaintiff in a cause of 'scandalous words' against Humphrey Nichols of Lincoln's Inn, promoted such a cause of office against Guy Moulsworth of St. Andrew Holborn and William Garfoote of the Inner Temple, who met him near the gate of the Inner Temple, and derided and scoffed at him for taking Nichols to the Court of Chivalry.[3]

Should it be necessary to commit for contempt of the

---

[1] e.g. *Baleston* v. *Snell* (1639), Cur. Mil. Boxes 6/151.

[2] (1639), Cur. Mil. Boxes 6/141.

[3] *Bowen* v. *Nichols* (1635), Cur. Mil. Boxes 9/4/63; *Bowen* v. *Moulsworth*, ibid. 9/4/24. Moulsworth said: 'This is one of the gentlemen that petitioned my L: Marshall', swearing in a deriding manner, 'Zounds, what a redd face hee hath! itt would make a man forfeite fiue hundred poundes to looke upon him and his face, Zounds I cannott looke aside on him but hee will complayne to my L: Marshall on mee, and I shall forfeite my fyue hundred pound bond. I care not for your complainte, nor for my 500 li bond.' The opening sentence was a reference to Robert Napper of the Middle Temple who had taken proceedings against Moulsworth and Garfoote for challenging him to a duel. The defendants were convicted and imprisoned for some days before they were released on giving security for their good behaviour, in spite of which they derided and scoffed at Napper and challenged him again (*Napper* v. *Moulsworth* (1635), Cur. Mil. Boxes 9/4/31).

Court of Chivalry at the present time, the inherent jurisdiction of the High Court to punish contempts of inferior courts could be invoked. An 'inferior court' for this purpose is one which the High Court has power to correct by *certiorari* or prohibition.[1] The Court of Chivalry, although commonly dignified by the epithet 'High', is an 'inferior court' in this respect, for it is well settled that it can be controlled by prohibition.[2] Such an inferior court is protected by writ of attachment for contempt issued by a Divisional Court of the Queen's Bench Division.[3]

Having dealt with the cases in which the Court of Chivalry had jurisdiction, it is necessary to turn to a class of case in which the Court has been wrongly supposed to have jurisdiction, namely peerage cases.

Round's paper, 'Peerage Cases in the Court of Chivalry', was written with the object of establishing that under Elizabeth I and James I the recognized forum for the trial of claims to peerage dignities, on reference from the Crown, was the Court of Chivalry.[4] Since the Court of Chivalry is a civil-law court, it would be surprising to find that it had any jurisdiction over dignities, which are incorporeal hereditaments subject to limitations unknown to the civil law and which have been held to be tenements within the statute *De Donis Conditionalibus*.[5]

Round based his theory upon the assertion by Cruise that the court to which the crown usually referred such claims was that of the high constable and earl marshal where cases were determined by the rules and customs of chivalry.[6]

[1] *R.* v. *Davies*, [1906] 1 K.B. 32, 43; *R.* v. '*Daily Mail*' (*Editor*), *Ex parte Farnsworth*, [1921] 2 K.B. 733, 752.

[2] *Russel* v. *Oldish* (1692), 1 Show. K.B. 353. Prohibition also lay against the 'High' Court of Admiralty (*Jurado* v. *Gregory* (1669), 1 Sid. 418).

[3] *R.* v. '*Daily Mail*' (*Editor*), *supra; Ex parte Bishop of Norwich*, [1932] 2 K.B. 402.

[4] *Peerage and Pedigree*, i. 69–102. *C.P.* iv, App. H, 694, tacitly accepts Round's proposition by referring to 'the many peerage cases which have come before the ancient Earl Marshal's Court and the modern Committee for Privileges'. Round reiterated his view in *The King's Serjeants*, p. 78.

[5] *In re Rivett-Carnac's Will* (1885), 30 Ch. D. 136.

[6] W. Cruise, *A Treatise on the Origin and Nature of Dignities* (2nd ed., London, 1823), p. 249.

Cruise in his turn quoted the following statement by Milles:

For the desciding of sutes concerning honours, and for the preservation unto euery man the right of his fame or Dignity, the naturall *Tribunall*, seat or *Court* for the *Nobility* is euery where called by this name, *Militaris* (that is to say) the Martial or Military Court, and commonly the Court of Chivalry.[1]

The year before Cruise's work was published Moule had observed that Milles's *Catalogue* requires to be 'quoted with caution'.[2] It was indeed but a slender foundation for Round's 33-page paper. The expression 'sutes concerning honours' is hardly appropriate to claims to peerages, and in the next sentence Milles makes it apparent that he is writing of suits *inter partes*.[3] Read in their context the words 'sutes concerning honours' must mean suits in which the honour of the parties is involved, and not peerage claims, where there is no *lis inter partes*, but only a petition to the Crown.[4]

Both Cruise and Round support their theory by reference to a number of sixteenth- and seventeenth-century cases. Of these the earliest is the claim made towards the end of the reign of Henry VIII by Thomas Wymbish, the husband of Elizabeth, Baroness Tailboys, to be summoned to Parliament as a baron *jure uxoris*. This case is cited for the answer given by the two Chief Justices

that the common law dealeth little with the titles, and customs of chivalry. But such questions have always been decided before the constables and marshals of England.

Despite this statement, Wymbish's claim was not referred to the Earl Marshal (there being no Lord High Constable at that time), but was decided by the King himself,

---

[1] T. Milles, *The Catalogue of Honor* (London, 1610), p. 82.
[2] T. Moule, *Bibliotheca Heraldica* (London, 1822), p. 68.
[3] '. . . any plaintife either in case of dignity or of Armes, or of any other sute or Controuersie concerning *Nobility* and *Honour*, may sue the defendant'.
[4] In any event Milles was not purporting to be stating the position in his own time, for although the passage quoted by Cruise is in the present tense, Milles expressed the hope that James I would 'repaire the lamented ruines of that Iurisdiction' (op. cit., p. 83), and attributed the condition of the heralds to 'the want of the *Martiall Court*, or *Court of Chiualry*' (p. 86).

with the advice of the two Chief Justices, the Bishop of Winchester, a doctor of civil law and canon law, and Garter King of Arms.[1]

There seems to be no recorded instance of a peerage claim being decided before the Constable and the Marshal, but even if there were such a case, it would not follow that the Constable and the Marshal were sitting together in the Court of Chivalry. There were undoubtedly many peerage claims referred to the Earl Marshal or to Commissioners for executing his office during the period after there ceased to be a permanent Lord High Constable. Round gives particulars of fourteen such cases between 1569 and 1626, and goes on to state that it would be possible to compile 'an even fuller and more instructive list if the records of the Earl Marshal's court, in the custody of the College of Arms, were open to the public'.[2] In fact the records of the Earl Marshal's Court do not contain a single example of such a case. It would be rash to draw from the absence of records the conclusion that there were no such cases in that Court, for there is very little evidence of any kind of the work of the Court during the period covered by Round's list of cases. What can be stated with certainty is that none of the cases cited by Round contains any mention of the Earl Marshal's Court. This still leaves open the question whether the Earl Marshal (or the Commissioners) when dealing with peerage cases was sitting as the judge of the Court of Chivalry or in some other capacity.

The answer to this question is indicated in the proceedings relating to the barony of Dacre of the North in 1569. In that year the infant Lord Dacre died, leaving as his coheirs three sisters. His heir male was an uncle, who assumed the title. The stepfather of the coheirs was the Earl Marshal, Thomas, Duke of Norfolk, and he 'for avoiding all manner of suspicion of fauour to be shewed to them' petitioned the Queen to appoint some of her Council to determine the right to the Dacre barony,

[1] Collins, *Proceedings, Precedents and Arguments on Claims . . . concerning Baronies by Writ*, p. 11.
[2] Op. cit., p. 72.

'although the trial thereof of very right did belong to him *by reason of his office of Earl Marshal of England*, as matter incident to be decided before him *in respect of his said office*'. His position was made clear by the terms of the commission, which contained a proviso

> sauing always that the same should not be by any manner of means prejudicial, but that in such like causes of debate and controuersie that at any time hereafter shall happen or come in question, the said Duke, *by virtue of his said office of Earl Marshalship*, may hear, determine and adiudge the same, as though this Commission had been never granted.[1]

Similarly the letter sent by the Earl of Essex E.M. to Sampson Lennard in 1598 citing him to appear at the hearing of his claim to the barony of Dacre of the South contained a recital

> Whereas her Ma^te vppon yor humble peticon to enioy by her gratiouse fauo^r ye honor, and title of the Baronye of Dacres of ye South . . . hath comaunded me as Earle Marshall of Englande to heare, and examyne yor title, and claime thereunto.[2]

Despite the Earl Marshal's claim in 1569 that the trial of a peerage claim belonged to him 'of very right', there was no original jurisdiction in such matters inherent in his office. It was held in the Star Chamber in *Earl of Kent* v. *Rotherham* in 1597 that whilst the title to arms should properly be decided by the Earl Marshal and the Lord High Constable, the right to titles of honour and dignity, such as baronies and the like, was to be decided by the Crown as the fountain of honour.[3] Claims to peerages were made by petition addressed to the Crown. Putting the matter at its highest in favour of the Earl Marshal, it can only be said that to refer such petitions to him had become a well-recognized practice. Thus when the Earl

---

[1] C. G. Y[oung], 'Additions to Dugdale's Baronage' in *Coll. Top. et Gen.* v (1838), p. 323.

[2] Coll. Arm. MS. R. 19, f. 108.

[3] J. Hawarde, *Les Reportes del cases in camera stellata* (London, 1894), p. 66. This was supported by a reference to a dispute between the Earls of Arundel and Devon, which was a case of precedence (*C.P.* i. 249).

of Rutland claimed the barony of Roos of Hamlake in 1618 he asked in his petition that the matter should be referred to the Commissioners for executing the office of Earl Marshal.[1] This was done, but the decision was given by the King by letters patent and not by the Commissioners.[2] Similar requests for reference to the Commissioners were made in the petitions concerning the barony of Dacre in 1596, 1604, and 1612.[3]

The true nature of such a reference is shown by the subscription to the petition of Sampson Lennard for the Dacre peerage in 1604, which is in the following form:

> *Our pleasure is* that the Commissionours Marshall shall consider of this peticon and report to us the Trueth of the Case that we may determyne our pleasure.[4]

The existence of this practice seems to have led to some contemporary confusion of thought. Sir William Segar, Garter King of Arms, in a paper entitled 'The Earl Marshal his Office both in Peace and War',[5] after giving a general account of the 'Court Marshal', states that a claim to a dignity was made by petition to the King, who referred it to be 'iudicially heard in the Court Marshal'. That this identification of the Earl Marshal acting upon a reference from the Crown with the Earl Marshal sitting as judge of the Court of Chivalry is inaccurate is shown by the fact that the reference to the Earl Marshal of a petition for a peerage was not a matter of course.

When Sir Thomas Fane petitioned for the barony of

---

[1] Collins, op. cit., p. 162.

[2] Ibid., p. 172. In the *Dacre Peerage Case* (1604) the decision was given by the Commissioners with the 'privity and assent' of the King (ibid., p. 29).

[3] Ibid., pp. 26, 29, 30.

[4] Coll. Arm. MS. I. 25, f. 27.

[5] Bodl. MS. Ashm. 856, p. 431, printed in J. Guillim, *A Display of Heraldry* (6th ed., London, 1724), p. 40. Internal evidence shows that this paper was written after the accession of Charles I and therefore after the Earl Marshal had 'restored and settled' the procedure of the Court of Chivalry (see p. 46 *ante*), yet Segar states that the lawyers practising in the Court were 'Serieants and Counsellors of the Law, and sometimes Doctors and Proctors of the Ciuil Law, as the Cause doth require'. This is untrue so far as the 'Serieants and Counsellors of the Law' were concerned and tends to cast doubt upon the legal accuracy of the remainder of Segar's account of the Court.

Abergavenny in 1588 he submitted the cause to the Queen and 'the learned doom and censure of such, as she shall be pleased to appoint hearers and discussers thereof'.[1] Round does not draw attention to these words in Fane's petition, but states: 'That his claim would come before the Marshal's Court he seems to have taken for granted.'[2] In support of this statement Round quotes the following passages from Fane's petition:

> Forasmuch as the state of this challenge and claim is for the title of a barony, being a matter of nobility and chivalry, . . . the high constable and marshal of England the usual judges thereof in time past. . . .[3]

> That the question touching the barony of Bargavenny is not determinable by the common laws of this realm may well be proved by sundry presidents of pleadings in the like cases, usually wont to be heard and determined in the court of chivalry before the high constable and marshal of England.[4]

Fane was not taking it for granted that his claim would come before the Earl Marshal's Court. He was saying that his claim was the kind of claim of which the Constable and Marshal in the Court of Chivalry were the usual judges *'in time past'*. His reason for saying that was to found an argument that because the Constable and Marshal did not proceed according to the common law, his claim was not determinable by the common law. This is made clear by the words omitted by Round from the first passage in the petition which he cited. The omitted words are italicized.

> Forasmuch as the state of this challenge and claim, is for the title of a barony, being a matter of nobility and chivalry, *the questions thereof, and the manner of trials, are not wont to be made by juries after the course of the common law, but by depositions and proofs, after the manner of the civil law; and therefore* the high constable and marshal of England, the usual judges thereof in time past, *were accustomed to call divers doctors in the civil law, and officers of armes to assist them.*

---

[1] Collins, op. cit., p. 61. [2] *Peerage and Pedigree*, i. 79.
[3] Collins, op. cit., p. 63. [4] Ibid., p. 64.

Fane's petition is not authority for the proposition that the Earl Marshal's Court was the recognized forum for peerage cases in his own day. As an authority for the proposition that the Constable and Marshal were the usual judges of such cases 'in time past' (which could only refer to a period before the death of the Earl of Derby in 1504, since when there had been no *de facto* Constable) it is of very doubtful validity in the absence of any record of such a case tried by them.[1] Furthermore, Fane's statement is at variance with the refusal of the Court of Star Chamber in *Earl of Kent* v. *Rotheram* to adjudicate upon the descent of a barony on the ground that it should be decided by the Crown as the fountain of honour.[2] His argument that peerage claims were not determinable by the common law is not borne out by other cases. In deciding Thomas Wymbish's claim to the barony of Tailboys *jure uxoris* Henry VIII sought advice as to the common law from the two Chief Justices and as to the civil law from the Bishop of Winchester and in making his decision preferred the common law.[3] The Earl of Essex E.M. told the claimant to the barony of Dacre of the South that he would hear what might be said 'by the lawes of this realme, or the lawes and customes of honor and armes'.[4]

The position is accurately stated in the introductory part of Fane's petition quoted above before he proceeds to discuss the law applicable to the case. The matter was submitted to the Queen and those whom she would be pleased to appoint 'hearers and discussers' of it. The 'hearers and discussers' were frequently the Earl Marshal or the Commissioners for executing his office. In 1569 the Earl Marshal claimed that this was so as of right,[5] but that this claim of right was not accepted by the Crown is shown by the proceedings on the claim of Richard Bertie to the barony of Willoughby in 1580. His petition

---

[1] The procedure for the determination of peerage claims before 1504 is examined in Appendix XXVII, p. 276 *post*.

[2] See p. 156 *ante*.

[3] Collins, op. cit., p. 11.

[4] Coll. Arm. MS. R. 19, f. 108. See p. 156 *ante*.

[5] See p. 155 *ante*.

was referred to Lord Burleigh, Lord High Treasurer, the Earl of Sussex, Lord High Chamberlain, and the Earl of Leicester.[1] This case and the claim of Henry Vernon to the barony of Powys, which was referred to Burleigh and Sussex in 1584, were cited by Round as examples of peerage cases in the Court of Chivalry.[2] These peers were not, however, Commissioners for executing the office of Earl Marshal. Both in 1580 and 1584 the Earl Marshalship was held by the Earl of Shrewsbury, and if the claim made by his predecessor in 1569 had been regarded as valid, it would have been he to whom the Willoughby and Powys claims should have been referred.

When James I set up his new order of baronets he referred disputes concerning it to the Commissioners, but here again, although Round suggests that the jurisdiction of the Court of Chivalry included claims to baronetcies,[3] such matters only came before the Commissioners by virtue of special references from the King. Thus in 1620 Sir Francis Crane petitioned the King to refer to the Commissioners a dispute with Sir Samuel Tryon, who had promised to pay £2,100 on Crane's procuring him to be made a baronet, like Sir Nicholas Bacon, but refused to do so because of some difference between his patent and Bacon's.[4]

Although not cited by Round, some support for his view is at first sight to be found in *Edisbury* v. *Broughton*,[5] where the right to a baronetcy was called in question in a cause of office. The grant of the baronetcy in 1644 had not been enrolled, but the right was established by the

---

[1] Collins, op. cit., p. 23.

[2] Op. cit., pp. 73, 74.

[3] *Peerage and Pedigrees*, i. 69. Round supports his argument by reference to the case of Sir Thomas Harris (which he wrongly dates 1662), where the King directed the Earl Marshal that proceedings should be 'according to the customs and usage of the Court Marshal', but in that case the matter in dispute was not Harris's right to the baronetcy, but whether he was qualified as a gentleman of blood and coat armour to receive a baronetcy: see *Leeke* v. *Harris* (1623), Her. Cas. 1.

[4] *C.S.P.D. 1619–1623*, p. 141. Tryon was imprisoned by the Commissioners for breach of an interlocutory order (ibid., p. 246).

[5] (1690), Her. Cas. 71.

production of the original letters patent.[1] Such a proceeding is, however, not to be confused with a claim to a baronetcy. The allegation against the defendants was that one of them falsely pretended to be a baronet and the other a baronet's widow. The case was in form and in substance similar to the causes of office promoted against those who falsely pretended to be esquires or gentlemen,[2] and bore no resemblance to a claim to a baronetcy.

[1] G.E.C., *Complete Baronetage* (Exeter, 1903), iii. 303, citing Le Neve's MS. Baronetage, states that an erasure in the patent over which the words 'Edward Broughton' had been inserted 'appeared plainly', but the case, however, was dismissed as being 'a matter of record' and accordingly belonging to the common law. This does not agree with the entry in the Act Book, which is the only extant record of the case in the Court of Chivalry.

[2] See p. 139 *ante*.

XII

THE LAW OF ARMS

THE Court of Chivalry is a civil-law court[1] and can proceed only in accordance with that law.[2] Conversely the common law does not apply to matters which fall within the jurisdiction of the Court of Chivalry.[3] As Fineux C.J. said in the *Duke of Buckingham's Case*,[4] the common-law judges have no experience of the 'ley darmes'. We may accept the reason given by Selden in his *Ad Fletam Dissertatio* why the civil law was received and retained in this Court, namely, that in military matters foreigners accustomed to the civil law were as frequently involved as natives.[5]

The basic rule is that the Court of Chivalry proceeds according to the customs and usages of the Court, except in cases omitted, and there it is governed by the civil law, *secundum legem armorum*.[6] Beyond this general statement it is not easy to go. There is no report of a case in which a judge of the Court has set out the reasons for his decision earlier than the present century.[7] Indeed, there is nothing to indicate that the early civilians paid any heed to the doctrine that 'no court can give a proper decision in any case without formulating to itself at the time of the

---

[1] Duck, *De Usu et Authoritate Iuris Civilis*, p. 395. Cf. Ridley, *View of the Civile and Ecclesiastical Law*, pp. 86, 89.

[2] Statutes 8 Ric. II, c. 5; 13 Ric. II, st. 1, c. 2.

[3] *R. v. Parker* (1668), 1 Sid. 353.

[4] (1514), Keil. 170, 172.

[5] D. Ogg, *Joannis Seldeni Ad* Fletam Dissertatio (Cambridge, 1925), p. 157. And see p. 13 *ante*.

[6] 4 Co. Inst. 125. Brydall, *Law of England relating to the Nobility and Gentry* (London, 1675), p. 66, contains no more on this point than a quotation from Coke. In *Blount's Case* (1737), 1 Atk. 295, this proposition is reversed, Lord Hardwicke L.C. stating that 'the Court of Chivalry proceed according to the rules of the Civil law, except in cases omitted, and there they are governed by the course and customs of chivalry and arms', but he cites Coke as his authority.

[7] *Manchester Corporation* v. *Manchester Palace of Varieties Ltd.*, [1955] P. 133 was the first such case.

decision the reasons on which such decision is based'.[1] Reasoned judgments do not appear to have been delivered in any of the courts in which the civilians practised before the eighteenth century.[2] Certainly the judges in the civil-law and ecclesiastical courts in England, unlike the common-law judges, did not regard themselves as bound by precedent until the end of that century.[3] The first ecclesiastical-law reporter, Dr. Joseph Phillimore, whose earliest case is dated 1809, stated that he first undertook the then unprecedented work of reporting the decisions of the ecclesiastical courts in the face of much opposition.[4]

Not only did the practitioners in the Court of Chivalry not produce reports, but they were not moved to write books on the law which they practised there.[5] We are therefore in the position of the historian of the common law before the Year Books, who has as primary evidence only the formal records of the courts.

Before considering what light is thrown on the substantive law administered in the Court of Chivalry by the surviving records of the Court, it is desirable to consider the general nature of that law. Although the Court proceeds according to the rules of the civil law, this does not mean that it is rigidly governed by the law of ancient Rome. Whilst the study of Roman law never entirely ceased, even during the darkest centuries of the Middle Ages, it lacked practical application until the great revival in the law schools of southern France and northern Italy in the eleventh century.[6] The outcome of this revival was the general acceptance throughout Western

---

[1] *Sullivan* v. *Sullivan*, [1947] P. 50, per Lord Merriman, P. at p. 51.

[2] Lee's *Reports*, which were not published until 1833, show that reasoned judgments were being delivered in the ecclesiastical courts as early as 1752. Sir William Burrell's *Reports*, published in 1885, are evidence for the practice in the Court of Admiralty from 1766.

[3] E. G. Roscoe, *Lord Stowell* (London, 1916), pp. 35–38.

[4] Phillimore's preface to Lee's *Reports*, p. ix. Lee's *Reports* were the notes made by a judge of the cases which he decided and were not the work of a reporter.

[5] For an account of the scanty literature on the subject see pp. 279–83 *post*.

[6] P. Vinogradoff, *Roman Law in Medieval Europe* (Oxford, 1929), pp. 41, 43.

Europe of a common stock of legal principles founded upon a basis of Roman law, which has been called 'the common law of all well governed Nations'.[1] It is not to be identified in every particular with the law of the *Corpus Juris Civilis*, but it was known as civil law and those who professed it were known as civilians. This revived civil law was no longer the law of an empire embracing most of the known world, and it had to be adapted by its practitioners to the needs of a diversity of nations.

In some matters this could only be done by agreeing to differ. The medieval civilians held it to be a rule of their law that titles and matters of honour and dignity were to be ordered and ruled according to the custom of every particular country.[2] 'In honoribus decernendis inspicienda est consuetudo regionis.'[3]

The result of the application of this rule in England was that for all practical purposes it was only the procedure of the Court of Chivalry that was governed by the civil law. The substantive law was recognized to be English. Thus in *Grey* v. *Hastings* one John Reppeley, whose evidence is of particular value because he was a notary, deposed in 1408 that he had heard ancient men at arms and heralds of arms discussing the parties' rights and concluded that the defendant had the better right 'according to the law of arms as used in England'.[4] This law was not only English, but peculiar to the Court of

---

[1] T. Ridley, *View of the Civile and Ecclesiastical Law*, p. 2. Cf. Senior, *Doctors' Commons*, p. 2; Lord McNair, *International Law Opinions* (Cambridge, 1956), iii. 408, 420.

[2] A. Collins, *Proceedings . . . on Claims . . . concerning Baronies by Writ*, p. 63; cf. ibid., pp. 5, 39, and the authorities there cited.

[3] An unnamed civilian cited in 'A Tract concerning the Court of the Earl Marshal of England' (B.M. MS. Add. 9021, ff. 58–59). Similarly there were matters in which the canon law in England differed from the canon law in operation on the Continent. For examples see R. C. Mortimer, *Western Canon Law* (London, 1953), p. 53.

[4] Wagner, *Heralds and Heraldry*, p. 24, citing Coll. Arm. MS. Processus in Curia Marescalli, ii. 491. The deposition of this witness does not appear in the printed *Account* of the case by C. G. Young (1841), but the pleadings there printed show that the case was to be tried according to the 'droict ley custume & usages Dengleterre' (p. 20), and Sir William Hoo in his evidence speaks of 'la custume d'armes Dengleterre' (p. 26).

Chivalry: cases were tried 'secundum legem et consuetudinem curie nostre militaris'.[1]

Although not administered by the common-law courts, this amalgam of English custom and civil-law procedure was recognized by the common lawyers. In 1459 Nedham J. said: 'The law of the Constable and Marshal is the law of the land and the law of our Lord the King. . . . We take notice of it.'[2] Nevertheless, its true nature was sometimes imperfectly understood. Gerard Legh said 'fewe Herehaughtes knowe the lawe of armes, neyther yet manye Ciuilians',[3] and then showed that he was in the same plight by observing that 'the lawe of Armes is most part directed by ye Ciuile lawe'.[4] Cruise went to the other extreme, saying that questions of chivalry 'were never determined according to the Roman law, but by the common law of England'.[5] There seems to have been some justification for the view expressed in argument in the *Abergavenny Peerage Case*[6] that 'to be a judge of marshal causes, and of cases of chivalrie . . . is a service that requireth more than ordinary understanding'. In truth, as might be expected from the fact that the lawyers who practised in the Court of Chivalry were learned in the canon and civil laws and practised in the ecclesiastical and admiralty courts, the relationship between the English law of arms and the civil law was exactly the same as that between English ecclesiastical law and the canon law on the one hand and that between English admiralty law and the civil law on the other. As Lord Blackburn pointed out in *Mackonochie* v. *Lord Penzance*,[7] the law administered in the ecclesiastical courts consists of such canons and constitutions ecclesiastical as have been allowed by general consent and custom within the realm. Once so allowed they are 'the King's ecclesiastical laws of

---

[1] *Puryman* v. *Cavendissh* (1397), Close Roll 21 Ric. II, p. 1, m. 5.
[2] *Paston* v. *Ledham*, Y.B. 37 Hen VI, Pasch., pl. 8.
[3] *Accedens of Armorie* (London, 1562), f. 35v.
[4] Ibid., f. 69v.
[5] W. Cruise, *A Treatise on . . . Dignities* (2nd ed., London, 1823), p. 250.
[6] (1588), Collins, op. cit., p. 71.
[7] (1881), 6. App. Cas. 424, 448.

England',[1] just as the law of the Constable and Marshal is 'the law of our Lord the King'.[2]

Similarly the civil law has no binding force or authority in English courts, though it may be quoted to illustrate principles generally admitted and received. Admiralty law is to be ascertained from the practice and judgments of its judges:[3] it is the English maritime law.[4] So the law of the Court of Chivalry is the English law of arms to be ascertained from the practice of the civilians who served it as judges and counsel. That law must be found or deduced from affirmative practice or judgments: neither principle nor proposition can be deduced from mere negative, i.e. by saying the point has never been treated in the Court of Chivalry.[5]

It must not be thought that the law of arms has always been concerned, as it now is, only with coats of arms and other heraldic matters. Cases concerning prisoners of war were described as being determined according to the law of arms,[6] as also were appeals of treason,[7] and it is a fair inference that the whole body of jurisprudence administered by the Court of Chivalry, covering what may be described as the business side of medieval warfare, was embraced within this expression.[8] It so happens, however, that the only medieval cases in the Court of which detailed accounts have survived are heraldic cases, so that the following attempt to deduce something of the law of arms from the records of the Court must inevitably fail to cover the whole subject.

---

[1] *Caudrey's Case* (1591), 5 Co. Rep. 1, 9. This passage appears not to be part of the decision, but of Coke's comment upon it. Cf. Mortimer, *Western Canon Law*, p. 59.   [2] See p. 165 *ante*.

[3] *The Gas Float Whitton No. 2*, [1896] P. 42, per Lord Esher, M.R., at p. 48.

[4] *The Gaetano and Maria* (1882), 7 P.D. 137, 143.

[5] Cf. *The Gas Float Whitton No. 2*, *supra*, at p. 48.

[6] *Totesham* v. *Garenseres* (1351), *Foedera*, v. 716; *Lydell* v. *Louthre* (1359), ibid. vi. 116.

[7] 'Solonc la ley & vsage d'Armes': *Rot. Parl.* iii. 604.

[8] The law of arms cannot, however, be defined as the law of the Court of Chivalry, for it was also administered by other tribunals, e.g. by the Council (see p. 12 *ante*) and the Seneschal of Gascony and Marshal of Bordeaux (Gascon Roll, 15 Nov. 1347, cited in Prynne, *Animadversions on the Fourth Institute*, p. 338).

In seeking light on the substantive law from the records of the Court we are not only hampered by the fact that there is no record of the reasons for the decisions, but also by the fact that in many, if not the majority, of cases no record of the decision itself survives. We are therefore to a great extent thrown back upon the pleadings and the depositions. This entails making the assumption that in general the pleaders applied their minds to the law correctly and that the evidence was directed to relevant matters. Such an assumption seems at first sight to be a rash one, but it becomes more reasonable when it is remembered that the Bar in Doctors' Commons was a very small one,[1] and that many of the advocates were also judges [2] In these circumstances it is not unfair to regard the pleadings and depositions as reflecting that *communis opinio* among the lawyers which is evidence of what the law is.[3] This view can be taken more confidently when it is found that the pleadings and depositions contain evidence of rules which are familiar to the modern practitioner in the Probate, Divorce, and Admiralty Division of the High Court of Justice. Thus in the numerous cases of 'scandalous words provocative of a duel' we frequently find provocation by the plaintiff set up as a defence.[4]

---

[1] e.g. there were only 38 advocates 'exercent' in 1684 (E. Chamberlayne, *Second Part of the Present State of England* (12th ed.), pp. 289–90), and 35 in 1714 (*The Laws of Honour*, pp. (35)–(36)).

[2] Nineteen of the 38 advocates in 1684 and 15 of the 35 in 1714 held judicial offices. Cf. Charles Dickens, *David Copperfield*, chap. xxiii: 'They are like actors: now a man's a judge, and now he is not a judge; now he's one thing, now he's another! now he's something else, change and change about; but it's always a very pleasant, profitable little affair of private theatricals, presented to an uncommonly select audience.'

[3] *Isherwood* v. *Oldknow* (1815), 3 M. & S. 382, 396; *Manchester Corpn.* v. *Manchester Palace of Varieties Ltd.*, [1955] P. 133, 149.

[4] e.g. *Argent* v. *Crayford* (1638), Cur. Mil. I, 187. In *Locke* v. *Grove* (1638), Cur. Mil. Boxes 11/32/2, the provocation was alleged to have come from the plaintiff's wife, who was alleged to have abused the defendant in a very immodest manner, saying to him in 'an upbraydeinge manner that her father was noe pissepott maker'. It would be difficult to find a provocation to a duel more remote than that in which Thomas, Earl Rivers, alleged that an actor, Richard Weekes, had said in the presence of one of the Earl's kinsmen, 'I am a better gentleman or as good a gentleman as any Darcy in England' (*Rivers (Earl)* v. *Weekes* (1635), Cur. Mil. Boxes 18/1*i*).

Here we have the 'conduct conducing' so often pleaded by the respondent in a divorce suit based on adultery. Similarly we find that a cause of action could be lost by condonation.[1] The defendant in *Claxton* v. *King*[2] set up a recriminatory plea that the words libellate were spoken in an ale-house while the parties were drinking and tippling together with other company.

By a parity of reasoning we can deduce that scandalous words were justiciable whether spoken to the plaintiff himself[3] or to a third party.[4]

Publication of the words was an ingredient of the cause of action, for in *Chaloner* v. *Heylin*[5] the defendant pleaded that the words complained of were sent in a sealed letter which was not published by the defendant to any third party and the plaintiff could have concealed its contents had he so desired. The mere fact that the words were such that they might provoke someone to a duel was not sufficient. The circumstances in which the words were spoken had to be such that the plaintiff would be likely to be so provoked. This is presumably why there are no cases of this kind in which the defendant was a woman. In *Greaves* v. *Knyveton*[6] the defendant pleaded that his admitted striking of the plaintiff was not intended to provoke a duel because the plaintiff was a clergyman.[7]

---

[1] e.g. *Bacchus* v. *Mountford* (1638), Cur. Mil. I, 141–53, where a witness deposed that the parties drank together after the speaking of the words complained of. Cf. *Coffyn* v. *Steevens* (1638), Cur. Mil. I, 55, where the defence alleges that the parties subsequently drank together and pledged each other. In *Sherard (Lord)* v. *Mynne* (1638), Cur. Mil. Boxes 10/12/2, the defendant pleaded a reconciliation before the Earl of Chesterfield.

[2] (1638), Cur. Mil. II, 250.

[3] e.g. *Rudd* v. *Lumley* (1637), Cur. Mil. I, 172.

[4] e.g. *Wortley* v. *Allott* (1638), Cur. Mil. I, 222, where the words were spoken to the plaintiff's servant. In *Jervoise* v. *Heather* (1637), Cur. Mil. Boxes 3/25, the plaintiff was a justice of the peace and the defendant told a constable that he was serving 'a Jackanape his warrant'. In *Knyveton* v. *Greaves* (1639), Cur. Mil. Boxes 8/14, the plaintiff was beyond the seas when the words were spoken in England.

[5] (1638), Cur. Mil. II, 28.

[6] (1638), Cur. Mil. Boxes 18/2*l*.

[7] This plea, though it may have been sound in law, was somewhat disingenuous, for the defendant brought cross-proceedings for scandalous words spoken by the clergyman (*Knyveton* v. *Greaves* (1638), Cur. Mil. Boxes 19/4*b*).

Edward Heylin of Minster Lovell pleaded that the letter which he wrote to Henry Chaloner of Oxford could not have been provocative of a duel because when it was written he was a sick man and altogether unfit for single combat, and he called a bachelor of medicine to give evidence as to his state of health at the time.[1]

The common-law doctrine of privilege for words spoken during judicial proceedings cannot have applied in proceedings in the Court of Chivalry. In *Bodurda* v. *Griffith*[2] the plaintiff complained that whilst he was being examined under a commission directed out of the Court of High Commission, one of the commissioners 'of set purpose in a disgraceful manner' told him that his evidence was 'a base untruth'. Similarly in *Le Strange* v. *Styleman*[3] the defendant was sentenced in respect of a petition tending to the scandal of the plaintiff delivered to the judges of assize.[4] In *Constable* v. *Constable*[5] the plaintiff's complaint was that the defendant, knowing him to be an esquire, had caused him to be styled 'gentleman' in a Star Chamber bill.[6] The defendant in *Claxton* v. *Tunstall*[7] went out of his way to be unnecessarily offensive when he said in his pleading in an action for debt that the plaintiff 'being heir apparent to a worthy knight had degenerated from his gentility'. His defence that these words were included by his counsel without his instructions or knowledge does not seem very convincing.[8]

It would be interesting to know whether the clergyman pleaded his cloth, but his defence, if any, has not survived. In *Morrice* v. *Fowlkes* (1639), Cur. Mil. Boxes 17/5*f*, the plaintiff alleged that when he said that he could not fight with a man clad in clerical attire, the defendant replied 'that if that was all the matter hee would pull of his Cassock and putt on his mans frize suite and then fight with mee'.

[1] *Chaloner* v. *Heylin* (1637), Cur. Mil. Boxes 1/4/7; Cur. Mil. II, 1–24.

[2] (1637), Cur. Mil. Boxes 3/13.   [3] (1639), Cur. Mil. Boxes 4/46.

[4] Cf. *Powell* v. *Rhodes* (1637), *C.S.P.D. 1637*, p. 569, where the defendant, a clergyman, had presented one of his parishioners to the ordinary for drunkenness and incontinency.   [5] (1640), Cur. Mil. Boxes 5/116.

[6] Cf. *Hooke* v. *Hatt* (1637), Cur. Mil. Boxes 13/10, where the defendant was alleged to have exhibited bills in the Court of Chancery against the plaintiff by the name of Humphrey Hooke alias Lyon in order to insult and injure him. The defendant did not plead that this disclosed no cause of action, but that it was done without his instructions (ibid. 13/2*e*).

[7] (1637), Cur. Mil. Boxes 8/8.   [8] Ibid. 17/4*j*.

The chief value of causes of 'scandalous words' for the present inquiry lies in the fact that the foundation of the jurisdiction was that the plaintiff was a gentleman[1] or an esquire.[2] An allegation to this effect was common form in every libel, and traverses of this allegation were very frequent. Sometimes the plaintiff went further and alleged that the defendant was of plebeian stock. The object of such an allegation on the part of the plaintiff seems to have been to discredit the defendant generally, for the Court's jurisdiction did not depend upon the defendant's lack of gentility, and there are many cases in which both the parties were of undoubted gentility.[3] Indeed, it was expressly found in *Roberts (Lord)* v. *Samuel*[4] that although the unsuccessful defendant had been alleged not to be a gentleman, he was a gentleman born of an ancient family bearing arms.

Such pleadings let in much evidence concerning the parties and their ancestors and kinsfolk. Whilst the evidence is often of great genealogical value, it also throws light upon the juristic character of the English gentleman. John Ball's famous question was sociological in intent, but it reflects a question of law. When Robert Willymot, yeoman, was disclaimed at the visitation of Derbyshire in 1611 he was found to have taken upon him the name and title of a gentleman 'contrary to the lawes of Armes in this Kingdome'.[5] If the taking of the name and title of a gentleman by Willymot was contrary to the laws of arms, the laws of arms must have provided who was entitled to

---

[1] In *Bland* v. *Clarke* (c. 1636), Cur. Mil. Boxes 7/23, the plaintiff was ordered to 'clear his gentility' in the current term on pain of his suit being dismissed, and it was ordered that he and his counsel should have access to his ancestor's patent and his pedigree which were in court as exhibits in another cause. Cf. *Baker* v. *Spenser* (1637), Her. Cas. 29.

[2] In *Nunne* v. *Chamberlaine* (1638), Cur. Mil. Boxes 7/50, the plaintiff alleged in his petition that he was Serjeant of the Carriage Horse to the King and so an esquire 'by his place', upon which the King's Advocate subscribed the petition: 'I take the Petitioner to bee sufficiently qualified to seeke his remedy in my L. Marshall's Court.'

[3] e.g. *Stepney* v. *Williams* (1638), Cur. Mil. I, 8–36, 88–138; *Leonard* v. *Engham* (1640), Cur. Mil. II, 46–47.

[4] (1638), Cur. Mil. Boxes 4/12, 18.

[5] *Chitting* v. *Willymott* (1635), Her Cas. 20.

that name and title. During the period covered by the bulk of the records of the Court of Chivalry, whether a man was a gentleman was a question of law of practical importance and it was an issue raised in many of the cases before the Court. At first sight it is not easy to discover from the records how the law stood. What is immediately apparent is that A. C. Fox-Davies stated it much too narrowly when he wrote:

> Nothing a man can do or say can make him a gentleman without formal letters patent of gentility—in other words, without a grant of arms to himself or to his ancestors, either near or far removed.[1]

It is true that the possession of a coat of arms was sometimes put forward in the Court of Chivalry as evidence of gentility,[2] but it was evidence of gentility, not because the possession of a coat of arms made a man a gentleman, but because only a gentleman was qualified to bear arms.[3] The more usual course was for a litigant to prove his gentility by evidence that he had always lived in the manner of a gentleman and was so reputed.[4]

This is in accord with the opinion of Doderidge J. (d. 1628), which was:

> Gentlemen have their beginning, either of blood, as that they are borne of worshipfull Parents, or that they had expedited some-

---

[1] 'X', *The Right to Bear Arms*, p. 32.

[2] The libel in *Tichbourne* v. *Allden* (1688), Cur. Mil. Boxes 21/3, in order to show that the plaintiff was qualified to take proceedings for 'scandalous words', opens with an allegation that he was entitled to the arms shown in an annexed painting. In *Garton* v. *Bland* (*No. 2*) (1636), Her. Cas. 116, a witness deposed that he was a gentleman 'having purchased his Armes'. In *Richardson* v. *Hardwicke* (1640), Cur. Mil. 1631-40, 139-42, the plaintiff's apprentice deposed that he had seen an escutcheon of arms which the plaintiff said he had had from the heralds.

[3] *Duck* v. *St. George* (1638), Her. Cas. 33 (cause of office against Norroy and Somerset in which it was alleged that they had granted arms to one who was not a gentleman). It is to prevent this that the Earl Marshal's warrant is required before arms can be granted: see *Leigh* v. *Lye* (*No. 2*) (1688), Her. Cas. 53, 56, 57.

[4] e.g. *Eure* v. *Harris* (1640), Cur. Mil. II, 123-9. In *Rodes* v. *Slater* (1637), Cur. Mil. I, 268, 277, the defendant supported such evidence of general reputation by calling a witness to prove that his father and grandfather had been freeholders and headman of their parish, that the father had been collector of a subsidy and headborough and constable, and that the defendant's grandmother was descended from the Eyres of Keeton.

thing in peace or warre, whereby they deserve to have armes, and to be accounted Gentlemen.

But in these dayes he is a Gentleman, who is so commonly taken, and reputed, Doctor *Ridley* 96. And whosoever studieth in the Vniversities, who professeth the liberall sciences, and to be short, who can live idly, and without manuall labour, and will beare the Port, charge, and countenance of a Gentleman, he shall bee called Master: For that is the title that men give to Esquires, and other Gentlemen: For true it is with us, as one said; *Tanti eris aliis quanti tibi fueris*: and if need be, a King of Heralds shall give him for money armes newly made, and invented with the Creast and all: the title whereof shall pretend to have bin found by the said Herauld, in the perusing and viewing of old Registers, where his ancestors in time past had beene recorded to beare the same: or if he will doe it more truly, and of better faith, hee will write, that for the merits of, and certaine qualities that he doth see in him, and for sundry noble acts which he hath performed, hee by the authority which he hath, as King of Heralds in his Province, and of armes, giveth unto him and his heires, these and these heroicall bearings in arms, *vide Smith de Republic. Anglorum.*[1]

John Brydall, writing in the second half of the seventeenth century, sought to rationalize this by dividing gentlemen into four sorts, namely (1) gentlemen by birth; (2) gentlemen by office; (3) gentlemen by reputation; and (4) gentlemen by creation.[2] There is, however, no evidence of such a classification in the records of the Court of Chivalry. Apart from the comparatively few cases in which a right to arms was relied upon as direct proof, the evidence is simply evidence of reputation— primary facts from which an inference of gentility could

---

[1] *The Magazine of Honour* (1642), pp. 147–8. This work, which is stated on the title-page to be 'collected by Master Bird, But, perused and enlarged by ... Sir Iohn Doderidge Knight, one of his Majesties Iudges of the Kings Bench', consists of the argument of Doderidge, Sjt. (as he then was) in the *Abergavenny Peerage Case* (1588) (T. Moule, *Bibliotheca Heraldica* (London, 1822), p. 130; Round, *Peerage and Pedigree*, i. 77). The pagination is eccentric. Moule states that there are 158 pages, but there are 223, the numbers 105–58 being repeated on what should be pp. 171–223. The passage cited begins on the second p. 147.

[2] Brydall, *Law of England relating to the Nobility & Gentry*, p. 57. Cf. the elaborate classification of gentlemen in Ferne, *Blazon of Gentrie*, pp. 89–90. Both Brydall and Ferne were common lawyers.

be drawn.[1] Conversely a man could be a gentleman even though he was not entitled to arms.[2]

The definition of a gentleman in the Court of Chivalry seems to have been 'one who is reputed to be a gentleman' —a definition reminiscent of the well-known definition of an archdeacon as one who performs archidiaconal functions. Whilst the imprecision of such a definition may be distasteful to the common lawyer, it was a concept which would have been readily acceptable by the practitioner in the Court of Chivalry by reason of his work in the ecclesiastical courts. There he had to deal with cases, such as presentments for fornication, which were decided by reference to 'common fame' or 'public fame'.[3]

Whatever may have been the original meaning of the word 'gentleman',[4] Fox-Davies was centuries behind the times when he wrote:

The less abrupt gradation of ranks, and a mistaken 'courtesy' adopted by society in general, have caused the word 'gentleman' to be applied in an idiotic manner to anyone whose education, profession, or perhaps whose income, raises him above the lower level of ordinary trade or menial service, or even to a man of polite and refined manners and ideas. Such an idea is absolutely wrong.[5]

This 'absolutely wrong' idea is an accurate statement of the law administered in the Court of Chivalry.

Many and varied were the facts adduced to found an inference that a man was or was not a gentleman. The defendant in *Wheeler* v. *Sheffield*[6] produced a certificate

---

[1] For the distinction between primary facts and the inferences to be drawn from them see per Denning J. in *Bracegirdle* v. *Oxley*, [1947] K.B. 349, at p. 358; per Denning L.J. in *British Launderers' Research Association* v. *Borough of Hendon Rating Authority*, [1949] 1 K.B. 434, at p. 471; and per Lord Evershed M.R. in *Chivers & Sons Ltd.* v. *Cambridge County Council*, [1957] 2 Q.B. 68, at p. 77.

[2] *Stepkin* v. *Dobbins* (1638), Her. Cas. 30, 32, 33. The three Kings of Arms certified that the defendant was not a gentleman of coat armour, but the defendant obtained a suspension of the execution of the definitive sentence which had declared him not to be a gentleman on the ground that the Kings of Arms had never denied that he was a gentleman.

[3] R. Burn, *Ecclesiastical Law* (4th ed, London, 1781), iv. 23–24.

[4] For some account of changes in the meaning see Sir George R. Sitwell, 'The English Gentleman' in *The Ancestor*, i (1902), 58–103.

[5] 'X', *The Right to Bear Arms*, p. 31.

[6] (1640), Cur. Mil. II, 181.

under the hand and seal of arms of the Earl of Mulgrave
that he was of kindred to the Earl. Sometimes military
rank was relied on. Thus the defendant in *Vicars* v.
Hudson[1] added to his statement that he lived in the 'ranke,
quality, fashion and reputation of a gentleman' that he
was captain of a trained band of soldiers in Surrey, whilst
the plaintiff in *Mascall* v. *Sole*[2] was alleged to be lieutenant of a troop of horse in Sussex. In *Longvyll* v. *Hawthorne*[3] the defendant pleaded that he had been named
with the addition of 'gentleman' amongst other commissioners in various commissions for the examination of
witnesses issuing out of the Star Chamber and the Court
of Chancery.

Reliance was frequently placed on the father's position,
it being considered relevant that he was a justice of the
peace[4] or a barrister,[5] or that he was educated in the
University of Oxford and was afterwards taught the law
of the land,[6] or even that he was called 'Mr. Rigby' and
never 'Goodman Rigby'.[7] In *Temple* v. *Ayleworth*[8] the
'scandalour words' complained of were that the defendant
had said that the plaintiff was no gentleman, but the son
of an abbot's bailiff.

Sometimes the mother's descent was relied upon,[9] and
occasionally a remoter relation was prayed in aid by a
litigant, as in *Rumsey* v. *Rogers*,[10] where the plaintiff showed
that his uncle had been High Sheriff of Brecknock about
twenty years previously, and in *Stepkin* v. *Dobbins*,[11] where
the defendant relied on deeds in which his great-grand-

---

[1] (1639), Cur. Mil. Boxes 14/3*n*.

[2] (1637), Acta Cur. Mil. (4), 32.

[3] (1634), Her. Cas. 9.

[4] e.g. *Leeming* v. *Clopton* (1637), Her. Cas. 25; *Long* v. *Sticklowe* (1638), Cur.
Mil. II, 142–9.

[5] *Hudson* v. *Vicars* (1638), Cur. Mil. II, 91–97.

[6] *Stepkin* v. *Dobbins* (1638), Her. Cas. 30.

[7] *Rigby* v. *Hardham* (1640), Cur. Mil. 1631–42, 220–7. Cf. *Rodes* v. *Slater*
(1637), Cur. Mil. I, 268–77, where some of the defendant's father's neighbours
called him 'Mr. Slater' and some 'Goodman Slater'.

[8] (1634), Her. Cas. 7.

[9] e.g. *Leeming* v. *Clopton, supra,* at p. 26; *Stepkin* v. *Dobbins* (1638), Her. Cas.
30.

[10] (1639), Cur. Mil. I, 5–6.   [11] (1638), Her. Cas. 30.

father and great-great-grandfather had been described as gentlemen.

There was a similar variety in the evidence by which it was sought to negative gentility. In *Ivat* v. *Harding*[1] the defendant sought to apply the strictly heraldic test, saying that he had searched 'some office in London' for it and had not found that the plaintiff was a gentleman. Usually, however, the criteria were less precise. In *Eyre* v. *Keresforth*[2] it was deposed that the defendant could not be a gentleman because his mother used to ride to market upon a pair of panniers to sell butter or soap. In *Norton* v. *Buggs*[3] the defendant pleaded that the plaintiff was but an apothecary, who was said to have obtained the title of 'Doctor of Physick' at Padua 'or some other part beyond the seas'. The defendant in *Ingepen* v. *Penny*[4] pleaded that he lived in 'the rank, quality and fashion of a gentleman', but that the plaintiff lived as a yeoman, alleging that he

laboureth in husbandry ordinarily with his owne hands, holdeth the plough, maketh hay, selleth his Corne att the markett himselfe, and keeps noe man or attendant on him but such as are imployed in laboureing and husbandry, and in the parrish rates and other writeings hee is only written Richard Inckpen without the addition of gentleman to his name.[5]

Richard Ingepen seems to have been of the same standing as William Crispe of Winchingham, co. Cambridge, who was described as 'an ordinary country fellowe'.[6] The defendant in *Warner* v. *Cadyman*[7] said that the plaintiff's kinsmen were none but butchers and graziers, and whilst it was admitted that some called the defendant in *Killiow* v. *Cullis*[8] 'Master', it was pleaded that he was not reputed to be a gentleman.

Allegations that plaintiffs were esquires were supported by evidence which was more precise. John Pincombe

[1] (1637), Cur. Mil. II, 71–84. [2] (1638), Cur. Mil. Boxes 11/38*e*.
[3] (1638), ibid. 9/3/6. [4] (1638), ibid. 9/3/5.
[5] Of more local interest is the plea in the same case that Regarders of the New Forest are for the most part yeoman and not gentlemen.
[6] *Castell* v. *Crispe* (1639), Cur. Mil. Boxes 2/128.
[7] (1639), Cur. Mil. Boxes 2/125.
[8] (1639), Acta Cur. Mil. (4), 106–10.

of Poughill, co. Devon, called a witness to depose
that he 'was and is commonly accounted reputed and
taken to bee an Utter Barrister having studyed in y^e
Middle Temple London and therefore an Esqr as hee
believeth for hee is commonly called by the name of
Esqr'.[1] In order to prove that he was an esquire, Robert
Dixon, Secretary to the Lord Privy Seal, exhibited a
certificate by the clerk of the peace that he was in the
commission of the peace and of the quorum for the city
and liberties of Westminster.[2] Of a more specialized
nature was the statement in the petition of Henry Nunne
of St. Martin-in-the-Fields, co. Middlesex, that he had
been Gentleman of the Carriage Horse, first to Prince
Henry and then to Prince Charles, and afterwards sworn
Serjeant of the Carriage Horse to the King, whereby he
had been since the beginning of the reign of Charles I an
esquire 'by his place'.[3]

The effect upon gentility of engaging in trade gave rise
to much controversy. Trade in itself was not inconsistent
with gentility. One who was a clothier by trade could still
allege that he was a gentleman and proceed against
another clothier who denied it.[4] Edward Done of Duddon,
co. Chester, deposed that he was 'a gentleman by birth
and a linen draper by trade'.[5] One of the matters in issue
in *Leeming* v. *Clopton*[6] was the possibility of a soap-boiler
being also a gentleman. The defendant pleaded that the
plaintiff was not accounted a gentleman, but a soap-
boiler. Against this the plaintiff contended that 'many
Citizens of great worth and esteeme discended of very
ancient gentile familyes' were soap-boilers, and that
citizens so descended (notwithstanding their trade of
soap-boiling) enjoyed the privilege and dignity of gentlemen. This was supported by one of the defendant's
witnesses, who in answer to interrogatories said that those

[1] *Pincombe* v. *Prust* (1640), Cur. Mil. Boxes 16/4c.
[2] *Dixon* v. *Hulker* (1638), Cur. Mil. Boxes 18/3e.
[3] *Nunne* v. *Chamberlaine* (1638), Cur. Mil. Boxes 7/50.
[4] *Mantell* v. *Samson* (1635), Her. Cas. 21.
[5] *Done* v. *Babington* (1640), Cur. Mil. Boxes 8/13.
[6] (1637), Her. Cas. 25.

who were gentlemen and soap-boilers did not lose their gentility, adding that the plaintiff maintained his wife and children as became the degree of a gentleman. The key to the matter seems to lie in the defendant's plea in *Starkey* v. *Bestney*[1] that the plaintiff had publicly exercised 'base and mechanical arts' as a tailor and broker and seller of remnants of cloth. The line between 'base and mechanical arts' and occupations consistent with the rank of gentleman must have been a difficult one to draw precisely. The attempt to draw it led to such niceties of argument as are found in *Brome* v. *Woodman*,[2] where the plaintiff replied to a plea that he was a goldsmith and sometimes worked 'at the forge and anvill' with a witness who deposed that he had never seen him wear a leather apron.

Sometimes an allegation of gentility was traversed on the ground that it had been lost. In *Mantell* v. *Samson*[3] the defendant sought to impugn the plaintiff's gentility on the ground that one of his paternal ancestors had been attainted and executed for his part in Sir Thomas Wyatt's rebellion in 1554. Gentle rank could not only be lost by attainder. A sentence by the Court of Star Chamber to stand in the pillory not only deprived the party sentenced of all offices, titles, and dignities, but also made him and his posterity 'incapable of bearing arms or assuming the degree and dignity of gentlemen'.[4] In *Sibthorpe* v. *Hursler*[5] the plaintiff alleged that the defendant had lost his gentility by being Groom of the Stable to the King.

It would appear that not only must the plaintiff in a cause of scandalous words have been a gentleman, but that the defendant must have known or have had reasonable ground to believe that he was, for in *Woodcocks* v. *Bacon*[6] a witness deposed that he did not know 'by what manifest signes it should appeare unto the defendant or his neighbors that the Plaintiff was or is a gent.', but added that the plaintiff had worn 'such decent habit as befitted his quality'.

---

[1] (1634), Her. Cas. 10.   [2] (1640), Cur. Mil. 1631–42, 162–9.
[3] (1635), Her. Cas. 21.   [4] *Garton* v. *Bland* (1636), Her. Cas. 23 n.
[5] (1640), Cur. Mil. 1631–42, 120.   [6] (1640), Cur. Mil. II, 240–9.

The records of the Court of Chivalry also afford evidence from which the law of England on the right to bear arms can be deduced. This is a matter which has given rise to much controversy—controversy which has been quite barren because the antagonists have failed to remember that the law of England on heraldic matters is not necessarily the same as the law of other countries.[1]

The contention that a man may take such arms as he pleases without any grant, subject only to the proviso that they have not been borne by anyone else before, is of respectable antiquity, being founded upon a passage in the *De Studio Militari* of Nicholas Upton written in the first half of the fifteenth century.[2] This passed freely into currency by being copied later in the fifteenth century by the author of the *Book of St. Albans*.[3] However, although Upton was an Englishman, his work was based upon that of a fourteenth-century Italian civilian, Bartolus of Sasso-Ferrato, reputed to be the earliest writer on heraldry. It is unfortunate that so much misunderstanding should have been propagated through the centuries in England by reason of Upton having been acquainted with the writings of Bartolus, for his view was not universally held, even on the Continent. There was a rival school of civilian writers which, in the words of Sir George Mackenzie of Rosehaugh, Lord Advocate of Scotland, 'very justly maintain'd, that none can assume Arms, but that all must owe them to Authority'.[4]

This may be the reason why not all English writers on arms followed the doctrine of Bartolus as slavishly as did Nicholas Upton. Thus John 'de Bado Aureo', whom

---

[1] See p. 164 *ante*. The following account of the law relating to the acquisition of arms is based upon the writer's *The Law of Arms in England* (East Knoyle [1953]).

[2] 'Meny by their owne auctoritie take armys upone them and to ther heyres. Nevertheless soche arms may frely and lawefully be borne, yff they be not borne by someother:' *Nicholas Upton's* De Studio Militari . . . *Translated by John Blount* . . . (*c. 1500*) (1931), p. 48. The original work was written before 1446 (*D.N.B., sub nom.* 'Upton').

[3] First printed in 1486; reprinted in Dallaway, *Inquiries into . . . Heraldry*, App. V, where the relevant passage is at p. cxii.

[4] *The Science of Herauldry, Treated as a part of the Civil Law, and Law of Nations* (Edinburgh, 1680), p. 11, and authorities there cited.

Professor E. J. Jones would identify as John Trevor, Bishop of St. Asaph, modified Bartolus's account of the manner in which arms may be acquired, saying that arms may be given by the King, a prince (i.e. one of the greater nobility), a king of arms, or a herald.[1]

One of the most important works on English medieval heraldry is the unpublished *Tractatus nobilis de lege et exposicione armorum*, written in the 1450's by Richard Strangways of the Inner Temple. Strangways expounded the law of arms from the English point of view in some detail. He was acquainted with the writings of Bartolus, to which he refers.[2] Yet he held that a man could not take arms 'without an herowd or percyvant'.[3]

In the next century another Inner Templar, John Ferne, flatly contradicted Upton's statement that a man may take arms of his own authority, blaming Bartolus for having led Upton astray.[4]

When we turn from the literary to the documentary evidence we find nothing to suggest that Bartolus's view had any legal validity in England and much to suggest that the English civilians applied an entirely different rule.

One of the earliest causes of arms in the Court of Chivalry of which a detailed record survives is *Scrope* v. *Grosvenor*, which commenced in 1385.[5] Each party called numerous witnesses to prove that he and his ancestors had used the disputed arms over a long period. Some have seen in this merely a contest as to which party's ancestor had first assumed of his own motion the golden bend on the azure shield, regarding the case as evidence for the acceptance in England of the law as laid down by Bartolus and his school.[6]

[1] E. J. Jones, *Medieval Heraldry* (Cardiff, 1943), p. 142.
[2] H. S. London, 'Some Medieval Treatises on English Heraldry', in *Ant. Journ.* xxxiii (1953), 174.
[3] B.M. Harl. MS. 2259, f. 109*b*. I am grateful to Mr. H. Stanford London, Norfolk Herald Extraordinary, for giving me a transcript of the portions of this manuscript relevant to the present inquiry.   [4] *Blazon of Gentrie*, p. 224.
[5] The record is printed in Nicolas, *The Scrope and Grosvenor Controversy* (1832), i. 1–357.
[6] e.g. W. Paley Baildon, 'Heralds' College and Prescription', in *The Ancestor*, viii (1904), 122.

The form in which the evidence is given makes it clear that *Scrope* v. *Grosvenor* is not an authority for this view of the law. Many of the witnesses stated that the arms had been borne from beyond the time of living memory by the ancestors of the party for whom they were giving evidence. The year 1385 also saw the beginning of another great armorial cause, *Lovel* v. *Morley*, where the arms in dispute were *Argent, a lion rampant sable, armed and crowned or.* In this case it was expressly pleaded by the plaintiff that his ancestors had borne the arms in question 'del tempe dont memoire ne court'.[1] These cases, it is submitted, show that an attempt was being made to prove user from time immemorial, which would give a good title under the civil law as under the common law.[2]

Under the common law time immemorial was deemed to date from the accession of Richard I in 1189, but the wording of the depositions in *Scrope* v. *Grosvenor* indicates that in the Court of Chivalry the Conquest was regarded as the limit of legal memory.[3] This is borne out by the case of *Carminow* v. *Scrope*, the only reliable account of which is to be found in the depositions of John of Gaunt, Duke of Lancaster, and other witnesses in *Scrope* v. *Grosvenor*.[4] According to these witnesses it was proved that Carminow's ancestors had borne *Azure, a bend or* since the time of King Arthur and that Scrope's ancestors had borne the same coat since the time of William the Conqueror. On this evidence, the nature of which is not specified, it was adjudged that both might bear the arms entire. This decision is only explicable on the basis that

[1] Coll. Arm. MS. Processus in Curia Marescalli, ii. 2.

[2] W. W. Buckland and A. D. McNair, *Roman Law and Common Law* (Cambridge, 1936), p. 103. Cf. Ferne, op. cit., p. 60.

[3] e.g. John Warde deposed that the disputed arms belonged to Scrope 'par discent de droit lynee & heritage depuis le Conquest' (*Scrope and Grosvenor Controversy*, i. 118), whilst Rauf de Ivre deposed that the arms had descended to Scrope 'par droit lynee & par descent de heritage dount memoir ne court' (ibid. i. 120). The same inference may also be drawn from the quitclaim by Walter Haywode in 1403 of the arms 'from the Conquest always borne' by the tenants of the fee, lands, and tenements of Haywode (*Collection of Miscellaneous Grants* (Harl. Soc. lxxvii, 1926), p. 220).

[4] Nicolas, op. cit., pp. 50, 62, 125, 146, 214. The relevants parts of these depositions are reprinted in *Visit. Cornwall* (Harl. Soc. ix, 1874), pp. vi, vii.

both parties were entitled to the coat by virtue of user from time immemorial. Had the right depended on prior assumption, Carminow would have been solely entitled to the exclusion of Scrope.[1] In *Lovel* v. *Morley* the plaintiff pleaded that the disputed arms had been borne by 'touts ses auntecessours devant luy de la Conquest'.[2] Again in *Grey* v. *Hastings*[3] in 1407 the plaintiff alleged that the arms in dispute—*Or, a maunch gules*—had been borne 'par temps dount memoire de home nest del contraire' and 'franchement et sans ascun chalenge ou contradiction dascun devant le Conquest'.

There is thus a substantial body of evidence that a right to arms was obtained by user from time immemorial and that in the Court of Chivalry time immemorial was deemed to date from 1066, and not from 1189.[4]

Confirmation of the view that self-assumed arms were not regarded as lawful in the medieval period is to be found in a writ directed by Henry V to the Sheriffs of Hampshire, Wiltshire, Sussex, and Dorset on 2 June 1417.[5] By this writ the Sheriffs were ordered to proclaim that no one should bear a coat of arms on the forthcoming expedition unless he possessed or ought to have possessed it in right of his ancestors, or by the grant of someone having sufficient power to make it, and that such a one should show by whose grant he held his arms, those who had borne arms with the King at the battle of Agincourt

---

[1] One of the witnessess in *Scrope* v. *Grosvenor* (John Topclyffe, p. 214) explains the decision in *Carminow* v. *Scrope* on the unconvincing ground that Cornwall was once a separate kingdom. There is another account of *Carminow* v. *Scrope* in *A Complete Parochial History of the County of Cornwall* (Truro, 1867–72), iii. 275–6. This is taken from a manuscript by William Hals (1655–1737) and states that Carminow was sentenced to bear the arms with a label for a difference. Hals's account bears signs of anachronism and may be an attempt to explain the label which was undoubtedly used by some of the later Carminows.

[2] Coll. Arm. MS. Processus in Curia Marescalli, ii. 10.

[3] *Account*, p. 8.

[4] As late as 1639 we find William Hamersley of Hamersly, co. Stafford, pleading that he and his ancestors had been gentleman bearing arms ever since the Conquest (*Hamersley* v. *Cliffe*, Her. Cas. 42).

[5] Printed in *The Right to Bear Arms*, pp. 44–45. Although Fox-Davies's interpretations cannot always be accepted, his book is a valuable repository of the texts of a number of documents of heraldic interest.

only excepted. In view of what will appear later it is important to observe the exact wording of the relevant part of this writ:

Quod nullus cujuscunque status, gradus, seu conditionis fuerit, hujusmodi Arma sive Tunicas Armorum in se sumat, nisi ipse jure antecessorio, vel ex donatione alicujus ad hoc sufficientem potestatem habentis, ea possideat aut possidere debeat.

Some have read into this a statement that previously men had assumed arms of their own motion and have construed the writ as an attempt by the Crown to prevent this for the future, with a saving for those who fought at Agincourt. The writ was not, however, legislation, its object being to regulate the army on a particular expedition, and it seems more consistent with that object to regard the exception of those who had fought at Agincourt, not as conferring a sort of 'battle honour' upon all who had fought there, but as showing that they had for the purposes of that occasion proved their right to their arms, and relieving those of them proceeding on the later expedition from the necessity of repeating the proof.[1] Whatever may have been the position of those who fought at Agincourt, the writ does not warrant the suggestion that Englishmen in general had any right to use a new coat otherwise than by virtue of a legally valid grant.

The heralds acted upon the principle above deduced from *Carminow* v. *Scrope* and *Scrope* v. *Grosvenor* in confirming arms. Thus in 1454 Clarenceux King of Arms confirmed to John Aleyn the arms which 'his progenitours out of mind have borne'.[2] In 1456 Guyan King of Arms

---

[1] An intermediate view is suggested in Nicolas, *History of the Battle of Agincourt*, p. 170, namely that the use of arms at the battle was constituted by the writ a sufficient title for their being continued, but did not create any privilege of subsequently adopting arms in consequence of their service on that occasion. The story told by Juvenal des Ursins that Henry V promised to ennoble such of his company as were not already noble, and so that their nobility might be known, gave them permission to wear collars of SS. of his livery, might suggest a somewhat different interpretation of the 1417 writ, but it seems better to accept the view put forward by Nicolas (op. cit., p. 98) that 'the improbability of this circumstance is too obvious to entitle it to any credit'.

[2] *Collection of Miscellaneous Grants* (Harl. Soc. lxxvi, 1925), p. 2.

confirmed arms which John Bangor and his progenitors 'time out of mind had borne',[1] and in 1470 Norroy King of Arms certified to the Prior of Bridlington certain arms 'which armes of their family were for there ancesters by what right they were due to them for ever neither can tongue expresse or the memory of man recollect'.[2]

Proof of actual user from so remote a time as before 1189 must have presented extreme difficulty, whilst proof of user before 1066 was, of course, impossible. The nature of the evidence of user adduced in *Scrope* v. *Grosvenor* shows that the Court of Chivalry was prepared to hold that evidence of user during the time of living memory raised a presumption that the user had continued for the necessary period.[3] This is reflected in the wording of confirmations of arms, which after the fifteenth century cease to refer to 'time out of mind' and use vaguer expressions, such as 'ancient'. This modification of the wording of confirmations did not, however, reflect any change in the law, and as late as 1633 Garter Burroughs confirmed a coat as having been borne 'tyme out of mind'.[4]

Meanwhile persons who unlawfully assumed arms were prosecuted in the Court of Chivalry,[5] but little is to be gleaned from the records of these prosecutions as to the rules of law applicable until towards the end of the seventeenth century, when an innovation in the procedure provides a remarkably good substitute for the reasoned judgments given in the common-law courts.

In earlier times the articles merely set out the facts constituting the alleged offences, but Dr. William Oldys, who was appointed King's Advocate when the Court was revived in 1687, started a new practice of beginning his

---

[1] *Misc. Gen. et Her.* i (1868), 54.

[2] *Heraldic Visitation of the Northern Counties in 1530* (Surtees Soc. xli, 1863), App., p. xxxviii.

[3] The common-law courts met this difficulty in the same way: see per Lush J. in *Angus* v. *Dalton* (1877), 3 Q.B.D. 85, at pp. 89–90.

[4] See a collection of extracts from confirmations in *The Ancestor*, viii (1904), 124–41.

[5] e.g. *St. George* v. *Tuckfield* (1637), Her. Cas. 24; *Prust* v. *Saltren* (1637), Her. Cas. 25.

articles with a statement of the rule of law alleged to have been infringed. It could not, of course, be suggested that implicit reliance is to be placed on a statement of law made by counsel in a pleading, but when we find the King's Advocate, whose position in the Court of Chivalry corresponded to that of the Attorney-General in the common-law courts, making the same statement of law in case after case and obtaining convictions upon it, we are entitled to regard his statement as authoritative.

During the first few years after the revival Oldys pleaded the law in the following form:

Quod nemo potest gerere Arma, Insignia, Galeam et Cristam, nisi ea quae sunt ei, et familiae suae propria, et spectantia aut sunt ei authoritate legitima rite et legitime concessa et confirmata.[1]

It will be seen that Oldys only recognized two ways in which a right to arms could be enjoyed—by birth[2] or by grant by 'lawful authority'. Like the other advocates in Doctors' Commons, Oldys was also an ecclesiastical lawyer, and we may perhaps see in his use of the words *authoritate legitima* a reflection of the ecclesiastical use of the expression 'lawful authority'. In their ecclesiastical context the words 'lawful authority' have given rise to much controversy,[3] but in the present context they must refer to the 'authority, power and licence' to grant arms conferred by the Crown on the kings of arms in their patents of appointment.[4]

Later Oldys altered the form of his articles, and put his allegation of law in these words:

Quod de jure et per Leges Armorum nullus hujus Regni Angliae subditus cujuscunque status, gradus, sive conditionis

---

[1] *Oldys* v. *Tyllie* (1687), Her. Cas. 59; *Oldys* v. *Mowbery* (1689), Her. Cas. 61.

[2] The word 'birth' is used advisedly, for both 'descent' and 'inheritance' imply heirship, and 'heir' has technical meanings which differ in the common law and the civil law, but neither of which embraces the conception of the transmission of arms to all male issue: see J. Cowel, *Institutes of the lawes of England* (London, 1651), p. 128.

[3] See ' "Lawful Authority", a Memorandum' in *The Canon Law of the Church of England* (London, 1947), pp. 215–23.

[4] For a modern instance see the patent of William Henry Weldon, Norroy King of Arms, printed in *The Right to Bear Arms*, pp. 104–8.

fuerit, Arma, sive Insignia Armorum in se sumere aut gerere debet nisi ipse jure antecessorio, vel ex donatione alicujus personae ad hoc sufficientem potestatem habentis ea possideat, vel possidere debeat.[1]

The meaning is the same as in the earlier form—no right except by birth or by grant. The interesting feature of the new form is that the wording of the essential parts of it is identical with that of Henry V's writ of 1417. It looks as though research, perhaps by Dr. Robert Plot, who was at this time the Register of the Court of Chivalry, had revealed the 1417 writ, and Oldys, recognizing in it an authoritative statement of the law, administered in the Court, preferred the ancient wording to his own.[2]

Thus Oldys, who was one of the leading heraldic lawyers of his day, recognized only two kinds of right to arms—a right by birth and a right by grant.

Of grants it is unnecessary to say more. Arms acquired by birth must have originated either in a grant or in use beginning before the time of legal memory. It is therefore necessary to consider what kind of use in fact will support an inference of use from time immemorial.

The extent of the antiquity of user required to support a claim based upon user from time immemorial is shown by a letter written by Sir William Dugdale, Garter King of Arms, on 15 June 1668, in which he states:

As for Mr. Raynes, if I can find anything in our books at the office to justifye the arms you drew with his descent, I will do it, but I have allready perused some books and can find nothing out; therefore it will be requisite that he do look over his own evidences for some seals of arms, for perhaps it appears in them; and if so and that they have used it from the beginning of Queen Elizabeth's reigne, or about that time, I then allowe thereof, for our directions are limiting us so to do, and not a shorter prescription of usage.[3]

[1] *Oldys* v. *Booth* (1693), Her. Cas. 79. This is the earliest example of this form of pleading which has been found.

[2] It may be that the research was undertaken for the purposes of fighting the cases of *Oldis* v. *Donmille* (1692), Show. P.C. 58 and *Russel's Case* (1692), 4 Mod. 128, in which it was held by the House of Lords and the Court of King's Bench respectively that the Court of Chivalry had no jurisdiction to deal with painters charged with painting arms and marshalling funerals without licence from the kings of arms. See pp. 97, 98 *ante*.

[3] B.M. MS. Lansdowne 870, f. 88, printed in *The Ancestor*, ii (1902), 45.

A few weeks before this letter was written the Commissioners for executing the office of Earl Marshal had been authorized by letters patent dated 26 May 1668 to make rules to be observed by the officers of arms. The 'directions' referred to by Dugdale were no doubt the rules then in course of preparation. When the rules were finally made on the following 22 November they did not mention the beginning of the reign of Elizabeth I, but required that all certificates and other attestations of arms made by the officers of arms should contain 'a certain and particular reference to some Books in the Office of Arms ancient Deeds Records Monuments or other authentic Memorials of Antiquity justifying the same'.[1] It would therefore appear that the law still required user from time immemorial to found a right to arms, but that this could be presumed on proof of user dating back to about the beginning of the reign of Elizabeth I, i.e. beyond the actual period of living memory.[2]

The standard of proof required for certificates and other attestations of arms made by the officers of arms was slightly relaxed respecting visitations, the rule relating to the entering of arms at visitations being as follows:

... and that in all Cases wherein the Arms claimed by any person or persons ... shall not be registred or entred in the Office of Arms or allowed by some former King of Arms or where a lawful Grant of the same made by a King of Arms shall not be exhibited or shall not be made out and proved either by some ancient Monument Glass Windows Impressions of Seals or other credible Testimony that the same Arms have been born and used by the Ancestors of the Party claiming them for the space of sixty years at the least before the time of that his claim; such Arms shall not be allowed or entred.[3]

---

[1] Printed in *Roos Peerage Case* (1804), Minutes of Evidence, p. 335.

[2] For the distinction between time immemorial and the period beyond living memory, cf. per Sir William Scott (afterwards Lord Stowell) in *Walter* v. *Gunner & Drury* (1798), 1 Hag. Con. 314, 322.

[3] *Roos Peerage Case*, p. 333. It will be observed that in the absence of previous registration or a grant arms had to be 'made out and proved' before the visiting heralds would accept them. Fox-Davies, *The Right to Bear Arms*, p. 130, inverted the true position by contending that arms became legal, not by virtue of usage, but 'on the strength of their being recorded, or of their confirmation at the

This acceptance of sixty years' user for the purposes of future visitations did not, however, affect the requirement of proof dating back to a more remote period in all other cases.

W. P. W. Phillimore sought to place another construction on Dugdale's letter. He suggested that Dugdale 'by a good-natured laxity' was praying in aid the well-known legal fiction of a 'lost grant'.[1] The doctrine that user which does not go back as far as time immemorial is evidence upon which it can be found that the user originated in a grant which has since been lost was acted upon in the common-law courts at least as early as the beginning of the seventeenth century.[2] It was familiar to the later English civilians, for it was applied in the ecclesiastical courts to presume lost faculties.[3] It was a rule of law and did not depend upon 'good-natured laxity'.

No trace of the application of this rule by the Court of Chivalry to presume a lost grant of arms has been found. Even if a lost grant of arms could be presumed from user, it would be an impossible presumption to make in cases where the user could not be proved farther back than 1673, for in that year the regular recording of grants of arms began.[4] It is true that the records of grants are not absolutely complete.[5] Nevertheless, a party arguing for the presumption of a lost post-1673 grant would be asking the Court to find that not only had there been a grant

---

Visitations'. On the contrary, the visitation records abound in instances of the heralds refusing to enter arms for which no proof could be adduced, and an entry in a visitation book shows that the arms were already borne lawfully by virtue of either a grant or presumed user from time immemorial.

[1] *Heralds' College & Coats of Arms* (London, 1904), p. 18.

[2] See *Dalton* v. *Angus* (1881), 6 App. Cas. 740, 811. This must be distinguished from the later doctrine under which adverse possession as of right for more than twenty years was not merely evidence of, but gave rise to, a presumption of a lawful origin. The later doctrine is first mentioned in a case of 1761 (*Dalton* v. *Angus*, at p. 812), and so can never have applied in the Court of Chivalry, which had previously last sat more than twenty years earlier.

[3] e.g. *Walter* v. *Gunner & Drury, supra.*

[4] A. R. Wagner, *The Records and Collections of the College of Arms* (London, 1952), p. 21.

[5] Mr. H. S. London has kindly called my attention to two unrecorded grants published by him in *Misc. Gen. et Her.* 5 S, x (1939), 56, 80.

which had been lost, but also that the proper officer of the College of Arms had failed in his duty to record it. The latter would be an impossible finding, for the law presumes against misconduct.[1] We may therefore dismiss Phillimore's interpretation of Dugdale's letter.

Others have drawn a very different deduction from Dugdale's statement, arguing that because a period of 100 years had elapsed between the beginning of the reign of Elizabeth I and the date of Dugdale's letter, the use of arms for a period of 100 years gave a prescriptive right to them.[2] This argument is based on a misunderstanding of the history of the law of prescription. Originally user for a long period did not of itself confer any right either under the civil law as administered in the Court of Chivalry or the common law. It was only evidence from which user from time immemorial, which alone gave rise to a right, could be inferred. It was not until the Prescription Act, 1832, that the modern form of prescription was introduced. Under that Act, the enjoyment of certain easements for specified periods gave a right to those easements, but the Act had no application to arms and is quite irrelevant for our purpose.

We return to our proposition that user to support a claim by prescription must be such as will justify an inference that the user commenced before the time of legal memory.

To prove such a user today would be a matter of considerable difficulty. During the century and a half between 1530 and 1687 every county in England was visited by the heralds on more than one occasion, so that every armigerous person had the opportunity of entering his arms. Any coat which has been in use from time immemorial must *ex hypothesi* have been in use during that period, and the fact that a coat now alleged to have been in use from time immemorial does not appear in any

---

[1] This was as true in a civil-law court as in a common-law court: see per Dr. Lushington in *Lloyd* v. *Roberts* (1858), 12 Moo. P.C. 158, at p. 165.

[2] See 'The Prescriptive Usage of Arms', in *The Ancestor*, ii (1902), 45. W. Paley Baildon, 'Heralds' College and Prescription', ibid. viii (1904), 144, stated that 'a reasonable length of user' was all that was required.

visitation record must raise a *prima facie* presumption that
the coat was not in use during that period. Doubtless
there are persons now living whose ancestors were entitled
to arms and failed to obey the heralds' summons; but the
onus of proving their right would be a heavy one. Even if
there were evidence of user, regard would have to be had
to the nature of the user. Evidence of a mere private user,
e.g. on family plate, would not be enough. It would have
to be shown that the arms had been borne *coram publico*,
e.g. on tombstones, for it is an old and well-established
rule, both in the civil law and the common law, that no
reliance can be placed on clandestine user to support a
claim to an incorporeal right. The evidence would have
to be that the arms had been borne (to use the words of
some of the witnesses in *Scrope* v. *Grosvenor*) 'publike-
ment, pesiblement et quietment'.[1]

The laws of arms not only govern the right to arms but
also the manner in which lawful arms are to be used. The
extent to which the use of lawful arms is controlled by law
is somewhat obscured by the way in which modern grants
of arms are drafted. The modern common form *habendum*
is 'to be borne and used for ever hereafter by [the grantee]
and his descendants with due and proper differences
according to the Laws of Arms'. At first reading it might
appear that it is only the 'due and proper differences'
which are to be according to the laws of arms, but that this
is not so is clearly shown by the wording used in early
grants. There are a number of sixteenth- and seventeenth-
century grants of arms to be borne according to the laws
of arms without any mention of differences.[2] It is the arms
(including the differences, if any) and not merely the
differences which are to be borne according to the laws
of arms. So we find Gerard Legh putting 'as a case of

---

[1] *Scrope and Grosvenor Controversy*, i. 296–7. These words are reminiscent of
the civil-law rule that user upon which a claim of right is founded must have been
'nec vi, nec clam, nec precario'.

[2] e.g. 'to have hould use beare enjoye and shew forth att all tymes hereafter
accordinge to the Auncient Lawes of Arms' (1574) (*Collection of Miscellaneous
Grants* (Harl. Soc. lxxvi, 1925), p. 14); 'to be by them and every one of them
born according to the Law of Armes forever' (1637) (ibid., p. 107). The form of
habendum mentioning differences occurs as early as 1595 (ibid., p. 29).

the law' the question of the marshalling of the arms of a woman who is heiress of her mother but not of her father.[1]

Whilst it is clear that the manner in which arms are to be used is a matter of law, the records of the Court of Chivalry throw very little light on the subject. Most of the armorial causes related to the illegal assumption of arms. The only cause in which an undoubtedly armigerous defendant was accused of misusing arms is *Oldys* v. *Feilding*.[2] The defendant, Robert Feilding, better known as the notorious 'Beau Feilding', was charged with four heraldic malpractices. The first was that he bore his arms upon the breast of an imperial eagle with a ducal coronet upon the shield.[3] The second was that he wrongfully used a quartering of the arms of Hastings, and the third was that another quartering was incorrectly blazoned. Only the fourth charge raised a question of principle. Feilding had married the daughter and heiress of the Marquess of Clanricade, by whom he had no issue. He was charged with displaying the Burgh arms on an escutcheon of pretence, although, so it was alleged in the articles, 'by the laws of arms no person can use and bear in his coat armour any arms on an escutcheon of pretence but when such person has married an heiress and had a child by such heiress'. Feilding pleaded that he was advised that he had a right to bear the arms on an escutcheon of pretence. Unfortunately the records do not disclose the decision on this point, but the then current edition of Guillim's *Display of Heraldry*[4] states the rule as pleaded by the promoter, though more modern heraldic writers do not mention the birth of issue as a condition precedent to displaying the arms of an heiress upon an escutcheon of pretence.[5]

---

[1] *Accedens of Armorie* (London, 1562), f. 167.

[2] (1702), Her. Cas. 102.

[3] The imperial eagle no doubt referred to the alleged descent of the Feildings from the Hapsburgs, though the defendant alleged that he was entitled to it in right of his former wife, the daughter and heiress of Viscount Carlingford.

[4] (London, 1679), p. 294.

[5] e.g. Porny, *Elements of Heraldry* (London, 1777), pp. 11, 121; J. E. Cussans, *Handbook of Heraldry* (London, 1893), p. 166; W. H. St. John Hope, *A Grammar of English Heraldry* (2nd ed., Cambridge, 1953), p. 28.

XIII

THE PROCEDURE OF THE COURT

PRESUMABLY because the work of the Court has never been sufficiently heavy and the practitioners in it have never been sufficiently numerous to make the undertaking a commercial proposition, no treatise on the practice of the Court of Chivalry has ever been published. The only way in which something can be learnt of its procedure is by examining the records of the Court in order to see what in fact happened.

The business of the Court fell into three main classes:

(A) Instance: the hearing of cases between party and party.
(B) *Ex officio*: the correction of faults by the judge by virtue of his 'office'.
(C) Appeals of treason and murder.

(A) *Instance*

Whilst the number of causes of office was substantial, the great bulk of the surviving records of the Court relate to business which arose *ad instantiam partium*, and we may conveniently begin with an account of the procedure in such causes.

So far as the medieval period is concerned, this task has already been performed by the anonymous author of 'The Manner of judicial Proceedings in the Court of Constable and Marshal (or Court Military) touching the Use and Bearing of Coats of Arms; observed and collected out of the Records of the Tower of London', printed in Hearne's *Collection of Curious Discourses*.[1] This is based upon the documents relating to the appeals in *Grey* v. *Hastings*, *Lovel* v. *Morley*, and *Scrope* v. *Grosvenor*, together with entries in the patent rolls relating to other

---

[1] 1775 ed., ii. 243–9.

appeals from the Court of Chivalry. Although it is not dated, it seems very likely that the materials for this paper were collected in 1622 at the time when the Earl Marshal was instructed to 'restore and settle' the procedure of the Court.[1]

What follows is a similar attempt to 'restore and settle' the procedure of the Court based upon its surviving records of the seventeenth and eighteenth centuries.

At first sight this would appear to be a simple task, for there exists a set of rules of the Court.[2] These rules, entitled 'Orders to be observed in yᵉ E: Marshals Courte', purport to set out the steps to be taken by plaintiffs and defendants, i.e. in causes of instance. Unfortunately, however, the procedure described in the rules does not tally in detail with the procedure revealed by the surviving documents, and the only conclusion which can be drawn is that the rules are not actual rules of the Court, but a draft which never became effective. This conclusion is borne out by a note prefixed to the British Museum copy of the rules—'Book from Mr. Ryly Herauld'. William Ryley was Lancaster Herald from 1641 to 1667, though between 1646 and 1660 he was intruded into the office of Norroy King of Arms, so the note must have been written during the first or the last few years of his time as Lancaster. During the earlier period he is unlikely to have been much interested in the Court of Chivalry, since its sittings were suspended early in 1641,[3] but during the later period he may have been concerned in some scheme for reviving the Court and the 'Orders' may be a draft prepared at that time. This assumption has been made for the purposes of the present chapter. What follows is based upon the records of the Court and is for convenience written in the past tense.

A cause of instance was initiated by lodging with the Register a petition on paper addressed to the Earl Marshal,

[1] See p. 46 *ante*.
[2] B.M. MS. Harl. 4128, ff. 27–32.
[3] See p. 67 *ante*.

praying that process might be issued.[1] The plaintiff was required by statute to set out his alleged cause of action in the petition.[2]

The petition was usually signed by the plaintiff, but sometimes by his counsel.[3] Provided that it disclosed a cause of action within the jurisdiction of the Court, the petition was subscribed by the Earl Marshal or by the King's Advocate 'Let process issue as is desired' or some similar phrase.[4] A cause was deemed to have been commenced as soon as the petition was presented and before the fiat had been granted.[5] Before granting his fiat the Earl Marshal frequently consulted the King's Advocate. This consultation was normally oral, but occasionally the Earl Marshal received written advice, as in *Pendred* v. *Farr*,[6] where the petition is subscribed in the following manner:

May itt please yr Lp. I conceave the words in ye petition doe conteyne a fitt cause of action in yr Lps Court, the petitioner beinge a gentlman anciently descended. if itt shall please yr Lp a

[1] For an example of such a petition see Appendix IX, p. 246 *post*. Instead of petitioning for process out of the Court of Chivalry it was possible to obtain a warrant to convent an adversary before the Earl Marshal in private, but this was not very effective, since the witnesses could not be brought to a full proof without a legal proceeding. See *Jennings* v. *Hygate* (1640), Cur. Mil. Boxes 2/50, where the plaintiff had been advised by his counsel to petition for a warrant for process, but mistaking his directions obtained a warrant to convent the defendant before the Earl Marshal in private. Cf. *Sutton* v. *Denne* (1637), Cur. Mil. Boxes 3/200, where the plaintiff complained that the defendant had failed to appear on the day appointed for the hearing by the Earl Marshal and petitioned for the cause to be 'assigned over to the Court Military to be there judicially determined', whereupon 'process of Court' was granted.

[2] 13 Ric. II, st. 1, c. 2, s. 3. If the defendant contended that the cause of action alleged might be tried by the common law, he could obtain from the Crown a writ under the privy seal suspending the proceedings until the King's Council had discussed whether the cause was triable at common law or in the Court of Chivalry (ibid).

[3] e.g. *Southcote* v. *Spiller* (1639), Cur. Mil. Boxes 5/54, signed by Dr. Joseph Martin, who seems to have made a practice of signing his client's petitions. The civilians signed documents at the bottom on the *left*-hand side.

[4] Occasionally the subscription was in Latin 'Fiat processus' (e.g. *Wogan* v. *Nicholas* (1639), Cur. Mil. Boxes 6/124). It is referred to in the text as the fiat.

[5] *Dockwara* v. *Killingworth* (1640), Cur. Mil. Boxes 2/34, 35. The bond dated 29 Jan. states that the plaintiff has commenced a suit, but the fiat was not granted until 12 Feb.

[6] (1636), Cur. Mil. Boxes 3/12.

process may issue out of my L. Marshalls Court. wch I make bolde to certify beinge hindred from attendeinge of yr Lp May 13 1636.

ARTH. DUCKE

May 13 1636. Lett a Processe bee issued accordingly

H. MATRAVERS

The Earl Marshal could grant a fiat by himself, as in *Ballard* v. *Kestian*,[1] where the petition is subscribed:

Good Mr. Dethicke[2]
My lo: Marshall doth give order that Mr. Ballard shall have prosses against Richard Kestian

yr servant
JOHN COXE

Arundell House
21 Jany 1637

Apparently fiats of which the King's Advocate did not approve were sometimes issued in this manner, for on 18 October 1637 Dr. Duck sent an instruction to the Register:

If any desire a processe out of Court for Mr. Woodward against Edward Chute Esquire late high sheriff of Kent I desire to bee acquainted itt before the processe goe out that I may attende my L. Marshall about itt.[3]

Conversely the fiat was frequently signed by the King's Advocate alone.

In 1693 Henry, Duke of Norfolk E.M., made a rule that no cause of instance should be begun without a petition subscribed by the King's Advocate that the cause was cognizable in the Court of Chivalry.[4]

Consideration was had to the quality of the plaintiff as well as to the nature of his cause of action. In *Seagar* v. *Wademan*[5] the petition is subscribed:

The petitioner is a fit person to have his remedy in this Court and the words fit for an action there, let process issue

ARTH: DUCKE

---

[1] (1637), Cur. Mil. Boxes 3/176.   [2] Dethicke was the Register at this time.
[3] Cur. Mil. Boxes 3/129. There is no record of such a process being issued.
[4] Northamptonshire Record Office MS. I. C. 3311; Powell MS. The rule was presumably made for the Earl Marshal's protection on account of the decision in *Russel's Case* (1692), 4 Mod. 128: see p. 97 *ante*.
[5] (1637), Cur. Mil. Boxes 3/21.

In *Bunting* v. *Hughes*[1] the King's Advocate was willing to certify on a letter from the plaintiff's advocate to the Register.

If the cause presented difficulty, the Surrogate might also be consulted before the fiat was granted, as in *Hillyard* v. *Lawrence*,[2] where the fiat was in the following form:

Mr. Dethick this is the business in wch I have attended my L. Matravers and Sr H. Marten,[3] and I have their allowance hereof, and I pray Lett process goe out

ARTH: DUCKE

In *Hassall* v. *Fletcher*[4] the plaintiff asked in his petition not only for process, but also for an attachment, on the ground that the defendant was 'a fellow that upon any judicial process served on him [will] run clean out of the country or subduct himself' whereby the plaintiff would be 'hindered of a course of justice' against him.

In order to obtain such an attachment on mesne process the petition had to be supported by such affidavit evidence as would suffice, if true, to secure a sentence against the defendant. He could be taken into custody as soon as process had been issued.[5]

A supporting affidavit was also required if the plaintiff desired to be admitted to sue *in forma pauperis*.[6]

A petition could be presented on behalf of an infant by his next friend.[7] Two plaintiffs could join in proceedings against one defendant.[8] It was also possible to join additional plaintiffs at later stages in the proceedings.[9]

---

[1] (1637), Cur. Mil. Boxes 3/90.   [2] (1637), ibid. 3/102.
[3] The Surrogate.   [4] (1640), Cur. Mil. Boxes 5/124.
[5] *Hopton* v. *Dawes* (1638), Cur. Mil. Boxes 6/38, where the defendant was discharged from the custody of the Messenger on the ground that there was only a single affidavit which was not sufficient testimony to convict him, there being depending between the deponent and the defendant suits which had been prosecuted 'with much asperity and violence'. The plaintiff had to pay the defendant, who had been brought from Ludlow, £10 for his costs and charges, but the payment was suspended until the cause had been heard.
[6] *Loris* v. *Tabor* (1640), Her. Cas. 49, where the plaintiff, a septuagenarian, attributed his poverty to the trouble which he had had in recovering his wife's portion: he was assigned two advocates as his counsel.
[7] e.g. his mother, as in *De la Ware* v. *Crutchman* (1635), Her. Cas. 12.
[8] *Andrewes* v. *Morris* (1637), Cur. Mil. Boxes 17/3d.
[9] In *Sidenham* v. *Cruse* (1639), Cur. Mil. Boxes 4/32, it was ordered that the depositions already taken should stand for all the plaintiffs.

Dissimilar causes of action against different defendants could be joined in one petition.[1]

A fiat was required in all causes of instance, including those promoted by the officers of arms.[2]

There was an alternative summary method of commencing a cause of instance whereby the defendant was taken into the custody of the Messenger of the Court and brought before the Earl Marshal, who took a complaint on oath, but this seems to have been rarely done.[3]

The Earl Marshal's fiat was the Register's authority for issuing the monition or citation. The citation was in Latin and engrossed on parchment under the Earl Marshal's seal. Unlike a modern writ of summons in an action in the High Court, it was not addressed to the defendant, but to all justices of the peace, sheriffs, bailiffs, constables, and officers of the Crown, and all faithful subjects, especially the Mandatory or Marshal of the Court, requiring them to cite the defendant or to cause him to be cited peremptorily.[4] It was frequently executed by the Marshal,[5] but he sometimes gave a letter of deputation to someone to act on his behalf,[6] and there are cases in which it was executed by one of the general classes of persons to whom it was addressed, for example, the Bailiff of the Hundred of Chelmsford[7] or a 'faithful subject'.[8] A constable, and presumably any other person to whom it was addressed, was under a duty to execute a citation and failure to do so laid him open to proceedings.[9]

---

[1] *Carnabie* v. *Johnson* (1640), Her. Cas. 47. The plaintiff alleged that the first defendant had called him a base knight and that the second defendant, his kinsman, had refused to give his arms with due distinction and had falsely boasted himself to come of a branch of the family superior to the plaintiff.

[2] *Officers of Arms* v. *Fogg* (1637), Cur. Mil. Boxes 3/129.

[3] *Andrews* v. *Morris* (1638), Cur. Mil. Boxes 18/3m.

[4] For an example see Appendix X, p. 247 *post*.

[5] e.g. *Oldys* v. *Tillie* (1687), Cur. Mil. Boxes X/23/5.

[6] e.g. *Peacock* v. *Quainton* (1690), Cur. Mil. Boxes X/23/28.

[7] *Rud* v. *Lumley* (1638), Cur. Mil. Boxes 17/4f.

[8] *Lusher* v. *Vandeburge* (1639), Cur. Mil. Boxes 12/3j (the plaintiff's brother-in-law).

[9] *St. George* v. *Hill* (1687), Act Book, 9, 21, and 24 Nov. Hill, the constable of the precinct of Thames Street in the parish of St. Michael Crooked Lane, refused to execute a warrant issued by Clarenceux King of Arms summoning

Execution of the citation was effected by showing it to the defendant and by leaving with him a notice of the time and place at which he was to appear and of the nature of the cause.[1] If the process-server could not find the defendant, he made an affidavit to that effect and an order was made for the affixing of the citation to the outside of the defendant's dwelling-house. The original was then hung upon the latch for a quarter of an hour and a copy was left behind.[2]

Process-serving has always been a hazardous occupation. When George Perkins, the deputy to the Messenger of the Court, went to serve a citation on William Merriell, he found his quarry going home from church and ran after him. The defendant thought (so he said) that Perkins meant to do him harm and there was a struggle in which Perkins received a blow on the head. The parish constable then appeared and commanded Perkins in the King's name to keep the peace. When Perkins refused, the constable drew a little dagger and struck at him. Merriell and the constable later had to answer for their conduct in a cause of office in which they were fined £100 and ordered to pay £100 damages and £30 costs, but that can have been but small consolation to the process-server.[3] Sometimes he met with no more than hard words, but even so the defendant could be committed on proof by affidavit of his contempt.[4]

The original citation was retained and returned to the plaintiff with a certificate of its execution. Sometimes the certificate of execution was endorsed on the citation and made on oath[5] and sometimes it was contained in an

certain persons to appear before him, but the same principle would apply to a citation issued by the Earl Marshal. Hill submitted and was discharged on payment of costs.

[1] For an example, see Appendix XI, p. 249 *post*.

[2] *Oldys* v. *Loving* (1693), Cur. Mil. Boxes X/23/37, 39; *Oldys* v. *Ellwill* (1701), Her. Cas. 97.

[3] *Hungate* v. *Merriell* (1639), Cur. Mil. Boxes 15/4*r*, 19/7*b*.

[4] For examples of such affidavits see *Lusher* v. *Vandeburge* (1639), Cur. Mil. Boxes 12/3*j*, and *Some* v. *Vandeburge* (1639), ibid. 12/3*l*, in each of which cases the defendant told the process-server that the plaintiff was 'a rogue and a knave'.

[5] e.g. *Spyller* v. *Manning* (1688), Cur. Mil. Boxes X/23/19.

affidavit.[1] The Marshal of the Court usually endorsed the citation with his certificate of execution and then swore to it in open court.[2]

A cause could not proceed after execution of the citation until the original citation with the certificate of execution was brought into court.[3] This was done by the plaintiff's proctor. Proclamation was then made for the defendant by the Cryer. If the defendant appeared, he might submit, in which event he could be condemned immediately in damages and costs.[4] If he appeared and did not submit, the judge monished him to appear to receive the libel at the next sitting.[5]

The plaintiff had to give a bond for the due prosecution of the cause, and the defendant had to give a bond to appear and to pay any costs and damages awarded against him and to make submission.[6] The plaintiff's bond was usually given after the fiat had been granted, but there are cases in which the bond was dated earlier than the fiat.[7] Such bonds were usually for £100, but occasionally for other sums. In 1637 a bond for the large sum of £2,000 was given by a defendant for his appearance.[8] The bond was sometimes by the party alone, sometimes with two sureties,[9] and sometimes one surety.[10] Carew Raleigh of East Horsley, co. Surrey, was required to give a bond with two sureties to be of good behaviour and keep the peace and not to go within the verge of the King's Court without special licence, as well as to appear on the first court day of the next term.[11] In *Bland* v. *Clarke*[12] the Earl Marshal caused both parties to be bound with sureties to abide his censure. The defendant could be arrested and

[1] e.g. *Oldys* v. *Mowbery* (1688), Cur. Mil. Boxes X/23/10.
[2] e.g. *St. George* v. *Bowater* (1688), Act Book, 10 Mar.
[3] *Oldys* v. *Mowbery* (1688), Act Book, 23 Feb. and 3 Mar.
[4] *Hamilton* v. *Spernick* (1688), Act Book, 15 Mar.
[5] *Wase* v. *Newman* (1688), Act Book, 23 Feb.
[6] For submissions see p. 212 *post*.
[7] e.g. *Hungerford* v. *Broad* (1639), Cur. Mil. Boxes 6/108, 109.
[8] *Kingston (Earl)* v. *Copley* (1637), Cur. Mil. Boxes 3/7.
[9] e.g. *Bacchus* v. *Mountford* (1637), Cur. Mil. Boxes 3/46.
[10] e.g. *Jones* v. *Lloyd* (1640), Cur. Mil. Boxes 5/11.
[11] *St. Ravie* v. *Raleigh* (1639), Cur. Mil. Boxes 5/41.
[12] (*c.* 1636), Cur. Mil. Boxes 7/23.

kept in custody until he produced the necessary bond,[1] provided that the complaint against him was made on oath.[2] If the cause was settled or dismissed by agreement, the bonds were delivered to the parties by decree.[3] The same course was taken if referees were able to conclude the matter.[4]

The next document was the plaintiff's pleading, known as the libel. This was normally addressed to the Earl Marshal[5] and usually commenced with an allegation of the plaintiff's gentility, sometimes coupled with an allegation of the defendant's plebeian condition. The evidence in support and contradiction of these allegations frequently contains detailed genealogical and biographical information. The libel then went on to state the facts necessary to constitute the cause of action, and concluded with a prayer setting out the relief sought. Times and dates were pleaded as widely as possible. Thus it was usually alleged that the plaintiff and his ancestors had been gentlemen for such periods as '10. 20. 30. 40. 50. 100. 200 pluresque annos elapsos', whilst the date of the cause of action was expressed in the form 'mensibus Decembris Januarij Februarij et Martij Anno Domini 1635 seu mensibus Martij et Aprilis Anno Domini 1636 seu in eorum uno'.[6]

The libel was written on parchment in Latin with an English translation of any words alleged to have been spoken by the defendant, and was usually signed by the plaintiff's advocate.[7]

The contents of a libel in the Court of Chivalry followed the general rule versified by Henry Conset as follows:

Each Plaintiff and Defendant's Name,
And eke the Judge who tryes the same;

---

[1] *Molins* v. *Waters* (1636), Cur. Mil. Boxes 7/91.

[2] *Andrewes* v. *Morris* (1637), Cur. Mil. Boxes 17/3d.

[3] *Scoles* v. *Nutt* (1637), Cur. Mil. Boxes 7/38; *Midleton* v. *Delieu* (1638), ibid. 3/14. [4] *Bodurda* v. *Griffith* (1637), Cur. Mil. Boxes 13/1m.

[5] In *Pudsay* v. *Johnson* (1637), Cur. Mil. II. 62a, the libel was addressed to Henry, Lord Matravers, Lieutenant of Thomas, Earl of Arundel and Surrey, E.M.

[6] *Bacchus* v. *Mountford* (1637), Cur. Mil. I. 139.

[7] Sometimes two advocates signed the libel, e.g. *Copley* v. *Mountney* (1638), Acta Cur. Mil. (5), 102.

> The thing demanded, and the right whereby
> You urge to have it granted instantly:
> He doth a Libel right and well compose,
> Who forms the same, omitting none of those.[1]

Libels were not dated, though the Register sometimes endorsed them with the dates on which they were lodged with him.

If there were two or more plaintiffs, they could put in joint or several libels.[2] If a plaintiff was added after the original plaintiff had pleaded, he exhibited an additional libel.[3]

A libel could be amended by the Register in pursuance of an order of the Court.[4]

Upon the defendant's appearance he obtained a copy of the libel from the Register,[5] but he was not usually required to give his answer until after evidence had been given for the plaintiff,[6] although the Court had power to decree what was called a 'personal answer', as distinct from an answer signed by the defendant's advocate, at this stage.[7] The object of requiring a personal answer was to exonerate the plaintiff from the burden of proving undisputed facts.[8]

One of the distinctive features of the Court of Chivalry, as of the other courts in which the civilians practised, was that witnesses did not give evidence viva voce, but on commission.[9]

---

[1] H. Conset, *Practice of the . . . Ecclesiastical Courts*, p. 403. For an example of a libel see Appendix XVI, p. 254 *post*.

[2] *Andrewes* v. *Morris* (1638), Cur. Mil. Boxes 18/3m.

[3] *Sidenham* v. *Cruse* (1639), Cur. Mil. Boxes 18/1k.

[4] *Dorset (Earl)* v. *Riggs* (1640), Cur. Mil. Boxes 4/38.

[5] *Price* v. *Griffith* (1634), Cur. Mil. Boxes 7/59.

[6] That the answer was often not even drawn until after the plaintiff's witnesses had been examined is shown by frequent references to those witnesses by name in the answers.

[7] That a personal answer was filed before the examination of the plaintiff's witnesses is shown by the order of the items in the bill of costs in *Greaves* v. *Mathewes* (1639), Cur. Mil. Boxes 12/3e.

[8] J. T. Law, *Forms of Ecclesiastical Law* (London, 1831), p. 183.

[9] This continued to be the rule in the ecclesiastical courts until the passing of the Ecclesiastical Courts Act, 1854. There were occasional exceptions to the rule, see p. 206 *post*.

If the witnesses were in the country, the next step in the proceedings was the issue of a commission, termed 'letters commissory', prepared by the Register's clerk[1] in the name of the Earl Marshal, to a number of persons commanding them or some of them[2] to take evidence on behalf of the plaintiff. The commissioners were ordered to start the hearing on a named day,[3] at a named place (frequently an inn)[4] in the presence of the Register or a notary public nominated by him, and to return the evidence to the Court in the Painted Chamber in the Palace of Westminster[5] before a named date (usually the first sitting of the Court in the following law term). At the end of the document is the Register's nomination of a notary public to expedite the commission on his behalf. The place for taking the evidence was determined by the residences of the proposed witnesses rather than by those of the parties. Thus in *Stepkin* v. *Dobbins*[6] the plaintiff lived in Stepney, co. Middlesex, and the defendant in the City of London, but the letters commissory directed the evidence to be taken at Newent, co. Gloucester.

The persons named as commissioners were knights, esquires, gentlemen, or clerks in Holy Orders living in the neighbourhood where the evidence was to be taken. The number of commissioners varied, but was usually eight.[7] The names of the commissioners were set out in two groups, coupled with 'necnon', the first group having been chosen by the plaintiff and the second by the defendant.[8] The notary public employed as the Register's deputy was also usually a local man.

[1] *Meyrick* v. *Catchmaye* (1635), Cur. Mil. Boxes 7/71.

[2] It was exceptional for all the named commissioners to act.

[3] The date was usually three or four months after that of the letters commissory, but sometimes less than a month.

[4] Commissioners also sat in such places as the Court House in St. Brevell's Castle, co. Gloucester (*Somerset* v. *Perkins* (1634), Acta Cur. Mil. (5), 19) and the Town Hall in Pembroke (*Meyrick* v. *Catchmaye* (1636), Acta Cur. Mil. (4), 254).

[5] In *Folliott* v. *Forrest* (1640), Cur. Mil. I. 58 the depositions were to be returned to Arundel House in the Strand.

[6] (1638), Her. Cas. 30.

[7] There were only four in *Somerset* v. *Perkins, supra*.

[8] The manner of choosing the commissioners appears from a letter written to

If more than one commissioner in a group were present, it was not necessary for them all to sit for the whole of the examination; they could take it in turns and so facilitate late sittings.[1]

The commission was engrossed on parchment, and it and the libel, and any documents annexed to the libel, were fastened together by a parchment tag passing through slits cut in the lower edges of the documents, and were sealed with the seal of the Earl Marshal *ad causas*.[2] The sealed documents were then sent to the commissioners, presumably in the care of the notary appointed to act as the Register's deputy.

The time and place at which the commission was to be kept were nominated by the plaintiff,[3] notice being given to the defendant.[4] The witnesses attended either at the request of the plaintiff[5] or in response to a citation signed by the commissioners.[6]

---

the Earl Marshal by two of the commissioners chosen by the plaintiff in *Constable* v. *Constable* (1640), Acta Cur. Mil. (4), 63. It further appears from this letter that normally at least one of each of the two groups had to be present. This was necessary, for there seems to have been no requirement that the commissioners should be unbiased. Thus in *Mannaton* v. *Lampen* (1638), Cur. Mil. I. 207, two of the commissioners had the same unusual surnames as the plaintiff and the defendant. In *Seaward* v. *Ebdon* (1640), Acta Cur. Mil. (4), 224–31, none of the defendant's commissioners appeared, whilst in *Hungerford* v. *Broad* (1639), Acta Cur. Mil. (5), 144, one of the commissioners gave evidence. Although commissioners did not have to be unbiased, they had to act fairly to both parties (*Owen* v. *Lloyd* (1639), Cur. Mil. Boxes 6/141).

[1] One of the commissioners nominated by the plaintiff in *Constable* v. *Constable* (1638), Acta Cur. Mil. (4), 63, complained that he had had to sit from 4 p.m. until 10 p.m., whereas there were present four commissioners nominated by the defendant to 'ioyne or ease one another in despatch of the said Comicon'.

[2] Most of the surviving libels and letters commissory are now separated, but a few are still attached to each other with fragments of the seals remaining: e.g. *Kenn* v. *Robins* (1638), Acta Cur. Mil. (4), 250; *Done* v. *Babington* (1640), Cur. Mil. Boxes 9/2a–d; *Amcotts* v. *Shuttleworth* (1638), Cur. Mil. Boxes 11/27.

[3] *Morgan* v. *Morgan* (1635), Cur. Mil. Boxes 7/68.

[4] The length of the notice was prescribed by the Register. Ten days' notice was ordered in *Somerset* v. *Perkins, supra*, but only six days' notice in *Kenn* v. *Robins, supra*.

[5] A witness in *Brome* v. *Woodman* (1640), Cur. Mil. 1631–42, 162–9, said that the plaintiff told her that if she did not come to give evidence he would get a pursuivant sent for her.

[6] There is a citation endorsed with a certificate of service in *Argent* v. *Crayford* (1638), Cur. Mil. I. 186. In *Mansergh* v. *Moore* (1640), Cur. Mil. 1631–42, 25–38,

The proceedings before the commissioners opened with the reading of the commission by the notary public acting as the Register's deputy.[1] The plaintiff then appeared and produced his witnesses,[2] whose attendance could be enforced by 'compulsories'.[3] Each witness was examined on behalf of the plaintiff upon each of the allegations contained in the libel.[4] This examination was conducted by the plaintiff's advocate or by a notary public appointed by letters substitutional signed by the advocate.[5] The letters substitutional were exhibited to the commissioners by the substitute,[6] and were retained by the commissioners, who sent them to the Register with the other documents relating to the examination.

The deposition of each witness opens with his rank or occupation, age, and residence. Frequently it also states how long he has lived at his present place of abode and where he was born, and occasionally even gives intermediate residences with the period of each.[7] In addition the witness sometimes gives further personal details about himself, so that the potential biographical and genealogical value of the depositions is great.

After the examination-in-chief the witness was examined upon interrogatories which were usually drawn by

two of the witnesses stated that they were ordered to give evidence by one of the commissioners.

[1] *Constable* v. *Constable, supra*; *Meyrick* v. *Catchmaye* (1636), Acta Cur. Mil. (4), 266.

[2] In *Freeman* v. *Page and Hartell* (1637), Acta Cur. Mil. (4), 149, the plaintiff's son appeared on behalf of his father.

[3] *Anon.* (n.d.), Cur. Mil. Boxes 7/77.

[4] The examination was confined to these allegations. In *Kingston (Earl)* v. *Copley* (1636), Acta Cur. Mil. (5), 170, one of the commissioners sent a protest that the examination of two of the witnesses had not been so confined.

[5] It seems to have been usual to appoint a substitute when the examination was held out of London. There are many letters substitutional preserved amongst the records of the Court: e.g. *Meyrick* v. *Catchmaye* (1636), Acta Cur. Mil. (4), 251. Sometimes two substitutes were appointed *conjunctim et divisim*: e.g. *Stepkin* v. *Dobbins* (1638), Cur. Mil. II. 169.

[6] *Wortleye* v. *Allott* (1639), Cur. Mil. II. 133–41.

[7] e.g. in *Bacchus* v. *Mountford* (1637), Cur. Mil. I. 141–53, Francis Hughes of St. Botolph's, Cambridge, yeoman, aged 38, states that he has lived there for ten years, and previously in Peterborough for fourteen years, at Milton, co. Northampton, for five years, and in Shrewsbury, where he was born.

the defendant's counsel.[1] This was not cross-examination properly so called, for the questions were formulated and reduced to writing in advance and were not directed to the answers given by the witness on his examination-in-chief. The interrogatories were founded upon the allegations contained in the libel,[2] and frequently contained many common form questions, such as whether the witness was related to or in the employment of the plaintiff; whether he hoped for the plaintiff's success;[3] whether he was being paid by the plaintiff for giving evidence; how much he paid in taxes; and how much he was worth all his debts paid. The interrogatories were written on parchment and signed by the defendant's advocate. The common form parts were usually in Latin and the remainder in English.

The interrogatories were sent to the commissioners under seal not to be broken until the time of the examination.[4]

Outside London the interrogatories were administered to the witnesses by a notary public appointed by letters substitutional signed by the defendant's advocate.[5] The notary presented his letters substitutional to the commissioners and sought leave to administer the interrogatories.[6]

If these 'fishing' interrogatories did not suffice, the

[1] In *Smyth* v. *Wallis* (1637), Cur. Mil. Boxes 12/1*m*, the defendant's counsel did not send any interrogatories, so the defendant had some interrogatories drawn by a proctor of the Archdeaconry Court of Cornwall. Unfortunately for the defendant, the interrogatories drawn by the proctor were scandalous.

[2] *Price* v. *Griffith* (1634), Cur. Mil. Boxes 7/59.

[3] Francis Muncke of Mountsorrell, co. Leicester, yeoman, answered this question by saying that if it were in his power he 'would give the victorie in this suite according as the justice thereof should require in his understanding' (*Rugely* v. *Smith* (1640), Cur. Mil. Boxes, 11/34. John Barrowcloughe of Bradley Park, co. Derby, yeoman, although a witness for the plaintiff, frankly said that if it were in his power he had rather the defendant had the victory than otherwise (*Greaves* v. *Knyveton* (1638), Cur. Mil. Boxes 19/4*c*).

[4] The interrogatories in *Copley* v. *Mountney* (1638), Acta Cur. Mil. (5), 102, are endorsed 'Interrogatories on the behalfe of Mountney, theis are to remaine sealed untill the witnesses are sworne and are to be examined thereupon'. The interrogatories were usually sewn on to the letters commissionary: e.g. *Eyre* v. *Keresforth* (1638), Cur. Mil. Boxes 11/38; *Amcotts* v. *Shuttleworth* (1638), Cur. Mil. Boxes 11/27.

[5] *Meyrick* v. *Catchmaye* (1636), Acta Cur. Mil. (4), 251, 256.

[6] Ibid. 266.

notary appearing in place of the defendant's advocate could propound further interrogatories '*secundo loco*'. Interrogatories *secundo loco* were frequently directed to the characters of fellow witnesses.[1] They were written on paper and signed by the notary propounding them.[2] If the interrogatories *secundo loco* did not suffice, they could be supplemented by interrogatories *tertio loco* and so on.[3] The practice of the civilians did not give the producent of a witness an opportunity of examining in reply after the examination upon interrogatories.[4]

The evidence was taken down in writing by the notary public acting as the Register's deputy, or his clerk, signed by the witness, and counter-signed by the commissioners present.

When all the plaintiff's witnesses had been examined the depositions were fastened together with a certificate by the notary acting as deputy Register. This certificate frequently states the diocese in which the notary was born, and is authenticated by his signature and notarial sign, the latter often being an intricate piece of penwork with the notary's initials and a Latin motto. In addition there is frequently an ecclesiastical wafer seal.[5] The bundle was completed with a formal return to the Earl Marshal by the commissioners, reciting the due execution of the commission.

[1] e.g. that in *Garton* v. *Bland* (1636), Acta Cur. Mil. (4), 270–5, about Joan Page alias Hunt, which produced the answer that she was 'accounted no better than shee should be'.

[2] *Garton* v. *Bland, supra,* 267; *Killiow* v. *Cullis* (1639), Acta Cur. Mil. (4), 105a; *Badd* v. *Riggs* (1640), Acta Cur. Mil. (4), 221.

[3] In *Pincombe* v. *Prust* (1640), Cur. Mil. Boxes 16/4i, the defendant persisted until he had administered interrogatories *septimo loco*.

[4] Evidence of Dr. Lushington given before a Select Committee of the House of Lords in 1844 and reprinted in the *First Report of the Royal Commission on the Law of Divorce* (1853), Q. 91.

[5] e.g. the depositions in *Coffyn* v. *Steevens* (1638), Cur. Mil. I. 38–52, are sealed with the official seal of the Peculiar of Woodberry. The depositions in *Wortley* v. *Allott* (1639), Cur. Mil. II. 133–41, taken in Yorkshire, are sealed with the seal of the Commissary-General of the King's Free Chapel of Wolverhampton, co. Stafford, no doubt through the agency of the notary, who is described as being of the diocese of Coventry and Lichfield. This seal was also used by the same notary in the Warwickshire case of *Fullwood* v. *Greene* (1640), Acta Cur. Mil. (4), 289–93.

The bundle containing the depositions was then sent together with the libel and the commission and any interrogatories and letters substitutional to the Register.

There was an alternative procedure for the examination of a witness in the country by means of a deputation to a person of substance in the locality,[1] but this course does not seem to have been followed at all frequently.

In the case of witnesses examined in London a somewhat different procedure was followed. The evidence was taken down in writing by an examiner and was afterwards (sometimes some days afterwards) repeated and acknowledged before the Judge of the Court in the presence of a notary public.[2] Sometimes witnesses were examined in open court,[3] but this was unusual and it is not clear in what circumstances it was allowed.

It was not until the plaintiff's witnesses had been examined that the defendant was normally called upon to plead.[4] The answer was very similar in form to the libel. It was addressed to the Earl Marshal, engrossed on parchment, and signed by the defendant's advocate.[5] The answer consisted either of a traverse or of confession and avoidance, the most frequent form of the latter being that the words complained of were spoken by the defendant in response to the plaintiff's provocation.[6] The defendant could also allege that one or more of the plaintiff's witnesses were unworthy of credit.[7] He could also file a separate

---

[1] *Kings of Arms* v. *Fetherstone* (1635), Her. Cas. 8.

[2] Most of the surviving examples of this practice are from the first half of the year 1640, portions of the book in which the depositions were entered being bound up with other documents in Cur. Mil. 1631–42. In *Perrot* v. *Perrocke and Perrot* (1639) the evidence of one witness was taken in this manner (Cur. Mil. 1631–42, 228–9), the remainder being taken on commission in Carmarthen (Acta Cur. Mil. (5), 70–76). In *Watson* v. *Philcott* (n.d.), Cur. Mil. Boxes 7/31, a clerk to the Register acted as examiner and was alleged by the defendant to have put words into the examinations which the witnesses did not speak, on which the defendant prayed for the witnesses to be examined again by commission in the country.

[3] e.g. *Wise* v. *Holmes* (1634), Cur. Mil. Boxes 7/114*k*; *Bowne* v. *Throgmorton* (1634), Cur. Mil. Boxes 8/22*b*.   [4] See p. 200 *ante*.

[5] Occasionally two advocates sign the answer, e.g. *Rowden* v. *Mace* (1635), Cur. Mil. I. 221.

[6] *Garton* v. *Bland* (1636), Acta Cur. Mil. (4), 287.

[7] e.g. *Southcott* v. *Morrell* (1639), Cur. Mil. Boxes 13/3*b*, where the defence

document signed by his advocate (called 'letters remissional') containing exceptions to some or all of the plaintiff's witnesses.[1] If the libel contained criminal matter, so that the cause, though civil in form, was in the nature of a criminal prosecution, the defendant could not be ordered to give his answer upon oath.[2]

There then followed letters commissory to take evidence on behalf of the defendant, the procedure being the same (*mutatis mutandis*) as in the case of the plaintiff's commission. Documentary evidence in support of the allegations in the answer was exhibited by the defendant's advocate before the Judge after the issue of the letters commissory and before the examination of the witnesses.[3] Copies of documents referred to in the answer were annexed as schedules.[4] The letters commissory and the answer were annexed to each other by a sealed tag[5] and the evidence of the defendant's witnesses was taken in the same way as that of the witnesses for the plaintiff. The defendant's witnesses were sometimes examined in chief upon positions and articles (*positiones et articula*) exhibited by the defendant instead of (or perhaps in addition to) the allegations in the answer.[6]

After the evidence for both parties had been returned to the Court, the costs of the examination were taxed by the Judge of the Court.[7]

If it was desired to interrogate the opposite party,

alleged that two of the plaintiff's witnesses had each got his maidservant with child before his examination in the cause, whilst another had been the cause of the defendant being arrested and imprisoned for debt.

[1] *Rowden* v. *Mace, supra.* One witness had assaulted the defendant; another had attacked him with a multiplicity of frivolous suits and actions; a third was a tenant of the plaintiff or his brother and was a man of no faith; whilst a fourth was not only a household servant of the plaintiff or his father, but had also begotten two bastards.

[2] *Coventry (Earl)* v. *King* (1702), unrep., cited in *Blount's Case* (1737), 1 Atk. 295, at p. 297.

[3] e.g. *Leeming* v. *Clopton* (1637), Cur. Mil. I. 248; *Stepkin* v. *Dobbins* (1638), Cur. Mil. II. 165–6.

[4] e.g. *Le Strange* v. *Cremer* (1639), Acta Cur. Mil. (4), 358.

[5] e.g. *Rowden* v. *Mace, supra.*

[6] e.g. *Somerset* v. *Perkins* (1634), Acta Cur. Mil. (5), 16–17.

[7] There is a note of the taxation appended to the depositions in *Browne* v. *Atkinson* (1635), Acta Cur. Mil. (5), 53.

separate letters commissory were obtained for the purpose.[1] In addition there was issued in the name of the Earl Marshal a commission addressed to justices of the peace, mayors, sheriffs, bailiffs, constables, and other officers and to the King's faithful subjects requiring them to monish and cite the party to be interrogated to appear at a time and place appointed by the commissioners named in the letters commissory. The commissioners subscribed at the foot of the commission issued to the justices of the peace, &c., an appointment of the time and place for the interrogation.[2]

Even if a witness had not been interrogated, his evidence could be challenged as being false. Thus in *Sibthorpe* v. *Hurstler*[3] the defendant's witnesses stated that the plaintiff gave the first offence in a cause of scandalous words by making a great noise in his lodging above the defendant's kitchen. The plaintiff, who had not been present when the witnesses so deposed, petitioned for an inspection of the premises, whereupon two viewers were appointed and certified that the plaintiff's lodging was not above the defendant's kitchen.

A cause could be submitted to arbitration before the evidence was heard.[4] Alternatively the Earl Marshal could refer a cause to referees appointed by him. If the defendant refused to submit to the order of the referees, the plaintiff could present a further petition that the defendant should appear before the Earl Marshal to receive punishment.[5] In *Bodurda* v. *Griffith*[6] 'gentlemen of quality' in Anglesey were appointed referees at the

---

[1] *Chaloner* v. *Heylin* (1637), Cur. Mil. Boxes 17/3*f*.
[2] *Chaloner* v. *Heylin* (1637), Cur. Mil. II. 44.
[3] (1640), Cur. Mil. Boxes 15/4*c*.
[4] In *Longe* v. *Sticklowe* (1638), Cur. Mil. II. 107–8, the plaintiff appeared before the commissioners on 10 Mar. 1637/8 and offered to submit to the arbitration of Sir Edward Baynton, knight. The matter was then adjourned, but on 3 Apr. following the plaintiff produced his witnesses and the matter proceeded in the usual manner. *Cooper* v. *Billop* (1639), Her. Cas. 42, was referred to neighbours chosen by mutual consent, who proposed conditions of peace to which the parties agreed.
[5] *Wadham* v. *Cooke* (1640), Cur. Mil. Boxes 2/33.
[6] (1637), Cur. Mil. Boxes 3/1–3, 13; 13/1*m*.

request of the defendant, Owen Griffith, the King's Attorney in the Three Shires of North Wales, on the ground that he was attending the King's service in the Court of Great Sessions, as appeared by the certificate of the Justice of Assize. The referees were able to make an 'amiable and lovinge end' between the parties, who were brothers-in-law, and they asked that the plaintiff's bond for the prosecution of his complaint might be rendered up or 'indemnified'.[1]

It was the commissioners chosen by the parties to take the evidence who reconciled them in *Ingpen* v. *Penny*.[2] The reconciliation was witnessed by a release under the hand of the plaintiff, whereupon the cause was dismissed and the parties' bonds were delivered up to be cancelled.

A reference was usually to four persons, giving them or any two or three of them power to call both parties and their witnesses before them, and to examine the difference and end it if they could. If they found either of the parties refractory, they were to certify it and their opinion of the controversy.[3]

In *Hoblyn* v. *George*[4] four referees were appointed. Three of them heard the parties and examined witnesses and then certified the examinations to the Earl Marshal. The defendant did not submit to the arbitrament, but before the certificate was returned he secretly obtained an order of reference nominating one referee. This the defendant kept in his hands for six months and never endeavoured to have anything done upon it, 'supposing under colour thereof to delay the plaintiff's proceedings against him'. The plaintiff then obtained a fresh process against the defendant ordering him to make his personal appearance in court and to stand to and abide by such order as the Earl Marshal should think meet.[5]

---

[1] Cf. *Castell* v. *Crisp* (1640), Cur. Mil. Boxes 18/4*n*, where the referees made 'a loving & friendly end betweene them'.

[2] (1640), Cur. Mil. Boxes 7/28.

[3] *Hach* v. *Ratcliffe* (1639), Cur. Mil. Boxes 2/93.

[4] Cur. Mil. Boxes 2/91.

[5] *Heber* v. *Michell* (1640), Cur. Mil. Boxes 5/130, was another case in which the defendant obtained a fresh reference after refusing to submit to the original

Lewis v. *Jones*[1] was referred by the Earl Marshal to the examination of Jones J. of the King's Bench 'to end it if he could', otherwise the plaintiff should proceed in the Court Military for the foul language and should be left at liberty to proceed at common law for the pretended blows. Jones J. 'convented' the parties before him, but could not end the difference, so process was ordered by the Earl Marshal.[2]

All pedigrees entered in the books of the College of Arms had to be signed by the parties requesting the entries to be made, and an unsigned pedigree was not admissible in evidence in the Court of Chivalry.[3]

If any question upon which expert opinion was required arose during a cause it could be referred for report. Thus in *Burrough* v. *Tuckfield*[4] ten deeds produced by the defendant were referred to Sir Edward Dering, Sir Henry Spelman, and Ralph Whitfeld, serjeant-at-law, who reported that two of them were counterfeit and that five of the others had been tampered with. More usually such questions related to pedigrees and were referred to the officers of arms.[5] On 1 March 1695 the Earl Marshal, on motion on behalf of the kings of arms, ordered that all references should be directed to the kings of arms only, unless the other officers of arms showed cause to the contrary.[6]

If a cause was adjourned to a certain day, it was necessary to take some step on that day, even though it might only be a further adjournment. Thus on the death of Sir Thomas Exton, the other surrogate, Sir Richard Raines, being ill, the Earl Marshal appointed Sir Thomas Pinfold surrogate *ad hoc* to adjourn the Court on 6 December

---

reference. The plaintiff alleged enmity between himself and one of the defendant's referees, whereupon he was granted a process so that the cause could be heard judicially in court.

[1] (1639), Cur. Mil. Boxes 2/159.
[2] Jones J. was 'a person of admirable learning . . . in the British antiquities (Hearne, *Collection of Curious Discourses*, ii. 449).
[3] *Blount's Case* (1737), 1 Atk. 295, 297.
[4] (1635), Her. Cas. 19.
[5] e.g. *Constable* v. *Constable* (1640), Her. Cas. 35, 39.
[6] Act Book.

1688, to which date *Re Percy's Pedigree*[1] had been continued, 'else it would fall'.[2]

Some causes, although causes of instance in form, were in the nature of criminal prosecutions. A cause of this kind was that of the Earl of Coventry against Gregory King, Lancaster Herald, for having contrary to his oath and the duty of his office caused the arms of the Earl's father to be impaled with false arms.[3]

The decision of the Court was given in a formal document known as a definitive sentence. Each party put forward ('porrected') in writing the definitive sentence which he sought engrossed on parchment and signed in the bottom left-hand corner by his advocate, blanks being left for the insertion of the amounts of any fine or damages and the costs. When the sentence was pronounced, the Earl Marshal or his surrogate filled in the blanks in the sentence porrected by the successful party and signed it in the bottom right-hand corner.[4] Both the completed sentence and that porrected by the unsuccessful party were retained amongst the records of the Court.

Blackstone states that since the Court cannot meddle with anything determinable by the common law, it can give no pecuniary satisfaction or damages; 'inasmuch as the quantity and determination thereof is ever of common law cognizance'.[5] This statement, whilst in accordance with the law relating to the Court of Admiralty,[6] is not at all borne out by the records of the Court of Chivalry, where there are many cases in which damages were

---

[1] Her. Cas. 62.

[2] Misc. Cur. Mil. 235. Owing to this rule it is possible to ascertain the number of causes pending on any day for which the Act Book survives, see p. 56 *ante*.

[3] *Coventry (Earl) v. King* (1701), unrep., cited in *Blount's Case* (1737), 1 Atk., at p. 297. The 'false arms' were those ordered by King to be used as those of the Earl's stepmother at his father's funeral (*The Case of the Earl of Coventry*, reprinted in *Her. and Gen.* vii (1873), 100–4).

[4] According to T. Oughton, *Ordo Judiciorum* (London, 1728), i. 199, the judge wrote the word *justitiam* in his own hand in a space left for it in the porrected sentence, but the completed sentences surviving in the records of the Court of Chivalry do not appear to afford any evidence of such a practice in that Court. For the form of sentence, see Appendix XXI, p. 261 *post*. *Justitiam* is in the ninth line.

[5] *Commentaries*, iii. 104.   [6] *Sparks v. Martyn* (1668), 1 Vent. 1.

awarded.[1] Why there should have been this difference between the two courts, which resembled each other in so many other respects, is not apparent.

Fines also were imposed, sometimes in addition to damages. Here again the Court of Chivalry differed from the Court of Admiralty, which could only fine for contempt.[2] The fine might be much heavier than the damages and costs, as in *Ryvers* v. *Burley*,[3] where the fine was £40, the damages £6. 13*s*. 4*d*., and the costs 20 marks.[4]

One of the most frequent requirements of a definitive sentence was that the defendant should make a formal acknowledgement of his wrongdoing, known as a submission. In such cases the wording of the submission was laid down by an order of the Court, as in the case of Nathaniel Hawthorne of Cookham, co. Berks., who was required to say:

> Being but a yeoman & no gentleman and that notwithstanding that by the Officers of Armes in a visitation held at Ockingham in anno 1623 or thereabouts I was proscribed and proclaymed not to be a gentleman, yet that I have since . . . assumed and used the name and title of gentleman in contempt of the Lawes of Armes and of the Court aforesaid, I the said Nathaniel Hawthorne doe humbly confesse and acknowledge that in so doing I did much forgett my selfe and my duty and the honor and respect I ought to have had to the gentry lawes and officers of Armes of this kingedome, and doe promise henceforth not to arrogate use or assume any such title except I be lawfully called or intituled thereto hereafter.[5]

Nathaniel Hawthorne was required to make his submission at the Berkshire Quarter Sessions. Sometimes submission had to be made at assizes[6] or at borough

---

[1] e.g. *Temple* v. *Ayleworth* (1634), Her. Cas. 7 (20 nobles); *Starkey* v. *Bestney* (1634), Her. Cas. 10 (£10); *Duck* v. *Mosely* (1638), Her. Cas. 33 (200 marks).

[2] *Thomlinson's Case* (1604), 12 Co. Rep. 104; *Sparks* v. *Martyn* (1668), 1 Vent. 1.   [3] (1639), Cur. Mil. Boxes 10/9/3.

[4] The defendant in *Darcey* v. *Greene* (1640), Cur. Mil. Boxes 20/2*e*, was guilty of a serious underestimate of the possibilities when, on being told that the plaintiff would sue him in the Court of Honour, he sent a message that he had laid aside 20 marks to spend with the plaintiff in the Court of Honour, for he knew that was 'the worst the Court of Honour could do him'.

[5] *Longvyll* v. *Hawthorne* (1635), Cur. Mil. Boxes 4/2.

[6] e.g. *Coffin* v. *Stephens* (1638), Cur. Mil. Boxes 4/6 (Exeter).

sessions,[1] whilst defendants in London or Middlesex were required to appear in open court in the Painted Chamber.[2]

It was, however, not essential that the submission should be made in a court. A submission closely corresponded to the penance enjoined by an ecclesiastical court in a cause of defamation. What was desired was that the submission should be made in such a manner as to repair the plaintiff's reputation amongst those who knew him best.[3] In *Andrewes* v. *Farmer*[4] the submission had to be made in the hall of the Crown Inn in Oakham on the day of the next Rutland Assizes. The defendant in *Mantell* v. *Sampson*[5] had to make his submission near the Cross at Highgate, co. Kent. In *Andrewes* v. *Morris*[6] the submission had to be made at Barber-Surgeons' Hall in Mogwell Street, where the 'scandalous words' had been spoken. The defendant in *Carew* v. *Hellin*[7] was required to make his submission in three places as far apart as Tiverton, Haverfordwest, and Pembroke. In *Office of the Judge* v. *Underwood*[8] the submission was made at and recorded in the College of Arms, a certificate of the fact being filed amongst the records of the Court. In *Porter* v. *Larder*[9] the defendant had to make his submission on the day of the general meeting of the trained band of soldiers under the plaintiff's command in a place to be appointed by the plaintiff. In *Sidenham* v. *Cruse*[10] the defendant was ordered to stand bareheaded at the stile of Dulverton churchyard near to Widow Garleforde's house after morning prayer and sermon, between the hours of 10 a.m. and 1 p.m. on Sunday, 1 December 1639, and there to read a confession of his conviction in the Court.

An even less suitable place for the making of a submission was the parish church of Much Bentleigh, co.

---

[1] e.g. *Nest* v. *Greene* (1639), Cur. Mil. Boxes 13/3*z* (Pontefract).
[2] e.g. *Bowen* v. *Nicholls* (1636), Cur. Mil. Boxes 4/3.
[3] Cf. Oughton, *Ordo Judiciorum*, i. 392.
[4] (1640), Cur. Mil. Boxes 4/28.   [5] (1637), Cur. Mil. Boxes 15/1*w*.
[6] (1639), Cur. Mil. Boxes 4/24.   [7] (1635), Cur. Mil. Boxes 10/10/4.
[8] (1634), Her. Cas. 6.   [9] (1639), Cur. Mil. Boxes 4/39.
[10] (1639), Cur. Mil. Boxes 18/4*e*.

Essex. The vicar was furnished with the words of the submission signed by the defendant, which he read in church on Sunday morning, 16 July 1637. The defendant was supposed to repeat the words after the vicar, but he sat with his hat on and made various alterations in the words of the submission in a 'jeering and flering manner by way of scorne and derision' to the plaintiff. Not content with that, the defendant went to evening prayer that day and made several low obeisances before the plaintiff in his pew 'in way of derision', laughing in his face, which 'moved a great part of the Congregacion to a laughter'.[1] The result of all this was that the defendant was brought before the Court again in a cause of office for contempt and was fined £100 and ordered to pay £25 costs.[2]

In *Ryvers* v. *Burley*,[3] where the defendant had said that 'every Cobler might be a gentleman as well as . . . Mr. Ryvers', submission was ordered to be made to the officers of arms, as well as the plaintiff, on account of the 'contempt of the laws and officers of arms'.

Previous notice of the submission had to be given to the plaintiff, so that, if he so desired, he could attend and gloat over his defeated adversary. If notice was not given to the plaintiff, he could obtain another order of submission.[4]

If the defendant failed to make his submission as ordered, an attachment was granted against him.[5]

After the submission had been made a certificate signed by some responsible person present was returned to the Court.[6] This certificate was in its turn certified by the Register.[7]

[1] *Badcock* v. *Comin* (1637), Cur. Mil. Boxes 12/1*gg*.

[2] *Badcock* v. *Comin* (*No. 2*) (1637), Cur. Mil. Boxes 12/1*hh*; 15/20.

[3] (1639), Cur. Mil. Boxes 10/9/3.

[4] *Sidenham* v. *Cruse* (1639), Cur. Mil. Boxes 18/4*k*. The submission was performed on 12 Sep. 1639 and a certificate of it returned to the Court on the first day of Michaelmas term (ibid. 18/4*o*), but the plaintiffs alleged that they had not been given notice of the first submission and obtained another order of submission, which the defendant countered by an affidavit of service of notice.

[5] *Leigh* v. *Burnett* (1638), Cur. Mil. Boxes 4/19.

[6] e.g. *Brooke* v. *Gutch* (1640), Cur. Mil. Boxes 4/41 (Clerk of Assize): *Turney* v. *Wodden* (1635), ibid. 9/4/38 (Clerk of the Peace).

[7] e.g. *Huntingdon* (*Earl*) v. *Hawkes* (1640), Cur. Mil. Boxes 18/4*l*.

After sentence against him the defendant was required
to give a bond, usually with two sureties, for the payment
of the fine, damages, and costs and the performance of the
submission.[1] Sometimes only one surety was required,[2]
and with the approval of the King's Advocate sureties
could be dispensed with altogether.[3] Like most money
bonds, such bonds were usually for double the amount
secured. The bond could provide for payment by instalments. In *Wortley* v. *Allott*[4] the damages and costs were
to be paid in five instalments, the last being payable on
29 June 1642, so the defendant was saved from paying several instalments by the supression of the Court
in 1641. An allegation of poverty by the defendant in
Sidenham v. *Cruse*[5] resulted in an order for payment by
instalments, but the plaintiff was afterwards able to prove
that the defendant was a man of good estate, whereupon
the defendant was ordered to pay within a month not only
the original £40 damages, but also an additional £13. 6s. 8d.
for unnecessary costs.

Pending the giving of the bond the defendant could be
imprisoned in the custody of the Knight Marshal or his
deputy.[6] This was not always done. In *Collin* v. *Wigg*[7] the
defendant was sentenced in Trinity term 1640 in £20 costs
and £20 damages and to make submission, but apparently
was neither taken into custody nor required to give a
bond, for on his refusal to perform any part of the sentence
it was ordered on 14 September that he should make submission the next court day and pay the costs on 29 September and the damages on 4 December, failing which an
attachment should issue against him for his contempt.

---

[1] *Bacon* v. *Webb* (1639), Cur. Mil. Boxes 6/117.
[2] e.g. *Springnall* v. *Chapman* (1637), Cur. Mil. Boxes 3/66.
[3] *Freeman* v. *Page* (1637), Cur. Mil. Boxes 3/54.
[4] (1639), Cur. Mil. Boxes 6/90.
[5] (1640), Cur. Mil. Boxes 7/48.
[6] *Bowne* v. *Throgmorton* (1634), Cur. Mil. Boxes 7/6; *Office of the Judge* v.
Winchell (1634), Her. Cas. 6. In *Bowen* v. *Nicholls* (1635), Cur. Mil. Boxes 7/66,
67, the Earl Marshal ordered on 23 Dec. that upon the production of sufficient
sureties the defendant should be released from the Marshalsea 'against this good
time of Christmas'.
[7] (1640), Cur. Mil. Boxes 7/21.

Blackstone, following Holt C.J. in *Chambers* v.
Jennings,[1] states that the Court of Chivalry cannot imprison, 'not being a court of record'.[2] The reason why it is
not a court of record is that its proceedings are according
to the course of the civil law.[3] Nevertheless, whilst such
a court cannot pass a sentence of imprisonment, it can
imprison for contempt.[4] This power the Court of Chivalry
freely exercised, using it for the enforcement of sentences
to pay damages and fines and to make submission.[5] As
Francis Thynne, Lancaster Herald, wrote of the Constable
and the Marshal in 1605, 'if they should not have
authority to imprison, in vain it were then to determine
anything'.[6] Attachments were made by the Messenger of
the Court or his deputy.

It is stated in Giles Jacob's *New Law-Dictionary*[7] that
the Earl Marshal had a prison of his own, known as the
White Lion prison in Southwark. At first sight this
appears a convincing story, for the members of the
Mowbray family who held the Earl Marshalship at
various times during the fourteenth and fifteenth centuries gave for their arms *Gules, a lion rampant argent,*
whilst the white lion was used as a badge by the first
Howard Duke of Norfolk. However, when traced to its
source the story proves to be a myth. Jacob cites as his
authority William Nelson's *Abridgement of the Common
Law.*[8] Nelson, in his turn, states that Parker was 'committed by the Commissioners [for executing the office of

---

[1] (1692), 7 Mod. 125, at p. 128.
[2] *Commentaries*, iii. 105. No court can fine or imprison which is not a court of
record (*Godfrey's Case* (1614), 11 Co. Rep. 42*a*, 43*b*). Conversely the possession
of power to fine and imprison makes a court a court of record (*Kemp* v. *Neville*
(1861), 31 L.J. C.P. 158 (University Court)). As to fines see p. 212 *ante*.
[3] *Thomlinson's Case* (1604), 12 Co. Rep. 104; *Case of the Admiralty* (1609), 13
Co. Rep. 53.
[4] *Sparks* v. *Martyn* (1668), 1 Vent. 1.
[5] *Pace* Kekewich J. in *In re Croxich, Croxon* v. *Ferrers*, [1904] 1 Ch. 252, at p.
258: 'The Court of Chivalry only decided the facts, and decided in what sense the
law was, but it was a Court which had no power of enforceing its decrees.'
[6] 'A Discourse of the Duty and Office of an Herald of Arms' in Hearne,
Curious Discourses, i. 156.
[7] 10th ed. (London, 1782), s.v. 'Honour-Courts'.
[8] (London, 1726), ii. 935.

Earl Marshal] to their Prison, called the White Lyon in Southwark', citing *R. v. Parker*,[1] as reported in Siderfin. Unfortunately Nelson mistranslated Siderfin's report. Siderfin stated that Parker was committed 'al prison del marshal' (appell le White-Lyon in Southwark)'. Nelson failed to observe that in Siderfin's report the word 'marshal'' is followed by an apostrophe used as a mark of abbreviation, so that the prison referred to was not that of the Marshal, but that of the Marshalsea. This is confirmed by the return to the *habeas corpus*, which was made by John Lowman, Deputy Marshal of the Marshalsea of the King's Household, and expressly states that Parker was in the prison called 'Le Marshalsea'.[2]

In fact Parker's committal was in accordance with the usual practice. Thus William Holmes was in the custody of the Knight Marshal pending his trial for the murder of Thomas Wise,[3] and Sir James Tillie was committed to the Marshalsea for making an escape out of the custody of the Messenger of the Court in 1687.[4] In this, as in many other respects, the Court of Chivalry followed the practice of the Court of Admiralty, which committed for contempt to the prison of the Marshalsea of the Royal Household until its prisoners were removed in 1842 to the prison of the Marshalsea of the Court of Queen's Bench (then renamed the Queen's Prison).[5] The Court of Chivalry, however, sometimes made use of other prisons as well. William Holmes was imprisoned in the Poultry Compter before being transferred to the Marshalsea,[6] whilst Lord Rea and Donald Ramsey were committed to the Tower of London.[7] Presumably persons who were

---

[1] (1668), 1 Sid. 352.
[2] Coll. Arm. MS. R. 28 (not foliated). The warrant of commitment was addressed 'To the Keeper of the Prison of the Marshalsea' (ibid). The prison is not named the White Lion in any of the documents there copied, but if Siderfin was right in so naming it, some revision may be required of the account of the White Lion prison in *Survey of London*, xxv (1955), 17, where it is stated that it was the county jail for Surrey. The Marshalsea prison here referred to must not be confused with the prison of the Marshalsea of the Court of King's Bench.
[3] See p. 55 *ante*.   [4] Coll. Arm. MS. SML 3, p. 27.
[5] 5 & 6 Vict., c. 22, preamble and fig.
[6] See p. 53 *ante*.   [7] See p. 54 *ante*.

arrested by the Messenger of the Court in order to ensure their appearance were kept in temporary custody at the Earl Marshal's residence.

In addition to porrecting the definitive sentence which he desired, each party porrected his bill of costs on parchment signed by his counsel in the bottom left-hand corner, with a space left for the insertion of the sum at which the bill was taxed. Bills of costs were itemized, but were taxed at a lump sum. On taxation a bill was signed by the Earl Marshal or his surrogate. Sometimes the taxation was severe. Of the total of £88. 8s. 8d. claimed by the successful plaintiff in *Carewe* v. *Hellin*[1] only £6. 13s. 4d. was allowed on taxation. This is hardly surprising, for £60 of the total was made up of the travelling expenses from Somerset to London (£10), the expenses of the plaintiff in London (£33), the expenses of his servants (£7), and travelling expenses from London (£10). Added to this, the plaintiff's conduct was harsh and oppressive, for he refused to accept the defendant's tender of a submission in writing, although the defendant was a poor man.[2]

It was quite common for a cause to take a year or more from petition to sentence. The progress of a cause can readily be seen if there is a bill of costs surviving. A typical cause is *Dingley* v. *Maulton*,[3] where the plaintiff's bill of costs shows the steps term by term as follows: Hilary term, 1639: Petition, Monition, Execution of Monition; Easter term, 1639: Libel; Trinity term, 1639: Commission; Vacation following: Execution of Commission; Michaelmas term, 1639: Interrogatories; Vacation following: Examination on Interrogatories; Hilary term, 1640: Definitive Sentence.

(B) *Ex Officio*

Causes of office were of two kinds: (1) those on the necessary promotion of the King's Advocate,[4] and (2)

---

[1] (1635), Cur. Mil. Boxes 9/4/1.
[2] Ibid. 9/4/10. In *Le Strange* v. *Styleman* (1640), ibid. 14/1*h*, the plaintiff's bill of £140. 4s. 9d. was taxed at £8.   [3] (1639), Cur. Mil. Boxes 11/28.
[4] e.g. *Duck* v. *Hanslopp* (1637), Her. Cas. 27.

those on the voluntary promotion of the promoter.[1] They were commenced by articles exhibited against the defendant by the promoter. Apart from this difference in pleading, the procedure in causes of office was similar to that in causes of instance.

The case was proved by the depositions of witnesses as in causes of instance. Damages could be awarded in a cause of office as well as in a cause of instance. Thus in *Duck* v. *Mosely*[2] the defendant, who had caused arms and banners to be displayed at the funeral of his uncle without the direction of the officers of arms, was not only fined £200, but also sentenced to pay 200 marks damages to the officers of arms in respect of the fees which they had lost.

(C) *Appeals of Treason and Murder*

It is not necessary to describe in detail the procedure in an appeal of treason, for it is available in print in the report of *Rea* v. *Ramsey*,[3] and in Sir Henry Spelman's *Glossarium Archaiologicum*.[4]

The proceedings commenced with a bill of appeal in writing, which was read in open court, after which the party challenging threw down his glove for a pawn or pledge. The party challenged then threw down his glove, and the two gloves were taken up by Clarenceux King of Arms and delivered to the Lord High Constable, who with the Earl Marshal committed them to the custody of the Register. The Earl Marshal arrested both parties and released them on the production of sureties for the prosecution and defence of the challenge.[5]

The decision of such a cause by duel did not follow as a matter of course. The duel was the ultimate trial in default of all others, and even then it was in the arbitrament

---

[1] e.g. *St. George* v. *Tuckfield* (1634), Her. Cas. 24.

[2] (1638), Her. Cas. 33.   [3] (1631), 3 St. Tr. 483.

[4] 3rd ed. (London, 1687), pp. 99–103, s.v. 'Campus'. There is an English version with annotations by Sir John Burrough, Garter King of Arms, in Inner Temple MS., Petyt 538, and in P.R.O. State Papers Miscellaneous, vol. 10, ff. 49–78. See also p. 53 *ante*.

[5] 3 St Tr., at p. 501.

of the Court whether a duel should be granted or denied.[1] The Court heard evidence and could then determine the matter in one of three ways, namely (1) by absolving the accused; (2) by condemning the accused, when the truth of the crime alleged appeared by witnesses or in any other way; or (3) by way of public duel.[2]

When the Court decided to order a duel, the parties were required to state their acquiescence in the bill of appeal and answer respectively, and to sign them and seal them with their seals of arms.[3] Then the Lord High Constable put the bill of appeal into the challenger's glove, and the answer into the defender's glove. He then held the bill and glove in his right hand and the answer and glove in his left, and joining the bill and answer and the gloves and folding them together, he and the Earl Marshal adjudged a duel between the parties at a certain time and place.[4] After the duel had been adjudged, the Court made orders concerning the number of offensive weapons and their maximum dimensions,[5] and the presence in the lists of counsel, a surgeon with his ointments and instruments, bread, wine, or other drink, nails, hammer, file, scissors, bodkin, needle and thread, armourer and tailor with their instruments.[6]

The evidence concerning appeals of murder is scanty, there being records of only one case—*Wise* v. *Holmes* in 1634. A bill signed by the widow of the murdered man was presented in Court in the presence of the accused.[7] In this case the allegations in the bill were proved by witnesses and the accused was condemned without any battle.[8]

---

[1] *Per* Earl of Arundel E.M., 3 St. Tr., at p. 497.
[2] *Per* Earl of Arundel E.M., ibid. 506.   [3] Ibid. 506.
[4] Ibid. 507.
[5] Ibid. 511. The parties could use defensive weapons at their own discretion (ibid. 513).
[6] Ibid. 509, 510.
[7] Cur. Mil. Boxes 8/21a.   [8] See p. 55 *ante*.

XIV

APPEALS FROM THE COURT
OF CHIVALRY

ROM the earliest days of the Court of Chivalry
appeals lay to the King in Chancery. The work of
hearing and definitively determining such appeals
was delegated to commissioners specially appointed by
letters patent for each case. During the medieval period
the commissions were usually composed of knights and
doctors of law, with whom a few noblemen were sometimes associated,[1] though there were cases in which only
doctors of law were appointed.[2]

In more modern times the delegates were usually
common-law judges and civilians sitting together, and
were known as 'the High Court of Delegates',[3] though
there was nothing permanent about the constitution of the
Court, fresh delegates being appointed for each appeal.
The commissions were issued under the half-seal, i.e.
sealed with wax impressed with the upper part of each
half of the matrix of the Great Seal.[4]

If an unsuccessful party to an appeal wished to question
the decision of the delegates, he could obtain a commission of review appointing fresh delegates. This, of
course, could be used as a means of considerable delay.
One of the most striking examples was in *Haule* v. *Shakel*,
concerning the ransom of the Count of Denia, where on
24 July 1409 delegates were appointed to examine the

---

[1] e.g. the defendant's appeal in *Scrope* v. *Grosvenor* was delegated to the earls
of Kent, Salisbury, and Northumberland, John de Cobham and Richard Adder-
bury, knights, John Appleby, dean of St. Paul's, and John Barnet, Robert
Weston, and Nicholas Stoket, doctors of laws (*C.P.R. 1388–92*, p. 40).

[2] e.g. in *Grey* v. *Hastings* (1413), *C.P.R. 1413–16*, p. 9.

[3] Privy Council Appeals Act, 1832, preamble.

[4] 8 Eliz. I, c. 5. For an account of the practice of sealing with the half-seal see
Sir H. C. Maxwell-Lyte, *Historical Notes on the Use of the Great Seal of England*
(London, 1926), pp. 304–9. Maxwell-Lyte does not mention the use of the half-
seal on commissions of delegacy.

proceedings in the appeal which had been commenced by a commission issued nineteen years earlier (21 October 1390).[1] Commissions of review were abolished in 'civil and marine causes' by statute in 1566,[2] though they still continued in ecclesiastical cases.

Appeals from the Court of Chivalry were common in the medieval period, but they were rare during the periods when the Court was active in the seventeenth and eighteenth centuries.[3]

Until the procedure was altered in the nineteenth century[4] an appeal from the Court of Chivalry was initiated by means of a petition addressed to the Crown, by whom it was laid before the Lord Chancellor.[5] The appellant then had to obtain a commission of delegacy and bring it into the Court of Chivalry.[6] In considering whether to grant a commission the Lord Chancellor had not to try the merits of the cause or decide whether the judge of the Court of Chivalry had properly rejected an allegation, though he had to decide whether an appeal would lie or not.[7] The delegates by letters patent in the King's name, but under a special seal *ad causas*, required the Earl Marshal and the Register to transmit to them all the documents in the cause.[8]

---

[1] *C.P.R. 1388–92*, p. 324: *C.P.R. 1408–13*, p. 100. Yet another commission was issued on 22 Apr. 1412 (ibid., p. 391).

[2] 8 Eliz. I, c. 5.

[3] There are only four such appeals mentioned in *A Catalogue of Processes in the Registry of the High Court of Delegates from 1609 to 1823* (n.d.), but there were a few others known from other sources, e.g. *Leeke* v. *Harris* (1625), Her. Cas., at p. 5; *Blount's Case* (1737), 1 Atk. 295. According to the *Return of all Appeals in Causes of Doctrine or Discipline made to the High Court of Delegates* made to the House of Commons in 1868 there were seven instances of appeal from the Court of Chivalry of various dates from 1625 to 1739 in the extant records of the Delegates (p. xxiv).

[4] See p. 223 *post*.

[5] For a petition of appeal see Appendix XXV, p. 269 *post*.

[6] *St. George* v. *Howell* (1688), Act Book, 29 Mar. *King* v. *Coventry (Earl)* (1702), *Her. and Gen.* viii. (1873), 104. Such commissions were in the form of letters patent, e.g. *Harris* v. *Leeke* (1625), *Foedera*, xviii. 241.

[7] *Blount's Case* (1737), 1 Atk. 295, 297. In *Copley* v. *Kingston (Earl)* (1637), *C.S.P.D. 1636–1637*, p. 495, this question was referred to the Earls of Northumberland and Dorset and two other persons.

[8] *Harris* v. *Leeke* (1625), Coll. Arm. MS. R. 19, f. 226.

Appeals from decisions of the Court of Chivalry were not governed by any special custom, but had to be brought under the rules of the civil law with regard to appeal, so far as the civil law had been admitted in England.[1] In the civil law an appeal only lies where *gravamen est irreparabile*, in contrast with the canon law, where there is an appeal from all grievances in general. Accordingly the practice with regard to appeals from the Court of Admiralty was applicable to appeals from the Court of Chivalry.[2] An appeal from the Court of Chivalry would therefore only lie against a definitive sentence, or a final interlocutory decree having the force of a definitive sentence, or an interlocutory order which was *gravamen irreparabile*. It was *gravamen irreparabile* to order a defendant to give his answer upon oath in a cause which was in the nature of a criminal prosecution, for if he had made a confession upon oath the cause would have been over.[3] But the admission in evidence of an unsigned pedigree in a book in the College of Arms was not *gravamen irreparabile*, for that raised a question of law which could be taken on appeal after definitive sentence.[4]

The powers of the Court of Delegates were transferred to the King in Council by the Privy Council Appeals Act, 1832. Although it did not mention the Court of Chivalry by name, the effect of this Act was to substitute an appeal to the King in Council for the old appeal to the King in Chancery. By section 3 of the Judicial Committee Act, 1833, appeals to the King in Council were required to be referred by the King to the Judicial Committee of the Privy Council, though no special order of reference is now necessary.[5] In the event of an appeal from a decision of the Court of Chivalry the procedure would now be by way of a petition of appeal addressed to the Queen and lodged

---

[1] *Blount's Case, supra,* at p. 296.
[2] Ibid., at pp. 296, 298.
[3] *King* v. *Coventry (Earl)* (1702), unrep., cited in *Blount's Case, supra,* at p. 297.
[4] *Blount's Case, supra.*
[5] Judicial Committee Act, 1844, s. 11; Appellate Jurisdiction Act, 1908, s. 5 Statutory Rules and Orders, 1909, No. 1228.

with the Clerk of the Privy Council.[1] The appellant and respondent would then lodge their respective cases and the appeal would proceed in the same manner as any other appeal to the Privy Council.[2]

[1] Judicial Committee Act, 1844, s. 11.
[2] For the procedure in Privy Council apppeals see N. Bentwich, *The Practice of the Privy Council in Judicial Matters* (3rd ed, London, 1937).

APPENDIX I

The Records of the Court

UNTIL the setting up of the Public Record Office only the records of the Chancery were in the custody of the Master of the Rolls, the other public records being scattered in many different repositories in the hands of many different keepers. Under the Public Record Office Act, 1838, the records of the Courts mentioned in section 1 of that Act were transferred to the Master of the Rolls. The Court of Chivalry was not there mentioned and therefore none of its records is to be found in the Public Record Office.[1]

The fact that the records of the Court have not been in the custody of the keepers of the public records has led to the mistaken belief that the records no longer exist. Writing but little more than half a century after the Court had last sat, James Dallaway stated:

The history of the proceedings in the Court of Chivalry must, from a deficiency of authorities, remain almost unknown. Circumstances which cannot be ascertained have conspired to consign their records, during the early centuries, to a total oblivion. All that is preserved in the archives of the College of Arms appears to have been collected rather as private than official notices, and as memoranda made by the practitioners in that Court, in no instance giving more than a summary view of any particular cause, hereafter to be cited as a precedent.[2]

Dallaway's statement about the records 'during the early centuries' is true. In the early years of the seventeenth century an anonymous author could write—

'such hath byn the neglect & miscarridg of such who in their severall and respective tymes had the custody of the Records of that Court, That there are not above 4 or 5 processes in any cause in that Court of auncient tymes extant Saveing that there be amongst the Records in the Tower some appellations upon sentences there given, and Writts thereupon.[3]

[1] P. H. Winfield, *The Chief Sources of English Legal History* (Cambridge, Mass., 1925), p. 107, states that the records of the Court of Chivalry were transferred to the Master of the Rolls. This is the sole reference to the Court in that work.

[2] *Inquiries into the Origin . . . of Heraldry*, p. 290. Cf. Grazebrook, *The Earl Marshal's Court*, p. 13: 'We must accept the statement of all previous writers that the Records of the Earl Marshal's Court cannot be found.' Round, on the other hand, seems to have known of the existence of the records, for he complains of them not being open to the pubic (*Peerage and Pedigree*, i. 72).

[3] Lincoln's Inn MS. Hale X (not foliated).

It is, however, apparent from the dates of the ten cases cited by Dallaway as precedents[1] that he thought that the seventeenth-century records had also disappeared. In fact there is quite a substantial body of original records of the Court preserved in the College of Arms. How they came to be there is not certain. Presumably they were in the custody of the successive Registers of the Court until Mark Holman, who was the last Register until recently, died in 1754. It seems likely that Holman was allowed to keep the records in the College, where the Court usually sat in his time, and that they remained there during the long vacancy in the office of Register. It is, however, possible that the records came to the College at some later date, since they were not mentioned in the return made to the Select Committee on the Public Records by the Officers of Arms in 1800, though this may have been because they were not records of the College.[2] In addition there are a few records of the Court amongst those of the Court of Arches, which is doubtless explicable by the fact that during the reigns of Queen Anne and George I the Register of the Court of Chivalry was Henry Farrant, who was also Register of the Court of Arches.[3]

The main bulk of the records of the Court in the College of Arms is contained in two large wooden boxes, which appear to be no older than the beginning of the nineteenth century. Within the boxes the documents are made up into twenty-two parcels.[4] Many of the documents are now loose in the parcels, but in some cases they are filed on strings with metal tags resembling modern shoelaces. There was a separate file for each session in each term, but the contents of most of the files have been separated, there being only twenty-six files remaining.

In addition to the documents in the boxes, there are several volumes consisting of what were originally separate documents

---

[1] Op. cit. pp. 295–302.

[2] *Reports from the Select Committee appointed to inquire into the State of the Public Records* (1800), p. 82. The only reference to records of the Court of Chivalry in the return made by the Officers of Arms is that the Earl Marshal's Books 'contain some few proceedings in the Earl Marshal's Court from the time of Queen Elizabeth to that of Charles II inclusive'.

[3] During the war of 1939–45 these records were temporarily deposited in the Bodleian Library. Sir Edmund Craster, *History of the Bodleian Library, 1845–1945* (Oxford, 1952), p. 342, errs in stating that they were returned after the end of the war. They were deposited in the Lambeth Palace Library in 1958.

[4] Each box is inscribed 'Curia Militaris' and the documents are cited as 'Cur. Mil. Boxes', followed by the number of the parcel. Parcels 1 to 20 consist of documents dated between 1631 and 1640. Parcel 21 and an unnumbered parcel marked 'X' consist of documents dated between 1687 and 1710.

bound together. Some of these volumes have been lettered 'Acta Curiae Militaris', but this is misleading, for they contain miscellaneous documents and not the formal acts of the Court. The documents in these volumes probably came from files which have been dismembered.

With the exception of the sessional files, the documents in the boxes and the bound volumes are not arranged in their original order, but some of the parcels contain artificial collections of particular kinds of documents. Thus parcel 2 consists of 171 petitions and bonds, mostly of the year 1639, and parcel 4 consists of fifty orders of submission dated between 1635 and 1640.

Of the series of act books the only survivor in its original form is that for the years 1687 to 1702. There is an act book for 1636–8 so much damaged by damp as to be practically useless. There are also some fragments of act books amongst the miscellaneous documents, whilst parcel 1 contains some draft acts for a number of sessions between 1634 and 1640.

Most of the surviving depositions are the originals annexed to the returns of the commissioners before whom they were taken, but there is one volume containing copies of depositions taken between 1687 and 1692.

The system of sessional files must always have made it difficult to trace all the documents relating to any particular cause and the breaking up of the files has probably not increased the difficulty much, if at all. For the purposes of the present work an index of causes has been made. Many causes are now only represented by a single document, whilst at the other end of the scale are causes such as *Sidenham* v. *Cruse* (1639–40), for which there are eighteen documents dispersed amongst six parcels. There can never be any certainty that the surviving documents in any cause are complete.

Whilst not technically records of the Court of Chivalry, there are amongst the Chancery records in the Public Record Office copies of the Court of Chivalry records of two important heraldic causes—*Scrope* v. *Grosvenor* and *Lovel* v. *Morley*—and a few other causes in the Court which went to appeal. These copies, which are almost contemporary with the originals, owe their preservation to the fact that the processes were by writs of *certiorari* directed to be transmitted to the Chancellor, the rolls containing the returns to these writs being amongst the earliest of the Miscellanea of the Chancery.[1]

[1] P.R.O., C. 47/6/1–3.

APPENDIX II

Lists of Officers of the Court

THE following abbreviations are used:

adm.	admitted	d.	died
app.	appointed	ex.	executed
att.	attainted	occ.	occurs
cr.	created	succ.	succeeded

I. CONSTABLES OF ENGLAND[1]

Humphrey (de Bohun), Earl of Hereford and Essex, succ. as hereditary Constable of England 20 Jan. 1335/6; d. 15 Oct. 1361.

William (de Bohun), Earl of Northampton, by grant from his brother for life before 12 June 1338;[2] d. 16 Sept. 1360.

Humphrey (de Bohun), Earl of Hereford, Essex and Northampton, succ. 15 Oct. 1361; d. 16 Jan. 1372/3, leaving two daughters and coheirs.

Thomas of Woodstock, youngest son of Edward III, m. Eleanor de Bohun, elder daughter of the last; app. during pleasure 10 June 1376;[3] cr. Earl of Buckingham 16 July 1377; cr. Duke of Gloucester 6 Aug. 1385; arrested on a charge of treason 10 July 1397.[4]

Edward, Earl of Rutland, app. during pleasure 12 July 1397[5] and for life 9 Sept. 1397;[6] cr. Duke of Aumale 29 Sept. 1397; forfeited 1399.

Henry (Percy), Earl of Northumberland, app. for life 30 Sept. 1399;[7] in rebellion 1403.

John, 3rd s. of Henry IV, app. during pleasure 10 Sept. 1403[8] and for life 4 July 1410;[9] cr. Duke of Bedford 16 May 1414; d. 15 Sept. 1435.

Sir Henry Brounflete, app. to discharge the office of Constable pro tem. 11 Nov. 1438.[10]

[1] Appointments made for the purposes of coronations have not been included.
[2] *C.P.R. 1338–40*, p. 95.
[3] *C.P.R. 1374–7*, p. 279.
[4] *C.P.* v. 725.
[5] *C.P.R. 1396–9*, p. 171.
[6] Ibid., p. 359.
[7] *C.P.R. 1399–1401*, p. 12.
[8] *C.P.R. 1401–5*, p. 259.
[9] *C.P.R. 1408–13*, p. 211.
[10] *C.P.R. 1436–41*, p. 265.

John (Beaumont), Viscount Beaumont, app. 12 Nov. 1445.[1]

Henry (Percy), Earl of Northumberland, app. during pleasure 25 May 1450 in succession to Beaumont.[2]

Edmund (Beaufort), Duke of Somerset, app. 11 Sept. 1450;[3] d. 22 May 1455.

John (Tiptoft), Earl of Worcester, app. during pleasure 7 Feb. 1461/2.[4]

Richard (Woodville), Earl Rivers, app. for life with remainder to his son, Anthony, 24 Aug. 1467, on the surrender of Worcester;[5] ex. 12 Aug. 1469.

Anthony (Woodville), Earl Rivers, succ. 12 Aug. 1469; resigned.[6]

Richard (Plantagenet), Duke of Gloucester, app. for life 17 Oct. 1469.[7]

John (Tiptoft), Earl of Worcester, app. for life 14 Mar. 1469/70;[8] ex. 18 Oct. 1470.

Richard (Plantagenet), Duke of Gloucester, occ. 29 Feb. 1471/2[9] and 20 Aug. 1480.[10]

Sir William Parre, Sir James Haryngton, and Sir James Tyrell, knts. (one of whom in the absence of the others to be Vice-Constable), and Masters John Wallyngton, William Lacy, William Fuller, and George Warde, bachelors of laws, app. Commissioners 14 Nov. 1482.[11]

Henry (Stafford), Duke of Buckingham, app. for life 15 July 1483;[12] ex. 2 Nov. 1483.

Thomas, Lord Stanley, app. for life 18 Nov. 1483;[13] cr. Earl of Derby 27 Oct. 1485; reapp. Constable by Henry VII, 5 Mar. 1485/6,[14] d. 29 July 1504.

Edward (Stafford), Duke of Buckingham, claimed the office as of right 1514[15]; ex. 1521.

---

[1] J. Doyle, *The Official Baronage of England* (London, 1886), i. 146. *Sed cave*, for Doyle's dates, though given with apparent exactitude, cannot be relied upon when he cites no authority (*C.P.* iii. 263, note (*d*)). Beaumont occurs as Constable on 15 Nov. 1446 (*C.P.R. 1446–52*, p. 6).

[2] *C.P.R. 1446–52*, p. 326.   [3] Ibid., p. 401.

[4] *C.P.R. 1461–7*, p. 74.   [5] *C.P.R. 1467–77*, p. 19.

[6] *Excerpta Historica*, p. 241.   [7] *C.P.R. 1467–77*, p. 178.

[8] Ibid., p. 205.   [9] Ibid., p. 307.

[10] *C.P.R. 1476–85*, p. 230.   [11] Ibid, p. 317.

[12] Ibid., p. 361.

[13] Ibid., p. 367. For some reason which is not apparent Stanley was reapp. 16 Dec. 1483 (ibid., p. 381).

[14] *C.P.R. 1485–94*, p. 83.   [15] *Duke of Buckingham's Case*, 3 Dyer 285b.

Robert (Bertie), Earl of Lindsey, app. for the trial of *Rea* v. *Ramsey* 24 Nov. 1631[1] and for the trial of murders and homicides committed overseas 11 Feb. 1634.[2]

II. EARL MARSHALS AND DEPUTY EARL MARSHALS[3]

Thomas (Beauchamp), Earl of Warwick, app. during pleasure 10 Feb. 1343/4;[4] d. 13 Nov. 1369.

Edmund (Mortimer), Earl of March, occ. 6 Feb. 1373/4;[5] resigned 1376.[6]

Henry, Lord Percy, occ. 1 Dec. 1376[7] and 15 Mar. 1377.[8]

John, Lord Arundel, occ. 9 Apr. 1378;[9] d. Dec. 1379.

Thomas (Holand), Earl of Kent, app. 13 Mar. 1379/80;[10] discharged before 30 June 1385.[11]

Thomas (Mowbray), Earl of Nottingham, app. for life 30 June 1385[11] and in tail male 12 Jan. 1385/6;[12] cr. Duke of Norfolk 29 Sept. 1397; appealed of treason 30 Jan. 1397/8; d. 22 Sept. 1399.

Thomas (Holand), Duke of Surrey, app. during pleasure 30 Jan. 1397/8[13] and during the life of Thomas, Duke of Norfolk 17 Sept. 1398.[14]

Ralph (Neville), Earl of Westmorland, app. for life 30 Sept. 1399;[15] occ. 10 Jan. 1408/9;[16] apparently resigned in favour of the next.

John (Mowbray), Earl of Nottingham, occ. 9 Feb. 1410/11;[17] restored as Duke of Norfolk 30 Apr. 1425; d. 19 Oct. 1432.

John (Mowbray), Duke of Norfolk, succ. 19 Oct. 1432; d. 6 Nov. 1461.

John (Mowbray), Duke of Norfolk, succ. 6 Nov. 1461; d. 16–17 Jan. 1475/6, s.p.

Sir Thomas Grey, knt., app. Vice-Marshal 14 Nov. 1482.[18]

---

[1] Coll. Arm. MS. R. 19, f. 238v.   [2] Cur. Mil. Boxes. 7/114*i*.
[3] Appointments made for the purposes of coronations or other special occasions have not been included.
[4] *C.P.R. 1343–5*, p. 243. Warwick had a fresh commission 16 Oct. 1366 (*C.P.R. 1364–7*, p. 332).
[5] *C.C.R. 1374–7*, p. 70.   [6] *C.P.* viii. 446.
[7] Summons to Parliament (*R.D.P.*, App. I, p. 670).
[8] *C.P.R. 1374–7*, p. 491.   [9] *C.P.R. 1377–81*, p. 182.
[10] Ibid., p. 488.   [11] *C.P.R. 1385–9*, p. 11.
[12] *R.D.P.* v. 79.   [13] *C.P.R. 1396–9*, p. 339.
[14] Ibid., p. 413.   [15] *C.P.R. 1399–1401*, p. 9.
[16] *C.P.R. 1408–13*, p. 81.   [17] Ibid., p. 277.
[18] *C.P.R. 1476–85*, p. 317.

John (Howard), Duke of Norfolk, app. in tail mail 28 June 1483;[1] d. 22 Aug. 1485; att. 7 Nov. 1485.

William (Berkeley), Earl of Nottingham, during pleasure 26 Oct. 1485 and in tail male 19 Feb. 1485/6;[2] cr. Marquess of Berkeley 28 Jan. 1488/9; d. 14 Feb. 1491/2, s.p.s.

Henry, 2nd s. of Henry VII, occ. 31 Oct. 1494;[3] cr. Duke of York 31 Oct. 1494; occ. 23 Apr. 1496;[4] succ. to the Crown 21 Apr. 1509.

Thomas (Howard), Earl of Surrey, app. for life as from Michaelmas 1509, 10 July 1510;[5] cr. Duke of Norfolk 1 Feb. 1513/14; d. 21 May 1524.

Charles (Brandon), Duke of Suffolk, app. in reversion 4 July 1523.[6]

Thomas (Howard), Duke of Norfolk, app. in tail mail 28 May 1533, on the surrender of Suffolk;[7] att. 27 Jan. 1546/7.

Edward (Seymour), Duke of Somerset, app. for life 17 Feb. 1546/7;[8] deprived Oct. 1549.

John (Dudley), Earl of Warwick, app. for life 20 Apr. 1551;[9] cr. Duke of Northumberland 11 Oct. 1551; ex. 22 Aug. 1553.

Thomas (Howard), Duke of Norfolk, restored by Act of Parliament 1553;[10] d. 25 Aug. 1554.

Thomas (Howard), Duke of Norfolk, succ. 25 Aug. 1554; att. 16 Jan. 1571/2.

George (Talbot), Earl of Shrewsbury, app. for life 2 Jan. 1572/3;[11] d. 16 Nov. 1590.

William (Cecil), Lord Burleigh, Charles (Howard), Lord Howard of Effingham, and Henry (Carey), Lord Hunsdon, app. Commissioners 25 Jan. 1591/2.[12]

Robert (Devereux), Earl of Essex, app. 28 Dec. 1597;[13] ex. 25 Feb. 1600/1.

Thomas (Sackville), Lord Buckhurst, Charles (Howard), Earl of

[1] Ibid., p. 358.
[2] C.P.R. 1485–94, p. 74.
[3] C.P. (1st ed.), viii. 216.
[4] C.P.R. 1494–1509, p. 67.
[5] L & P. Hen. VIII (2nd ed.), i. 320.
[6] L. & P. Hen. VIII, iii. 1322.
[7] Ibid., vi. 261.
[8] C.P.R. 1547–8, p. 180.
[9] C.P.R. 1550–3, p. 126.
[10] 1 Mar. sess. 2, c. 13 (private) (printed in Statutes of the Realm (1810), i, p. lxxv).
[11] C.S.P.D. 1547–1580, p. 458.
[12] C. G. Young, Privy Councillors and their Precedence (1860), p. 48.
[13] Doyle, Official Baronage, i. 694.

Nottingham, and Edward (Somerset), Earl of Worcester, app. Commissioners 26 Dec. 1601.[1]

Thomas (Sackville), Lord Buckhurst, Lord High Treasurer, Lewis (Stuart), Duke of Lennox, Charles (Howard), Earl of Nottingham, Thomas (Howard), Earl of Suffolk, Edward (Somerset), Earl of Worcester, and Lord Henry Howard, app. Commissioners 4 Feb. 1603/4.[2]

Thomas (Sackville), Earl of Dorset, Lord High Treasurer, Lewis (Stuart), Duke of Lennox, Charles (Howard), Earl of Nottingham, Thomas (Howard), Earl of Suffolk, Edward (Somerset), Earl of Worcester, Charles (Blount), Earl of Devonshire, and Henry (Howard), Earl of Northampton, app. Commissioners 5 Feb. 1604/5.[3]

Thomas (Howard), Earl of Suffolk, Lord High Treasurer, Edward (Somerset), Earl of Worcester, Lord Keeper of the Privy Seal. Lewis (Stuart), Duke of Lennox, Charles (Howard), Earl of Nottingham, William (Herbert), Earl of Pembroke, and George (Talbot), Earl of Shrewsbury, app. Commissioners 16 Jan. 1615/16.[4]

Thomas (Howard), Earl of Suffolk, Lord High Treasurer, Edward (Somerset), Earl of Worcester, Lord Keeper of the Privy Seal, Lewis (Stuart), Duke of Lennox, Charles (Howard), Earl of Nottingham, William (Herbert), Earl of Pembroke, and Thomas (Howard), Earl of Arundel, app. Commissioners 25 Sept. 1616;[5] George (Villiers), Earl of Buckingham, added 8 Mar. 1616/17.[6]

Thomas (Howard), Earl of Arundel, app. for life 29 Aug. 1621;[7] d. 4 Oct. 1646.

Thomas (Wriothesley), Earl of Southampton, Lord High Treasurer (d. 16 May 1667), John, Lord Robartes, Lord Keeper of the

---

[1] Coll. Arm. MS. Heralds VIII, p. 212. Robert (Radcliffe), Earl of Sussex, is styled Earl Marshal in the Journal of the House of Lords, between 11 Oct. and 20 Dec. 1597 and again between 27 Oct. and 19 Dec. 1601 (*L.J.* ii. 191–213, 227–59), but he is not included in a catalogue of Earl Marshals made by Francis Thynne, Lancaster Herald, in 1602 (*C.S.P.D. 1601–1603*, p. 165), and when the Commissioners were appointed the office was stated to be vacant by the attainder of the Earl of Essex (ibid., p. 126).

[2] *C.S.P.D. 1603–1610*, p. 74.   [3] *Foedera*, xvi. 608.
[4] Ibid. xvi. 779.
[5] *C.S.P.D. 1611–1618*, p. 395.   [6] Ibid., p. 441.
[7] The patent did not pass the Great Seal until the end of September, but Arundel executed the office by virtue of the staff given to him by the King (*C.S.P.D. 1619–1623*, pp. 291–3).

Privy Seal, George (Monck), Duke of Albemarle (d. 3 Jan. 1669/70), Henry (Pierrepoint), Marquess of Dorchester, Montague (Bertie), Earl of Lindsey (d. 25 July 1666), Edward (Montagu), Earl of Manchester (d. 5 May 1671), Algernon (Percy), Earl of Northumberland (d. 13 Oct. 1668), and Charles (Howard), Earl of Carlisle, app. Commissioners 27 May 1662.[1]

Henry (Howard) Earl of Norwich, app. with special remainder by virtue of which the office has since devolved 19 Oct. 1672;[2] succ. as Duke of Norfolk Dec. 1677; d. 13 Jan. 1683/4.

Deputies

Henry (Somerset), Marquess of Worcester, Henry (Pierrepoint), Marquess of Dorchester, William (Russell), Earl of Bedford, James (Howard), Earl of Suffolk, Henry (Mordaunt), Earl of Peterborough, Charles (Howard), Earl of Carlisle, and Robert (Bruce) Earl of Ailesbury, app. June 1673.[3]

Henry (Howard), Duke of Norfolk, succ. 13 Jan. 1683/4; d. 2 Apr. 1701.

Thomas (Howard), Duke of Norfolk, succ. 2 Apr. 1701; d. 23 Dec. 1732.

Deputies

Charles (Howard), Earl of Carlisle, app. during the minority of the Duke of Norfolk 2 May 1701.[4]

Henry (Howard), styled Lord Walden, app. c. 27 Feb. 1705/6;[5] cr. Earl of Bindon 30 Dec. 1706; succ. as Earl of Suffolk 10 Nov. 1709; d. 19 Sept. 1718.

Henry Bowes (Howard), Earl of Berkshire, app. 12 Nov. 1718.[6]

Talbot (Yelverton), Earl of Sussex, app. 13 May 1725;[7] d. 27 Oct. 1731.

Francis (Howard), Earl of Effingham, app. 9 Dec. 1731.[8]

---

[1] *C.S.P.D. 1661–1662*, p. 381.

[2] Patent printed in 'X', *The Right to Bear Arms*, pp. 68–77.

[3] *C.S.P.D. 1673*, p. 414. Carlisle was to be 'the present deputy' and to carry the staff (*Letters . . . to Sir Joseph Williamson* (Camden Soc. 1874), i. 54).

[4] Act Book, 2 May 1701. The Duke attained his majority 11 Dec. 1704.

[5] Petition to the Queen for approval of appointment (W. Addison, *Audley End* (London, 1953), p. 229). *C.P.* xii, pt. i. 472, gives the date of appointment as 24 Aug. 1706.

[6] *C.P.* xii, pt. i. 476.

[7] Doyle, *Official Baronage*, iii. 491.

[8] Coll. Arm. MS. SML 3, f. 212. *C.P.* v. 12 gives the date as 13 Dec.

Edward (Howard), Duke of Norfolk, succ. 23 Dec. 1732; d. 20 Sept. 1773.

Deputy

Francis (Howard), Earl of Effingham, reapp.; d. 12 Feb. 1742/3.

* * * * *1

Bernard Marmaduke (Fitzalan-Howard), Duke of Norfolk, succ. 15 Feb. 1917. The present Earl Marshal.

III. LIEUTENANTS, ASSESSORS, AND SURROGATES

It is not possible to compile a record of the succession of Lieutenants, Assessors, and Surrogates of either the Constable or the Marshal, for these officers were appointed as and when required and sometimes acted on only one occasion. The only persons who can be regarded as permanent judges of the Court of Chivalry are:

Thomas Kent LL.D., app. Under-Constable of England for life 7 Jan. 1444/5.[2]

Edmund Isham D.C.L., app. *c.* 1728;[3] reapp. 23 Dec. 1731[4] and 1733;[5] succ. as 6th baronet 5 Mar. 1736/7; d. 15 Dec. 1772.

Rayner, Lord Goddard Hon. D.C.L., Lord Chief Justice of England, app. 24 Oct. 1954.

IV. KING'S ADVOCATES

Thomas Brouns.

Thomas Appulton, app. in succession to Brouns 8 Oct. 1469.[6]

Robert Rydon, app. 23 Oct. 1482.[7]

Arthur Ducke LL.D., app. before 24 Nov. 1623.[8]

[John Exton LL.D., adm. as 'Advocate of the Court or Promoter of Causes' by the Commissioners for executing the Ordinance of Parliament 14 Apr. 1646.][9]

---

1 The series of Earl Marshals and Deputy Earl Marshals have not been continued during the period when there was no sitting of the Court of Chivalry.

2 *C.P.R. 1441–6,* p. 348. Kent, being appointed by the Crown by letters patent during a vacancy in the Constableship, cannot be described with complete accuracy as a lieutenant, but he is included in this list since his functions were those of a lieutenant.

3 *Mag. Brit. Not.* (1728), p. 218.   4 Coll. Arm. MS. SML 3, f. 220.

5 Northamptonshire County Record Office MS. I.L. 1393.

6 *C.P.R. 1467–77,* p. 110.

7 *C.P.R. 1476–85,* p. 423.

8 B.M. MS. Add. 6297, p. 390.   9 Coll. Arm. MS. SML 3, f. 186.

[Walter Walker LL.D., app. by the Commissioners 28 Apr. 1648.][1]

William Oldys LL.D., adm. 5 Oct. 1687.[2]

Nathaniel Lloyd LL.D., adm. 26 Apr. 1707.[3]

Humphrey Henchman LL.D., app. *c.* 1727;[4] readm. 3 Mar. 1731/2.[5]

John Audley LL.D., occ. 1741 and 1745.[6]

V. REGISTERS

Richard Vaux, occ. 3 Aug. 1408.[7]

George Long, occ. 24 Nov. 1623.[8]

Thomas Long, occ. 1 June 1625.[9]

Gilbert Dethick, occ. 28 Nov. 1631[10] and 21 Feb. 1638/9.[11]

Humphrey Terricke, occ. 15 June 1639[12] and 9 Dec. 1639.[13]

William Lewin LL.D., occ. 4 Feb. 1639/40[14] and 30 Oct. 1640.[15]

[John Watson, adm. by the Commissioners for executing the Ordinance of Parliament 14 Apr. 1646.][16]

Robert Plot LL.D., adm. 5 Oct. 1687;[17] d. 30 Apr. 1696.

John Cheeke, acted as Register from 24 Nov. 1687, but not adm. until 12 July 1699; readm. 11 Feb. 1701/2.[17]

Henry Farrant, adm. 26 Apr. 1707;[18] d. 30 Oct. 1727.

Mark Holman, adm. 3 Mar. 1731/2;[19] d. 7 Jan. 1754.

Anthony Richard Wagner C.V.O., Richmond Herald, and Wilfrid Maurice Phillips, app. 27 Oct. 1954.

---

[1] Ibid., f. 195.   [2] Act Book.
[3] Coll. Arm. MS. RRG. LXIV A, f. 6.
[4] *Mag. Brit. Not.* (1727), p. 215.   [5] *London Gazette,* no. 7073.
[6] *Mag. Brit. Not.* (1741), p. 184; (1745), p. 272.
[7] *Ant. Journ.* xix. 422.   [8] B.M. MS. Add. 6297, p. 392.
[9] Coll. Arm. MS. R. 19, f. 266. Perhaps the same as the last.
[10] 3 St. Tr. 486.
[11] Cur. Mil. II. 190.
[12] Acta Cur. Mil. (4), 23.
[13] Ibid. 354.
[14] Cur. Mil. Boxes 9/2*d.*
[15] Ibid. 11/21*a.*
[16] Coll. Arm. MS. SML 3, f. 186.
[17] Act Book.
[18] Coll. Arm. MS. RRG. LXIV A, f. 6.
[19] Noble, *Hist. of the College of Arms,* p. 373.

VI. PROCTORS

Ralph Suckley, practised before 1641; readm. 5 Oct. 1687.[1]

[John Allen
[Mark Cottle
[John Oughton   } app. by the Commissioners 21 Apr. 1646.][2]
[Samuel Franklyn

Samuel Francklin LL.B.
Everard Exton LL.B.
Francis Nixon   } adm. 5 Oct. 1687.[1]
Robert Chapman
Samuel Wyseman

John Hill, adm. 3 Mar. 1687/8.[1]
Anthony Trehane, adm. before 15 Mar. 1687/8.[1]
Keate Waller, adm. 9 Apr. 1690.[1]
Edward Shaw, occ. 1702.[3]
Thomas Willymot, occ. 1702.[3]

George Sayer
Edward Cooke
William Jones   } adm. 26 Apr. 1707.[4]
Samuel Boheme
Edward Alexander

Edward Greenley
Brian Rushworth
John Rawson
Edward Smith
John Searle
William White
Linthwaite Farrant
William Browne   } adm. March 1731/2.[5]
Everard Sayer
John Phillips
John Cooke
Francis Boycot
William Skelton
Philip Champion de Crespigny
Arthur Zouch

---

[1] Act Book.   [2] Coll. Arm. MS. SML 3, f. 187.
[3] *Angliae Notitia* (1702), p. 606.   [4] Coll. Arm. MS. RRG. LXIV A, f. 6.
[5] Powell MS. The date is taken from Noble, *History of the College of Arms*, pp. 373–4, where some of the names are not mentioned, but the Powell MS. list must have been compiled before 11 Dec. 1733, when Linthwaite Farrant died,

VII. EARL MARSHAL'S PROCTORS

Francis Nixon.[1]
Godfrey Lee, adm. 26 Apr. 1707.[2]
William Jones, occ. 1728.[3]
Sandford Nevile, app. 29 Feb. 1731/2.[4]

VIII. SECRETARIES AND SEAL KEEPERS

Francis Negus, occ. 1694[5] and 1714.[6]
Samuel Stebbing, occ. 1718.[7]
Grey Longueville, occ. 1728.[8]

IX. SUB-MARSHAL OR SERJEANT MARSHAL

Thomas Barton, esquire, occ. 12 Nov. 1426.[9]
Henry Langton, junior, occ. 13 Jul. 1447.[10]
[John Allen, app. by the Commissioners 14 Apr. 1646.][11]
Thomas Housman, occ. 1734.[12]

X. MESSENGERS

Stephen Reed, occ. 24 Nov. 1623.[13]
John Coxe, app. *c.* 1625;[14] occ. 12 May 1640.[15]
[John Withie, app. by the Commissioners, 14 Apr. 1646.][16]
John Currey, occ. 4 Nov. 1687[17] and 1707.[18]

XI. MESSENGER AND CRYER

James Sheriff, app. 29 Feb. 1731/2.[19]

(Sir William Musgrave, *Obituary* (Harl. Soc. 1900), ii. 302), so it is probable that all these proctors were admitted at about the same time. Only White, Phillips, Skelton, and de Crespigny were surviving on 1 Jan. 1755 (W. Maitland, *History of London* (London, 1775), ii. 873).

[1] Referred to as Lee's predecessor in Nevile's appointment.
[2] Coll. Arm. MS. RRG. LXIV A, f. 6.
[3] *Mag. Brit. Not.* (1728), p. 218.   [4] Powell MS.
[5] *Angliae Notitia* (1694), p. 647.   [6] *Laws of Honour* (1714), App., p. 52.
[7] *Mag. Brit. Not.* (1718), p. 179.   [8] *Mag. Brit. Not.* (1728), p. 218.
[9] Coll. Arm. MS. Processus in Curia Marescalli, ii. 78.
[10] *C.P.R. 1446–52*, p. 62.   [11] Coll. Arm. MS. SML 3, f. 186.
[12] Seymour, *Survey of the Cities of London and Westminster*, i. 143.
[13] B.M. MS. Add. 6297, p. 391.   [14] Cur. Mil. Boxes 13/2w.
[15] Ibid. 15/4a.   [16] Coll. Arm. MS. SML 3, f. 187.
[17] Cur. Mil. Boxes X/23/5.
[18] *Present State of Great Britain* (1707), p. 138.   [19] Powell MS.

XII. USHER

Edmund Thorold of Easthamstead, co. Berks, gent., occ. 10 June 1640.[1]

XIII. CRYER AND USHER

John Ayres, app. 2 Mar. 1731/2.[2]

XIV. COURT KEEPERS

Samuel Wastell, occ. 10 Oct. 1707.[3]
Thomas Bowyer, occ. c. 1732.[4]

[1] Cur. Mil. Boxes 5/72. See also *Visit. London, 1633–5* (Harl. Soc., 1883), ii. 286.
[2] Cur. Mil. Boxes X/7.
[3] Coll. Arm. MS. RRG. LXIV A, f. 48.
[4] Powell MS.

APPENDIX III

Letters Patent dated 1st August 1622

JAMES by the Grace of God King of England, Scotland, France and Ireland, Defender of the Faith &c. To Our right trusty and right well beloved Cousin and Councellour Thomas Earl of Arundell and Surry Our Earl Marshal of England Greeting;

WHEREAS Wee have been informed that you have delayed to proceed juditially in some causes before you depending in the Court Marshal by Reason of some Doubts, which have been by some divulged, that the Earl Marshal was but a Minister to see the Preccpts, and Judgments of the Constable to be performed; in which respect, though for Ourself We never made the least Doubt of the absolute Power of the Earl Marshal, when there was no Constable; as also that He always was a Judge joined with the Constable, when there was one: We held it fit in a cause of so great weight to proceed with extraordinary Deliberation, And having now both by Ourself, and the Body of Our Privy Councill received ample satisfaction by many, and clear Proofs, that the Constable and Marshal were joint Judges together, and severally in the Vacancy of either: *WE DO* hereby authorize, will, and command you Our Earl Marshal, that from henceforth you proceed in all causes whatsoever, whereof the Court of the Constable and Marshal ought properly to take cognizance, as juditially and definitively, as any Constable, or Marshal of this Our Realm either jointly or severally heretofore have done: And that You do by all means endeavour to restore and settle the Honourable Proceedings of that Court, with addition of all the Rights thereto belonging; for which Our Pleasure is, that You assist yourself as much by antient Records, & Precedents as You may: And these Presents shall be your sufficient Warrant & Discharge in that Behalf: In Witness whereof We have caused these Our Letters to be made Patents. Witnesse Ourself at Westminster the first day of August in the XXth year of Our Reign of England &c and of Scotland the LVIth

EDMUNDS

Per breve de privato sigillo

[Coll. Arm. MS. SML 3, f. 228.]

APPENDIX IV

Letters Patent dated 13th August 1687

JAMES the Second by the Grace of God of England, Scotland, France and Ireland King Defender of the Faith &c *TO OUR* Right Trusty and Right Entirely beloved Cousin Henry Duke of Norfolk Our Earl Marshall of England Greeting *WHEREAS* there are several Causes onely proper to be heard and determined in a Court of Chivalry or Court of Constable and Marshall, to be holden before the Constable of England and Earl Marshall of England as Judges thereof, or during the Vacancy of either of the said Officers [*sic*], to be holden separatly before one or either of them; which said Court hath been disused ever since the horrid Rebellion which began in the year of Our Lord God One Thousand Six hundred forty and one or thereabouts; by reason whereof very many abuses not determinable in any other Court hath been unreformed and gon unpunished: For remedy whereof for the Future *OUR WILL* and pleasure is, and We do hereby authorize will and Command you Our Earl Marshall to call and hold from time to time as formerly hath at any time been lawfully used, a Court of Chivalry or Court of Constable and Marshall And that you henceforth proceed in all Causes whatsoever, whereof the Court of Chivalry or Court of Constable and Marshall ought properly to take Cognizance, as judicially and definitively as any Constable or Marshall of this Our Realm either joyntly or severally heretofore have or hath done: *AND* that you do by all means endeavour to restore and settle the Honorable Proceedings of that Court with the Rights thereunto belonging: For which Our pleasure is that you assist yor self as much by ancient Records and Presidents as you may; And these presents shall be yor sufficient warrant and discharge in that behalf. *IN WITNES* whereof We have caused these Our Letters to be made Patents *WITNES* Our self at Westminster the Thirteenth day of August in the third year of Our Reigne

Per Breve de Privato Sigillo

Exam^r per   BARKER

   ROB. PLOT Curiae Militaris Reg'rium
   GRE^M KING R.Dr: Collegij Armorum Reg'rium
[Misc. Cur. Mil. 243.]

APPENDIX V

Draft Bill for Declaring the Earl Marshal's Jurisdiction, c. 1707

WHEREAS some doubts have been lately made touching the power of Judicature in the Court military during the vacancy of the Office of Constable, whereby the ordinary course of Justice hath been in some measure obstructed. It is hereby declared & enacted. . . . That the Common Law of this part of this Realm called England is and always was & ought to be taken, that the Court Military of that part of Great Britain called England hath been, is, and lawfully may be holden before the Marshal of England or his deputy duely approved of by Her Majesty notwithstanding during the vacancy of and in the Office of Constable, And it is hereby further declared and enacted by the authority aforesaid that the said Marshal for the time being by himself or sufficient Deputy always had hath and of right ought to have use & execute authority, jurisdiction, execution of Laws and power of Judicature, and shall & may from henceforth as of right belonging to the said Office proceed judicially & definitely in all cases within the cognizance and jurisdiction of the Court Military of that part of Great Britain called England in as full large & ample a manner and to all intents construcions and purposes as if there was a Constable in being save only in cases of Appeals to be made of things done out of the Realm, which shall be tryed & determined according to the Statute in the first year of Henry the fourth made and provided.

[Coll. Arm. MS. R.19, f. 223.]

APPENDIX VI

Appointment of Lieutenant

THOMAS COMES ARRUNDELL ET SURREY Comes Marescallus
Angliae universis et singulis has litteras nostras patentes visuris et
audituris Salutem. Sciatis quod nos ex certis causis et considera-
tionibus animum nostrum in hac parte iuste moventibus dilectum
nobis [*sic*] Henricum dominum Matravers filium et heredem
apparentem meum [*sic*] Locumtenentem nostrum in Curia Militari fecimus nominavimus et constituimus sicque facimus nomi-
namus et constituimus per presentes damusque et concedimus eidem
Locumtenenti nostro plenam authoritatem et potestatem gene-
ralem vice loco et nomine nostris in omnibus et singulis causis et
negotijs in Curia predicta procedendi, mandata citatoria et attachia-
menta decernendi, libellum et libellos et alias quascunque materias
in jure concludendi admittendi, compulsoria contra testes et com-
missiones pro examinacione testium quorumcumque si opus fuerit
concedendi, testesque quoscumque productos admittendi, et iura-
mento corporali ad sancta Dei Evangelia de fideliter in ea parte
deponendo onerandi, eosque sic iuratos tam super libellis et
materijs super quibus respective producuntur quam super interro-
gorijs in ea parte ministrandis si que parte adversa ministrare
curaverit examinandi et repetendi, testium quorumcumque dicta
et deposiciones publicandi, et partibus copias decernendi, terminum
seu terminos ad audiendum sentenciam in causis predictis seu earum
aliqua assignandi, sentenciasque diffinitivas in scriptis dandi forendi
et promulgandi, easdemque executioni demandandi, expensas
quascumque taxandi et moderandi, decreta interloquutoria viri
sentencie diffinitive habentia interponendi, Curiamque predictam
et omnes et singulas causas et causarum assignationes ibidem de-
pendentes ad et in quemcumque diem competentem eius arbitrio
statuendi continuandi et prorogandi, omnesque et singulos quos in
ea parte intererit ad tunc et ibidem interessendi monendi Et gene-
raliter omnia et singula alia pro meliori causarum expedicione
faciendi et expediendi que in premissis necessaria fuerint seu
quomodolibet oportuna etiamsi mandatum et authoritatem magis
exigant speciale quam superius est expressum Ideoque omnibus et
singulis quorum in hac parte interest precipimus et firmiter inju-
gendo mandamus quatenus in premissis omnibus et singulis prefato

Locumtenenti nostro obedientes sint et debite intendentes Datum vicesimo sexto die Junij Anno Regni Domini nostri Caroli Dei gratia Anglie Scotie Francie et Hibernie Regis fidei defensoris &c decimo tertio Annoque Domini 1637

ARUNDELL & SURREY

[Endorsed] for Mr Walker.

[Cur. Mil. Boxes 8/15.]

APPENDIX VII

Appointment of Register

By the Right Honourable Thomas Lord Walden Deputy with her Maties Approbation to the Most Noble Thomas Duke of Norfolke Earle Marshall & Hereditary [Marshal] of England

In Trust and Confidence of the Ability and Skill of Henry Farrant Gentleman & Notary Publick for the Performance of the Office of Register of the Court Military I doe hereby Nominate Authorise and Appoint the said Henry Farrant to be Register of the said Court and duly to Enter in a Fair Book or Books all Causes Proceedings Acts and Decrees that shall be promoted prosecuted or Determined in the said Court before me or my Lieutenant or Surrogate (for the tyme being) from tyme to tyme as their shall be occasion To Hold the said Office and Place of Register (with all Fees perquisites and Emolluments thereto belonging) during my Pleasure Requiring that all Libells or Instruments of process and Records and Books that shall come to the Hands or Custody of the said Henry Farrant of Matters belonging to & transacted in the said Court be carefully preserved, And for his the said Henry Farrants acting accordingly this shall be a sufficient Warrant. Given under my Hand and seale the 28th Day of October in the year of our Lord 1706 & in the Fifth Year of the Reigne of Our Most Gratious Soveraigne Lady Anne by the Grace of God Queen of England Scotland France & Ireland Defender of the Faith &c.

[Coll. Arm. MS. RRG. LXIV A, f. 4.]

APPENDIX VIII

Appointment of Cryer and Usher

(L.S) To Mr. John Ayres By the Right Honourable Francis Earl of Effingham Deputy with the Royal Approbation to the Most Noble Thomas Duke of Norfolk, Marshall, & Hereditary Earl Marshall of England &c.

IN Trust and Confidence of your Care, Diligence and Fidelity, *(6d.* stamp) I do hereby nominate, authorise and appoint you the said John Ayres to be Cryer & Usher to the Court and Office of Marshall *(6d.* stamp) and Earl Marshall of England, with full power & authority to you, *(6d.* stamp) or your sufficient Deputy or Deputies, to execute such Orders as you shall from time to time receive from me, or my Lieutenant or Lieutenants, in as large & ample manner, as any other Cryer & Usher of the said Court or Office hath heretofore executed, or lawfully might or may execute the said Office; to hold the same to you the said John Ayres during my Will and Pleasure only; together with all Fees, Perquisites & Profits thereunto in any wise belonging. Given under my Hand and Seal of Office the Second Day of Marsh anno Dom 173½

EFFINGHAM, M.

By His Lordship's Command
  J. HUTCHENSON

[Papered Seal: Arms with coronet and supporters SIGILL · OFFICII · COMITIS · MARESCALL · ET · MARESCAL · ANGLIÆ]

[Cur. Mil. Boxes X/7.]

APPENDIX IX

Petition

To the right hoble Thomas Earle of Arundell and Surrey Earle Marshall of England

The petition of Ambrose Elton of Ledbury in the County of Hereford Esqr

HUMBLY sheweth That yor peticoner is a gentleman descended of an Auncient and generous family bearinge Armes and hath byn high Sheriffe of the County of Hereford aforesaid and is nowe one of his Maiesties Justices of the peace for the said County that one William Elton of Ledbury aforesaid in the moneth of January last past att the house of William Hodges an Inne in Ledbury aforesaid did publiquely abuse yor peticoner and then and there spake many disgracefull wordes to or of him and some then present speakinge about the referringe of a Cause hee the said William Elton said he would not Consent that the Cause or matter should bee referred to the petitioner for the petitioner Ambrose Elton was a rascally base fellowe or to that effect

Wherefore yor petitioner humbly prayeth processe may goe out of yor hono^{rs} Courte against the said William Elton to answeare the premisses &c

Mr. Dethick the petitioner being qualifyed as to armes I take the Cause to bee fitt for my L. Marshalls Court and I desire process may goe out.

Febr. 7. 1637

ARTH: DUCKE

[Cur. Mil. Boxes 8/1.]

APPENDIX X

Citation

HENRICUS DUX NORFOLCIAE Dominus Comes Mariscallus Angliae &c Universis et singulis Justitiarijs ad pacem, Vice Comitibus, Balivis, Constabularijs, et Officiarijs Necnon Regiae Majestatis subditis fidelibus quibuscunque presertim vero Johanni Currey Mandatario, sive Curiae Nostrae Mariscallo Salutem Vobis conjunctim et divisim comittimus, et firmiter injungendo mandamus quatenus citetis, seu citari faciatis peremptorie Dominum Jacobum Tillie Militem (antea se nominantem Jacobum Tillie de Pentillie Castle Armigerum) Quod compareat coram Nobis, Nostrove Locumtenente, aut alio Judice in hac parte competente in Curia Nostra Militari, in Camera depicta infra Palatium Westmonasteriensem, Locoque Judiciali ibidem Die Mercurij, nono vidzt die Mensis Novembris, Anno Domini Millesimo, sexcentesimo, octogesimo, septimo, hora nona antemeridiem ejusdem diei, certis Articulis concernentibus ejus contemptum authoritatis Nostrae, et Legum Armorum, et presertim in gerendo et ostentando, absque ullo Jure, aut titulo, Arma, Insignia, Galeam, et Cristam ad eum nullo modo spectantia, et assumendo, et gestare presumendo Telamones seu Angelos Insignia supportantes contra Leges Armorum, et in prejudicium procerum hujus Regni. Ad promotionem necessariam Guilielmi Oldys Legum Doctoris Serenissimae Regiae Majestatis in hac Curia Advocati, de Justitia responsurus, Ulteriusque facturus et recepturus quod Justum fuerit in hac parte. Et quid in premissis feceritis Nos, Nostrumve Locumtenentem aut alium Judicem in hac parte competentem debite certificetis, Una cum presentibus Datis, Ultimo die mensis Octobris Anno Regni Serenissimi Domini nostri Jacobi secundi Angliae, Scotiae, Franciae et Hiberniae Regis fidei Defensoris &c Tertio Annoque Domini Millesimo, sexcentesimo, octogesimo septimo

[Seal: Howard crest within a Garter surmounted by a Duke's coronet]

[Endorsed]

November ye 4th 87

This day I executed this warrant on Sr James Tillie in his own Chamber our the Middle Temple gate London to apeare in the painted Chamber in Westmr Hall to be there at nine a Clock in the morning being the ninth day of the same by me

JOHN CURREY

[Cur. Mil. Boxes X/23/5.]

APPENDIX XI

Notice of Citation

To Mr. Thomas Kynnersley sole Exec^r of the last Will &
Testament of Mary London of Islington decd.

BY virtue of the Citacon herewith shewed unto you under seale
you are cited to appear before the Right Honoble Henry Earle
of Bindon (by her Majestyes approbacon) Deputy Marshall of
England in the Common Hall of the Colledge of Armes comonly
called the Heraulds Office situate in the Parish of St. Benedict near
Pauls Wharfe London on Thursday the one & Thirtieth day of
this instant July between the hours of three and five in the afternoon of the same day then & there to answer to certaine Articles
to be objected and ministred to you att the promotion of the
Worshipfull Nathaniel Lloyd her Matis Advocate in the Court
Military touching & concerning your Contempt of the Jurisdiccon
& Authority of the Lord Marshall of England his Office of Armes,
& the Lawes of Armes more particularly for usurping bearing
useing & pretending to Armes or a Coat of Armes as the proper
Coat of Armes of the sd Mary London which of Right and by the
Lawes of Armes you ought not to do, and which in noe manner of
wise did or doe belong unto the sd Mary London And further to
do & receive as unto Law and Justice shall appertain

[Coll. Arm. MS. RRG. LXIV A, f. 17.]

APPENDIX XII

Order for Security

December 12th [1638]

WHEREAS Richard Morris one of the Company of Barber Chirurgions of the Citty of London was this day brought before mee to make Answer to two severall Complaints made against him, the one of Michaell Andrewes one of his Mats Chirurgions for uncivill and provokeinge language used to him by the said Morris in an open Courte held in Barber Chirurgions Hall London, and particularly for giveinge him the Lye, The other by John Woodhall an auntient Mr and an Assistant of the sayd Company, for a blowe given him by the sayd Morris wth his fist as they sate togeither in a Court kept wthin the said Hall. Both wch Complaints beinge proved upon Oath, forasmuch as the offences were publiquely committed in the face of a Court and to soe principall Members of the Society I conceive it most proper to bee brought to a publique tryall. And doe therefore order that the sayd Plts doe ioyntly or severally as their Councell shall advise them put in their Libells into the Court Marshall against the sayed Morris for the aforesaid abuses. And that Morris give Bond wth good Sureties to appeare and answer the sayed Complaints and to stand to and performe such Order as shalbee made by the sayed Courte and paye such fynes Costs and charges as shalbee assessed or awarded against him in the said Causes, and till that security bee given to remaine in the Custody of the Messenger

ARUNDELL & SURREY

[Cur. Mil. Boxes 18/3*m*.]

APPENDIX XIII

Appointment of Proctor

WHEREAS a Cause of Office is commenced and presented against me Sarah Radburne widow sole Exectrix of the last Will and Testament of my late Husband John Radburne late of Mark Lane London dec^d in the Court of Chivalry for bearing and using Armes, which are alleged not to belong to me or my said late Husband or to either of our Families

NOW Know all men by these Presents that I the said Sarah Radburne do hereby constitute and appoint Brian Rushworth Notary publick one of the Proctors exercent in the said Court to be my lawful Proctor for me and in my place to appear before the Right Hon^bl Francis Earl of Effingham by his Majesties Approbation Deputy Earl Marsal of England or his Assessor or any other Competent Judge in his behalf in the said Court and to oppose the admission of the Articles exhibited against me there if the same shall be admitted to give an answer thereto and generally to do and perform whatsoever else is necessary to be done and performed by me in the said Cause hereby promising to ratify and confirm whatsoever my said Proctor shall do or cause to be done therein by virtue of these presents. In Witness whereof I have hereunto set my hand and seal this 25 day of April 1732

SARAH RADBURN (L.S.)

Sealed and delivered ⎱ LEWIS GUILLEMAN
in the presence of us ⎰ ROBERT BROWN

[Coll. Arm. MS. SML 3, f. 234.]

APPENDIX XIV

Plaintiff's Bond

Noverint Universi per presentes Me Phillipum Darcy de Addington in Com' Northampton' gen' teneri et firmiter obligari Serenissimo in Christo Principi Carolo dei gratia Anglie Scotie Francie et Hibernie regi fidei defensori &c in Centum Libris bone et legalis monete Anglie solvendum eidem serenissimo in Christo Principi Heredibus sive Successoribus suis ad quam quidem solucionem bene et fideliter faciendam obligo me Heredes Executores et Administratores meos firmiter per presentes sigillo meo sigillatum Datum decimo sexto Die Mensis Junij Anno Regni Domini nostri Caroli predicti decimo sexto Annoque domini 1640

THE Condicon of this Obligacon is such that whereas the above named Phillip Darcy hath Commenced a suite in the Court Military before the right honble Thomas Earle of Arundell & Surrey Earle Marshall of England against Tobias Greene of the Citty of London Tanner if therefore the said Phillip Darcy shall duely prosecute the said Suite & personally as often as the Course of the Courte shall require or hee bee thereto lawfully called & otherwyse by his Councell lawfully authorized appeare in the said Courte in the paynted Chamber within the Pallace of Westminster from Courte Day to Courte Day during the proceeding & dependancy of & in the said suite & also doe pay such Costs & Charges & performe such order as the Courte shall in that beehalfe taxe & enioyne him the said Phillip Darcy to pay & performe Then this present Obligacon to bee void & of noe effect or else to stand & remaine in full power force & vertue

Signed sealed &

Delivered in the presence of   PHILLIP DARCY (L.S.)

     JO: WATSON

[Cur. Mil. Boxes 5/79.]

APPENDIX XV

Defendant's Bond

Noverint Universi per presentes Me Walterum Nash de Bran Castle in Com' Norfol' gen' teneri et firmiter obligari Serenissimo in Christo Principi et domino nostro Carolo dei gratia Angliae Scotiae Franciae et Hiberniae Regi Fidei Defensori &c in Centum Libris bonae et legalis Monetae Angliae solvendum eidem domino nostro Regi Haeredibus et Successoribus suis ad quam quidem solucionem bene et fideliter faciendam obligo Me et Haeredes Executores et Administratores meos firmiter per presentes Sigillo meo Sigillatum Datum undecimo die Mensis Junij Anno Regni domini nostri Caroli predicti decimo sexto Annoque domini 1640

THE Condicon of this present Obligacon is such that whereas Robert Talcot of Colchester in the County of Essex gent hath commenced a suite in the Courte Military before the right honourable Thomas Earle of Arundell & Surrey Earle Marshall of England against the abovebounden Walter Nash therefore the said Walter Nash shall personally soe often as the Course of the Courte shall require & hee shall bee thereunto lawfullie Called & at other tymes by his Councell lawfully Authorized Appeare in the said Courte in the paynted Chamber within the Pallace of Westminster from Courte day to Courte day duringe the proceeding & dependancy of and in the said Suite And shall pay such Costs Fyne & Damages and performe such Order as the Courte in that beehalfe shall taxe & inioyne him the said Walter Nash to pay & performe Then this present Obligacon to bee void and of noe effect Or else the same to stand and remayne in full power force & Vertue

WALTER NASH (L.S.)

Sealed Subscribed and
Delivered in ye presence of

JO: WATSON

[Cur. Mil. Boxes 5/73.]

APPENDIX XVI

Libel

In Dei Nomine Amen. Coram vobis Praenobili et Honorando viro Thoma Comite Arundell et Surrey Comite Marescallo Angliae vestrove Locumtenente In Curia vestra Militari. Ego Fulco Salisbury Civitatis Cestriae generosus contra Samuelem Marten Civitatis praedictae per viam Querelae in Jure Propono

1. IMPRIMIS Quod Ego praefatus Fulco Salisbury et Maiores mei per hos 50. 100. 200. 300 pluresque annos elapsos fuimus generosi antiqua generosaque Salisburiorum familia in Comitatu Denbighensi orti et propagati sicque communiter reputati ipseque per plures annos elapsos fui et sum unus Aldermanorum Civitatis praedictae, et per plures annos elapsos fui vicomes fuique et sum unus Coronatorum Civitatis praedictae, sicque communiter reputatus Dictusque Samuel Marten per plures annos elapsos fuit et est Mercator sericus, Anglice a Mercer, sicque communiter reputatus. Et pono coniunctim divisim &c.

2. Item Quod mensibus Aprilis, Maij, Junij, Julij, et Augusti Anno 1637 eorumve uno infra Civitatem Cestriae praedictae, aliaque loca vicina Praedictus Samuel Marten publice coram pluribus personis generosis et fidedignis dixit et asseruit me Fulconem Salisbury fuisse et esse Wallicum nebulonem seque fuisse et esse aeque dignum et digniorem Fulcone Salisbury, et Martinos fuisse prae Salisburijs magis generosos, seque esse aeque dignum licet toga violacea esset indutus. Anglice hee said that Salisburie was a Welch rogue, and hee was as good a man and a better gentleman then Salisbury, and that the Martens were better gentlemen then the Salisburys and said hee was as good a man as Salisbury though hee wore a violett gowne, seu similiter in effectum. Et pono coniunctim divisim &c.

3. Item Quod dictus Samuel Marten me et familiam meam (qua Ego ortus sum) denotabat et significabat dum verba praedicta seu similia protulit. Et per togam violaceam indumentum Aldermanorum Civitatis Cestriae significabat, eademque verba seu similia in effectum saepius in me protulit modo derisorio, et per

contumeliam et contemptum et per ea me ad duellum et certamen cum eo subeundum provocare conatus est. Et pono coniunctim divisim &c.

4. Item Quod praemissa omnia sunt vera publica notoria &c.

Unde Ego praefatus Fulco Salisbury a vobis Illustrissimo Domino vestrove Locumtenente aut alio Judice in hac parte competente Peto Jus et Justiciam Praedictumque Samuelem Marten ad satisfactionem restitucionemque famae et honoris mei faciendum, et ad solvendum mihi damna et expensas in hac causa factas seu illatas. Ulteriusque fieri quod iustum fuerit secundum leges et consuetudines Armorum et huius Curiae Condemnandum fore per Sententiam vestram. Praemissaque propono coniunctim et divisim non arctans me &c.[1]

ARTH: DUCKE

[Endorsed] Libellus Salisbury c.
      Martin dat 20 8ber 1638

[Cur. Mil. Boxes 11/32/5.]

---

[1] The prayer of a libel normally ends thus, but in *Somersett v. Perkins* (1634), Acta Cur. Mil. (5), 18, the '&c'. is expanded 'ad onus superfluae probaconis &c. Jurisque beneficio in omnibus mihi semper salvo'.

APPENDIX XVII

Articles (Necessary Promotion)

In Dei Nomine Amen. Nos Thomas Comes Arundell et Surrey Comes Marescallus Angliae Tibi Thomae Hanslopp parochiae de Aynhoe in Comitatu Northampton' articulos infrascriptos ad promotionem necessariam Arthuri Ducke Legum Doctoris Regij Curia nostra Militari Advocati obijcimus

1. IMPRIMIS Quod tu predictus Thomas Hanslopp et Maiores tui per 50. 100. 200 pluresque annos elapsos, et a tempore immemoriali fuistis et es plebes et non generosi, et non habuistis ius habendi et assumendi Arma et insignia maioresque tui predicti per totum tempus predictum gradum et titulum generosi nunquam fuerunt assecuti, et sic communiter reputati. Et obijcimus coniunctim divisim &c.

2. Item Quod tu predictus Thomas Hanslopp per hos septem Annos ultimo elapsos mensibusque in ijsdem annis spective concurrentibus eorumve uno infra parochiam de Aynhoe, et Comitatum predictum alijsque parochijs, locis, et Comitatibus huius Regni Angliae nomen et titulum generosi assumsisti, et arrogasti, teque verbis et scriptis generosum appellasti et descripsisti, seu appellari et describi procurasti, teque pro generoso gessisti. Et obijcimus coniunctim divisim &c.

3. Item Quod premissa omnia sunt vera publica, notoria &c.

Unde prefatus Arthurus Ducke a Nobis nostrove Locumtenente aut alio Judice in hac parte competente petit Jus et Justitiam teque predictum Thomam Hanslopp ob premissa debite puniendum et pro plebeio et non generoso publice declarandum et proclamandum, et ne in posterum nomen aut titulum generosi, aut arma et insignia assumere aut arrogare presumas monendum et iniungendum, et in expensis huius litis solvendum ulteriusque fieri quod iustum fuerit secundum leges et consuetudines Armorum et huius Curie condemnandum esse per sententiam nostram. Premissaque proponit coniunctim et divisim non arctans se &c.

ARTH: DUCKE

[Cur. Mil. Boxes 15/1/0.]

APPENDIX XVIII

Articles (Voluntary Promotion)

In Dei Nomine Amen. Nos Thomas Comes Arundell et Surrey Comes Marescallus Angliae Tibi Thomae Tuckfield de Crediton in Comitatu Devoniae ad promotionem voluntariam D. Willielmi Le Neve Militis Regis Armorum Clarencieux Australium, Orientalium et Occidentalium partium huius Regni Angliae hos articulos obijcimus et articulis alias [*sic*] Coram Nobis per Henricum S. George Militem Richmond Heraldum exhibitis adijcimus

Quod tu prefatus Thomas Tuckfield post mortem patris tui predicti Arma et insignia in prioribus articulis expressa gentilitia et familiae tuae ut pretenditur licet minus vere propria non solum supra Monumenta Patris tui predicti verum etiam in alijs locis dictae Ecclesiae et alibi supra Muris, parietibus, fenestris, sigillis, vasis alijsque rebus appingi, insculpi, et apponi procurasti, eaque tanquam Arma tua propria, et ad te familiamque tuam spectantia assumsisti et arrogasti per hos 15.10.5 seu unum annum elapsos in Comitatu predicto, alijsque locis infra hoc regnum Angliae, Et obijcimus conjunctim et divisim &c.

Item quod tu prefatus Thomas Tuckfield post articulos contra te in hac Causa datos ad justificandum et probandum Jus tuum in Armis predictis et in assumendo titulo, et nomine generosi et Armigeri varia scripta et munimenta exhibuisti, quae a viris doctis et peritis inspecta notorie fuisse falsa et fictitia deprehensa sunt. Praemissaque omnia sunt vera, notoria &c.

Unde prefatus D. Willielmus Le Neve Petit Jus et Justiciam &c.

ARTH: DUCKE

[Cur. Mil. Boxes 20/2*d*.]

APPENDIX XIX

Defence

In dei nomine Amen Coram vobis prenobili et Honorando viro domino Thoma Comite Arrundelli et Surrey Comite Marescallo Anglie vestrove locumtenente in Curia vestra militari Ego Willielmus Crayford Generosus ad omnem quemcunque iuris effectum exinde quovismodo sequi valentem ac omnibus melioribus via modo et iuris forma quibus melius potui aut possim pro defensione mei ipsius Willielmi Crayford in negotio querele contra me prefatum Willielmum Crayford in Curia vestra militari per quendam Willielmum Argent proposito et excipiendo contra quoscunque testes pretensos ex parte dicti Willielmi Argent in negotio predicto et in eadem Curia Contra me productos dixi allegavi et proposui et in his scriptis dico allego et in iure propono Coniunctim divisim et articulatim prout sequitur

INPRIMIS quod ego prefatus Willielmus Crayford maioresque mei per hos 10: 20: 50: 100: 200: pluresque annos elapsos fuimus generosi et ex antiqua generosa familia oriundi et propagati sicque Communiter reputati Et pono ut supra

Item that immediately or at least within a moneth next before the words libellate are pretended to be spoken by me the said William Crayford the said William Argent and the Lady Mary Nevinson his wife did at diverse severall tymes or at least before the words libellate are pretended to be spoken use diverse scandalous and disgracefull speeches to and of me the said William Crayford vizt the said Mr Argent called me foole and badd me come to dinner Will foole and hath often wished their servants or mine the said William Crayfords servants to call Will foole to dinner he the said Argent speaking of and meaninge me the sayd William Crayford Hocque fuit et est verum publicum Notorium et manifestum Et pono ut supra

Item that immediately or within a moneth before the words libellate are pretended to be spoken the said William Argent came into my Chamber at the house of the said William Argent in Estry in Kent where I and my wife (she beinge then great with Child) were togeather and there without any provoakation he the said Mr

Argent in a furious angry and outragious manner flue at and struck
me the said William Crayford diverse and severall blowes or at
least one on the face and head with his fist and drew blood on me
and I did by reason of the sayd blow or blowes bleed soe much and
soe exceedinglie that my said wife was soe affrighted therewith that
it caused her to swoune and fall to the ground to the great danger
of her life Hocque fuit et est verum publicum notorium et manifestum Et pono ut supra

Item that in case I the said William Crayford did at any other
tyme utter or speake any of the words libellate quod non fateor sed
penitus diffiteor et nego yet the sayd words were by me soe spoken
uppon great wronge abuse and provocation offered and given me
by the sayd William Argent immediately or within a moneth
before such the speakinge thereof vizt I and my wife living and
cohabitinge with the sayd William Argent at the said William
Argents house in Eastry in the Countie of Kent when I the sayd
William Crayford have gone abroad about my afaires and business
at my returne he the sayd William Argent hath kept me out of
doores & not suffered me to come to my said wife Et pono ut supra

Item quod premissa omnia et singula fuerunt et sunt vera &c.

TH. EXTON

[Cur. Mil. I. 187.]

APPENDIX XX

Kings of Arms' Report

To the right ho^{ble} Thomas Earle of Arundell and Surrey Earle Marshall of England

WHEREAS your LoP was pleased by your Order made in the Court of Chivalrie the 9th day of May last past to command us to certifie your LoP what we beleve of the veritie validitie or invaliditie of certain Evidences Instruments and Exhibits, as allso of an Escochene of Armes Exhibited on the part of Daniell Dobbins in a Cause wherein John Stepkin gent is plaintiff against the said D: Dobbins and whether the said Escochen of Armes do by hereditary right belong unto the sayd Dobbins and by what right the sayd Dobbins doth call himself Esquire and assume the name of Esquire

May it please your LoP

In obedience to your LoP^s said Order and directions we have maturely considered of all the premises and do humblie Certifie your LoP that we do not find by anything exhibited in Court or otherwise produced before us That the sayd Daniell Dobbins is or any of his Auncestors were gentlemen of Coate Armour yet we find that his Grandfather & som others of his name inhabiting about the place where his father now dwelleth were written Gentilmen in divers Evidences And we do not fynde the Escochen of Armes produced by the sayd Dobbins in Court to belong to him or his Auncesters nor that the sayd Dobbins hath any right to call himself Esquire or to assume the name or title of Esquire. Dated at the Office of Armes the first day of June 1638

JOHN BORROUGH	WM LE NEVE	HEN: ST GEORGE
Garter	Clarencieux	Norroy

[Cur. Mil. Boxes 13/2s.]

APPENDIX XXI

Definitive Sentence (Cause of Instance)

In Dei Nomine Amen. Auditis visis et intellectis per Nos Henricum Dominum Matrevers Locumtenentem Excellentissimi Domini Domini Thomae Comitis Arundell et Surrey Comitis Marescalli Angliae, et Exercitus Regij Generalis Meritis et circumstantijs cujusdam Querelae coram Nobis in Curia Militari per Johannem Syddenham de Dulvreton in Comitatu Somersett' generosum contra Willielmum Cruse de Dulvreton predict' mercatorem tabernarium intentatae et prosecutae Partibus predictis coram Nobis comparentibus et Justitiam fieri respective petentibus QUIA per acta et probationes in hac causa factas invenimus dictum Johannem Syddenham intentionem suam in Libello suo in hac causa dato penes Registrarium Curiae predictae remanente deductam sufficienter probasse nihilque effectuale ex parte dicti Willielmi Cruse in contrarium allegatum et probatum fuisse et esse IDCIRCO Nos Henricus Dominus Matrevers Locumtenens, et Judex antedictus Christi Nomine invocato, et cum Jurisperitorum consilio cum quibus in hac parte communicavimus, predictum Willielmum Cruse tempore et loco in hac causa Libellatis dixisse et asseruisse Hugonem Syddenham fratrem Johannis Syddenham predicti fuisse et esse vilem et scabiosum homuncionem omnesque fratres suos fuisse viles, scabiosos, et fraudulentos homunciones, et prefatum Johannem Syddenham fuisse et esse prae reliquis omnibus vilissimum Anglice, that Hugh Syddenham brother to the said John Syddenham was a base scurvy fellowe and all his brothers were base scurvy cheating fellowes, & John Syddenham the eldest of them was the basest of them all, seu similiter in effectu; Predictaque verba seu similia in effectu fuisse prolata per prefatum Willielmum Cruse maliciose contra pacem Domini nostri Regis, et in offensionem et contumeliam prefati Johannis Syddenham pronunciamus, decernimus et declaramus Eundem igitur Willielmum Cruse ad submissionem et satisfactionem tam Nobis et huic Curiae quam prefato Johanni Syddenham modo et forma per Nos aut alium Judicem in hac parte competentem quemcunque designandis peragendam, et ad interponendam cautionem cum fidejussoribus per Nos et hanc Curiam approbandis de bene se gerendo durante beneplacito nostro et hujus Curiae. Necnon in damnis et

expensis prefati Johannis Syddenham, quae damna ad summam . . .
quadraginti librarum . . . et expensis ad summam . . . *triginti
librarum* . . . taxamus, et moderamus, et sub salva custodia deti-
nendum donec sufficienter cum fidejussoribus per Nos et hanc
Curiam approbandis de perimplendo hanc nostram Sententiam
diffinitivam sive hoc nostrum finale decretum fidejusserit, etiam
pronunciamus, decernimus et declaramus quam sive quod fecimus
et promulgavimus in hijs scriptis

ARTH: DUCKE   H. MATRAVERS

[Cur. Mil. Boxes 16/19.]

APPENDIX XXII

Definitive Sentence (Cause of Office)

In Dei nomine Amen. Auditis, visis, et intellectis ac plenarie, et mature discussis per Nos Henricum Ducem Norfolciae Dominum Comitem Mariscallum Angliae &c. Meritis et Circumstantijs cujusdam negotij Officij quod coram Nobis in Judicio inter venerabilem virum Guilielmum Oldys Legum Doctorem, Serenissimae Regiae Majestatis in hac Curia Militari Advocatum Promotorem Officij in hac parte, et partem dictum negotium promoventem ex una, et Dominum Jacobum Tyllie Militem (antea se nominantem Jacobum Tyllie de Pentillie Castle Armigerum) partem, contra quam idem negotium promovetur, partibus ex altera vertitur et pendet indecisum, rite et legitime procedentes, dictoque Guilielmo Oldys Legum Doctore coram Nobis Comite Mariscallo comparente et Sententiam ferri et Justitiam fieri pro parte sua petente dicto vero Domino Jacobo Tyllie Militi trina vice procognizato et non comparente RIMATOQUE primitus processu in hoc negotio habito et facto, et diligenter recensito, Servatisque per Nos de Jure in hac parte servandis, ad nostrae Sententiae diffinitivae, sive nostri finalis decreti prolationem in hoc negotio ferendae sic duximus procedendum fore, et procedimus in hunc, qui sequitur, modum. QUIA per acta inactitata, et confessata in hoc negotio comperimus luculenter et invenimus dictum venerabilem virum Guilielmum Oldys Legum Doctorem Promotorem Officij in hac parte intentionem suam in quibusdam Articulis ex parte sua in hoc negotio ministratis praesentibusque annexis deductam (quos quidem Articulos pro hic lectis et inscriptis habemus et haberi volumus) ex confessatis dicti Domini Jacobi Tyllie in hac parte factis sufficienter et ad plenum (quoad infra pronuncianda) fundasse pariter et probasse IDCIRCO NOS praefatus HENRICUS DUX NORFOLCIAE DOMINUS COMES MARISCALLUS ANGLIAE &c. Judex antedictus (Christi nomine primitus invocato, ac ipsum solum Deum oculis nostris praeponentes, et habentes) deque et cum consilio Jurisperitorum (cum quibus in hac parte communicavimus matureque deliberavimus) Praefatum Dominum Jacobum Tyllie Militem infra tempus in hac parte articulatum, Arma, Insignia, Galeam, et Cristam in Scuto Armorum sub pictura praesentibus annexa, sculpta, et discripta, tanquam Arma, Insignia, Galeam et Cristam sibi propria de facto, absque ulla tamen authoritate aut ullo Jure, gessisse, et ostentasse atque binos Angelos, expansis Alis, dicta Arma, et Insignia supportantes gestare utcunque et ostentare praesumpsisse, in magnum praejudicium Procerum et Generosorum hujus Regni, et in contemptum authoritatis nostrae, et Legum et Officij Armorum, ad omnem juris effectum pronunciamus decernimus et declaramus prefatum igitur Dominum Jacobum Tillie Militem nullum jus, titulum, aut interesse ad gerendum et ostendandum dicta Arma, Insignia, Galeam, Cristam et Angelos supportantes habuisse, et habere eaque a dicta pictura separanda publice dilaceranda Et ubicunque extiterint rodenda Eumque pro tanto suae temeritatis excessu in praemissis juxta leges et consuetudines Armorum debite corrigi, et puniri ad omnem Juris effectum pronunciamus, decernimus, et declaramus, Eique inhibemus stricteque mandamus Ne imposterum dicta Arma, Galeam et Cristam et Angelos supportantes gestare praesumat, praefatumque Dominum Jacobum Tyllie Militem in summa Ducentarum librarum legalis monetae Angliae in usum Serenissimi Domini nostri Regis solvenda nomine mulctae et poenae necnon in summa Viginti librarum similis monetae pro Expensis ex parte dicti venerabilis viri Guilielmi Oldys Legum Doctoris Promotoris Officij in hac parte factis et faciendis, eique solvendis condemnandum fore decrevimus, et condemnamus per hanc nostram Sententiam diffinitivam sive hoc nostrum finale decretum quam sive quod ferimus et promulgamus in his Scriptis

WLM. OLDYS.   NORFOLKE & MARSHALL

[copy] Lecta lata et promulgata fuit haec sententia in Camera depicta infra Palatium Westmonasteriensem Vicesimo Octavo die mensis Januarij Anno Domini (stylo Angliae) 1687

ROBTUS PLOTT Reg'rius

[Original: Cur. Mil. Boxes X/12/3; copy: Coll. Arm. MS. SML 3, f. 27.]

APPENDIX XXIII

Bill of Costs

EXPENSAE Litis facte et faciende ex parte Jevan Gwyn generosi in quadam Causa querelae per eum contra Johannem Lloyd generosum in hac Curia motae sequuntur.

Termino Trinitatis 1638

Inprimis pro peticione	5s	
pro feodo Advocati	20s	
pro citacione primaria	16s	
pro execucione eiusdem	20s	
pro ordinibus Curie	6s	
pro Comissione	30s	
pro substitucione	2s	6d
pro concepcione Libelli	20s	
	6— 0—0 [*sic*]	

Tempore vacacionis

Item pro expensis Comrior'	5li		
pro expensis testium	3li		
pro salario registrarij	6li	13s	4d
pro expensis substituti	20s		
	15—13—4		

Termino Michaelis 1638

Item pro feodo Advocati	20s
pro ordinibus Curie	6s
pro copijs deposicionum	20s
pro sollicitacione cause	20s
	3— 6—0

Termino Hillarij 1638

Item pro feodo Advocati	20s	
pro ordinibus Curie	6s	
pro copia materie defensive	6s	8d
pro substitucione	5s	
pro sollicitacione cause	20s	
	2—17—8	

Tempore vacacionis

Item pro interr'	20s
pro examinacione desuper	3li
pro expensis Comrior'	5li

9— 0—0

Termino Pasche 1639

Item pro feodo Advocati	20s
pro ordinibus Curie	6s
pro copijs deposicionum	26s
pro sollicitacione cause	20s

3—12—0

Termino Trinitatis 1639

Item pro feodo Advocati	20s
pro ordinibus Curie	6s
pro concepcione sententie et bille	10s
pro feodo sententie et officiarijs Curie	40s
pro concepcione ordinis submissionis	10s
pro copia eiusdem	6s 8d
pro attachiamento	16s
pro execucione	5li
pro sollicitacione	20s

11—10—8 [*sic*]

Summa totalis huius Bille lij li

THO: EDEN

Taxamus ad summam viginti librarum

H. MATRAVERS

[Cur. Mil. Boxes 16/1*e*.]

APPENDIX XXIV

Receipt and Warrant of Discharge from Custody

RECEIVED this 10th January 1687 of Mr. John Coker £220 to be Entred as Sr James Tillies fine & Costs in the Court of Chivalry whereon at his request within twenty days he is to have his dismission and discharge out of the said Court & forthwith to be Released out of Prison which if he be not sett at Liberty forthwith I promise to repay the said £220 on demand

> To Mr. Christopher Lowman Keeper of the Prison of the Marshalsea in Southwark there

I Henry Duke of Norfolk Earl Marshal of England send Greeting &c. Whereas Sr James Tillie knt has been committed into your Custody for making an escape out of Custody without performing what was enjoyned in our Court of Chivalry, which since he has done as also by his Proctor given Caution to pay such further Fees Costs & Charges as shall by Law be due and I tax and approve of the same Whereupon you are hereby required in his Majestys name without asking or demanding any Fees or sums of Money forthwith immediately on sight hereof to discharge & sett at Liberty the said Sr James Tillie Knt for which this shall be your Warrant & discharge and your Contempt herein you shall answer Given under my hand & seal this 10th January 1687

Memorandum that upon the 15th day of March in the Year of Our Lord God 1687 (English Style) Anthony Trehane, Gent did in my Presence & Sight by virtue of a special proxy to him in this behalf committed by Sr James Tillie Knt appear before his Grace Henry Duke of Norfolk E. Marshall of England in this his Court of Chivalrie & did by Virtue of the said Proxy in the Name & on the behalf of the said Sr James pay into the said Court then sitting in the College of Arms scituate within the Parish of St Benedict near Pauls Wharf London into the hands of Docter Robert Plott Register of the said Court the sum of Two hundred pounds Sterling being in full for the Fine or Mulct to his Majesty sentenced & adjudged agt the said Sr James Tillie in a Cause of Office promoted agt him by Dr. William Oldys his Majesties Advocate in the said Court & also the sum of Twenty Pounds like Money taxed against

him for Costs of Suit in the said Cause; And the said Dr Robt Plott
had & received of the said Anthony Trehane the said Sum of two
hundred and twenty pounds so paid as afores^d. Witness my hand the
day & Year above written

J[OHN] C[HEEKE]

[Copy: Coll. Arm. MS. SML 3, f. 27.]

APPENDIX XXV

Petition of Appeal

To the King's Most Excellent Majesty
The humble Petition of Henry Howel Citizen and Painter-
Stainer of London

Most humbly Sheweth

That your Petitioner hath been bred up in the Art and Mistery
of Painting, (having served seven years Apprentiship in the Art)
and being free of the Company of Painters of London who have
for him beyond the memory of Man according to their Charter and
Usages of the said Company exercised painting of Escocheons
Ensigns and Arms without the interruption or molestation of any
other of your Maties Subjects but notwithstanding the same his
Grace the Duke of Norfolk Earl Marshal of England (at the
instance and promotion of Sr Henry St George Clarenceux King
of Arms for painting Escocheons at the Funeral of Sr Francis
Mannock (as is pretended) falsely tho' a Seal of the Coat of Arms
was brought to him for his directions) hath in the Court of Chivalry
proceeded against your Petitioner and given Sentence against him
and therein not only pronounced your Petitioner to have without
any Authority against the Laws of Arms and in his Jurisdiction to
the great prejudice of the said Sr Henry St. George and Office of
Arms painted the same but also fined him and condemned him in
Expences and deprived him and made him utterly uncapable of
painting Arms &c for the future without the especial Licence
Authority and Direction of the said Sr Henry St. George to the
utter ruin of your Petitioner and his Family and the great damage
of the whole Company from which Sentence he hath appealed to
your Matie

> Your Petitioner doth therefore most humbly pray your most
> Sacred Matie to grant to him a Commission of Appeal directed
> to such Noblemen of this Kingdom and learned Judges of the
> Common Law and Civilians as hath been used in the like Cases
> any two to proceed in ordinary Acts with such a Quorum &c
> to be present and consenting to the Difinitive Sentence or to give
> your Pet^r such relief therein as to your Matie shall seem meet
> And your Pet^r shall ever pray &c

Att the Court at Whitehall March 29th 1688

His Matie is graciously pleas'd to referr this Petition to the Right Honble the Lord Chancellor of England to give such Order therein as his Lo^p shall think fit or else to report the state of the matter together with his opinion to his Matie who will then declare his further pleasure

SUNDERLAND P.

12 Ap. 1688

I do appoint to hear the business upon these Peticons on Saturday next at nine o'Clock in the morning of which give notice forthwith to all parties concerned

JEFFREYS C.

[Coll. Arm. MS. Heralds IX, f. 449.]

APPENDIX XXVI

Tables of Fees

(a) Fees authorized c. 1624

To the Register

for every writ of summons, attachment, execution or commission	2s.
for entering every appearance	[*blank*]
for the filing of bills and other pleadings	[*blank*]
for copies therof	8d. per sheet
for stipulations, bonds or recognizances	2s.
for return of commissions, for writing and taking the oath	4d.
for copies of depositions and examinations	8d. per sheet
for recording and copies of exhibits	8d. per sheet
for every order other than decretal	3s.
for copies thereof	2s.
for drawing of decrees	8d. per sheet
for entering and copy thereof	8d. per sheet
for exemplifications thereof	8d. per sheet
for entering of appeals and copies of the same	8d. per sheet
for transcripts and certificates to commissions of appeal	8d. per sheet
for entering of every procuration	1s.

To the Procurator

for his fee	3s. 4d.
for drawing of every bill and other pleading	4d. per sheet
for engrossing thereof in parchment	2d. per sheet

To the Usher

out of every writ of summons	3d.
upon every order in court	4d.

To the Cryer

out of every writ of summons	3d.
upon every order in court	4d.

To the Serjeant or Sub-Marshals
[*blank*]

For the Seals of the Court

for the petty seal to every writ	6d.
for the grand seal to every exemplification, etc.	2s. 6d.

For fees of imprisonment and other things not before
mentioned the Earl Marshal shall take such order
as he shall think fit

[Folger Shakespeare Lib. MS. 393.4]

(b) *A Table of Fees in the High Court of Chivalry according to a
Regulation and Report thereof made by Sir Thomas Exton and
Sir Richard Raines to his Grace the Duke of Norfolk, Earl
Marshall of England etc.*[1]

	£	s.	d.
For the Earl Marshall Subscription or Fiat upon every Petition . .	oo	10	oo
For the Entring thereof	o	2	6
For the Advocates Fee	1	oo	o
For the Proctors Fee	o	5	o
For the Consignation of every Original Citation . . .	o	2	4
For a Copy thereof	oo	1	o
For Sealing the same	o	10	o
For Serving any Mandate of ye Court . .	oo	6	8
For a Certificate and Oath	o	3	4
For each Proxy	o	2	8
For every Ordinary Act of Court . .	o	o	8
For every Act out of Court . . .	o	1	o
For Bail to prosecute	o	5	o
For Bail or Caution to answer . . .	o	5	o
For the Copy of every Libel, allegation or Article	o	5	o
For entring the Answer of a Party Principal	o	3	6
For the Copy thereof	o	2	o
For a Commission for Answer . . .	1	o	o
For a Commission to answer Witnesses . .	1	o	o
For a Commission to take Bail . . .	1	o	o
For the Bail Bond or Stipulation . . .	o	2	6

[1] This table must have been drawn up between 9 Nov. 1687, when Exton and
Raines were appointed Surrogates (Act Book), and Nov. 1688, when Exton died
(*D.N.B.*).

	£	s.	d.
For the Examination of every Witness upon any Libel, Allegation or Article	0	5	0
and upon Interrogatories	0	3	4
For the copy of every Deposition	0	2	0
For every Affidavit	0	1	0
For the Copy thereof	0	1	0
For every Compulsory under Seal	0	10	0
For every Sentence	02	0	0
For every Interlocutory Decree having the force of a Sentence	2	0	0
For every Dismission after Issue joined	2	0	0
For every Dismission before Issue joined	0	13	4
For every Monition to pay charges in Case the Party do not pay it in Court	0	10	0
For every Attachment under Seal	0	10	0
For a Copy of every Act	0	1	0
For the Register's Subscription there unto, or to anything else	0	5	0
For the Copy of every Sentence, Interlocutory Decree (having the force of a Sentence) or Dismission after Issue joined	0	5	0
For the copy of every Order of Submission	0	5	0
For the Copy of a Petition	0	3	4
For the transmitting the Proceedings of any Cause appealed, with the Seal, (and four pence p[er] Leaf besides)	0	10	0
For Copying or Registring any Writing or Exhibit to be paid to the Register according to the length thereof, after the rate of 4^D p[er] Leaf			
For Serving any Mandate out of London according to the distance 8^D p[er] Mile, besides the fee of	00	6	0

[Powell MS.]   NORFOLK & MARSHALL

(c) *A Table of Fees in the Court of Chivalry established by his Grace the Most Noble Prince Henry Duke of Norfolk Earl Marshall of England etc.*[1]

	£	s.	d.
For the Fiat in every Cause of Instance to the Secretary	0	5	0

[1] This table was drawn up in 1693 (Northamptonshire County Record Office MS. I.C. 3311).

	£	s.	d.
For every Original Citation . . .	0	3	10
Vizt. to the Register 2^S–4^D, Cryer 8^D, Usher 8^D, Court Keeper 2^D			
To the Register for a Copy thereof . .	0	1	0
For the Seal thereof to the Secretary . .	0	6	8
To the Marshal for serving every Original Citation and making a Certificate thereupon	0	10	0
To D^o for every original Citation that is to be served ten miles out of London which the Party is to get executed	0	6	8
To D^o for executing every Attachment if in London 10^S if out of Town 8^D p[er] Mile			
To the Register for every Ordinary Act of Court	0	0	8
To him for every Act out of Court . .	0	1	0
For every Bail	0	8	6
Vizt. to the Register 5^S, to the Cryer and Usher 1^S–3^D apiece and to the Court Keeper 1^S			
To the Register for the Copy of every Libel, Allegation or Articles	0	5	0
For Entring the Answer of a Party Principal .	0	3	6
Vizt. to the Judge 1^S and to the Register .	0	2	6
To the Register for every Copy thereof .	0	2	0
For every Commission either for Answers, Examination of Witnesses, or taking Bail	0	16	8
Vizt. to the Seal 10^S and to the Register 6^S–8^D			
To the Register for a Bail Bond . . .	0	2	6
To the Register for examining every Witness upon any Libel, Allegation or Article	0	5	0
And upon Interrogatories	0	3	4
To him for every Copy of a Deposition .	0	2	0
And for every Affidavit or Copy thereof .	0	1	0
For every Compulsory Attachment, or Monition to pay Charges	0	15	0
Vizt. for the Seal 10^S and to the Register 5^S			
For every Sentence, Interlocutory Decree (having the force of a Sentence) or Dismission after Issue joined	2	0	0
Vizt. to the Judge 20^S, to the Register 10^S, to			

	£	s.	d.
the Cryer and Usher 4^S apiece and to the Court Keeper 2^S.			
For every Dismission before Issue joined . Vizt. to the Judge 6^S–8^D, to the Register 4^S–4^D to the Usher and Cryer 1^S apiece, and to the Court Keeper 4^D	0	13	4
To the Register for the Copy of every Act .	0	1	0
To him for his Subscription thereunto or to anything else	0	1	0
To the Register for the Copy of every Sentence, Interlocutory Decree, having the force of a Sentence, or Dismission after Issue joined	0	5	0
To the Register for the Copy of every Submission	0	5	0
To D^o for the Copy of a Petition . . .	0	5	0
To D^o for transmitting the Proceedings of any Cause appealed 4^D p[er] Leaf			
And for the Seal 10^S to the Secretary			
For Copying or Registring any Writing or Exhibit to be paid to the Register according to the length thereof			
An Advocate's Fee	1	0	0
A Proctor's Fee	0	5	0

No Cause of Instance to be begun
but by Petition subscribed by the
King's Advocate that the Cause therein
mentioned is cognizable in the Court of Chivalry.

[Powell MS.]   NORFOLK & MARSHALL

APPENDIX XXVII

Peerage Claims before 1504[1]

In order so see whether there was any truth in the allegation made by Sir Thomas Fane in his petition for the barony of Abergavenny in 1588 that 'the high constable and marshal of England [were] the usual judges [of a claim to a barony] in time past',[2] an attempt has been made to gather together particulars as to the manner in which peerage claims were determined when 'the high constable and marshal of England' held office concurrently, i.e. before the death of Thomas, Earl of Derby in 1504.[3]

The earliest case in which there is a record of the procedure is the claim made in 1339 by Lawrence Hastings to the earldom of Pembroke as heir to his uncle, Aymer de Valence. In the letters patent confirming and approving that Hastings should assume and have the name of Earl of Pembroke Edward III stated that he was acting on the declaration of learned persons (*peritorum*) whom he had consulted.[4] Presumably these *periti* were lawyers, but whether civilians or common lawyers does not appear.

There seems to be no other record of a claim to a peerage for nearly a century, when there were several in the course of a few years.

The first of these was the claim to the dukedom of Norfolk made by the Earl Marshal in 1425. The petition was considered in Parliament with the assistance of the judges, the serjeants-at-law, and other learned members of the Council.[5]

In 1428 Richard Neville claimed the earldom of Salisbury *jure uxoris* on the death of his father-in-law. The matter was considered by the Privy Council, which took the opinion of the judges, who advised in favour of the claim. This opinion was laid before the Lords in full Parliament, who consented to Neville having the

---

[1] The first draft of this Appendix was prepared by the late Sir Geoffrey Ellis, Junior Counsel to the Crown in Peerage and Baronetcy Cases from 1922 to 1954.

[2] See p. 158 *ante*.

[3] Edward, Duke of Buckingham, who was executed in 1521, is usually regarded as the last regular Lord High Constable, but he only filled that office by appointment for the coronation of Henry VIII, his claim to be Lord High Constable as of right being rejected in 1514 (*Duke of Buckingham's Case*, 3 Dyer 285*b*).

[4] *R.D.P.* v. 40.   [5] *Rot. Parl.* iv. 274.

name and dignity of Earl of Salisbury and a place in parliaments and councils until the King should come of age.[1]

In 1433 the petition of John, Lord Mautravers, for the earldom of Arundel, which was opposed by the infant Duke of Norfolk, was first considered by the Dukes of Bedford and Gloucester, with the serjeants-at-law, the King's Attorney, and others of the Council learned in the law, and later in Parliament with the advice of the judges and others learned in the law.[2] It is also to be observed that the Duke of Norfolk's counter-petition refers to his case being proved 'after the cours and fourme of your commone lawe'.[3]

This collection of medieval peerage claims may not be complete, but the search for it has not disclosed any case of a peerage claim being tried before the Lord High Constable and the Earl Marshal. All the evidence points to the Crown having been always, as it now is, the judge in such matters. The only respect in which there has been any change during the course of the centuries is that the sources from which advice has been sought have varied. The fact that advice has from time to time been sought from the Earl Marshal or those executing his office is not, it is submitted, evidence from which it can be deduced that the Court of Chivalry was in the Middle Ages the recognized forum for the trial of peerages cases or that they were determined by the civil law.

[1] *Proc. P.C.* iii. 325. Henry VI recognized Neville as Earl of Salisbury after attaining his majority (*C.P.R. 1441–6*, p. 111).
[2] *R.D.P.* v. 228, 229.   [3] Ibid. 227, 231.

BIBLIOGRAPHY

I. MANUSCRIPTS

1. *Court of Chivalry Records*

Act Book, 1687–1702
Acta: Curia Militaris (4)
„ „ „ (5)
Curia Militaris Boxes
Curia Militaris, 1631–1642

Curia Militaris I
„ „ II
Deposition Book, 1687–1692
Miscellanea: Curia Militaris

2. *Court of Arches Records*

Arches L.3

3. *Public Record Office*

Chancery Miscellanea (C. 47/6).
Documents presented to P.R.O.
(P.R.O. 30/26)

State Papers Domestic James I
(S.P. 14/124; 153; 185)

4. *College of Arms*

MS. Heralds II
„ III
„ IV
„ V
„ VIII
„ IX
MS. I. 25
MS. I. 26
MS. J.P. 199

MS. Processus in Curia Mares-
calli
MS. R. 19
MS. R. 28
MS. RRG LXIV A
MS. SML 3
„ 64
„ 65

5. *British Museum Manuscripts*

Additional MS. 6297
„ 9021
„ 9022
Cotton MS. Faustina C. VIII

Cotton MS. Vitellius A. XVI
Hargrave MS. XCIV
Harleian MS. 2259
Lansdowne MS. 870

6. *Bodleian Library*

MS. Ashmole 832
„ 836
„ 840
„ 856
„ 857

MS. Ashmole 862
„ 1137
MS. Rawlinson B. 378
MS. Tanner 236

7. *Cambridge University Library*

MS. Dd. III. 64   MS. Mm. VI. 69

8. *Inner Temple Library*

Petyt MS. 538

9. *Lincoln's Inn Library*

Hale MS. X

10. *Oxford, Exeter College*

MS. CLXIX

11. *Oxford, The Queen's College*

MS. CXXII

12. *Folger Shakespeare Library, Washington, D.C.*

MS. 393.4

13. *Kent County Record Office, Maidstone*

MS. U. 601. o. 3

14. *Northamptonshire County Record Office, Lamport Hall*

MS. I.C. 3311   MS. I.L. 1393

15. *Lord Northbrook*

MS. volume containing copies of documents and lists of officers of the Court of Chivalry, *c.* 1733, inscribed 'Rous Caleb Powell His Book Anno Dom: 1740' (cited as 'Powell MS.').

16. *Dr. A. R. Wagner, Richmond Herald*

MS. volume containing collections by John Anstis the elder for his projected work, *Curia Militaris*. This appears to be the volume referred to in Moule, *Bibliotheca Heraldica*, p. 259, as having belonged to the Marquess Townshend.

II. PRINTED BOOKS

The writings of only two civilians with practical experience of the Court of Chivalry seem to have found their way into print. The first of these was Dr. Arthur Duck, whose *De Usu et Authoritate Iuris Civilis Romanrum in Dominiis Principum Christianorum* was published posthumously in 1653.[1] This work dealt with the place of the civil law in all the countries of the civilized world. Of its 474 pages, ninety relate to England, and of these but a dozen[2] concern the Court of Chivalry. Duck was the King's Advocate in the Court of Chivalry and in addition had a large private practice there at a time when the Court was at its busiest, so that it is disappointing that he wrote so little upon it.

The other civilian whose work on the Court is in print was Dr. Robert Plot. Plot, who is perhaps best known by his *Natural History of Oxfordshire* (1677) and his *Natural History of Staffordshire* (1686), was not a practising lawyer, although he had the necessary academic qualification for membership of Doctors' Commons by holding the degree of D.C.L. of Oxford.[3] When the Court of Chivalry was revived in 1687 Plot was appointed its Register. A few years afterwards the Court's jurisdiction was questioned in cases in the Exchequer and King's Bench.[4] The main point raised in these cases was whether the Court was competent to try proceedings against painter-stainers for marshalling funerals and painting arms without the leave and licence of the kings of arms. There was, however, a subsidiary point that the Earl Marshal had no jurisdiction of any kind in the absence of a Lord High Constable. This latter point moved Plot to address to Sir John Somers, then Attorney-General, a long memorandum in which he sought to justify the jurisdiction of the Earl Marshal's Court in the vacancy of the office of Constable. This memorandum was later printed in the second edition of Thomas Hearne's *Collection of Curious Discourses*.[5] Plot's writing has not the objectiveness of Duck's work and he does not describe the work of the Court in his own time, but he had read widely on the subject in the public records and his work is a valuable guide to some of the sources for the early history of the Court.

Also printed in the second edition of the *Collection of Curious*

---

[1] It was reprinted by the Elzevirs at Leyden in 1654. The page references are to that edition. A translation of the text, omitting the notes, appeared as an appendix to C. J. de Ferrière's *History of the Roman or Civil Law* (London, 1724). Duck is said to have been much assisted in this work by Dr. Gerard Langbaine (A. Wood, *Athenae Oxonienses* (London, 1692), ii, col. 67).

[2] pp. 386–97.

[3] Like many other Oxford graduates in law, Plot usually described himself as LL.D.

[4] *Oldis v. Donmille* (1696), Show. P.C. 58; *Russel's Case* (1692), 4 Mod. 128. These cases were almost contemporary, but the first took more than four years to reach the House of Lords, See pp. 96, 98 *ante*.

[5] (London, 1775), ii. 250–76. Not included in the first edition published in 1720.

Discourses is a short anonymous and undated paper entitled 'The Manner of Judicial Proceedings in the Court of Constable and Marshal'.[1] This is founded upon medieval records then in the Tower of London and does not appear to be the work of a practitioner in the Court.

Written from the common-law point of view is Sir Edward Coke's description of the Court in the Fourth Part of his *Institutes*, first published in 1644, which must be read in the light of William Prynne's *Brief Animadversions on . . . The Fourth Part of the Institutes*, published in 1669.

Nothing else of importance written whilst the Court was active seems to have found a publisher. William Hawkins's *Treatise of Pleas of the Crown*, published in 1716, contains a chapter on the Court, but it is chiefly of value as a collection of references. *The Practice, Proceedings and Lawes of Armes* by Dr. Matthew Sutcliffe, Dean of Exeter, published in 1593 is not, as its title might suggest, a treatise on the Court of Chivalry. It begins with a discourse of what causes make wars just or unjust and the remainder of the work is concerned with military science. Rules of military discipline are set out in chap. xxi, part 9 of which deals with courts martial and the duties of the provost marshal.

A Whip for the Marshalls Court, and their Officers. The Petition of Robert Robins Gent to the House of Commons Against the Abuses, practised in the Marshals Court And a Discovery of the Jurisdiction and Priviledge of that Court[2] is another disappointing title. It relates to the Knight Marshal's Court which was held in Southwark weekly on Fridays. *Deep Mourning. Wig v. Blackball. Trial of Henry Hunt, Esquire, for Defamation, in the Earl Marshal's Court, On Monday, October 20, 1828* is a twelve-page satire concerning the Earl Marshal's order of 14 October 1828 for 'deep mourning' for the Queen Dowager of Wurtemburg.

By the second half of the eighteenth century the heraldic jurisdiction of the Court of Chivalry had made it an object of antiquarian interest. James Dallaway's *Inquiries into the Origin and Progress of the Science of Heraldry in England*, published in 1793, contains fifteen pages devoted to the Court, mostly consisting of copies and abstracts of documents.[3]

It is not until the end of the nineteenth century that we get a book solely devoted to the Court. This is *The Earl Marshal's*

[1] ii. 243–9.
[2] n.d., but George Thomason's copy in the British Museum is dated in manuscript 7 Dec. 1648.
[3] pp. 289–303, See also pp. 55, 80, 93.

Court in England by George Grazebrook, enlarged from a paper read before the Historic Society of Lancashire and Cheshire and privately printed in 1895. This work is a slim volume of sixty-four pages, of which twenty are devoted to a discussion of the College of Arms and the heralds' visitations, but there are some useful copies and abstracts of documents in an appendix. The scope of the work is, however, indicated by a sentence on p. 13: 'We must accept the statement of all previous writers that the Records of the Earl Marshal's Court cannot be found.'

In the present century there have been contributions to the history of the Court by two scholars of eminence. L. W. Vernon Harcourt's *His Grace the Steward and Trial of Peers* contains a chapter entitled 'Trial of Peers in the Fifteenth Century: The Court of Chivalry',[1] whilst J. H. Round included a paper 'Peerage Cases in the Court of Chivalry' in his *Peerage and Pedigree*.[2]

No account of the literature of the Court of Chivalry would be complete without some mention of two books which were never written. The first of these was *The History of the Office of Earl Marshal of England*, which was to have dealt with the jurisdiction of the Court 'at large, out of the Records of the Tower, Rolls, Exchequer, &c. and from other Authentick Evidences, in the Cottonian, Dugdalean and Ashmolean Libraries'. This was said to be 'now preparing for the Press' in a rare anonymous tract printed in 1689 and entitled *A Discourse concerning the Reasonableness of the Revival and Continuation of the Earl-Marshal's Court*.[3] This tract is directed to demonstrating the variety of causes within the jurisdiction of the Court for which no remedy could be obtained in the common-law courts. There is an elaborate analytical classification of causes, designed to give the impression of a considerable jurisdiction, much of which was either obsolete or non-existent. The argument is supported by copious citations of cases and other authorities, both medieval and modern, but they are used so un-

[1] pp. 363–99. See pp. 10–11, 26–28 *ante.*
[2] i. 69–102. For some observations on this paper see pp. 153–161 *ante.* There is a chapter entitled 'The Court of Chivalry' in R. J. Mitchell, *John Tiptoft* (London, 1938). This consists almost wholly of an account of the tournament between Lord Scales and the Bastard of Burgundy, which was, of course, not a judicial proceeding, but a sporting event. Cf. the theory that 'the Court of Chivalry had at first only an unofficial character, something like that which the Jockey Club now exercises in its own sphere' (G. Neilson, *Trial by Combat* (London, 1890), p. 179).
[3] 'In the Savoy. Printed by Edward Jones.' There is a copy bound in B.M. MS. Add. 47979, no. 61, which formerly belonged to Stephen Martin Leake, Garter King of Arms.

critically that the work cannot be said to have any value otherwise than as a curiosity. If, as seems likely, the *History* then 'preparing for the Press' was by the same hand, the abandonment of the project does not seem to be a cause for much regret.

It is more to be wished that we had the other projected work. This was *Curia Militaris: or a Treatise of the Court of Chivalry* by the elder John Anstis, a barrister of the Middle Temple, who was later to become one of the best known Garter Kings of Arms. The first sentence of his book was to have been:

> Among the variety of subjects on which learned men have employed their thoughts and industry it seems strange to me that there hath not hitherto appear'd a just Treatise of the Court Military: *Especially* since the Laws thereof being a part of the Law of Nations are a study not below the Noblest persons.

Unfortunately Anstis planned his work on too large a scale. He made an immense collection of materials for the history of the offices of every kind of constable and marshal, not only in England, but abroad as well, very little of which was germane to the comparatively small topic of the jurisdiction exercised by the Lord High Constable and the Earl Marshal of England in the Court of Chivalry. The result was that only a few pages of the book were ever written. In 1702 Anstis had the title-page printed together with the dedication to the Earl Marshal, table of contents, and an introduction of forty-one pages containing some 'animadversions' on two discourses on the office of Earl Marshal in the 1695 edition of Camden's *Britannia*, but that was all that ever appeared.[1] The book is, nevertheless, a well-established 'ghost', which has found a place in more than one bibliography.

(Law reports, works of general reference, and books mentioned incidentally are not included. Unless otherwise indicated books are published in London.)

(a) Record Publications

Acts of the Privy Council of England, 1890–.
Acts of the Privy Council of England, Colonial Series, 1909–12.

[1] Dr. A. R. Wagner has Anstis's own copy of this printed matter bound up with several hundred pages on which Anstis has written many notes and references together with drafts of a few pages of the projected work. The title-page and table of contents were reprinted by Sir Egerton Brydges in *Censura Literaria* (1809), ix. 225–32. There is the beginning of an attempt by Anstis to fill in the outline in B.M. MS. Add. 9022, ff. 6–35. Noble, *History of the College of Arms*, p. 378, states that the whole work was printed, 'probably only for private friends', but this seems very unlikely.

Calendar of Close Rolls, 1892–.
Calendar of Letters and Papers, Foreign and Domestic, Henry VIII, 1864–1932.
Calendar of Patent Rolls, 1891–.
Calendar of State Papers, Domestic, 1856–.
Foedera, Conventiones, Litterae, &c., 1816–69.
Proceedings and Ordinances of the Privy Council of England, 1834–7.
Rotuli Parliamentorum, 1771–83.

(b) *Other Books and Articles*

[J. ADDAMS], *A Catalogue of Processes in the Registry of the High Court of Delegates from 1609 to 1823*. [1824.]
W. ADDISON, *Audley End*. 1953.
S. P. ADYE, *A Treatise on Courts Martial*. 8th ed. 1810.
ANON., *A Discourse concerning the Reasonableness of the Revival and Continuation of the Earl-Marshal's Court*, 1689.
—— *Cabala Sive Scrinia Sacra*. 3rd ed. 1691.
—— *The Case of the Earl of Coventry, &c. Upon the Appeal of Gregory King, Lancaster Herald, from the Court of Chivalry to the Court of Delegates*. [c. 1702.]
—— *Laws of Honour*. 1714.
—— *The Parliamentary or Constitutional History of England*. 23 vols. and index. 1751–61.
—— 'The Family of the First Countess of Coventry; and the Matrimonial Relations of Gregory King, Lancaster Herald', in *Her. and Gen.* vii (1873), 97.
—— 'The Prescriptive Usage of Arms', in *The Ancestor*, ii (1902), 45.
W. R. ANSON, *Law and Custom of the Constitution*. 4th ed. 1935.
W. P. BAILDON, 'Heralds' College and Prescription', in *The Ancestor*, viii (1904), 122.
J. F. BALDWIN, *The King's Council in England during the Middle Ages*. Oxford, 1913.
F. P. BARNARD (ed.), *Essential Portions of Nicholas Upton's De Studio Militari . . . Translated by John Blount . . . (c. 1500)*. Oxford, 1931.
[S. BENTLEY (ed.)], *Excerpta Historica: or Illustrations of English History*. 1831.
W. BLACKSTONE, *Commentaries on the Laws of England*. 4 vols. 1765–9.
J. BRYDALL, *The Law of England relating to the Nobility and Gentry*. 1675.

S. E. Brydges, *Censura Literaria*. 10 vols. 1805–9.

E. Chamberlayne, *Angliae Notitia*, 1694, 1702.

J. Chamberlayne, *Magnae Britanniae Notitia*. 1718, 1727, 1728, 1741, 1745.

S. B. Chrimes, 'Richard II's Questions to the Judges', in *L.Q.R.* lxxii (1956), 390.

Clarendon, Edward, Earl of, *Life*. 2 vols. Oxford, 1817.

C. M. Clode, *The Military Forces of the Crown*. 2 vols. 1869.

G. E. C[ockayne], *Complete Baronetage*. 5 vols., and index. Exeter, 1900–9.

—— *Complete Peerage*. 1st ed. 8 vols. 1887–98; 2nd ed. 1910–.

E. Coke, *Institutes of the Laws of England*. 4 vols. 1628–44.

A. Collins, *Proceedings, Precedents and Arguments on Claims and Controversies concerning Baronies by Writ, and other Honours*. 1734.

[W. Combe?], *History and Antiquities of the City of York*. 3 vols. 1785.

H. Conset, *The Practice of the Spiritual or Ecclesiastical Courts*. 3rd ed. 1708.

W. Cruise, *A Treatise on the Origin and Nature of Dignities*. 2nd ed. 1823.

J. Dallaway, *Inquiries into the Origin and Progress of the Science of Heraldry in England*. Gloucester, 1793.

Dillon [Harold Arthur], Viscount, 'A MS. Collection of Ordinances of Chivalry of the Fifteenth Century', in *Archaeologia*, lvii (1900), 61.

J. Doderidge, *The Magazine of Honour*. 1642.

J. Doyle, *The Official Baronage of England*. 3 vols. 1886.

A. Duck, *De Usu et Authoritate Iuris Civilis*. Leyden, 1654.

W. Dugdale, *Origines Juridiciales*. 3rd ed. 1680.

W. A. D. Englefield, *History of the Painter-Stainers' Company*. 2nd ed. 1950.

C. D'O. Farran, 'An Ancient Court Revived', in *L.Q.R.* lxxi (1955), 187.

J. Ferne, *The Blazon of Gentrie*. 1586.

C. H. Firth and R. S. Rait, *Acts and Ordinances of the Interregnum*. 3 vols. 1911.

A. Fitzherbert, *La Graunde Abridgement*. 1577.

W. Forsyth, *Cases and Opinions on Constitutional Law*. 1869.

J. W. Fortescue, *A History of the British Army*. 7 vols. 1899–1912.

[A. C. Fox-Davies, *ps*. 'X'], *The Right to Bear Arms*. 1900.

G. GRAZEBROOK, *The Earl Marshal's Court in England*. Liverpool, 1895.

J. GUILLIM, *A Display of Heraldry*. 6th ed. 1724.

M. HALE, *History of the Common Law*. 3rd ed. 1739.

L. W. VERNON HARCOURT, *His Grace the Steward and Trial of Peers*. 1907.

P. H. HARDACRE, 'The Earl Marshal, the Heralds, and the House of Commons, 1604–1641', in *International Review of Social History*, ii (1957), 106.

J. HAWARDE, *Les Reportes del cases in Camera Stellata*. 1894.

T. HEARNE (ed.), *A Collection of Curious Discourses written by Eminent Antiquaries*. 2nd ed. 2 vols. 1775.

HERALDRY SOCIETY, *Full Report of the Case of the [Lord] Mayor, Aldermen and Citizens of the City of Manchester versus The Manchester Palace of Varieties Limited*. East Knoyle, 1955.

HISTORICAL MANUSCRIPTS COMMISSION, *The Manuscripts of the House of Lords, 1690–1691*. 1892; *1695–1697*. 1903.

W. S. HOLDSWORTH, 'Martial Law Historically Considered', in *L.Q.R.* xviii (1902), 117.

—— *A History of English Law*, vol. i. 7th ed. 1956.

E. J. JONES, *Medieval Heraldry*. Cardiff, 1943.

Journals of the House of Commons. n.p., n.d.

Journals of the House of Lords. n.p., n.d.

T. W. KING (ed.), *Lancashire Funeral Certificates*. Chetham Society, 1859.

W. LANGTON (ed.), *The Visitation of Lancashire . . . 1533*. Chetham Society, 2 vols. 1876–82.

J. T. LAW, *Forms of Ecclesiastical Law*. 1831.

J. S. LEADAM and J. F. BALDWIN, *Select Cases before the King's Council*. Selden Society, 1918.

G. LEGH, *Accedens of Armorie*. 1562.

W. A. LITTLEDALE (ed.), *Collection of Miscellaneous Grants*. Harleian Society, 2 vols. 1925–6.

H. S. LONDON, 'Some Medieval Treatises on English Heraldry', in *Ant. Journ.* xxxiii (1953), 174.

—— and G. D. SQUIBB: 'A Dorset King of Arms', in *Proc. Dorset Natural History and Archaeological Society*, lxviii (1947), 58.

N. LUTTRELL, *A Brief Historical Relation of State Affairs from September 1678 to April 1714*. 6 vols. Oxford, 1857.

G. MACKENZIE OF ROSEHAUGH, *The Science of Herauldry*. Edinburgh, 1680.

W. Maitland, *The History and Survey of London*. 2 vols. 1775.
R. G. Marsden, *Select Pleas in the Court of Admiralty*. Selden Society, 1894.
G. Meige, *Present State of Great Britain*. 1707.
T. Milles, *The Catalogue of Honor*. 1610.
[J. Mottley, *ps*. 'R. Seymour'], *A Survey of the Cities of London and Westminster*. 2 vols. 1734–5.
G. Neilson, *Trial by Combat*. 1890.
N. H. Nicolas, *History of the Battle of Agincourt*. 2nd ed. 1832.
—— *The Scrope and Grosvenor Controversy*. 2 vols. 1832.
M. Noble, *A History of the College of Arms*. 1805.
W. Notestein (ed.), *The Journal of Sir Simonds D'Ewes*. New Haven, Conn., 1923.
D. Ogg, *Joannis Seldeni* Ad Fletam Dissertatio. Cambridge, 1925.
G. Ormerod, *History of Cheshire*. 2nd ed. 3 vols. 1882.
R. O'Sullivan, *Military Law and the Supremacy of the Civil Courts*. 1921.
J. Percy, *The Case of James Percy, Claymant to the Earldom of Northumberland*. 1685.
R. Phillimore, *Ecclesiastical Law*. 2nd ed. 2 vols. 1895.
W. P. W. Phillimore, *Heralds' College and Coats of Arms*. 1904.
W. Prynne, *Brief Animadversions on . . . the Fourth Part of the Institutes*. 1669.
Report of the Departmental Committee . . . to inquire into certain matters connected with the Baronetage. 1907.
T. Ridley, *A View of the Civile and Ecclesiastical Law*. 1607.
[H. C. Rothery], *Return of all Appeals in Causes of Doctrine or Discipline made to the High Court of Delegates*. 1868.
J. H. Round, *Peerage and Pedigree*. 2 vols. 1910.
—— *The King's Serjeants and Officers of State*. 1911.
J. P. Rylands (ed.), *Cheshire and Lancashire Funeral Certificates*. Lancashire and Cheshire Record Society, 1882.
W. H. Rylands (ed.), *Grantees of Arms*. Harleian Society, 2 vols. 1916–17.
T. Rymer and R. Sanderson, *Foedera*. 20 vols. 1704–32.
W. Senior, *Doctors' Commons and the Old Court of Admiralty*. 1922.
H. Spelman, *Glossarium Archaiologicum*. 3rd ed. 1687.
G. D. Squibb (ed.), *Heraldic Cases in the Court of Chivalry*. Harleian Society, 1956.
R. R. Steele, *Bibliography of Royal Proclamations (Bibliotheca Lindesiana)*. 2 vols. Oxford, 1910.

M. Sutcliffe, *The Practice, Proceedings and Lawes of Armes.* 1593.

T. Twiss (ed.), *The Black Book of the Admiralty.* Rolls Series, 4 vols. 1871–6.

A. R. Wagner, 'A Fifteenth-Century Description of the Brass of Sir Hugh Hastings at Elsing, Norfolk', in *Ant. Journ.* xix (1939), 421.

—— *The Records and Collections of the College of Arms.* 1952.

—— *Heralds and Heraldry in the Middle Ages,* 2nd ed. Oxford, 1956.

J. Warkworth, *A Chronicle of the . . . Reign of King Edward the Fourth.* Camden Society, 1839.

J. de Waurin, *Recueil des Croniques.* Rolls Series, 5 vols. 1864–91.

J. Whitelocke, *Liber Famelicus.* Camden Society, 1858.

C. G. Y[oung], 'Additions to Dugdale's Baronage', in *Coll. Top. & Gen.* v (1838), 312.

—— 'Claim of James Percy, the Trunk-maker, to the Earldom of Northumberland', in ibid. vi (1840), 266.

C. G. Young, *An Account of the Controversy between Reginald Lord Grey of Ruthyn and Sir Edward Hastings.* Privately printed, 1841.

—— *Privy Councillors and their Precedence.* n.p., 1860.

INDEX

Abdy, Humphrey, 62.
Abergavenny, Lord, 33.
Abergavenny peerage, 158, 276.
Addis, Giles, 38.
Adjournment, 210.
Admiral, Lord High, 13.
Admiralty, Court of, 12, 13, 17, 54, 89, 132, 135, 136, 138, 163, 211, 217.
Admiralty Court of the North, 20.
Advocates, 133–5, 167.
Agincourt, battle of, 77, 181–2.
Ailesbury, Robert, Earl of, 79, 85, 233.
Albemarle, George, Duke of, 74, 77, 84, 233.
Aldermen, precedence of, 33.
Alexander, Edward, 236.
Aleyn, John, 182.
Allen, John, 236, 237.
Amery, John, 143.
Ancaster, Duke of, 109.
Andrewes, John, 250.
Andrews, Dr., 111, 112, 113, 116.
Anglesey, Christopher, Earl of, 50.
Annuity, non-payment of, 18.
Anson, Sir William, 102.
Anstis, John, Garter King of Arms, 110–14, 118, 119, 279, 283.
Answer, 124, 206–7: *see also* Defence.
Apothecary, not a gentleman, 175.
Appeal of murder, 22, 25, 54, 120, 128, 138, 147, 150, 191.
Appeal of treason, 22, 25, 26, 29, 52, 120, 128, 138, 147, 191.
Appleton, Thomas, clerk of the Constableship, 22, 132, 234.
Arbitration, 208.
Archbishop, funeral of, 140.
Arches, Court of, 88, 89, 90, 110, 133, 136, 226.
Argent, William, 258–9.
Armorial bearings, disputes concerning, 16, 17, 30, 32, 34, 61, 125, 138; evidence of gentility, 171; grants of, 171, 172, 184; right to, 178–89; unlawful assumption of, 61, 91, 183, 249, 257; unlawful painting of, 139,

280; use of for commercial purposes, 119, for ornamental purposes, 125, from time immemorial, 180–1, 185–9, on seals, 126.
Arms, deed or action of, 22, 23, 125.
Articles, 183, 219, 256–7.
Articles of War, 5.
Arundel, Earl of, 156; earldom of, 277; Henry, Earl of, 73; John, Lord, 230; Thomas, Earl of, 45, 73, 199, 232, 239, 242, 246, 250, 252, 253, 256, 257, 258, 260, 261.
Ashton, Ralph, 70; Sir Ralph, 70; Sir Thomas, 30; William, 70; Sir William, 70.
Aske, —, 34.
Attachment, 195.
Attainder, 177.
Attorney-General, 48, 51, 52, 114, 130, 149, 151, 280.
Audeley, James, Lord, 27.
Audley, Dr. John, 235.
Aumale, Edward, Duke of, 228.
Ayres, John, 238, 245.

Bacon, Sir Nicholas, 160.
'Bado Aureo', John de, 178.
Balfour, Sir William, 53.
Ballard, —, 194.
Bangor, John, 183.
Bantam, East Indies, 151.
Barbados, 61.
Bardolf, Thomas, Lord, 25.
Barkstead, John, 94; Mrs., 94.
Barnet, John, 132.
Baronet, funeral of, 140.
Baronetcies, claims to, 121, 160–1.
Barrister, audience in Court of Chivalry, 125, 133–4, in Court of Common Pleas, 135; competence to sign articles under Clergy Discipline Act, 135; green bag, 63; whether an esquire, 176.
Barrobie, John, 92.
Barrowby, Dr., 113.
Barrowcloughe, John, 204.
Bartolus of Sasso-Ferrato, 178.
Barton, Thomas, 237.

PRINTED IN GREAT BRITAIN
AT THE UNIVERSITY PRESS, OXFORD
BY VIVIAN RIDLER
PRINTER TO THE UNIVERSITY

Date Due

SEP 2 3 1959			
	PRINTED	IN U. S. A.	